Open Source Investigations in the Age of Google

Security Science and Technology – Vol. 4

Open Source Investigations in the Age of Google

Editors

Henrietta Wilson
SOAS University of London, UK

Olamide Samuel
University of Leicester, UK

Dan Plesch
SOAS University of London, UK

World Scientific

NEW JERSEY • LONDON • SINGAPORE • BEIJING • SHANGHAI • HONG KONG • TAIPEI • CHENNAI • TOKYO

Open Source Investigations in the Age of Google is a remarkable accomplishment, a conceptual introduction that is also a useful guide to navigating a new era of transparency, making a unique and critical contribution to addressing global human security.

— Ambassador Robert Gallucci, Distinguished Professor in the Practice of Diplomacy at Georgetown University's Walsh School of Foreign Service

Corruption and atrocities are harder to keep secret thanks to the exciting new methods of open source research to reveal patterns and incidents that are vital to justice and accountability. This book sets out the advantages and limitations of open source investigations through detailed case studies ranging from human rights abuses to weapons of mass destruction. But it also details the misuse of these techniques and how to develop better governance and ethical guidelines. Essential reading for defenders of open societies.

— Heather Grabbe, Director of the Open Society European Policy Institute, Brussels

As an OSINT specialist for decades, the importance of a book like this cannot be stressed enough. Whether you are starting in OSINT or online investigations or a veteran, this book will give you great insights into practical approaches, understanding ethical and legal dilemmas and the power of proper intelligence collection.

— Nico Dekens | Dutch_OsintGuy

This is a timely collection of essays on the uses of open source information about everything from nuclear weapons to human rights violations. The book's splendid introduction provides a sophisticated guide to major issues of reliability, accountability through transparency, governance and ethics, and highlights the promise and the perils of using ever more powerful technologies to gather and assess information. This volume is a major contribution to our understanding of this rapidly developing field and essential reading for policy-makers and citizens.

— Kennette Benedict, Senior Advisor, *Bulletin of the Atomic Scientists*

Open source information is a potential goldmine for security researchers but poses a host of questions related to transparency and research methodology, among many others. *Open Source Investigations in the Age of Google* captures the state of the art on these questions in a thoughtful manner and should be on the bookshelf of every serious researcher interested in the topic.

— Stephen Coulthart, Associate Professor, University at Albany

A carefully crafted and engaging collection by world-leading experts that will instantly prove a foundational resource for anyone interested in open source investigations.

— Dr Filippa Lentzos, Reader, King's College London

The stunning revelations from novel open source research methods and journalism can make these approaches seem more like magic than a craft. You have to engage with practitioners to really understand how these tools can be used, how they are changing today's information ecosystem, how norms around their use are evolving and how they affect international security. This volume brilliantly brings together that conversation, with contributions from the most insightful practitioners in open source analysis.

— Benjamin Loehrke, Stanley Center for Peace and Security

This excellent collection of essays from leading thinkers in the field is a must-read primer for open source investigators and people who want to understand their work. Human rights defenders, investigative journalists, policy-makers, law enforcement professionals, students, teachers and many more will find this exciting book an invaluable resource to understand powerful new monitoring approaches, and how they are making a difference to global governance, justice and accountability.

— Professor Andrew Futter, University of Leicester

This is a timely book! It offers radical new ways to achieve justice and accountability in the face of growing authoritarian governments, human rights abuses and misinformation. It is essential reading for anyone working at the intersection of technology, media and human rights.

— Saijai Liangpunsakul, Practitioner and Advocate Working against Hate Speech and for Responsible AI and Technology for Democracy

With the huge growth in modern monitoring methods and tools, more and more institutions and individuals are generating insight akin to what intelligence communities have long considered 'actionable intelligence' – including monitoring nuclear weapons proliferation and tracking ongoing military operations. These techniques are now increasingly available for public consumption with no government oversight. Because of the significance of the findings of these new approaches, and the direct-to-public conduit of dissemination, it is critical that practitioners and consumers of this work carefully reflect upon best practices, publication standards and ethical implications of this emerging tradecraft, which was once so closely associated with spycraft. This book is such a reflection: Everything from the much-needed discussion about who is qualified to practise, why quality of content is important, ethical implications of the work, the need for public literacy to the very name of this field is explored. Indeed, this book helps to define this emerging field of global security sense-making and its role in democratizing insight that affects us all.

— Allison Puccioni, Principal and Founder at Armillary Services

My experience as Executive Secretary to the Comprehensive Test Ban Treaty Organization has confirmed to me that enhanced transparency is crucial to uphold global efforts to prevent the harms of nuclear weapons proliferation. This book highlights novel opportunities to build transparency and accountability. The methods and issues covered within this book make it an indispensable read for policy-makers, scholars, journalists and open source professionals.

— Lassina Zerbo, Former Prime Minister of Burkina Faso, and Executive Secretary Emeritus, Comprehensive Test Ban Treaty Organization

Publishers' page

Publishers' page

Publishers' page

Publishers' page

© 2024 World Scientific Publishing Company
https://doi.org/10.1142/9781800614079_fmatter

Preface and Acknowledgements

Producing a book takes a lot of people, a lot of ideas and a lot of work. We are hugely indebted to the many colleagues, partners and friends who have helped to make this volume a reality.

Our journey towards creating the book began in 2018–2019, when we interviewed several people about their work with the international weapons inspections that took place in Iraq between 1991 and 2003. These conversations made us think afresh about the potential of inspection regimes in the digital age; thank you to Hans Blix, Pierce Cordon, Rolf Ekéus, Robert Gallucci and Nikita Smidovich for setting us on this path. Then, in 2020, we organized a webinar series for the Strategic Concept for the Removal of Arms and Proliferation (SCRAP) weapons programme at SOAS University of London. *Verification in the Age of Google* comprised seven fortnightly virtual events, which showcased global open source investigations that track weapons and other risks to human security, and reflected as well as strengthened our appreciation of this fast-growing field. We would like to thank all the speakers, respondents and audience participants for their fascinating talks and stimulating discussions.

The vision motivating the webinars, subsequent events and publications, and now this book, has been to capture and explore the richness, diversity and implications of open source research — that is, analyses that rely on publicly available tools and information. Rather than compartmentalizing different open source investigations in terms of what they monitor, or the specific tools or sources that they use, our research aims to recognize and examine the complexity, nuance and interconnections within and between different strands, for example, by highlighting and examining the links between tracking global weapons flows and how weapons are used, or between corruption in the arms trade and subversions of democracy, or between the evolution of violent extremism and political violence. The chapters here reflect these considerations, each delivering insights into particular open source investigations and together demonstrating synergies and connections.

We are enormously grateful to everyone who has helped us engage with and understand the world of open source investigations. In particular, we are honoured by the contributions of the chapter authors, who, in keeping with academic models of publishing, contributed their words *pro bono*, although many in the team work outside the security and non-monetary reward structures of full-time academic positions or well-funded think-tanks. We have been overwhelmed by their generosity in sharing their time, expertise and words, enabling us to experience at first-hand the broader goodwill and collaborative tendencies that drive much of the non-governmental open source research community. Our warm thanks to Muhammad Idrees Ahmad, Brian Balmer, Veronika Bedenko, Jonathan Bellish, Andrea Carboni, Yi Ting Chua, Geoffrey L. Duke, Andrew Feinstein, Lindsay Freeman, María Garzón Maceda, Richard Guthrie, Zuzanna Gwadera, Paul Holden, Alexa Koenig, Matt Korda, Hans M. Kristensen, Dan Liu, Robert J. Mathews, Rhona Michie, Ildikó Pete, Clionadh Raleigh, James Revill, Alexandra Smidman, Benjamin Strick, Aric Toler, Christiaan Triebert, Kathleen M. Vogel, Viet Anh Vu, Lydia Wilson and Jamie Withorne. It has been great working with you all.

The book has also benefitted from many research conversations, interactive events and workshops that were conducted on a non-attributable basis. The fact that we cannot name the people involved in these activities does not detract from our gratitude to them, and their importance in shaping our ideas and outputs. Special mention goes to: the open source research practitioners and experts that Henrietta Wilson interviewed from 2020 to 2022 in the context of her research on the global spread and diverse framings of open source research; the participants in a series of virtual interactive cafes we ran in 2020–21 with the goal of supporting the international epistemic community of open source researchers; and the organizers of, and participants in, a workshop run by the Stanley Center for Peace and Security held in Amsterdam in May 2022.

All our efforts on these diverse outputs originated in the SCRAP weapons programme at SOAS University of London, and we are grateful for the support of the core SCRAP team: Martin Butcher, Aashika Doshi, Zahraa Kapasi, Eloisa Romani and Lucy Tiller. Thank you to them, to SOAS University of London for its institutional support and to SCRAP's funders – the Joseph Rowntree Charitable Trust, the Marmot Charitable Trust and the Network for Social Change. We are also extremely grateful that these funders, along with Professor Plesch's enterprise fund, have provided the resources needed to make the e-book of this volume open access.

Alongside the commitment of SCRAP's paid staff, the project has also been enriched by the involvement of its amazing student volunteers. Three teams of students from Worcester Polytechnic Institute Massachusetts worked with us to produce a prototype Global Weapons Tracking Portal website – thank you to: Jack Ayvazian, Emily Bubencik, Kimberly Coudrey, Reese Haly, Jack Hoover, Evan Llewellyn, Benjamin Lunden, Victor Mercola, Julia Ormerod, Donovan Tames, Natasha Ussrey, Maxwell Westreich and Hayley Wigren, alongside their advisers Joel Brattin, John-Michael Davis, Dominic Golding and Sarah Stanlick. Back in Europe, we are also grateful to the SCRAP student volunteers and project partners who helped run the *Verification in the Age of Google* webinars and virtual cafes: Julia Auf dem Brinke, Philip Chennery, Jack Cinamon, Paul Gruet, Jonathan Poupon, Ruth Rohde, Anant Saria and Marla Zgheib.

Several of our authors illustrate their chapter with images taken from a range of sources. We are grateful to the copyright owners for their permission for these uses, as acknowledged by name in the different chapters. Where we have been unable to identify and get formal permissions from copyright holders, we have instead used an artist's impression of imagery – warm thanks to Aiden Page for their careful depictions.

The fantastic staff at World Scientific Publishing have supported the book's development from start to finish; many thanks to Logeshwaran Arumugam, Michael Beale, Adam Binnie, Shezmin Miah, Ana Ovey, Koe Shi Ying, Andreea Zaharia and above all Laurent Chaminade who has provided guidance and friendship at every stage.

On top of all these, we owe our families and friends a very special thank you, for their constant encouragement and love. Several have also provided vital support and guidance on the processes involved in editing a book: Thank you to Maike Bohn, James Brady, Filippa Lentzos, Gill Nineham and Leigh Shulman. Most of all, we are indebted to Seth Bullock for his steadfast interest and belief in the book, as well as his guidance on content and style – his constant willingness to help think through the many different choices that we faced along the way has been invaluable.

Thank you to everyone involved. It wouldn't have happened without you.

Henrietta Wilson
Olamide Samuel
Dan Plesch

© 2024 World Scientific Publishing Company
https://doi.org/10.1142/9781800614079_fmatter

About the Authors

Muhammad Idrees Ahmad is a Senior Lecturer in Journalism, University of Essex. He writes for *Foreign Policy*, the *New York Review of Books, Washington Post, Guardian*, and the *Times Literary Supplement* among others. He is writing a book for Columbia University Press on the war of narratives over Syria. E-mail: m.i.ahmad@essex.ac.uk.

Brian Balmer is Professor of Science Policy Studies in the Department of Science and Technology Studies, University College London. He was formerly a Research Associate at the Harvard Sussex Program. He has published extensively on the history of biological and chemical warfare. E-mail: b.balmer@ucl.ac.uk.

Veronika Bedenko is a Regional Issues Strategist at the Vienna-based Open Nuclear Network, a programme of the One Earth Future Foundation. Veronika is an expert in the use of open source information to understand military capabilities and support nuclear risk reduction, working at the intersection of research and analysis and outreach efforts. E-mail: vbedenko@oneearthfuture.org.

Jonathan Bellish is the Executive Director and Chief Operations Officer at One Earth Future, a philanthropic foundation that supports economic stabilization and inclusive diplomacy for peace. He has a JD from the University of Denver Sturm College of Law and an MBA from Millsaps College. E-mail: jbellish@oneearthfuture.org.

Andrea Carboni is the Head of Analysis at the Armed Conflict Location & Event Data Project (ACLED). He is also a Research Fellow in the School of Global Studies at the University of Sussex. He previously worked as a humanitarian analyst at Mercy Corps. He specializes in the use of conflict data and in the politics and institutions of African countries. E-mail: a.carboni@sussex.ac.uk.

Yi Ting Chua is an Assistant Professor at the University of Alabama. Her research focuses on the role of the internet in criminal offending and is shaped primarily by the increasing role of technology and cyberspace in criminal and deviant behaviours. Her current work spans three research areas: (1) individual pathways into cybercrime; (2) the impact of social networks and structures on the evolution of subcultural values, beliefs, and behaviours; and (3) countermeasures against cybercrime. E-mail: ychua@ua.edu.

Geoffrey L. Duke is the Head of the Secretariat of the South Sudan Action Network on Small Arms. His experience and research interests span community security, security sector reform, humanitarian disarmament, and arms control. He has been featured by *The New York Times, BBC, Al Jazeera*, and major national media outlets in South Sudan, and has contributed to regional, national and international policy-making. E-mail: dukegeff@gmail.com.

Andrew Feinstein is Executive Director of Shadow World Investigations (formerly Corruption Watch UK) and the author of *The Shadow World: Inside the Global Arms Trade*. A former ANC Member of Parliament in South Africa, Andrew was identified by the non-governmental organization Action On Armed Violence (AOAV) as one of the hundred most influential people globally working against armed violence. He was recently the co-recipient of the Gavin McFadyen Award, and has been named amongst South Africa's Whistleblowers of the Year and as one of the country's Anti-corruption Heroes of the Year. E-mail: andrew@shadowworldinvestigations.org.

Lindsay Freeman is the Director of Technology, Law, and Policy at the Human Rights Center, UC Berkeley School of Law. Freeman is an international criminal and human rights lawyer with experience working at the International Criminal Court and the Extraordinary Chambers in the Courts of Cambodia. She specializes in the use of technology, digital evidence and online investigations for justice and accountability purposes, particularly in the investigation and prosecution of atrocity crimes. Freeman led the drafting team of the *Berkeley Protocol on Digital Open Source Investigations*, which the Center co-published with the UN Office of the High Commissioner for Human Rights. E-mail: lfreeman@berkeley.edu.

María Garzón Maceda is the research assistant for the Weapons of Mass Destruction and Space Security Programmes at the United Nations Institute for Disarmament Research (UNIDIR), where she focuses on biological and chemical weapons. Before joining UNIDIR, María was a Policy Fellow at the European University Institute, where she worked on strengthening the participation of the Global South in WMD regimes. Previously, María was a civil servant at the Argentine Ministry of Foreign Affairs, where she worked on the implementation of the Chemical Weapons Convention. María holds a master's degree in international affairs from the Graduate Institute in Geneva. E-mail: maria.garzon@un.org.

Richard Guthrie is an international security policy researcher, primarily focused on technology control and innovation issues that relate to materials and technologies that can have hostile as well as peaceful uses. He runs CBW Events, a project that aims to create a record of events to enable and encourage understanding of how policies on issues relating to chemical and biological warfare (CBW) and its prevention are developed. He worked at the Harvard Sussex Program 1990–2003. E-mail: richard@cbw-events.org.uk.

Zuzanna Gwadera is a Research Assistant at the Centre for Science and Security Studies (CSSS), King's College London. She holds a BA in Philosophy, Politics and Economics from Durham University and an MA in Arms Control and International Security from King's College London. Her research interests include issues related to nuclear arms control and emerging technologies as well as China's defence and security policies. E-mail: Zuzanna.e.gwadera@kcl.ac.uk.

Paul Holden is Director of Investigations at Shadow World Investigations and has worked with Andrew Feinstein for over a decade on arms and corruption related matters. He was voted an Anti-corruption Hero of the Year alongside Andrew. Paul has written five books, including two national best-sellers in South Africa, and was a Network Fellow at the Safra Centre for Ethics at Harvard University. Paul has recently been closely involved in investigating the Gupta family's corrupt 'capture' of South Africa, which has included giving extensive evidence before a Judicial Commission of Inquiry investigating the issue. E-mail: paul@shadowworldinvestigations.org.

Alexa Koenig, JD, PhD, is Executive Director and co-faculty Director of UC Berkeley's Human Rights Center (winner of the 2015 MacArthur Award for Creative and Effective Institutions) and a Lecturer at UC Berkeley's School of Law and School of Journalism. She co-founded the Human Rights Center's Investigations Lab and directed the development of the *Berkeley Protocol on Digital Open Source Investigations*. Her recent books include *Digital Witness* (Oxford University Press, 2020), and *Graphic: Trauma and Meaning in Our Online Lives* (Cambridge University Press 2023). E-mail: kalexakm@berkeley.edu.

Matt Korda is a Senior Research Associate and Project Manager for the Nuclear Information Project at the Federation of American Scientists, where he co-authors the *Nuclear Notebook* with Hans M. Kristensen. Matt is also an Associate Researcher with the Nuclear Disarmament, Arms Control and Non-proliferation Programme at the Stockholm International Peace Research Institute (SIPRI). Previously, he worked for the Arms Control, Disarmament, and WMD Non-Proliferation Centre at NATO headquarters in Brussels. He received his MA in International Peace and Security from the Department of War Studies at King's College London. E-mail: mkorda@fas.org.

Hans M. Kristensen is the Director of the Nuclear Information Project at the Federation of American Scientists (FAS) in Washington, DC. His work focuses on researching and writing about the status of nuclear weapons and the policies that direct them. Kristensen is a co-author of the world nuclear forces overview in the *SIPRI Yearbook* (Oxford University Press) and a frequent adviser to the news media on nuclear weapons policy and operations. He has co-authored the *Nuclear Notebook* since 2001. Inquiries should be directed to FAS, 1112 16th Street NW, Suite 600, Washington, DC, 20036 USA; +1 (202) 546–3300. E-mail: hkristensen@fas.org.

Dan Liu is an investigator for Conflict Armament Research. He specializes in applying open source investigative techniques towards countering illicit trade, proliferation and arms trafficking. His experience extends across government, non-profit and academic sectors.

Robert J. Mathews is an Associate Professor at the University of Melbourne Law School. He was formerly scientific adviser to the Australian delegation, both during the negotiation of the Chemical Weapons Convention (CWC) in Geneva (1984–1992) and subsequently during the implementation of the CWC in The Hague (1993–2017). He is also a former member of the Organisation for the Prohibition of Chemical Weapons Scientific Advisory Board. E-mail: bobmathews17@hotmail.com.

Rhona Michie is the Director of Projects and Planning at Shadow World Investigations. She joined Shadow World Investigations in May 2019, coordinating various projects including their Investigative Methods Training, alongside organizational and financial management. She is a co-Founder and Coordinator of the Corruption Tracker and was listed as an Emerging Expert by the Forum on the Arms Trade in 2022. E-mail: rhona@shadowworldinvestigations.org.

Ildikó Pete received her PhD in computer science at the University of St Andrews, and has worked at the intersection of cybersecurity and machine learning, applying machine learning methods to investigate network attacks and using NLP techniques to explore communities on underground forums. E-mail: pildip23@gmail.com.

Dan Plesch is Professor of Diplomacy and Strategy at SOAS University of London where he leads the Strategic Concept for the Removal of Arms and Proliferation (SCRAP weapons programme), and is a 'door tenant' at the legal chambers of 9 Bedford Row in London. His research expertise spans disarmament and human rights. His books include: *Women and the UN: A New History of Women's International Human Rights; Human Rights after Hitler*; and *America, Hitler and the UN: How the Allies Won World War II*. E-mail: dp27@soas.ac.uk.

Clionadh Raleigh is the President of the Armed Conflict Location & Event Data Project (ACLED). She is also Professor of Political Violence and Geography in the School of Global Studies at the University of Sussex. Her primary research interests are the dynamics of conflict and violence, African political environments, and elite networks.

James Revill is the Head of the Weapons of Mass Destruction and Space Security Programmes at the United Nations Institute for Disarmament

Research (UNIDIR). His research interests focus on the evolution of regimes dealing with weapons of mass destruction, and he has published widely on this topic. He was previously a Research Fellow with the Harvard Sussex Programme at SPRU, University of Sussex, and completed research fellowships with the Landau Network Volta Centre in Italy and the Bradford Disarmament Research Centre in the United Kingdom. He holds a PhD focused on the evolution of the Biological Weapons Convention from the University of Bradford, UK. E-mail: james.revill@un.org.

Olamide Samuel is a Track II diplomat with a specialist focus on arms control, international security and nuclear politics. He is currently a Research Associate in Nuclear Politics at the University of Leicester, and a Senior Strategic Adviser to Centre de Recherche et d'Information pour le Désarmement et la Sécurité (CRIDS). Twitter: @olamideDIY.

Alexandra Smidman, an Associate of Shadow World Investigations, is a researcher and writer who has experience working with a number of non-profits on issues related to corruption, corporate lobbying and the consequences of armed conflict. She currently has a focus on environmental investigations. E-mail: alexandra@shadowworldinvestigations.org.

Benjamin Strick is a digital investigator with a background in law, the military and technology, specializing in open source intelligence (OSINT), investigations, influence operations, data and maps. He has applied his skills to document human rights abuses across the world, working with international media to create multi-award-winning investigative documentaries and assist civil society groups. He shares his passion for open source investigations through free YouTube tutorials to democratize diverse tools and techniques. Ben is the Director of Investigations for both the Centre for Information Resilience and Myanmar Witness. He was previously an open source investigator with BBC Africa Eye, is a Bellingcat contributor, and co-founder of the Ocelli Project. In 2021 he was awarded Open Source Intelligence Champion of the Year for investment, commitment and contribution to the field. E-mail: benjaminstrick@protonmail.com.

Aric Toler is the Training and Research Director at Bellingcat, an online publication that uses open source, digital research techniques to investigate topics around the world. He focuses on investigations into Russia and

Ukraine, including research into Russian intelligence operations, the ongoing war in Ukraine, and the 2014 downing of Malaysian Airlines Flight 17 over the Donbas. He received a Master's in Slavic Languages & Literatures from the University of Kansas in 2013. E-mail: arictoler@bellingcat.com.

Christiaan Triebert is a Reporter on the Visual Investigations team at the *New York Times*. His work, which combines traditional journalism with open source methods to break news and hold the powerful to account, includes a series exposing Russian airstrikes on Syrian hospitals and the Pentagon's flawed system of investigating allegations of civilian casualties, both of which were awarded with the Pulitzer Prize for International Reporting in respectively 2019 and 2022. He has digitally investigated airstrikes in Afghanistan, Armenia, Ethiopia, Gaza, Iraq, Libya, Nigeria, Somalia, Syria, and Yemen. Prior to joining the *Times*, he worked as a Senior Investigator and Lead Trainer at the investigative collective Bellingcat, and also worked on verifying United States-led coalition airstrikes causing civilian harm in Iraq and Syria for the monitoring group Airwars. E-mail: christiaan.triebert@nytimes.com.

Kathleen M. Vogel is Professor in the School for the Future of Innovation in Society at Arizona State University (ASU). She is also a Senior Global Futures Scientist, Julie Ann Wrigley Global Futures Laboratory at ASU. Vogel's overall research interests relate to the study of knowledge production on security and intelligence problems. E-mail: kathleen.vogel@asu.edu.

Viet Anh Vu is a Research Student in Computer Science at the University of Cambridge. His interest is in cybersecurity, particularly collecting, watching, and measuring bad things that happen on the internet. His current work focuses on cybercrime and its response to externalities such as the pandemic, war, law enforcement interventions and disruptions. He is also interested in cyberlaw and internet policy. E-mail: anh.vu@cst.cam.ac.uk.

Henrietta Wilson conducts policy-relevant research on armaments and arms regulations and teaches undergraduate and postgraduate modules on politics and international relations at UK universities. Originally trained as a physicist, her career spans three decades of collaboration with major non-governmental organizations and universities in the UK and Germany. She is Senior Analyst for the Strategic Concept for the Removal of Arms and

Proliferation (SCRAP weapons programme) at SOAS University of London, and is a Visiting Research Fellow and PhD student at King's College London. E-mail: henrietta.wilson@kcl.ac.uk.

Lydia Wilson researches extremism and motivations to join armed groups, and is an editor and writer at *New Lines Magazine*. She is currently writing a book on the industry of countering violent extremism. E-mail: lsmw2@cam.ac.uk.

Jamie Withorne is an Affiliate and Research Assistant with the Oslo Nuclear Project. She is pursuing a Master of Philosophy degree in Peace and Conflict Studies at the University of Oslo, where her work focuses on emerging technology, monitoring, and verification. E-mail: jamiewithorne@gmail.com.

© 2024 World Scientific Publishing Company
https://doi.org/10.1142/9781800614079_fmatter

Contents

Preface and Acknowledgements   ix

About the Authors   xiii

Part 1: Open Source Investigations in the Age of Google: Introduction, Context and Overview   1

1. Open Source Investigations in the Age of Google: How Digital Sleuths Can Strengthen Human Security   2
   Henrietta Wilson, Olamide Samuel and Dan Plesch

Part 2: Transparency and Accountability   23

2.1. Tracking Human Rights Abuses through Online Open Source Research   24
   Benjamin Strick

2.2. Open Source Investigations on the Ground: Reflections on Experiences from South Sudan   45
   Geoffrey Lou Duke

2.3. Monitoring Nuclear Weapons Developments with Open Source Intelligence   63
   Hans M. Kristensen and Matt Korda

2.4. Remote Scrutiny: How Online Information Can Help to
    Investigate Airstrikes   83
    Christiaan Triebert

2.5. Links in the Chain: How The Berkeley Protocol is
    Strengthening Digital Investigation Standards in
    International Justice   108
    Lindsay Freeman and Alexa Koenig

Part 3: Information and Societies   127

3.1. Open Source Journalism, Misinformation and the War
    for Truth in Syria   128
    Muhammad Idrees Ahmad

3.2. Saviour or Menace? Crowdsourcing Open Source
    Research and the Rise of QAnon   147
    Aric Toler

3.3. Collecting Conflict Data Worldwide: ACLED's Contribution 166
    Andrea Carboni and Clionadh Raleigh

3.4. OSINT and the US Intelligence Community: Is the Past
    Prologue?   183
    Kathleen M. Vogel

Part 4: Global Governance   199

4.1. Open Source Investigations before the Age of Google:
    The Harvard Sussex Program   200
    Henrietta Wilson, Richard Guthrie and Brian Balmer

4.2. The Verification of Dual-Use Chemicals under the
    Chemical Weapons Convention through Open Source
    Research: The Pugwash-SIPRI Thiodiglycol Project   217
    Robert J. Mathews

4.3. The Role of Open Source Data and Methods in Verifying
    Compliance with Weapons of Mass Destruction Agreements   234
    James Revill and María Garzón Maceda

4.4. Current OSINT Applications for Weapons Monitoring
and Verification — 252
Dan Liu and Zuzanna Gwadera

Part 5: Data, Methods and Platforms — **271**

5.1. Identifying and Collecting Public Domain Data for
Tracking Cybercrime and Online Extremism — 272
Lydia Wilson, Viet Anh Vu, Ildikó Pete and Yi Ting Chua

5.2. Assessing the Relationship between Machine Learning
and Open Source Research in International Security — 293
Jamie Withorne

5.3. Shadow World Investigations: Tracking Corruption in
the Arms Trade — 309
*Rhona Michie, Paul Holden, Andrew Feinstein and
Alexandra Smidman*

5.4. Democratization of OSINT: The Vision, Purpose, Tools
and Development of the Datayo Platform — 328
Veronika Bedenko and Jonathan Bellish

Part 1

Open Source Investigations in the Age of Google: Introduction, Context and Overview

© 2024 World Scientific Publishing Company
https://doi.org/10.1142/9781800614079_0001

Chapter 1

Open Source Investigations in the Age of Google: How Digital Sleuths Can Strengthen Human Security

Henrietta Wilson, Olamide Samuel and Dan Plesch

Abstract

A growing number of digital investigators, analysts, activists and agencies are electing to observe and understand the world through open source research, revealing detailed information that would otherwise remain unknown and unanalyzed. Their work is made possible by technological advances that enable people to access and process conventional and novel data sources that, while publicly available, may be too obscure, voluminous or dynamic to be handled using more traditional methods. These emerging practices provide new opportunities for innovative monitoring, post-hoc investigation and sense making, and suggest radical possibilities for global justice, accountability and governance. This book brings together chapters from leading open source research practitioners and experts, describing and analyzing this fast-growing sector from multiple perspectives, as well as showcasing specific investigations, methods and tools, and examining how findings can be applied across a very wide set of contexts. This opening chapter frames the contributions that follow by identifying and exploring common themes and challenges, and assessing the opportunities for, barriers to, and significance of this exciting new field.

Introduction

On 11 March 2022, Chris Kubecka tweeted:

> #FF Special thank you to @dutch_osintguy who helped myself & 25 other people get out safely from Kyiv #Ukraine to the border with Romania. We would not be

---

This is an open access article published by World Scientific Publishing Europe Ltd. and distributed under the terms of the Creative Commons Attribution-NonCommercial 4.0 International (CC BY-NC 4.0) License.

alive today if he hadn't tracked my phone & rerouted our convoy moments before imminent Russian bombing. Dankjewel![1]

A *Vice* article later gave more details, describing how a group of open source researchers (including Nico Dekens – @dutch_osintguy) used 'a mix of manual and semi-automatic tools' to find and analyze publicly available information in order to identify danger zones in Ukraine, follow the location of Chris and her 25 companions, and guide them along safe paths out of the country. Chris, Nico and others subsequently teamed up to help additional people to leave Ukraine safely using similar techniques.[2]

This anecdote provides a dramatic example of a wider trend: The way in which we find out about the world is changing profoundly. Digital technologies are transforming the production, dissemination and scrutiny of public domain information, providing an unprecedented capability to 'see' and interact with events around the world, with radical implications for the creation and consumption of global news, and the analysis and comprehension of world events. These new practices have been dubbed 'open source investigations', 'open source research', 'open source intelligence' (OSINT) and similar, each label emphasizing their reliance on open (non-classified) tools, data and materials.[3]

Whatever the name, there is widespread and growing excitement about the rise of open source approaches, despite or perhaps because of the

---

[1] Kubecka C. (@SecEvangelism). #FF Special thank you to@dutch_osintguy who helped myself & 25 other people get out safely from Kyiv #Ukraine... *Twitter*. 11 March 2022. Available from: https://twitter.com/SecEvangelism/status/1502339767668809737 [Accessed 28 August 2022].

[2] Geiger G. and Skov Andersen S. Inside the OSINT Operation to get Foreign Students Out of Ukraine. *Vice*. 18 March 2022. Available from: https://www.vice.com/en/article/epx88p/inside-the-osint-operation-to-get-foreign-students-out-of-ukraine [Accessed 4 June 2022]; Personal communication, Nico Dekens to Henrietta Wilson [email] 25 April 2022.

[3] There is no single agreed term for the sector. While some practitioners refer to OSINT (open source intelligence), many avoid this, wanting to avoid any association with the endeavours of national intelligence agencies. Some prefer 'open source research' (although others think this misleadingly implies a connection with collective software development projects, or feel that the word 'research' should be reserved for academics), and yet others use 'open source investigations' (although some people think that this should only be applied to projects hunting down facts about particular incidents in the past), open source analysis, open source verification, or similar. This book does not attempt to resolve this variation; each chapter specifies its preferred term/s and definitions. This chapter uses the terms open source investigations and open source research interchangeably, using both to mean analyses that use publicly available tools and data.

multiple different understandings of their nature and significance. This book explores these matters from a range of perspectives, collecting together a set of new chapters by leading practitioners and experts, each of which presents diverse experiences and insights. In the remainder of this chapter, we will frame these contributions by considering some common characteristics, trends and contradictions that run through the emerging open source research sector. We begin by exploring what open source research is, how it is done and who is involved. We then review ethical dimensions of the work, detail some of its advantages and limitations, and consider how societies can best benefit from it. These discussions cross-reference the book's other chapters, and an overview of the structure of the rest of the book is provided in the penultimate section. We conclude by examining the wider context around this developing field and argue that societies should take steps to understand and harness the full potential of open source research.

Sleuthing in the Age of Google: What, How and Who?

Open source investigations involve finding publicly available information sources, checking their accuracy, and piecing them together to build insights into events or situations. Before the widespread use of the internet, open source research involved collecting information from traditional media (e.g. newspapers, TV and radio broadcasts), publications (e.g. books, academic journals) and other materials (e.g. industry brochures).[4] Digital technologies and resources – such as the World Wide Web and camera phones, as well as digital data repositories, online databases and live satellite feeds – have dramatically increased the scope and reach of this work, allowing practitioners to locate, harvest, process, organize and store large quantities of data much more easily.[5] New technologies have facilitated vastly improved access to traditional media from around the world, and they have also opened a window on entirely novel data sets such as from satellite imagery and social media posts.

---

[4] See the chapters by H. Wilson *et al.* and Mathews in this volume (Chapters 4.1 and 4.2) for examples of open source research that predates recent developments in digital technologies.

[5] Tools that integrate multiple different aspects of this process are also available, for example, allowing automated searches to be undertaken alongside live visualizations of emerging research results.

Some investigations focus on making sense of a single event, such as the murder of two women and two young children in Cameroon,[6] an airstrike on a mosque in Syria[7] or the use of a nerve agent against Russian opposition politician Navalny.[8] By contrast, other investigations monitor trends over time, for example, the evolution of online extremism,[9] global numbers of nuclear weapons[10] or trade in materials that could have illicit uses.[11] Tracking these patterns is valuable in itself, and can also enable researchers to identify 'red flags' that indicate possible wrongdoing, prompting targeted follow-up investigations. Whether examining individual events or broader trends, and depending on the interests and resources of the practitioners involved, investigations can generate a near-real-time picture of developments, or may involve longer-term study to gain useful insights.

Uncovering details of incidents or patterns is not always straightforward or clear. Most data provide only partial or ambiguous fragments of a bigger picture; once sources have been authenticated as being genuine and accurate, investigations usually need to combine diverse data relevant to the target scenarios, rather than finding single items of conclusive evidence. Practitioners generally use multiple approaches to discover and analyze several data sources, and cross-check these against each other to generate robust insights. For example, videos circulated on social media can be compared to satellite imagery to 'geolocate' and 'chronolocate' their content (pinpoint the exact place and time of the recorded events);[12] global trade and export data can be aggregated and scrutinized for discrepancies that could indicate illicit weapons proliferation or corruption;[13] and newspaper reports in multiple languages can be collated to reveal patterns of political

---

[6] This was the focus of a BBC Africa Eye investigation *Anatomy of a Killing* that Benjamin Strick contributed to. See the chapters by Strick and Toler in this volume (Chapters 2.1 and 3.2).

[7] See the chapter by Triebert in this volume (Chapter 2.4).

[8] Bellingcat uncovered details of this assassination attempt. Bellingcat Investigative Team. 'If it Hadn't Been for the Prompt Work of the Medics': FSB Officer Inadvertently Confesses Murder Plot to Navalny. *Belllingcat*. 21 December 2020. Available from: https://www.bellingcat.com/news/uk-and-europe/2020/12/21/if-it-hadnt-been-for-the-prompt-work-of-the-medics-fsb-officer-inadvertently-confesses-murder-plot-to-navalny/ [Accessed 19 July 2022].

[9] See the chapter by L. Wilson *et al.* in this volume (Chapter 5.1).

[10] See the chapter by Kristensen & Korda in this volume (Chapter 2.3).

[11] See the chapters by Mathews and Liu & Gwadera in this volume (Chapters 4.2 and 4.4).

[12] See the chapters by Strick and Triebert in this volume (Chapters 2.1 and 2.4) for more information on these techniques.

[13] See the chapter by Liu & Gwadera in this volume (Chapter 4.4).

violence.[14] The resulting mosaic of evidence that develops may be more or less complete; while the findings of some investigations may be unequivocal and authoritative, others may be less categorical or conclusive. Relatedly, different investigations may *require* different levels of confidence in their results; while some projects may need near certainty regarding their discoveries, others may be able to act on a potential breach based on information that passes a lower threshold of proof.[15]

Open source research is being pursued by an increasing number of actors and institutions, including governments, law enforcement agencies, journalists and commercial enterprises, as well as think-tanks, civil society groups, universities and international organizations such as the United Nations and its associated agencies. The complexity and multifaceted nature of investigations mean that they tend to be both labour- and time-intensive, and require a combination of skills, expertise and attention[16] that is often beyond the scope of a single researcher. Consequently, they often involve teams of individuals or multiple organizations that may extend across cities, countries and time zones, and might comprise paid staff, volunteers or a mixture of the two. Just as digital technologies facilitate the actual data collection, management and analysis that drive open source research, they are key to enabling this kind of distributed collaboration,[17] and are catalysing the emergence of virtual support communities that network together practitioners, welcome and integrate newcomers, coordinate informal peer review and share tips about, and training in, different techniques.[18]

---

[14] See the chapter by Carboni & Raleigh in this volume (Chapter 3.3).

[15] See the chapter by Freeman & Koenig in this volume (Chapter 2.5).

[16] It took approximately 10 people working 10 hours a day, every day for a month, to uncover the details of the murder of two women and two young children in North Cameroon. Personal communications, Nico Dekens to Henrietta Wilson [email] 25 April 2022, and Benjamin Strick Centre for Information Resilience to Henrietta Wilson [email] 22 June 2022. The murder investigation is recorded in BBC Africa Eye. *Anatomy of a Killing* [video online]. 2018. Available from https://www.youtube.com/watch?v=XbnLkc6r3yc [Accessed 14 May 2023], and is described in the chapters by Strick and Toler in this volume (Chapters 2.1 and 3.2).

[17] For example, teams coordinate their work through Twitter, Slack, Discord, WhatsApp, Telegram, Signal, etc.

[18] See, for example, training materials and community support provided by Bellingcat, Available from https://www.bellingcat.com/category/resources/ [Accessed 14 May 2023]; OSINT Curious, Available from: https://osintcurio.us/ [Accessed 20 July 2022]; OSINT Combine, Available from https://www.osintcombine.com/ [Accessed 14 May 2023]; Benjamin Strick, Available from https://benjaminstrick.com/youtube/ [Accessed 14 May 2023]; and SOAS University of London's webinar series *Verification in the Age of Google*. Available from: https://www.scrapweapons.com/verification-in-the-age-of-google-earth-webinar-series/ [Accessed 20 July 2022].

While some collaborations emerge organically in response to specific events (such as the use of chemical weapons[19] or airstrikes[20] in Syria), others are more formally constituted – deliberately assembled and explicitly managed in order to systematically research and capture evidence about particular issue areas or situations.[21,22] For projects targeting particular geographic regions or spatially located events, local monitors are often essential; many projects would be impossible without on-the-ground investigators sharing testimony about events or circumstances in their area, or explaining specific cultural or linguistic contexts.[23]

Open source research practitioners can face risks to their physical and mental well-being. While remote monitors' work is often far removed from the events and situations that they investigate, they may nevertheless receive physical threats and develop PTSD as a result of observing atrocities and other distressing material, e.g. via video feeds.[24] However, local investigators in troubled regions are likely to face the biggest dangers in the open source research community. They may risk their physical safety in documenting and sharing evidence of wrongdoing in their community, whilst also often being the least protected and the most motivated to engage with and document dangers.[25]

Practitioner diversity within the open source research community is often raised as an issue; innovation in online remote investigation has been predominantly driven by practitioners based in open societies in the Global North.[26] Many open source researchers are aware of this, and aim to build more heterogeneous communities by actively recruiting and supporting partners local to the settings being investigated, providing free training and

---

[19] See the chapters by Freeman & Koenig, Ahmad, and Revill & Garzón Maceda in this volume (Chapters 2.5, 3.1 and 4.3).

[20] See the chapter by Triebert in this volume (Chapter 2.4).

[21] See chapters by Carboni & Raleigh, Mathews, and Bedenko & Bellish for examples (Chapters 3.3, 4.2 and 5.4).

[22] There is anecdotal evidence that some domains are more amenable to spontaneous collaborations; e.g. investigations into human rights atrocities often attract attention and volunteers.

[23] See the chapter by Duke in this volume (Chapter 2.2).

[24] Higgins E. *We Are Bellingcat; An Intelligence Agency for the People.* London: Bloomsbury. 2021, p. 189.

[25] See the chapter by Duke in this volume (Chapter 2.2).

[26] See the chapters by Revill & Garzón Maceda and Liu & Gwadera (Chapters 4.3 and 4.4).

paid work where possible. But there remain numerous barriers to participation in open source research, and the community's current demographics reflect underlying inequalities. Remote monitoring requires expensive equipment and reliable internet connections, as well as sufficient time, skills and confidence to learn and apply the relevant techniques. Some potential practitioners do not have sufficient resources to become involved.

There are also structural constraints. Non-governmental open source research benefits from legal environments within which people have the right to use the internet without reprisal, and cultures with a tradition of holding authorities to account. By contrast, closed societies are less likely to tolerate this sort of work, and are more likely to dismiss its results. In July 2022, for example, Russia prohibited the open source investigation collective Bellingcat from working inside its territory.[27]

Ethics and Best Practice

The issues of practitioner well-being and diversity (discussed above) are two examples of ethical challenges inherent to open source research. There are of course many others. Sloppy or incompetent open source research can harm societies and individuals, for example, by arriving at false conclusions about events, triggering vigilante actions, and/or undermining truth and trust.[28] However, even well-meaning and rigorous research faces numerous ethical dilemmas. When deciding whether to publish the results of an investigation, researchers need to weigh up the benefits of the increased transparency that publication will bring against the dangers of revealing witness identities and locations,[29] or the risk that it could compromise long-running investigations by alerting research targets to the fact that they are being watched. Practitioners also need to consider the morality of their methods; for example, does uncovering wrongdoing justify potentially violating the terms of use

---

[27] Reuters. Russia bans news outlet Bellingcat, labels it a security threat. *Reuters*. 15 July 2022. Available from: https://www.reuters.com/world/europe/russia-bans-news-outlet-bellingcat-labels-it-security-threat-2022-07-15/ [Accessed 30 August 2022].

[28] See the chapter by Toler in this volume (Chapter 3.2).

[29] The ethical dilemmas faced in open source investigations echo those in national intelligence collection, e.g. national intelligence agencies also have to think carefully about what and when to publish, and how to protect what they need to protect. See Fabre C. *Spying Through a Glass Darkly: The Ethics of Espionage and Counter-Intelligence*. Oxford: Oxford University Press. 2022.

of the various service providers involved in the investigation, or deceiving online Captcha systems in order to automate the mass collection of data from specific online communities?[30] Moreover, at a basic level, how should practitioners choose which issues or events to focus on, whilst ensuring that these choices do not simply reflect and reinforce their own or other people's biases, thereby perpetuating wider discrimination and exploitation?

Various strategies to address the ethics of open source research are being developed and pursued at individual, organizational and community levels. Recognizing that unambiguous 'right answers' may not exist for all ethical issues, approaches generally focus on establishing processes and structures that can guide practice effectively on a case-by-case basis, for example, setting up ethics committees and advisory boards, or setting out ethical criteria to inform decision-making.[31] A prominent example of the latter is the *Berkeley Protocol on Digital Open Source Investigations*, a global leader in understanding and codifying the working practice of online open source analyses, which emphasizes ethical principles and provides methodological guidelines and advice on professional practice.[32] The Stanley Center for Peace and Security has also contributed to ethical open source research practice, developing a process (accompanied by a set of free training materials) with which practitioners can recognize, understand and address the ethical conundrums that they encounter.[33]

As well as being 'the right thing to do', ethical practice in open source research is often recognized as a key element of wider best practice and

---

[30] See the chapter by L. Wilson *et al.* in this volume (Chapter 5.1).

[31] See, for example, the chapters by Duke, Freeman & Koenig, Ahmad, L. Wilson *et al.*, Withorne, Michie *et al.*, and Bedenko & Belish for discussion of the centrality of ethics to open source research, and ways to address this (Chapters 2.2, 2.5, 3.1, 5.1, 5.2, 5.3 and 5.4).

[32] 'Ethical Principles', pp. 14–17 of the *Berkeley Protocol on Digital Open Source Investigations* ('Berkeley Protocol'). Human Rights Center UC Berkeley School of Law and UN Office of the High Commissioner for Human Rights. 2020. Available from: https://www.ohchr.org/sites/default/files/2022-04/OHCHR_BerkeleyProtocol.pdf [Accessed 14 May 2023]. See also the chapter by Freeman & Koenig in this volume (Chapter 2.5).

[33] Hanham M. *Setting Your Moral Compass: A Workbook for Applied Ethics in OSINT*. Stanley Center for Peace and Security. August 2022. Available from: https://stanleycenter.org/publications/osint-applied-ethics-workbook/ [Accessed 1 September 2022]. See also Loehrke B., Kenausis L., al-Kaisy A., Terrill D., and Smits K. *Feeling the Burden: Ethical Challenges and Practices in Open Source Analysis and Journalism*. Stanley Center for Peace and Security. 2022. Available from: https://stanleycenter.org/publications/ethics-osint-analysis-journalism/ [Accessed 1 September 2022]. scu.edu/ethics/ethics-resources/ethical-decision-making/a-framework-for-ethical-decision-making/.

can improve the intrinsic quality and outcomes of analyses. There is broad agreement that open source investigations should be transparent and replicable, to enable others to reproduce and check the accuracy of findings, and that practitioners should be honest about their work and acknowledge the contributions of everyone involved.[34] Adherence to such standards can help ensure that the findings of an open source investigation are more likely to meet the requirements of national and transnational justice and governance bodies or other stakeholders.

At the time of writing (2022–2023), individuals and organizations unilaterally consider whether and how they will address the ethical aspects of their work, whilst at the same time a number of voluntary community-wide approaches are being developed, often linked to specific sectors or end uses (for example, the above-mentioned *Berkeley Protocol* was designed to help investigators to meet the evidentiary needs of the International Criminal Court). In the future, there may be calls to further institutionalize best practice, analogous to the creation of professional bodies and codes of conduct in fields such as engineering, journalism and medicine.[35]

Without some form of recognized quality assurance, it may be difficult to harness the full potential of open source investigations; for example, international weapons treaties may not mandate the use of non-governmental open source research unless it has been formally validated.[36] On the other hand, the current decentralized self-organizing community of open source researchers has value in generating multiple overlapping methodologies and practices, providing redundancies in capacity and fuelling the creativity and flexibility of the work. As the sector develops, it is important that it resolves the competing demands of maintaining its richness whilst striving to attain the highest standards of work and ethical practice throughout the community.

---

[34] Numerous chapters emphasize the importance of these qualities. See, for example, the chapters by Ahmad and Withorne (Chapters 3.1, 5.2), etc.

[35] Maria Robson Morrow considers the different indicators of professionalization in private sector intelligence. See Robson Morrow M. Private Sector Intelligence: on the long path of professionalization. *Intelligence and National Security*. 2022, 37 (3), pp. 404–422.

[36] Wilson H. and Lentzos F. Workshop on OSINT for Treaty Verification [discussion document - confidential]. King's College London. 17 March 2022.

Advantages and Limitations of Open Source Investigations

Open source investigations are proving that they can outperform other forms of monitoring.[37] For example, non-governmental open source researchers were among the first groups to publicly recognize Russia's unprovoked invasion of Ukraine,[38] were the source of the first public findings about new Chinese nuclear weapons capabilities[39] and provided in-depth analyses of the Capitol Hill riots in Washington US.[40] Investigations can be agile and flexible, quickly pivoting to look at diverse issues and geographies.[41] Moreover, because they rely on publicly available information, open source investigations can be easier to cite, as they can be referred to without revealing details of classified intelligence processes and sources.[42]

As well as being responsive and flexible, the sector is impressively creative. Practitioners are innovative in devising novel techniques, finding and exploiting new information sources and methods to get around impediments they encounter. While some practitioners focus on specific issues, geographical areas or methodologies, many do not restrict themselves in this way, instead engaging with a range of approaches in order to tackle an evolving set of diverse research targets. Regardless of the specificity of a practitioner's work, it will often tend to span traditional disciplinary boundaries. For example, one group has explored the interconnections between organized crime, weapons proliferation and illegal wildlife poaching in Africa.[43]

---

[37] See Kemsley H. In OSINT we trust? *The Hill.* 9 January 2021. Available from: https://thehill.com/opinion/national-security/569738-in-osint-we-trust/amp/#click=https://t.co/fSze2tmRLe [Accessed 16 July 2022].

[38] For example see Jeffrey Lewis' investigations, reported in Lerman R. On Google Maps, tracking the invasion of Ukraine. *The Washington Post.* 27 February 2022. Available from: https://www.washingtonpost.com/technology/2022/02/25/google-maps-ukraine-invasion/ [Accessed 15 July 2022].

[39] See the chapter by Kristensen & Korda in this volume (Chapter 2.3).

[40] Philp R. How Open Source Experts Identified the US Capitol Rioters. *Global Investigative Journalism Network.* 15 January 2021. Available from: https://gijn.org/2021/01/15/how-open-source-experts-identified-the-us-capitol-rioters/ [Accessed 15 May 2023].

[41] Vogel (Chapter 3.4 in this volume) documents that the US intelligence community recognizes the flexibility and speed of open source research.

[42] See the chapter by Revill & Garzón Maceda in this volume (Chapter 4.3).

[43] Acharya N. and Mühlen-Schulte A. *The Final Round: Combating Armed Actors, Organized Crime and Wildlife Trafficking.* Bonn International Centre for Conflict Studies BICC. 2016. Available from: https://www.bicc.de/publications/publicationpage/publication/the-final-round-combating-armed-organized-crime-and-wildlife-trafficking-648/ [Accessed 1 September 2022].

Another has pioneered work combining architectural expertise with digital research techniques to build 3D reconstructions of bombings that deliver insights into the details of atrocities.[44]

However, alongside their advantages, open source investigations inevitably face technical, political and systemic challenges. Even the most advanced technologies do not guarantee perfect access to all the information needed to understand particular activities or trends. Satellites do not monitor all places at all times; clouds may obscure key sites; companies or governments may intentionally blur images to disguise sensitive military sites or events.[45] Moreover, people can evade overhead scrutiny by simply covering their activities; for example, Syria shielded its clandestine nuclear weapons programme from satellite observations by placing it in a large building at Al Kibar.[46]

Additional technological blind spots reflect the fluidity of contemporary technology and information landscapes. For example, social media are inherently dynamic. Although posts may be readily available, they can be easily revised, removed or ignored. Communities use social media in very specialized ways – juxtaposing regular text with slang, emojis, abbreviations, images, videos and loan words and often using different terms to refer to the same thing – and their habits can quickly shift, making it hard to decode original meanings. Moreover, open source investigations are in a 'cat-and-mouse' relationship with the groups that they monitor. When practitioners publish details of their work, they cannot avoid revealing what data sources they are accessing and how they are extracting information from them. It is likely that determined wrongdoers can use these details to take steps to evade future scrutiny. Further, practitioners may find their options are restricted by changes to the functionality or terms of use of the data or tools that they employ,[47] and, as indicated above, their work can be constrained by the political, legal and cultural contexts in which it takes place.

---

[44] Forensic Architecture, based at Goldsmiths, University of London. Available from: https://forensic-architecture.org/ [Accessed 15 July 2022].

[45] For example, see the chapters by Triebert and Strick in this volume for details of blocks on satellite data in Palestine and China (Chapters 2.4 and 2.1).

[46] Narang V. *Seeking the Bomb: Strategies of Nuclear Proliferation*. Princeton and Oxford: Princeton University Press. 2022, p. 1.

[47] See the chapter by Strick in this volume (Chapter 2.1).

Even in territories with permissive and protective legal frameworks that are currently more conducive to open source research, there is no guarantee that such conditions will remain in the future.

More fundamentally, what practitioners 'see' depends on what they are looking for. While attention is inevitably drawn to 'hotspots' – such as the Malaysian Airlines Flight 17 MH17 crash on 17 July 2014[48] – other atrocities are underreported and overlooked. But 'non-observations' in an area could generate a false impression that there is nothing to worry about there. In some contexts, the absence of evidence is interpreted as evidence of absence.[49]

Meanwhile, the digital technologies that underpin the positive contributions of open source research may also have harmful consequences, whether arising from misuse that is inadvertent, mischievous or malicious. Such misapplications include the creation of deepfake frauds, and the doxing or trolling of individuals.[50] Digital technologies also exacerbate the potential for misinformation and disinformation campaigns, many of which have enormous reach (whether they are credible or not), undermining societies' health, trust and political processes. Damaging in themselves, they also complicate open source investigations, adding to the challenges of checking the accuracy and provenance of data, muddying the information landscape and confounding the difficulties of distinguishing between genuine and inaccurate reports.

Continuity of funding is also an issue for open source investigators. Many innovations derive from non-governmental groups and individuals who rely on short-term funding, some of which is conditional on practitioners undertaking particular projects, or achieving designated outcomes, that can therefore impose an influential power dynamic (for example, human rights investigations can attract more funding than those focussed on tracking

---

[48] Higgins E. MH17 – The Open Source Evidence. *Bellingcat.* 2015. Available from: https://www.bellingcat.com/news/uk-and-europe/2015/10/08/mh17-the-open-source-evidence/ [Accessed 15 July 2022].

[49] Personal communication, Gabriele Kraatz-Wadsack to Henrietta Wilson [email] 24 June 2022.

[50] See also the chapter by Toler in this volume (Chapter 3.2) for details of how the conspiracy theory movement QAnon misused open sourced research techniques in activities that ultimately led to the 6 January 2021 US Capitol Hill Riots.

small arms and light weapons in Africa).[51] Without sustained funding with no strings attached, there are limits to the work that can be done, and the people that can be involved.[52]

Overcoming Challenges: Innovation and Hybrid Approaches

While these challenges are to an extent unavoidable, the intrinsic nature of open source research offers some tools that can help to mitigate them. Perhaps most significantly, the use of varied methods across fluid communities provides some inherent redundancy in open source research practice, enabling broad coverage of multiple areas from multiple perspectives, and the possibility of self-organizing checks and balances that can assure quality, guard against bias, and reduce the size and number of blind spots. Some funders are beginning to recognize the strengths and potential of the sector and are supporting its sustained growth with core funding.[53]

The heterogeneous, multifarious nature of open source research sometimes stretches to include the use of 'closed' materials. For example, some open source investigations can be steered by a general awareness of classified sources, while others use more explicitly 'hybrid' approaches that directly involve both open and closed sources.[54] While practitioners have different attitudes to whether and when they are prepared to use closed material, this decision is not always obvious. For instance, there is not always a clear divide between open and closed sources; 'closed' sources can become 'open' through being leaked or declassified. Further, an 'open' data source need not necessarily be easily available: Numerous publicly available sources are obscure, either because they are difficult to understand, or

---

[51] See the chapter by Duke in this volume (Chapter 2.2).

[52] See the chapter by Vogel in this volume (Chapter 3.4) for discussion of bureaucratic factors impeding the US intelligence community's adoption of open source research.

[53] Walker J. Bellingcat to establish new office in The Hague after €500,000 funding win through Dutch postcode lottery. *PressGazette*. 2019. Available from: https://pressgazette.co.uk/bellingcat-to-establish-new-office-in-the-hague-after-e500000-funding-win-through-dutch-postcode-lottery/ [Accessed 8 September 2022].

[54] For example, see the chapters by H. Wilson *et al.* and Michie *et al.* in this volume (Chapters 4.1 and 5.3).

because getting hold of them is costly, time-consuming or requires specialist knowledge.[55]

Using multiple techniques and multiple sources helps practitioners to collect sufficient information to build reliable results. The contrasting experiences of national intelligence collection and international disarmament inspections in Iraq from 1991 through to the early 2000s are instructive on this point. The 1991 Iraq war ended on the condition that Iraq declared and eliminated its nuclear, chemical and biological weapons and long-range missiles, and that it do so under the supervision of international inspectors.[56] Three different groups were appointed for this: UNSCOM (1991–1999) and UNMOVIC (1999–2007) were tasked with finding and destroying Iraq's chemical and biological weapons and long-range missiles, and the IAEA was given responsibility for uncovering and eliminating Iraq's nuclear weapons (1991–2007).[57] Despite Saddam Hussein's deliberate and blatant attempts to obstruct and evade the ceasefire agreement that set out the disarmament requirements, the inspectors found and destroyed large quantities of Iraq's weapons of mass destruction and long-range missiles.[58] They did this by combining multiple innovative approaches[59] that included both open source information and circumspect use of classified material from national intelligence agencies. They carefully vetted all incoming intelligence; while some was invaluable, a lot was unreliable.[60]

By contrast, the UK and US governments used uncorroborated closed sources – some based on single human testimony – to make allegations

---

[55] See the chapter by H. Wilson *et al.* in this volume (Chapter 4.1) for a framework for understanding different categories of open and closed sources.
[56] UN Security Council Resolution 687. 3 April 1991. Available from: https://www.sipri.org/sites/default/files/2016-03/687.pdf [Accessed 12 September 2022].
[57] United Nations Security Council Resolution 1762. Available from: http://unscr.com/en/resolutions/doc/1762 [Accessed 11 January 2023]
[58] Trevan T. *Saddam's Secrets*. London: HarperCollins. 1999.
[59] Many of these techniques foreshadow contemporary open source investigations, including, e.g. pioneering the use overhead imagery similar to today's more widespread use of satellite imagery, and developing a 'material accountancy' approach that collected and compared known global exports of materials that could be used in weapons programmes with Iraq's holdings, similar to current trade investigations (described in the chapter by Liu & Gwadera in this volume, Chapter 4.4). Black S., Wilson H. and Lentzos F. UNSCOM's work to uncover Iraq's illicit biological weapons program: A primer. *Bulletin of the Atomic Scientists*. 2021, 77 (4). https://doi.org/10.1080/00963402.2021.1941592.
[60] Research conversations between Hans Blix and Henrietta Wilson, 2, 9 and 10 October 2018.

in 2002 that Iraq had resumed its illicit weapons programmes.[61] These allegations were not supported by the international inspection groups. UNMOVIC's Executive Chairman Hans Blix reported that the inspectors 'had found no evidence of the continuation or resumption of programmes of weapons of mass destruction'.[62] The IAEA Action Team discredited parts of the intelligence,[63] and on 7 March 2003 the IAEA Director General reported that 'After three months of intrusive inspections, we have to date found no evidence or plausible indication of the revival of a nuclear weapons programme in Iraq'.[64] Nevertheless, the UK and US governments went on to make a case for war, and on 19 March 2003 began military action with devastating consequences for Iraq, for security in the Middle East and for the legacies of Tony Blair and the George W Bush administration.

After Detection, What?

What happens once open source investigations have uncovered details about wrongdoing through diligent, robust and ethical research? How can their work be used to punish or prevent wrongdoing?[65] Different investigators have different approaches to these matters. Perhaps most prominently, open source investigations are impacting on global justice and accountability,

---

[61] Drogin B. and Goetz J. How U.S. Fell Under the Spell of 'Curveball'. *Los Angeles Times*. 2005. Available from: https://www.latimes.com/world/middleeast/la-na-curveball20nov20-story.html [Accessed 2 September 2022].

[62] UNSC Press Release, SC/7777. *UN Inspectors Found No Evidence of Prohibited Weapons Programmes as of 18 March Withdrawal, Hans Blix Tells Security Council* [press release]. 5 June 2003. Available from: https://press.un.org/en/2003/sc7777.doc.htm [Accessed 2 June 2023].

[63] See for example: Baute J. Timeline Iraq: Challenges and Lessons Learned from Nuclear Inspections. *IAEA Bulletin*. 2004, 46 (1). Available from: https://www.iaea.org/sites/default/files/publications/magazines/bulletin/bull46-1/46102486468.pdf; and the account of inspector Frank Pabian's findings on aluminium tubes found in Iraq, described in Gellman B. *Angler: The Cheney Vice Presidency*. London: Penguin, 2008.

[64] ElBaradei M. The Status of Nuclear Inspections in Iraq: An Update (7 March 2003). *International Atomic Energy Agency*. Available from: https://www.iaea.org/newscenter/statements/status-nuclear-inspections-iraq-update [Accessed 8 September 2003].

[65] This is a recurrent question in arms control and disarmament. Iklé F.C. After Detection – What? *Foreign Affairs*. January 1961. Available from: https://www.foreignaffairs.com/articles/1961-01-01/after-detection-what [Accessed 16 July 2022].

providing findings that have been used in successful national[66] and international prosecutions.[67] Moreover, the growth and successes of open source research have informed innovations in justice itself. For example, in 2017, the International Criminal Court (ICC) issued an arrest warrant in response to evidence primarily derived from social media.[68]

Open source research also has a track record in contributing to robust national and international policy-making and implementation. Expertise built from open sources can provide ways for non-governmental groups to connect to spaces where policy decisions are made: Once connected, they can use their expertise to understand and inform decisions.[69] Policy-making can also benefit from 'early warnings' of impending crises delivered by open source research, for example, in the context of political unrest and violence,[70] climate disruption and environmental degradation[71] or food security.[72]

Beyond contributing to legal and policy-making systems, shining a light on wrongdoing can trigger additional actions by governments, international organizations, legal institutions, citizens groups and individuals. Open source research has compelled governments both to admit their own liability and to impose fines on others,[73] and has led social media platforms to remove accounts associated with attempts to distort democratic elections.[74] It can also strengthen regional and national democratic processes, including

---

[66] See, for example, the chapter by Carboni & Raleigh in this volume, for information about how their work contributed to legal proceedings in the USA (Chapter 3.3), and the chapter by Strick for information on how his work contributed to the arrest, prosecution and conviction of murderers (Chapter 2.1).

[67] See the chapter by Freeman & Koenig in this volume (Chapter 2.5).

[68] Freeman L. Prosecuting Atrocity Crimes with Open Source Evidence: Lessons from the International Criminal Court. Dubberley S., Koenig A., and Murray D. (eds.). *Digital Witness*. Oxford: Oxford University Press. 2020, pp. 48–67.

[69] See the chapters by Duke, Mathews, and H. Wilson *et al.* in this volume (Chapters 2.2, 4.2 and 4.1).

[70] See the chapter by Carboni & Raleigh in this volume (Chapter 3.3).

[71] See for example World Meteorological Organization. Early Warning Systems Must Protect Everyone Within Five Years [press release]. *World Meteorological Organization*. 23 March 2022. Available from: https://public.wmo.int/en/media/press-release/%E2%80%8Bearly-warning-systems-must-protect-everyone-within-five-years#:~:text=%E2%80%9CThis%20is%20unacceptable%2C%20particularly%20with,warning%20systems%20within%20five%20years [Accessed 6 June 2023].

[72] See for example UNCTAD. CropWatch Innovative Cooperation Programme. Available from: https://unctad.org/project/cropwatch-innovative-cooperation-programme [Accessed 20 July 2022].

[73] See the chapters by Strick and Triebert in this volume (Chapters 2.1 and 2.4).

[74] See the chapter by Strick in this volume (Chapter 2.1).

by providing citizens with accurate information and correcting false narratives, for example, by revealing drone strikes and chemical weapons use in Syria,[75] generating reliable insights into otherwise secret details of global nuclear weapons,[76] establishing fatality numbers in Yemen[77] and refuting allegations of suspected centrifuge activity linked to illegal nuclear weapons proliferation in Iran.[78]

But a word of caution: While transparency can and does lead to positive outcomes, it is not always desirable. Better results are sometimes achieved by choosing not to reveal wrongdoing. The demand for too much transparency can limit options at politically sensitive moments, and reduce the chances of achieving policy objectives.[79] For example, exerting pressure on countries behind closed doors can result in them abandoning illicit nuclear weapons programmes, while 'going public' can result in determined proliferators doubling down on their activities.[80]

Nevertheless, when used wisely, transparency can change behaviours that are harmful to societies and individuals. Publishing information about the costs of infrastructure projects has reduced corruption in public procurement,[81] and the mere threat of such publication can be a restraining influence – if potential wrongdoers believe that their actions are visible and therefore that they can be held to account for them, they may be more likely to stop short of illicit behaviours. Transparency is also seen as essential to minimizing the risks associated with nuclear weapons, achieving effective irreversible nuclear non-proliferation and disarmament,[82] and more broadly,

---

[75] See the chapters by Triebert, Ahmad and Revill & Garzón Maceda in this volume (Chapters 2.4, 3.1 and 4.3).

[76] See the chapter by Kristensen & Korda in this volume (Chapter 2.3).

[77] See the chapter by Carboni & Raleigh in this volume (Chapter 3.3).

[78] See the chapter by Withorne in this volume (Chapter 5.2).

[79] Coe A. J. and Vaynman J. Why Arms Control is so Rare. *American Political Science Review*. 2020, 114 (2), pp. 342–355.

[80] Nutt C. G. and Pauly R. B. C. Caught Red-Handed: How States Wield Proof to Coerce Wrongdoers. *International Security*. 2021, 46 (2), pp. 7–50. Available from: https://direct.mit.edu/isec/article-abstract/46/2/7/107694/Caught-Red-Handed-How-States-Wield-Proof-to-Coerce [Accessed 2 September 2022].

[81] "Why CoST?", CoST Infrastructure Transparency Initiative. Available from: https://infrastructuretransparency.org/about-us/our-mission-and-vision/why-cost/ [Accessed 2 September 2022].

[82] Podvig P. *Transparency in Nuclear Disarmament*. UNIDIR. 2012. Available from: https://unidir.org/sites/default/files/publication/pdfs/transparency-in-nuclear-disarmament-390.pdf [Accessed 2 September 2022].

helping to stabilize antagonistic relationships. During the Cold War, for example, the USA and USSR informed each other about military matters to reduce risks of nuclear weapons' use, and accepted intrusive transparency and verification measures within international disarmament agreements. Contemporary open source investigators are developing new ways to build transparency and connect with diverse end users and other stakeholders in the pursuit of improved justice, accountability and governance systems.

Overview of the Book

This book collects together a set of detailed examples of open source investigations written by prize-winning practitioners and rising stars in open source research, as well as accounts from expert commentators. Between them, they detail investigations from around the world that target numerous different risks to human security, including human rights abuses, paedophilia, corruption, murder, weapons of mass destruction (WMD), influence operations, destruction of communities, political violence, conventional weapons, dual-use exports, online extremism, cybercrime and terrorism.[83] As wide ranging as this list is, it is by no means exhaustive. Future volumes could address open source investigations focussed on, for example, environmental destruction, food security and public health.

The chapters in Part 2 deal with the related topics of Transparency and Accountability. Strick (2.1), Kristensen and Korda (2.3), and Triebert (2.4) show how they conduct open source research at a distance to uncover information on human rights abuses, global nuclear weapons and airstrikes in Syria, respectively. Complementing these, Duke (2.2) describes work involving local investigators who observe small arms and light weapons in South Sudan, arguing that on-the-ground information is essential in providing local context for investigations, as well as for tracking items and events

---

[83] The book complements technical manuals (such as the books by Michael Bazzell, Available from: https://inteltechniques.com/books.html [Accessed 10 June 2022]), as well as a growing literature on the nature and significance of open source research. See, for example, Dubberley S., Koenig A. and Murray D. (eds.). *Digital Witness: Using Open Source Information for Human Rights Investigation, Documentation, and Accountability*. Oxford: Oxford University Press. 2020; Hobbs C., Moran M. and Salisbury D. *Open Source Intelligence in the Twenty-First Century*. London: Palgrave Macmillan. 2014.

that are too small to be detected by satellites or that are not flagged on social media. Freeman and Koenig (2.5) bridge these accounts, describing how diffuse efforts from distributed networks of remote and local investigators can coordinate via the *Berkeley Protocol*, and that doing so can help ensure that investigation results deliver evidence which meets the standards needed by the International Criminal Court.

Part 3 of the book presents four chapters that address the role of open source research in understanding Information and Societies, exploring the social impacts of open source investigations – both good and bad. Ahmad (3.1) shows that the rise of open source investigations has been driven by, and is helping to address, modern crises in investigative journalism, and in doing so, can counter the proliferation of harmful misinformation and disinformation. By contrast, Toler (3.2) details a darker side to the uptake of new digital techniques, detailing the dire consequences of QAnon's misapplication of open source research techniques. Following this, Carboni and Raleigh (3.3) detail ACLED's work compiling political violence datasets that have been used to correct false narratives about worldwide conflicts, demonstrating ways in which a project's choice of research methods affects its findings. Vogel (3.4) rounds off this section of the book by documenting the attitude of the US intelligence community to open source intelligence, and explains why its acceptance has been slow, despite a stated commitment to the contrary.

The penultimate group of chapters addresses the topic of Global Governance and considers open source investigations in the context of WMD disarmament and non-proliferation. The first two chapters describe the role of open source research in efforts to ban chemical and biological warfare. Here, H. Wilson *et al.* (4.1) and Mathews (4.2) show that international treaties can benefit from non-governmental research, and more broadly, that open source research expertise can enable non-governmental groups to access and contribute to national and international policy-making. Revill and Garzón Maceda (4.3) and Liu and Gwadera (4.4) examine whether and how WMD treaties can make use of open source research, and analyze obstacles to, and possibilities for, harnessing this potential.

The final chapters delve into the specific details and general challenges related to Data, Methods and Platforms. L. Wilson *et al.* (5.1) describe automated tools for collecting and compiling data on cybercrime and violent extremism, while Withorne (5.2) introduces a framework with which to understand when and how to apply machine learning in open source research. Both chapters emphasize that while digital tools facilitate working with large volumes of data, doing this effectively remains a non-trivial task. Automated tools must be guided by human expertise, and can produce misleading results if not carefully constructed and implemented soundly. Person-led approaches are also complex, as shown by Michie *et al.* (5.3) in their overview of how they uncover corruption in the arms trade by finding, scrutinizing and piecing together multiple data sources, and by Bedenko and Bellish (5.4) who present a new platform for coordinating crowdsourced research into nuclear weapons risks, and remind us that ethical issues are front and centre of open source investigations.

The book's chapters present a unique set of experiences, understandings and insights into open source investigations. Together, they provide a snapshot of the state of the art in open source research at the time they were written (2021–2023). Consequently, they represent a record of current trends and a benchmark against which future developments can be assessed.

Summing Up and Conclusions

The rapid growth and development of open source research is one manifestation of the changes to society stemming from the rise of digital technologies and the way in which their application is upending conventional assumptions and understandings about the world.[84] Whereas powerful states could once be confident that they could keep their secrets secret and manage public perceptions by controlling the flow of information, the enhanced transparency afforded by the combination of digital technologies and human skill and effort means that others – including less powerful states, non-governmental organizations, commercial groups and ultimately the public – can now track and report on global events to an unprecedented degree.

---

[84] See, for example, Moore R. Human Intelligence in the Digital Age [speech transcript]. IISS. 30 November 2021. Available from: https://www.iiss.org/events/2021/11/human-intelligence-digital-age [Accessed 16 July 2022].

For optimists, the rise of open source research signals a new era of transparency and accountability, empowering diverse communities and enabling them to shine a light on atrocities, corruption and illicit actions, bring perpetrators to some form of justice, achieve robust disarmament and extend international controls against WMD. By contrast, pessimists emphasize the difficulty of achieving this vision, highlighting the challenges inherent to exploiting the relevant technologies in ways that are robust and replicable, the fact that the digital information landscape is replete with misinformation and disinformation, and the complexities of arriving at clear conclusions about contested circumstances in tight timescales.

Whichever side of this fence proves more relevant at any particular moment, the scale and variety of open source investigations suggest that they will be unignorable across justice, transparency and governance systems. Decision-makers, experts and the general public need to understand this fast-developing field – including the nuances that determine what it can and cannot be expected to do – to maximize the realization of its potential and to mitigate the dangers of its misuse. The following chapters are a good starting point, outlining the possibilities and challenges afforded by this complex, aspirational and brave new field.

Part 2
Transparency and Accountability

© 2024 World Scientific Publishing Company
https://doi.org/10.1142/9781800614079_0002

Chapter 2.1

Tracking Human Rights Abuses through Online Open Source Research

Benjamin Strick

Abstract

This chapter details common open source research techniques that can reveal important information about human rights abuses. It explains how practitioners working far away from atrocities can establish where they took place, when they happened and who was responsible for them. It illustrates how these methods are used with examples from investigations into events across the globe, including murders, forced detentions, violent destruction of communities and influence operations that undermine democracy. These investigations have led to enhanced transparency and justice outcomes, such as successful prosecutions, the removal of harmful content from social media and greater visibility of atrocities. They also demonstrate the challenges of this sort of work, and the importance of strong collaborative teams in achieving the best results.

Introduction

In recent years, open source researchers have pioneered new applications of digital technologies to uncover the truth about murder, torture, violent destruction of villages, civil unrest, influence campaigns that undermine democracy and other human rights abuses. This chapter will detail how they do this, explaining core open source tools and illustrating their use with examples from investigations by me and others into events in Afghanistan, Cameroon, China, Ethiopia, Indonesia, Myanmar and Nagorno-Karabakh.

This is an open access article published by World Scientific Publishing Europe Ltd. and distributed under the terms of the Creative Commons Attribution-NonCommercial 4.0 International (CC BY-NC 4.0) License.

The chapter shows how common open source research[1] techniques are used to provide evidence-based answers to questions about where atrocities took place, when they happened and who was involved in them. Investigators use these methods to build insights into events across the globe, far removed from where they are based. Because of this, online open source research has become especially useful in cases where practitioners can't visit areas of interest in person because it is too difficult, costly or dangerous for them to do so – for example, areas in war zones, inaccessible regions or repressive regimes.

While online open source investigative methods are undoubtedly useful, it would be wrong to exaggerate their role. In fact, overrelying on particular approaches could prevent investigators from realizing monitoring and transparency possibilities – it remains the case that working collaboratively across different knowledge networks is the most effective way to harness the full potential of the information space of given events. The best results in investigations are usually achieved through hybrid mechanisms, for example, when remote online open source investigators work alongside, or in partnership with, other information, such as from on-the-ground contacts and/or closed sources.

Given that caveat, this chapter will outline frequently used online open source research techniques, looking at past investigations to show how different methods can shine a light on important and simple, yet often unclear, questions about human rights abuses: where and when they happened, and who was responsible.

Where Did It Happen?

Investigations are often triggered by online user-generated content, such as photos or videos posted to social media that suggest an atrocity has taken place. After confirming that the content is authentic and not part of some information campaign, open source researchers work to establish the exact details about what it shows. Investigations into serious wrongdoing need to generate a high level of evidence if they are to successfully trigger wider

---
[1] This chapter defines open source research as research that uses publicly available tools and information.

systems of accountability and justice, such as criminal prosecution,[2] not least as they often encounter concerted attempts to subvert their findings, including through denials of responsibility or the spreading of false rumours.

The first step is usually to establish *where* an event took place, by geolocating it. At its core, geolocation is 'the identification or estimation of the location of an object, an activity or the location from which an item was generated', as defined in the *Berkeley Protocol on Digital Open Source Investigations*.[3] It involves a detailed process of matching online content with a location on satellite imagery, much of which is freely available, by first finding reference points on the image or video and then linking these to features on satellite data. This process aims to establish unique identifiers between the user-generated content and satellite imagery, confirming that that the location identified is the only place that a video or photo could have been taken. Depending upon the nature of the footage or photo, elements such as trees (see Fig. 1), mountains, buildings, street signs, holes in a road

Figure 1: Matching trees to a panorama from footage of the execution video from Cameroon's far north. This image served as part of the evidence for proof of location during the investigation of BBC Africa Eye – *Anatomy of a Killing*.[4]

---

[2] See the chapter by Freeman & Koenig in this volume (Chapter 2.5) for more information about these systems.

[3] *Berkeley Protocol on Digital Open Source Investigations* ('Berkeley Protocol'). Human Rights Center UC Berkeley School of Law and UN Office of the High Commissioner for Human Rights. 2020. p. 66. Available from: https://www.ohchr.org/sites/default/files/2022-04/OHCHR_BerkeleyProtocol.pdf [Accessed 14 May 2023].

[4] BBC Africa Eye. *Anatomy of a Killing* [video online]. 2018. Available from: https://www.youtube.com/watch?v=XbnLkc6r3yc [Accessed 14 May 2023].

or other features create a set of characteristics that provide a unique match between an image and a specific geographical area.

The practice of geolocation allows open source researchers to rigorously test claims about the location of alleged incidents. Moreover, once user-generated content has been geolocated, researchers can further explore what may have happened in the area by scrutinizing additional satellite imagery. Geolocation has been used in numerous cases, including Europol's work finding the locations of child abuse content through crowdsourced efforts,[5,6] discovering missing hikers during search and rescue operations,[7] identifying US military bases overseas[8] and authenticating social media evidence used by the International Criminal Court.[9]

One example of how geolocation can be effective in analyzing footage to a standard that is able to withstand criticism is analyst Nathan Ruser's work authenticating images of '3-400 detainees handcuffed & blindfolded at a train station' in China's Xinjiang region, who were led by guards and positioned in lines, with their heads facing the ground.[10] Ruser geolocated the footage using satellite imagery on Google Earth, identifying a clear match between objects seen in the footage with those in satellite imagery of a train station in Xinjiang. Ruser also went on to analyze when the video was recorded, using chronolocation techniques similar to those described below. The verification, showing exactly where and when the video was filmed, was extremely important given the serious

---

[5]Gonzales C. Two Europol StopChildAbuse Images Geolocated: Part II – Cambodia. *Bellingcat*. 17 December 2019. Available from: https://www.bellingcat.com/news/2019/12/17/two-europol-stopchildabuse-images-geolocated-part-ii-cambodia/ [Accessed 14 May 2023].

[6]For more information on Europol's work, see the chapter by Toler in this volume (Chapter 3.2).

[7]Kovacik R. Missing Hiker Found After Man Using Computer at Home Pinpoints His Location. *NBC Los Angeles*. 15 April 2021. Available from: https://www.nbclosangeles.com/news/california-news/missing-hiker-mt-waterman-photo-search/2572468/ [Accessed 15 May 2023].

[8]Kwai I. What He Did on His Summer Break: Exposed a Global Security Flaw. *The New York Times*. 30 January 2018. Available from: https://www.nytimes.com/2018/01/30/world/australia/strava-heat-map-student.html [Accessed 14 May 2023].

[9]Bellingcat Investigation Team. How a Werfalli Execution Site Was Geolocated. *Bellingcat*. 3 October 2017. Available from: https://www.bellingcat.com/news/mena/2017/10/03/how-an-execution-site-was-geolocated/ [Accessed 14 May 2023].

[10]Ruser N. 4 days ago a video showing 3–400 detainees handcuffed & blindfolded at a train station in Xinjiang was uploaded to YouTube. *Twitter*. 21 September 2019. Available from: https://twitter.com/Nrg8000/status/1175353408749891584?s=20 [Accessed 14 May 2023].

claims by human rights organizations[11] about China's treatment of different minority groups. Ruser's work has been relied upon as evidence by international media[12] questioning Chinese government representatives on the content of the video and allegations of human rights abuses in Xinjiang.

This is not the only use of open source research to identify locations of interest in China's Xinjiang region. BuzzFeed News[13] identified more than 200 prison and internment camps that China had built, contradicting public claims that detainees were being set free.[14] It did this even though relevant areas on Chinese Baidu Maps had been blanked out (see Fig. 2). While the effectiveness of open source investigations is generally contingent on the availability of high-quality data, which was missing in this case, the BuzzFeed team managed to identify many prisons and camps by cross-referencing the blanked out areas with other satellite imagery. This showed that the tiles were covering the locations of prisons and internment camps.

Using technology to geolocate events for justice and accountability purposes does not come without challenges. Often, it can be difficult for investigators to get high-quality images for an area. Access to high-quality satellite imagery can be limited by several factors – it is sometimes deliberately restricted for political reasons, as seen in the Baidu Maps experience; or it might be subject to physical constraints, for example, cloud cover or

---

[11] Amnesty International. China: Draconian repression of Muslims in Xinjiang amounts to crimes against humanity. *Amnesty International*. 10 June 2021. Available from: https://www.amnesty.org/en/latest/news/2021/06/china-draconian-repression-of-muslims-in-xinjiang-amounts-to-crimes-against-humanity/ [Accessed 14 May 2023].

[12] BBC Politics. #Marr asks Chinese ambassador to the UK Liu Xiaoming to explain footage from China of handcuffed and blindfolded detained people. *Twitter*. 19 July 2020. Available from: https://twitter.com/BBCPolitics/status/1284784810200838145?s=20 [Accessed 14 May 2023].

[13] Rajagopalan M., Killing A., and Buschek C. Built To Last. *BuzzFeed News*. 27 August 2020. Available from: https://www.buzzfeednews.com/article/meghara/china-newinternment-camps-xinjiang-uighurs-muslims [Accessed 14 May 2023].

[14] Wang Y. China claims everyone in Xinjiang camps has 'graduated'. *AP News*. 9 December 2019. Available from: https://apnews.com/article/religion-terrorismap-top-news-international-news-politics-27f00e4feaa2755f25ab514cecda7add [Accessed 14 May 2023].

Figure 2: Artist's impression showing a masked tile on Baidu Maps, by Aiden Page, June 2023. The original image was shown in a BuzzFeed News article.[15]

gloomy days can impede the quality of images; or there might simply be an absence of recent satellite imagery of an area.

The August 2021 US withdrawal from Afghanistan, and the Taliban's subsequent quick rise to power, provides an interesting example of the availability of satellite imagery and capability levels of open source research. Before the withdrawal, Google Earth satellite images of the area were extremely limited in terms of their frequency and clarity. Bing maps' imagery was also low quality, with data on large areas of the country being unavailable, blurred or out of date. However, towards the end of August and beginning of September 2021, satellite imagery was made available on Google Earth,[16] opening up access to recent, high-resolution satellite imagery (see Figs. 3a and 3b). This changed the reporting space

---

[15] Killing A., Rajagopalan M., and Buschek C. Blanked-Out Spots On China's Maps Helped Us Uncover Xinjiang's Camps. *BuzzFeed News*. 27 August 2020. Available from: https://www.buzzfeed.com/alison_killing/satellite-images-investigation-xinjiang-detention-camps [Accessed 14 May 2023].

[16] Strick B. Praise be. Someone opened the tap on Afghanistan satellite imagery on @googleearth. *Twitter*. 3 September 2021. Available from: https://twitter.com/BenDoBrown/status/1433717564325220353?s=20 [Accessed 14 May 2023].

Figure 3: (a) and (b) show what an area of Afghanistan looked like on Google Earth before and after the August/September 2021 update. This is satellite imagery on Google Earth of the same location. *Source*: Map data 2021 ©Google.

on Afghanistan, allowing researchers to map conflicts in Panjshir Valley,[17] and enabling more open source investigative journalism on events in Afghanistan, such as a US drone strike that killed 10 civilians.[18]

In my own experience of covering conflicts around the world, the availability of imagery tends to differ dramatically between geographical areas. While an urban landscape in a western city may have regular, up-to-date satellite images, remote villages in less developed areas may severely lack the imagery required to ascertain key details. That said, the restriction of access to clear satellite imagery due to possible censorship ultimately benefitted the BuzzFeed investigation mentioned above, as the redacted parts of Baidu Maps signposted researchers to areas that needed analysis.

Other cases have been less fortunate in their access to suitable satellite imagery, and investigators must find alternative investigative methods. This happened in work aiming to geolocate footage of a massacre in Ethiopia's Tigray region,[19] which showed unarmed victims being killed. BBC Africa Eye, Bellingcat and Newsy worked to verify exactly where the footage was filmed, who the victims were and who was responsible for the killings. The challenge here was to confirm the location of a specific ridgeline seen in the footage, which could establish where exactly the atrocity had taken place. Ridgelines, formed by unique shapes in mountains or hills, can be seen on Google Earth using its 3D view; however, there are frequent issues with the way elevation points are rendered. For example, at times, satellite images clearly indicate jagged or sharp features, but Google Earth 3D view can present these as small hills.

This unevenness in landscapes, and patchiness of technical tools, means that while an investigator may have correctly identified where something was filmed, certain factors might not fit precisely – which can feel like having the right jigsaw piece for a puzzle that is nearly completed, but because

---

[17] Benjamin. Map update. Including dates, descriptions and colour Category's to visualize easier. *Twitter*. 18 September 2021. Available from: https://twitter.com/hengenahm/status/1439343008470667273?s=20 [Accessed 14 May 2023].

[18] New York Times Visual Investigations. *How a U.S. Drone Strike Killed the Wrong Person in Afghanistan* [video online]. 10 September 2021. Available from: https://www.youtube.com/watch?v=ZtecNyXxb9A [Accessed 14 May 2023].

[19] BBC Africa Eye. Evidence suggests Ethiopian military carried out massacre in Tigray. *BBC News*. 1 April 2021. Available from: https://www.bbc.co.uk/news/world-africa-56603022 [Accessed 14 May 2023].

the piece needs a firm push to fit into its place, one doubts whether it is correct. The lack of complete coherence can raise uncertainty and doubt about geolocation findings, or lead to confirmation anxiety.[20] In the investigation of the execution footage from Tigray, investigators used an alternative tool called PeakVisor that renders landscape features more precisely and clearly than is sometimes seen in Google Earth 3D landscapes.[21] This same method has been used in follow-up work (see Fig. 4) in Ethiopia's Tigray region where other mountain ranges have similar profiles, and for which using only Google Earth would result in flawed geolocation.[22]

When Did It Happen?

A second step and integral part of open source investigations is identifying *when* online content was produced, or when an event happened. This is commonly referred to as chronolocation, defined in the *Berkeley Protocol on Digital Open Source Investigations* (see footnote 3) as 'the corroboration of the dates and times of the events depicted in a piece of information, usually visual imagery'.

Chronolocating a piece of information can expand an investigator's lines of inquiry and geospatial awareness. For example, once a specific date of interest is precisely defined, it may flag up that an incident is part of a wider pattern, including by indicating that other incidents are related to the event shown in the original images. This can then be used in follow-up research on other pieces of footage. Identifying when something happened might also help shed light on who was responsible; for example, the date can be used to find out which militia might have been in control of an area at the time, or what military units were operating there.

Several overlapping tools can be used to narrow down the likely timeframe for an incident, and chronolocate it precisely. I will now outline

---

[20] Marciniak M. and Dubberly S. How to Crack Complex Geolocation Challenges: A Case Study of the Mahibere Dego Massacre. *Amnesty International*. 9 April 2021. Available from: https://citizenevidence.org/2021/04/09/geolocation-mahibere-dego/ [Accessed 14 May 2023].
[21] Bellingcat Investigation Team. Mahbere Dego: Clues to a Clifftop Massacre in Ethiopia. *Bellingcat*. 1 April 2021. Available from: https://www.bellingcat.com/news/2021/04/01/mahbere-dego-clues-to-a-clifftop-massacre-in-ethiopia/ [Accessed 14 May 2023].
[22] Strick B. Footage of debris of alleged 'Ethiopian Air Force C-130'… *Twitter*. 25 June 2021. Available from: https://twitter.com/BenDoBrown/status/1408441261212721155?s=20 [Accessed 14 May 2025].

Figure 4: Verification of debris of an 'Ethiopian Air Force C-130' in Tigray region. The top image shows a 3D representation of mountain ranges (screenshot from Peak-Visor), the middle image shows 3D data from Google Earth, and the bottom image is actual footage from the scene.

approaches that use hybrid methods, followed by an approach based entirely on satellite imagery.

Chronolocation using hybrid methods

One example of chronolocation through hybrid approaches is also a case in which it helped to uncover additional useful information, that is, the verification of footage showing the execution of two women and two young children in what appeared to be north Cameroon, which was circulated on the internet in 2018.

I was part of the BBC Africa Eye team that analyzed the video using open source techniques, to establish where and when the murder had taken place, and who was responsible. One challenge in geolocating and chronolocating the footage was that there was limited access to the area because of the neighbouring conflict in Nigeria and the associated heavy security presence. To make matters worse, the online discourse at the time was full of rumour, misinformation and attempts to discredit the footage, including from the Cameroonian government. As part of this, Cameroon's Minister of Communications, Issa Tchiroma Bakary, claimed that the men in the footage did not appear to be Cameroonian army soldiers and that their weapons and uniforms were not standard issue for the Cameroonian army in the north.[23] Reuters quoted the Minister as saying the video was 'nothing but an unfortunate attempt to distort actual facts and intoxicate the public. Its sincerity can be easily questioned', and reported that he described the footage as 'fake news'.[24]

Given the statements by the Cameroonian government, and the lack of access on the ground, the analysis of this footage demonstrates the important role that remote digital investigations can play in sorting fact from fiction. A small collaborative team made up of independent investigators that met on the Twitter platform, BBC Africa Eye, Bellingcat and Amnesty[25] was able to debunk a number of the Minister of Communications' claims by geolocating the footage to Cameroon's far north, near the village of Zelevet, close to Cameroon's border with Nigeria. The team was also able to show that Cameroonian army soldiers did use the types of weapons seen in the footage, and that the uniforms were consistent with those worn by the Cameroonian army in the north in multiple publicly available videos and images that were all geolocated to a vicinity close to where the killing happened.

The core of this investigation is a linear blueprint for open source verification work, that is, first geolocating the content, which in turn allows investigators to chronolocate it and then gives them leads to identify who was responsible. In this investigation, after fusing location tip-offs from sources with the ridgeline verification and geolocating exactly where the

---

[23] Reuters Staff. Cameroon investigates video showing apparent execution of women and children. *Reuters*. 12 July 2018. Available from: https://www.reuters.com/article/uk-cameroon-security-videoidUKKBN1K229A [Accessed 14 May 2023].
[24] *ibid.*
[25] BBC Africa Eye. *Anatomy of a Killing* [video online]. 24 September 2018. Available from: https://www.youtube.com/watch?v=4G9S-eoLgX4 [Accessed 14 May 2023].

two women and their children were executed, our team was able to chronolocate the footage using multiple complementary techniques.

Most of the verification work on the Cameroonian footage took part in a purpose-made Twitter Direct Message community comprising security experts, journalists, and open source verification and imagery intelligence specialists. This diverse team applied numerous chronolocation methods to the execution footage. For example, the video itself shows quite a dry Sahelian landscape, but trees appear to be green, which could indicate recent rainfall. However, Google Earth satellite imagery of the area shows that the area is quite lush green during the wet season, which suggested that the footage could have been filmed between certain temperate zones. Researchers also noticed that alongside the path the women and children were walked down, before they were executed, were signs that a type of crop had recently been cut or harvested. It looked as though this crop may have been a type of maize or corn that is harvested at certain times of the year and then dried on shelters or stacks.

While those two factors alone could help work out the season or month of the incident, we identified the year by looking for topographical features that were present in the footage, but missing in associated satellite imagery. The process is like a children's spot-the-difference exercise, in which two near-identical images are placed side by side, and a child notices the differences between them. The investigators followed the same approach, comparing the footage with satellite imagery from different dates. For example, the execution video shows a building at the top of the road where the women and children were led; this was identified as present in 2015 satellite imagery but was not visible in the 2014 data. Another building in the background of the video further narrowed down the possible date range, as it could be matched with satellite imagery from 2014, but was missing from the 2016 images. The footage also showed small paths that might have been used by villagers; these were not present in 2014 satellite imagery, but were visible in the 2016 images. All of these comparisons provided a clear indication that the footage was filmed during a dry season, after a harvest, between 2014 and 2016.

A common technique in chronolocation is to analyze the shadows seen in user-generated videos or footage. Shadows have played a significant role as indicators of time through history, with evidence of this dating back to 13th

Figure 5: Screenshot from BBC Africa Eye *Anatomy of a Killing*, where the nearest soldier in the image was turned into a sundial, using his measured height 'A' and the measured length of his shadow 'B' to identify angle 'X' for shadow calculations.

century BCE Ancient Egypt.[26] While generally the shadows of interest are cast by objects that have been purposely set, the use of humans as makeshift sundials has also been referenced, for example, in the 14th century writings of Geoffrey Chaucer, which describe someone estimating the time using their own shadow.[27] Open source investigations apply the same principles, using digital tools to obtain accurate readings of the sun's elevation in an image, as well as the azimuth, and where possible, the shadow's length and the height of the object causing it.

For example, in the Cameroon investigation, a soldier walking down a path was used as the object in an impromptu sundial as shown in Fig. 5 (see footnote 25). After geolocating the image, we had the necessary elements to identify the sun's azimuth and elevation before using purpose-made geo and sun calculators, such as suncalc.org, to give us the possible date range for the image and shadow in the footage.

---

[26] Universität Basel. One of world's oldest sun dial [sic] dug up in Kings' Valley, Upper Egypt. *ScienceDaily*. 14 March 2013. Available from: www.sciencedaily.com/releases/2013/03/130314085052.htm [Accessed 14 May 2023].

[27] Chaucer G. *The Pardoner's Prologue & Tale from the Canterbury Tales*. Cambridge: Cambridge University Press. 1994.

Chronolocation using only satellite imagery

The above techniques are not all possible when user-generated content is not available, and when instead only satellite imagery can be used for chronolocation. This is often the case in claims about bombings, destruction, fires or other events where change may be evident from overhead imagery.

For example, the Ocelli Project,[28] an initiative I co-founded to track events from above, collects signs of village destruction in Myanmar's Rakhine State, which was home to the majority of Myanmar's Rohingya population before mass violence and destruction forced them to leave. The first step for this work was to identify where change had occurred, by systematically looking through historical imagery on Google Earth Pro in the north of Rakhine state between January 2015 and December 2019, and identifying villages that can be seen at earlier dates but that are missing or significantly changed in later satellite imagery (see Fig. 6). Researchers looked for signs of the possible cause of any changes on the satellite imagery, such as signs of black scorched earth and traces of white which could indicate the possible ash left behind and which may suggest that villages have been burnt.

The benefit of using Google Earth in the Ocelli Project is that it has images with relatively high resolution that can be used to identify that a village has disappeared, and provides a rough time frame for when this happened. However, Google Earth imagery is irregular and sometimes there are big gaps in the dates between successive images. To narrow down the dates of the destruction, in the second stage of the project, researchers used freely available satellite data from Sentinel Hub. The images from this tend to be lower resolution, but can be looked at through different filters, and they are much more frequent than those on Google Earth, and so the two systems complement each other.

The Ocelli Project relies on humans to collect and process satellite data, and is very time- and labour-intensive. Its production of mass documentation, along with similar projects, is likely to contribute to realizing ambitions

---

[28] Strick B., De Ruiter K., and C4ADS. *Ocelli Project: Rakhine* [online]. Available from: https://ocelli.c4ads.org/ [Accessed 14 May 2023].

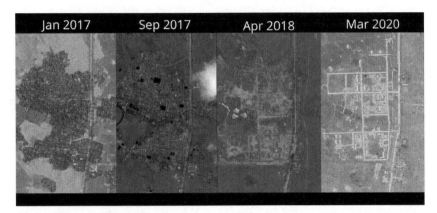

Figure 6: A geo/temporal analysis of a specific area in Myanmar's Rakhine State where thousands of buildings and villages were destroyed during the Myanmar Army's campaign on the Rohingya in the area. The image from September 2017 shows the entire village when it was burned to the ground. The area was later cleared and built over. *Source*: Map data ©2017 Google; ©2018 Google; ©2020 Google.

to develop automated data processing systems.[29] Machine learning models need to be trained on robust datasets – like those of Ocelli – through which algorithms 'learn' to perform specified tasks. Having prepared datasets will enable more machine learning to be incorporated in human rights monitoring. It is expected that machine learning will be able to greatly assist with processing the huge amounts of digital data now available, including by helping to identify signs of change from satellite imagery.[30] This aspect of automating data extraction from satellite imagery is already progressing in relevant use-cases such as building detection models[31] and deep learning elephant detection models.[32]

---

[29] Several other chapters in this volume present examples of projects involving mass data collection and processing, for example, the chapters by L. Wilson *et al.* (Chapter 5.1), Carboni & Raleigh (Chapter 3.3), and Bedenko & Bellish (Chapter 5.4). Chapter 3.2 (by Aric Toler) considers a problematic example of crowdsourced research, and whether/how it is possible to guard against such misuse.

[30] See also the chapter by Jamie Withorne in this volume (Chapter 5.2).

[31] Sirko W., Kashubin S., Ritter M., Annkah A., Bouchareb Y. S. E., Dauphin Y., Keysers D., Neumann M., Cisse M., and Quinn J. Continental-Scale Building Detection from High Resolution Satellite Imagery. *arXiv*. 2021. Available from: https://arxiv.org/abs/2107.12283 [Accessed 14 May 2023].

[32] Duporge I. and Isupova O. Deep Learning Detects Elephants in Maxar Satellite Imagery on Par with Human Accuracy. *Maxar Blog*. 12 January 2021. Available from: https://blog.maxar.com/earth-intelligence/2021/deep-learning-detectselephants-in-maxar-satellite-imagery-on-par-with-human-accuracy [Accessed 14 May 2023].

While the Ocelli Project looks for and codes changes over a large area, satellite-imagery-based chronolocation also applies to more detailed cases, where minor changes in an image may indicate when a video was filmed. For example, during the conflict in Nagorno-Karabakh in 2020, footage posted on Telegram of bodies lined up in the village of Zəngilan received critical responses and rebuttals, with claims it was filmed before 2020. However, through commercially obtained satellite imagery, a team of researchers was able to determine the window of time the footage was taken, as the same line of bodies could be seen in satellite imagery from 24 October 2020.[33]

Who Was Responsible?

Attribution of specific events remains one of the hardest tasks in digital open source investigations, not only because they rely on publicly sourced information but also because a high level of evidence is required to hold someone accountable for serious wrongdoing – assumptions do not make the cut. Open source investigations often use multiple approaches to collect and process information that can identify the specific actors responsible for human rights abuses; what is standard throughout effective investigations is transparency about working methods, through clear explanations detailing how researchers arrived at their results, which enable other people to check their methods and confirm or refute the findings.

For example, in the investigation of the footage of the execution of two women and their children in Cameroon's far north, the men responsible for shooting the victims were positively identified using multiple independent sources, which were cross-referenced to validate one another. The original footage showed the Cameroon soldiers using each other's nicknames, and those nicknames were found on Facebook accounts. Faces, rings and posture were also cross-referenced between the footage and social media profiles (see Fig. 7). After the investigation geolocated and chronolocated the footage, it looked at social media around the time of the event. Comments between friends, colleagues and loved ones established that the men

---

[33] Strick B. Geolocation of footage which shows bodies, some handcuffed, others unclothed, in Zəngilan, #Karabakh. *Twitter*. 30 October 2020. Available from: https://twitter.com/BenDoBrown/status/1322200787141971971?s=20 [Accessed 14 May 2023].

Figure 7: Still from the BBC Africa Eye investigation *Anatomy of a Killing* where three of the perpetrators responsible for shooting the women and children were identified.

had been in the area at the time of the killings. The names of those involved were also later confirmed in an announcement by the Cameroonian government as being under investigation. Almost two years after publishing our findings on BBC Africa Eye's *Anatomy of a Killing* (see footnote 25), four of the Cameroonian soldiers were sentenced to ten years imprisonment for their roles in shooting the two women and two children.[34] On a political level, as a result of this investigation and further reporting on Cameroon's human rights status, the United States government cut security and military aid to Cameroon[35] and the European Parliament passed a resolution condemning cases of torture, forced disappearances and extrajudicial killings perpetrated by governmental forces and armed separatists.[36]

In attribution investigations, unexpected challenges can arise. For example, data or analytic features are sometimes restricted by social media

---

[34] BBC News. Cameroon soldiers jailed for killing women and children. *BBC News*. 21 September 2020. Available from: https://www.bbc.co.uk/news/world-africa-54238170 [Accessed 14 May 2023].
[35] Browne R. and Hansler J. US to cut aid to Cameroon due to alleged human rights violations. *CNN*. 7 February 2019. Available from: https://edition.cnn.com/2019/02/06/politics/cameroon-security-assistance/index.html [Accessed 14 May 2023].
[36] European Parliament, Motion for a Resolution on Cameroon B8-0254/2019. April 2019. Available from: https://www.europarl.europa.eu/doceo/document/B-8-2019-0254_EN.html [Accessed 14 May 2023].

platforms, or are taken down after being previously viewable. The Cameroon investigation used Facebook's library graph system to identify information about the people who executed the women and children. Without that graph system, much of the information used to compile additional sources of evidence would not have been available to our research team, or we would have taken longer to find it. However, in June 2019, Facebook terminated this search function[37] which cut public access to tools and data integral to many ongoing investigations on war crimes, human rights abuses and investigations into child sex exploitation cases, to name a few. Facebook made its decision in order to protect user data and privacy; while this is important, it had the consequence of disabling important open source research tools, and made it harder to find the data required to make sufficiently robust attributions.

This challenge is not just a problem for human rights investigations. It is also an issue for attempts to attribute responsibility for the disinformation networks and influence operations that often surround human rights issues, including in situations where state actors attempt to manipulate narratives and distort facts. The attribution of those networks, in most cases, is now solely in the hands of social media platforms, as they have access to user-based data such as login IP addresses or verification details, as well as detailed account interaction data, which would assist in identifying the source of a campaign.

While this limitation of access to data is an obstacle to investigations, there are nevertheless examples of influence operations being successfully attributed using open source information. In one such example, co-investigator Elise Thomas and I were able to uncover the details of a well-funded and coordinated social media campaign comprising a network of more than 1,000 fake accounts on Twitter, Facebook, Instagram and YouTube. The campaign aimed to change international audience perceptions by misrepresenting the truth about events in the Indonesian province of

---

[37] Cox J. Facebook Quietly Changes Search Tool Used by Investigators, Abused By Companies. *Motherboard, Vice*. 10 June 2019. Available from: https://www.vice.com/en/article/zmpgmx/facebook-stops-graph-search [Accessed 14 May 2023].

Papua, as well as discredit people seeking Papuan independence, and undermine human rights activists that were involved in the dialogue on human rights abuses in West Papua. We successfully attributed the campaign to a digital marketing firm operating out of Indonesia.[38] A subsequent takedown of the network by Facebook identified that about $300,000 had been spent on Facebook ads to promote the campaign's content.[39]

The open source research in that case relied on off-platform information, as we were able to identify a blog site that the network was primarily promoting. The website registry information was not private, and included the email address, phone number and name of the person who registered the website (see Fig. 8). Further evidence was collected when the phone number of the individual was added to WhatsApp, which provided an associated profile picture. That picture was then used to find the person on freelancer sites and social media networks such as LinkedIn, enabling us to identify the place of work. That detail connected to other employees, photos, employers and alternative registry information. The company site also showed that it was running strategic campaigns using digital marketing techniques.

This information, once published, was confirmed via the takedowns of these networks by Twitter[40] and Google,[41] and shows the added strength of independent open source investigators and civil society groups collaborating or sharing findings with platforms.

---

[38] Strick B. and Thomas E. Investigating Information Operations in West Papua: A Digital Forensic Case Study of Cross-Platform Network Analysis. *Bellingcat*. 11 October 2019. Available from: https://www.bellingcat.com/news/rest-of-world/2019/10/11/investigating-information-operations-in-west-papua-a-digital-forensic-case-study-of-cross-platform-network-analysis/ [Accessed 14 May 2023].

[39] Gleicher N. Removing Coordinated Inauthentic Behavior in UAE, Nigeria, Indonesia and Egypt. *Meta Newsroom*. 3 October 2019. Available from: https://about.fb.com/news/2019/10/removingcoordinated-inauthentic-behavior-in-uae-nigeria-indonesia-and-egypt/ [Accessed 14 May 2023].

[40] Twitter Safety. Following an investigation originating from a @Bellingcat report on an information operation in Indonesia targeting the West Papuan independence movement, we removed 795 fake accounts.... *Twitter*. 2 April 2020. Available from: https://twitter.com/TwitterSafety/status/12456 [Accessed 14 May 2023].

[41] Huntley S. Protecting users from government-backed hacking and disinformation. *Google Threat Analysis Group*. 26 November 2019. Available from: https://blog.google/threat-analysis-group/protecting-users-government-backed-hacking-and-disinformation/ [Accessed 14 May 2023].

Tracking Human Rights Abuses through Online Open Source Research

Figure 8: One of the websites the influence operation was amplifying, which was a blog promoting pro-Indonesian propaganda about West Papua. The image on the right shows the registration details of the site, which linked to employees of the marketing firm responsible for the campaign.

Conclusion

Open source investigations have opened up opportunities for non-governmental groups and individuals to track where and when human rights abuses have taken place, and find out who was responsible for them. This chapter has demonstrated the possibilities of this work by outlining key tools and approaches, illustrated by case studies spanning investigations into enforced detention, executions, destruction of villages and influence operations aimed at undermining democracy.

This is a growing field, with increasing numbers of researchers working in different sectors to explore and develop new approaches that use online tools and information to monitor atrocities around the globe. The work is multi-dimensional, often involving collaborations between groups of people looking through diverse sources to build a compelling account about an event. As well as using multiple methods, open source investigations can lead to different outcomes, including successful prosecutions (for example, of the soldiers responsible for murdering two women and children in north Cameroon), changing behaviour (as when social media platforms take down accounts associated with influence operations), and enhanced transparency about atrocities in the global media (for example, in work exposing detention centres and the destruction of villages).

However, the work is neither easy nor straightforward. Open source researchers face a number of serious impediments to their work, including changing access to the tools and data that underpin their work. In order to maximize the potential for this field, societies should work with satellite imagery providers and social media companies to ensure that open source research can continue to access essential tools and data, while maintaining important privacy functions. In this way, open source research can contribute to global efforts to hold perpetrators to account, generate transparency and support for victims, and deter future human rights abuses.

© 2024 World Scientific Publishing Company
https://doi.org/10.1142/9781800614079_0003

Chapter 2.2

Open Source Investigations on the Ground: Reflections on Experiences from South Sudan

Geoffrey L. Duke

Abstract

This chapter demonstrates that open source research does not just involve advanced technologies and remote monitoring. Local knowledge is essential to effective investigations, as provided by trusted networks of people that have expert understanding of the local terrain and specific cultural, security and political contexts. However, such local expertise is often overlooked and undersupported. The chapter aims to rectify this by detailing work monitoring armaments in South Sudan, with a particular emphasis on small arms and light weapons (SALW). It considers the role of civil society organizations in verifying arms control instruments and discusses the possibilities of establishing global monitoring and verification mechanisms for arms control and humanitarian disarmament. The work of the South Sudan Network on Small Arms (SSANSA) is presented to showcase civil society work in South Sudan, demonstrating the value, reality and challenges of on-the-ground open source research.

Introduction

One of the main rationales for arms control is to prevent weapons from reaching the wrong hands, including criminals, private militaries, terrorists and, startlingly, some government groups. All of these have at times used weapons in ways that are contrary to international norms, for instance, against civilian groups and populations. Transparency about where weapons

This is an open access article published by World Scientific Publishing Europe Ltd. and distributed under the terms of the Creative Commons Attribution-NonCommercial 4.0 International (CC BY-NC 4.0) License.

are, who owns them and the circumstances in which they are used can be valuable to efforts to control illicit arms, and can contribute to bringing accountability to those responsible for illegal weapons proliferation and uses. Open source research conducted by civil society organizations is a key tool in facilitating such transparency.

Much of the conversation and excitement about open source research[1] in the realm of arms control and disarmament focuses on remote monitoring and its applications, for example, its potential to track illicit nuclear proliferation.[2] By contrast, this chapter focuses on work that monitors small arms and light weapons (SALW) and their ammunition, which are the weapons of choice of warlords and armed civilians in the Global South, and are the weapons wreaking violence there. For such investigations, remote monitoring by Google Earth alone is inadequate. On-the-ground open source observations are essential for establishing relevant facts, and they can also help remote open source investigations by providing crucial contextual information and corroborating evidence.[3] This suggests that it would be useful to build monitoring partnerships between the Global North and South. However, there are clear risks to local monitors seeking to elucidate the means of violence in their communities, and care must be taken to minimize such risks.

This chapter presents the work of the South Sudan Action Network on Small Arms (SSANSA), a network of civil society organizations working across South Sudan to bring peace and stability to the country, including by tracking SALW and ammunition proliferation and misuse, in order to lower, and ultimately stop, gun violence in the country. The chapter starts with an outline of the history of violence in South Sudan, which considers its civil

---

[1] This chapter refers to open source investigations and research as analyses that use publicly available tools and information, and the term open source verification is used to mean open source investigations that are aimed at monitoring compliance with weapons treaties. Echoing the categories identified by H. Wilson *et al.* in this volume (Chapter 4.1), much of our work involves 'open obscure' information, collected from local monitors who visually recognize and report on arms and truck movements in their communities.

[2] See for example The Economist. Open-source Intelligence Challenges State Monopolies on Information. *The Economist.* 7 August 2021, pp. 16–19.

[3] Other chapters in this volume also emphasize the central importance of local monitors to open source investigations. See, for example, the chapters by Wilson, Samuel & Plesch, Strick, Triebert, Freeman & Koenig, and Carboni & Raleigh (Chapters 1, 2.1, 2.4, 2.5 and 3.3).

war (2013–2018) and the conflicts predating its independence from Sudan in 2011. It then details SSANSA's methods, detailing what it monitors and how it goes about its work, as well as the risks it faces and how it works to mitigate these.

Context: The History of Violence in South Sudan

South Sudan gained independence from Sudan in 2011 after decades of civil strife. Before this, Sudan had several complex civil wars that in various forms and scales pitted Arabs against Africans, the North against the South, Muslims against Christians, as well as Northerners against Northerners, Christians against Christians, and Muslims against Muslims in various parts of the country. While there were various motivations for these conflicts – including, for example, political factors such as identity politics alongside other social and religious factors – one major aspect throughout has been the attempt to coercively control the country's abundant oil reserves and other natural resources.

On 13 December 2013, only two years after gaining its independence, South Sudan relapsed into another brutal civil war, which broke out following a split in government forces into two main factions: one allied to the government under President Salva Kiir and the other allied to Dr Riek Machar, who had previously been removed from his role as Vice President. The latter group eventually organized an armed rebellion under the name Sudan People's Liberation Movement/Army-In-Opposition (SPLM/A-IO).

The civil war between the government and the SPLM/A-IO lasted for years, leaving hundreds of thousands dead and millions displaced. A study by the London School of Hygiene and Tropical Medicine estimated 400,000 people had lost their lives from December 2013 to 2018.[4] In addition, 4.5 million people were displaced, including 2 million displaced internally as of 2019. The conflict exhibited indiscriminate violence, alongside targeted killings of civilians based on their ethnic origins which have been

---

[4]Checchi S., Testa A., Warsame A., Quach L., and Burns R. *Estimates of crisis-attributable mortality in South Sudan, December 2013–April 2018*. London School of Hygiene and Tropical Medicine. 2018. Available from: https://www.lshtm.ac.uk/south-sudan-full-report [Accessed 6 May 2021].

well documented and condemned by the United Nations[5] (UN) and various human rights groups.[6] The UN further evidenced gross violations and abuses of international human rights and humanitarian law that may amount to war crimes. These violations included the unlawful killing of civilians, attacks on humanitarian actors and facilities, forced displacement, unlawful destruction of property and pillage, as well as rape, sexual slavery and other forms of sexual violence.[7]

On 30 December 2013, the African Union established a Commission of Inquiry to investigate the human rights violations and other abuses committed during the armed conflict in South Sudan. The Commission's final report (published in 2014) established that there were reasonable grounds to believe that gross violations of human rights amounting to crimes against humanity had been committed against civilians during the violence that erupted in mid-December, including murder, rape and sexual violence, extermination, persecution, torture and other inhumane acts carried out by both government and opposition forces.[8] It concluded that these crimes were committed in a widespread systematic manner, and evidence suggested there were deliberate policies to launch direct attacks on civilians.

These war crimes, violations and abuses of human rights by the parties in conflict illustrate the irresponsible use of weapons which robust arms control, disarmament and non-proliferation seek to prevent.

Legacies of violence

South Sudan's civil war formally ended with a fragile peace agreement signed in 2018 – the Revitalized Agreement on the Resolution of the Conflict

---

[5]UNMISS. *UNMISS condemns targeted killings of hundreds of foreign and South Sudanese civilians in Bentiu* [press release]. Relief Web. 2014. Available from: https://reliefweb.int/report/south-sudan/unmiss-condemns-targeted-killings-hundreds-foreign-and-south-sudanese-civilians [Accessed 10 June 2021].

[6]Amnesty International. *South Sudan: Nowhere safe: Civilians under attack in South Sudan*. London: Amnesty International. 2014. Available from: https://www.amnesty.org/en/documents/AFR65/003/2014/en/ [Accessed 10 June 2021].

[7]UNMISS and United Nations Human Rights Office of the High Commissioner. *Indiscriminate Attacks Against Civilians in Southern Unity*. April–May 2018. Available from: https://www.ohchr.org/sites/default/files/Documents/Countries/SS/UNMISSReportApril_May2018.pdf [Accessed 16 May 2023].

[8]African Union. *Final Report of the African Union Commission of Inquiry On South Sudan*. 2014. Available from: https://www.peaceau.org/uploads/auciss.final.report.pdf [Accessed 10 June 2021].

in the Republic of South Sudan (R-ARCSS).[9] The R-ARCSS gave responsibility for implementing the peace-building process to a unity government composed of government and opposition leaders. Since then, the country has been on an indeterminate and slow transition from war to peace. However, the legacies of years of numerous civil wars are still playing out, and at the time of writing, the situation is fluid, armed, insecure and uncertain. For example, civilians armed with illicit weapons have continued to engage in cycles of local violence associated with cattle rustling, targeted killings and inter-communal clashes, making the security context even more precarious.[10]

One of the legacies of this recent history is that the country is awash with SALW. The instability and conflicts in South Sudan have been fuelled by millions of dollars' worth of arms and ammunition predominantly from China, and also from other countries including Russia and Ukraine, as well as from neighbouring countries.[11,12] Although often imported legally by South Sudan, many of these weapons have been used in the violations listed above, and have often ended up in the hands of civilians[13] and armed opposition forces, usually through battlefield captures or defections from government forces. These actions in effect constitute a diversion away from licensed end users to unauthorized ones.

---

[9]IGAD. *Revitalized Agreement on the Resolution of the Conflict in the Republic of South Sudan (R-ARCSS)*. Addis Ababa. 12 September 2018. Available from: https://docs.pca-cpa.org/2016/02/South-Sudan-Peace-Agreement-September-2018.pdf [Accessed 16 May 2023].

[10]At the time of writing (2021–2022), South Sudan is in a state akin to "no war, no peace", given the lack of political will demonstrated by the sluggish and selective implementation of the peace agreement and endemic low level violence.

[11]Conflict Armament Research. *Weapon Supplies into South Sudan's Civil War*. Conflict Armament Research. 2018. Available from: https://www.conflictarm.com/reports/weapon-supplies-into-south-sudans-civil-war/ [Accessed 28 April 2022].

[12]Leff J. and LeBrun E. *Following the Thread: Arms and Ammunition Tracing in Sudan and South Sudan*. HSBA Working Paper 32. Geneva: Small Arms Survey. 2014. Available from: https://www.smallarmssurvey.org/resource/following-thread-arms-and-ammunition-tracing-sudan-and-south-sudan-hsba-working-paper-32#. [Accessed 16 May 2023].

[13]Through leakages from government stockpiles due to inadequate security measures and sometimes deliberate diversions to civilians by senior members of organized forces.

The 2017 National Small Arms Assessment in South Sudan estimated that there were 232,000–601,000 weapons in civilian hands.[14,15] It is likely that this number has grown because there has not been any major civilian disarmament exercise since the report was written, while illicit imports continue. The scale and spread of SALW make it much harder to reduce the level of civilian armament, and meanwhile fuel criminality, inter-communal violence and repeated clashes between civilians and members of organized forces, including the military. Accordingly, death tolls in South Sudan remain alarmingly high.

Alongside this history have been several campaigns[16] aimed at reducing the number of weapons entering the country, promoting disarmament and encouraging the development of a peaceful and well-functioning society. For example, several partial civilian disarmament initiatives have been introduced since 2005. Some of these have focused on disarming various armed youth groups (especially those that posed a significant threat to the then newly established semi-autonomous government of Southern Sudan).[17] Further, a country-wide comprehensive disarmament plan was announced in 2008. This was ultimately unsuccessful; even though some individuals

---

[14] *National Small Arms Assessment in South Sudan*. UNDP. 2017. Available from: http://www.ss.undp.org/content/south_sudan/en/home/library/democratic_governance/national-small-arms-assessment-in-south-sudan.html [Accessed 6 May 2021].

[15] This was the first *National Small Arms Assessment in South Sudan* commissioned by UNDP and the South Sudan Bureau for Community Security and Small Arms Control (SSBCSSAC), and was conducted by the Small Arms Survey. The Assessment generated the first national estimates of the number of firearms in civilian hands in South Sudan, based on household survey and qualitative methodologies. The actual number could be higher than the estimates because the assessment was conducted in only six of the ten states of South Sudan, and there is good reason to believe that at least some of the four states not surveyed have higher than average rates of household firearms, as part of the reason these states weren't included was because of their high-level insecurity.

[16] See, for example, Human Rights Watch. *South Sudan: Joint Letter to President Obama regarding Arms Embargo*. 7 January 2014. Available from: https://www.hrw.org/news/2015/01/08/south-sudanjoint-letter-president-obama-regarding-arms-embargo [Accessed 5 May 2021]; Amnesty International. *South Sudan: Petition to members of the Intergovernmental Authority on Development – immediate embargo on arms supplies to South Sudan*. 4 November 2014. Available from: https://www.amnesty.org/en/documents/afr65/015/2014/en/ [Accessed 5 May 2021]; Amnesty International. *South Sudan: Joint Letter to the UN Security Council to impose an immediate arms embargo*. 4 November 2014. Available from: https://www.amnesty.org/en/documents/afr65/4505/2016/en/ (Accessed 5 May 2021).

[17] For example, see *Sudan Issue Brief. Anatomy of civilian disarmament in Jonglei State*. Geneva: Small Arms Survey. 2006. Available from: https://reliefweb.int/sites/reliefweb.int/files/resources/DC866C7CA6654FCB8525726100724E53-Full_Report.pdf [Accessed 29 April 2022].

and communities disarmed, they subsequently rearmed. Since then, civilian disarmament has tended to comprise government counterinsurgency in response to inter-communal violence. Consequently, South Sudan is stuck in a cycle of disarmament and rearmament.

At the international level, in June 2018, the UN Security Council imposed an arms embargo on South Sudan which specified that:

> Until 31 May 2019, all Member States shall immediately take the necessary measures to prevent the direct or indirect supply, sale or transfer to the territory of South Sudan from or through their territories or by their nationals, or using their flag vessels or aircraft, of arms and related materiel of all types, including weapons and ammunition, military vehicles and equipment, paramilitary equipment, and spare parts for the aforementioned; and technical assistance, training, financial or other assistance, related to military activities or the provision, maintenance or use of any arms and related materiel, including the provision of armed mercenary personnel whether or not originating in their territories.[18,19]

The UN Security Council later renewed the arms embargo until at least May 2023 (as at the time of writing),[20] as it determined that the situation in South Sudan continues to constitute a threat to peace and security in the region. As the sluggish implementation of the R-ARCSS peace agreement continued, the UN Security Council developed a system for assessing progress in the transition from war to peace, which could prompt it to 'review arms embargo measures, through *inter alia* modification, suspension, or progressive lifting of these measures, in the light of progress achieved on ... key benchmarks'.[21] History will tell if South Sudan will achieve these benchmarks

---

[18] Security Council Resolution 2428, S/RES/2428 (2018). 13 July 2018. Available from: https://undocs.org/en/S/RES/2428(2018) [Accessed 6 May 2021].

[19] The resolution to impose an arms embargo on South Sudan was adopted by a vote of 9 in favour and none against, with 6 abstentions. Côte d'Ivoire, France, Kuwait, the Netherlands, Peru, Poland, Sweden, the United Kingdom and the United States were in favour, while Bolivia, China, Ethiopia, Equatorial Guinea, Kazakhstan and Russia abstained.

[20] Security Council Resolution 2633, S/RES/2633 (2022). 26 May 2022. Available from: https://documents-dds-ny.un.org/doc/UNDOC/GEN/N22/363/06/PDF/N2236306.pdf?OpenElement [Accessed 10 July 2022].

[21] The key benchmarks issued by the Security Council are (a) the completion, by the Revitalized Transitional Government of National Unity (RTGNU), of Stages 1, 2 and 3 of the Strategic Defence and Security Review (SDSR) specified in the Revitalised Agreement; (b) the formation, by the RTGNU, of a unified command structure for the Necessary Unified Forces (NUF), the training, graduation and redeployment of the NUF, and allocation by the RTGNU of adequate resources for planning and implementing the redeployment of the NUF; (c) progress, by the RTGNU, on establishing and

and thereby enable the arms embargo to be lifted, or if it will continue to circumvent the embargo to acquire arms through other means.

In the meantime, South Sudan essentially remains trapped in its cycle of disarmament and rearmament, in which the indiscriminate use of violence by government forces undermines effective irreversible disarmament. 'The rampant unprofessional behavior of uniformed personnel is partly responsible for the drive within many communities in South Sudan to acquire small arms and light machine guns for their protection' wrote Lieutenant General (ret.) Kuol Deim Kuol, who led the Jonglei disarmament campaign launched by President Kiir in 2012.[22]

It is within this context that SSANSA's work takes place. The following sections detail SSANSA's practical work monitoring weapons flows through open source research and the ways these connect to local, regional and international arms control and disarmament initiatives, including the arms embargo.

The South Sudan Action Network on Small Arms (SSANSA)

SSANSA supports peace-building in South Sudan by monitoring illicit arms, reducing the numbers of weapons that fall into the wrong hands and campaigning against human rights abuses by members of the South Sudanese organized forces. Our work is compatible with several international weapons treaties and other instruments that mandate civil society to

---

implementing the disarmament, demobilization and reintegration (DDR) process, and in particular the development and implementation of a plan for collection and disposal of long- and medium-range heavy weapons, and development of a time-bound plan for the complete and verifiable demilitarization of all civilian areas; (d) progress by the South Sudanese defence and security forces on properly managing their existing arms and ammunition stockpiles, including by: establishing the necessary planning documents, protocols and training for the recording, storage, distribution and management of the weapons and ammunition; and by implementing the Joint Action Plan for the Armed Forces on addressing conflict-related sexual violence, with an emphasis on the training, sensitization, accountability and oversight of the defence and security forces.

[22] Kuol D. K. Confronting the Challenges of South Sudan's Security Sector: A Practitioner's Perspective. *Envisioning a Stable South Sudan*. 1 May 2018, pp. 39–46. Available from: https://www.jstor.org/stable/resrep19226.9?seq=1#metadata_info_tab_contents [Accessed 16 May 2021].

contribute to verifying treaty compliance, including the Nairobi Protocol,[23] the UN Programme of Action,[24] the Arms Trade Treaty,[25] South Sudan SALW policy and the Firearms Act.[26]

In South Sudan, most of the arms used both by state and non-state actors, including civilians, are SALW.[27] Unsurprisingly, SSANSA also largely focuses on SALW, and its work often connects to the repeated attempts to remove arms from civilians, which have resulted in the collection of some weapons, as well as in clashes between armed youth and government forces. For instance, in the 2012 civilian disarmament campaign, dubbed 'Operation Restore Peace in Jonglei', SSANSA documented high levels of human right violations and excessive use of force, including lethal force that resulted in unnecessary fatalities.[28] The incidents included beating youths, raping women and killings, and they constituted some of the drivers for rearmament.

One area we observe is armed youth. When we see young people handling weapons, we aim to assess whether their weapons match those carried

---

[23] Adopted in April 2004 by 11 governments of East and Horn of Africa, the Nairobi Protocol seeks to prevent, control and reduce the production of small arms and light weapons in the Great Lakes and Horn of Africa.

[24] The UN Programme of Action to Prevent, Combat and Eradicate the Illicit Trade in Small Arms and Light Weapons (UNPoA) is a globally agreed framework for activities countering the illicit trade in SALW and controlling their negative consequences. UNODA Regional Centre for Peace and Disarmament. *Programme of Action*. Available from: https://unrcpd.org/conventional-weapons/poa/#:\sim: text=The%20UN%20Programme%20of%20Action,Small%20Arms%20and%20Light%20Weapons [Accessed 29 April 2022].

[25] The 2014 Arms Trade Treaty is a multilateral treaty that regulates the international trade in conventional weapons from small arms to battle tanks, combat aircraft and warships. See https://www.un.org/disarmament/convarms/arms-trade-treaty-2/ [Accessed 29 April 2022].

[26] The Firearms Act 2016 is South Sudan's national law that sets the legal framework and administrative structures for firearms and their use, including possession by civilians.

[27] In the *National Small Arms Assessment*, the most reported type of firearm in armed households was 'automatic weapons (including AK47s)', which was acknowledged by 54% of those affirming household firearms; rifles/shotguns and handguns together accounted for an additional 22% of affirming respondents. See footnote 14.

[28] Duke G. L. and Rouw H. *The Catch 22 of Security and Civilian Disarmament: Community Perspectives on Civilian Disarmament in Jonglei State*. SSANSA. September 2013. Available from: https://protectionofcivilians.org/wp-content/uploads/reports/the-catch-22-of-security-and-civilian-disarmament.pdf [Accessed 16 May 2023].

by organized forces or armed opposition groups, by making daily small-scale local observations in public spaces, and carefully documenting and analyzing what we see. Often, we find that we can identify similarities in the types of weapons used, which may suggest that youth groups have acquired their weapons from the government – either because they have managed to access government stockpiles, or because some government elements have deliberately armed them.

Our work involves developing a trusted network of civil society monitors across the country. SSANSA members span national non-governmental organizations (NGOs) comprising youth groups, women's groups, faith-based organizations as well as individuals such as students, youth leaders and others with whom we have built good working relationships. When we have funding, we provide stipends to monitors, but often information exchanges continue even when there is no funding. We train our monitors to follow the guides for small arms identification and tracings provided by the Small Arms Survey,[29] Conflict Armament Research[30] and Bonn International Center for Conversion.[31] We also arrange external training (see Fig. 1). For instance, in December 2015, SSANSA convened a Community Security and Small Arms Control Bootcamp to equip our partners with skills and tools needed to recognize and track illicit weapons, including training delivered by experts from the Small Arms Survey and Conflict Armament Research.

These guides and training opportunities help civil society to recognize weapon types and compare the weapons held by civilians with those of authorized end users (e.g. the government). If we get a chance to handle the weapons and ammunition that we are monitoring, we look for serial numbers and markings which can facilitate efforts to trace their origins, the companies involved in any transfers and their intended end users. This can help to establish potential illicit diversion.

---

[29] Jenzen-Jones N. R. and Schroeder M. (eds). *An Introductory Guide to the Identification of Small Arms, Light Weapons, and Associated Ammunition*. Geneva: Small Arms Survey. 2018. Available from: https://www.smallarmssurvey.org/resource/introductory-guide-identification-small-arms-light-weapons-and-associated-ammunition [Accessed 16 May 2023].

[30] Conflict Armament Research. *Weapon Supplies into South Sudan's Civil War*. Conflict Armament Research. 2018. Available from: https://www.conflictarm.com/reports/weapon-supplies-into-south-sudans-civil-war/ [Accessed 28 April 2022].

[31] See for example *Training in Small Arms Control in South Sudan* [BICC-APFO Workshop Report]. 2006. Available from: https://www.files.ethz.ch/isn/131545/nairobi_workshop_report.pdf [Accessed 29 April 2022].

Figure 1: Training for SSANSA members delivered by Conflict Armament Research.

We equip our local partners to engage in field observations and related activities. Our open source investigations include tracking the following.

- Types of arms held by civilians and comparing them with those held by other non-state actors and government forces, to trace leaks and diversions.
- Weapons collection exercises which establish the types of arms collected and their markings and trace where civilians get them from, to prevent further diversions.
- Government agencies' compliance with legal commitments and policies for civilian disarmament. Such government actions need scrutiny; although government policy overtly stipulates that disarmament should be non-violent, government forces can in reality engage in forceful disarmament, resulting in civilian bloodshed.
- New arms flows into the country, comparing these with the requirements of the current UN Security Council arms embargo.
- Weapons used by criminals, to establish whether crimes are being committed using state-owned firearms.
- Misuse of arms by members of organized forces and civilians.
- Government compliance with legal and normative requirements for record-keeping, weapons marking and safe storage of munitions.
- Trends in the black market prices of SALW and ammunition to make sense of their correlation with conflict, arms availability and trafficking dynamics.

For these tasks, remote monitoring cannot provide the level of detail needed to ascertain what is really happening.

Practical challenges and dangers

SSANSA's work is complicated and time consuming, and we regularly face difficulties, such as the fact that some government agencies and opposition leaders prefer to cooperate with international researchers and journalists rather than work with local monitors. In fact, most government bureaucrats and military leaders do not accept local civil society involvement in weapons monitoring and handling, even when this is directly mandated by regional and international treaties. For example, the government refused to support our December 2015 Community Security and Small Arms Control Bootcamp by providing resources to train our network in how to trace and identify arms and ammunition. However even for international groups there is no guarantee of government cooperation; some governments and companies do not respond to requests from international institutes (such as the Small Arms Survey) for information about arms that are traced to their country.

Meanwhile, there are also a host of logistical challenges. These include basic access challenges, as some places are inaccessible due to poor infrastructure. Further, while some police arms are marked in order to keep track of them, once in the black market, criminals sometimes remove these markings, making it difficult to collect enough information to trace them. Moreover, while the army and National Security Services sometimes mark some of their portable weapons, they do not store information about the markings in a central database, although this is prescribed by law and regulations, and could ease oversight and tracking. In any case, most of the military's weapons – especially those outside the capital – are not marked. These circumstances, combined with the military and the police being among the lowest paid among government-organized forces, often make the military a source of arms supplies for civilians, through corrupt sales or transfers.[32]

Apart from these practical challenges are the risks our observers face; we encounter dangers on a daily basis. Monitors risk being arbitrarily arrested, detained and being made to disappear at the hands of National Security Services and other armed groups, including the police. While there is some level of transparency in the work of the latter, the former groups largely operate with very little transparency or accountability; for example, they never disclose how many people they have detained or disappeared, or give reasons for their actions. People deemed to be high value are most likely to be targeted – activists, political opponents and journalists. South Sudan's National Security Services have arrested and detained several civil society representatives, journalists and political dissidents. Some of these people

---

[32] See also the chapter by Michie *et al.* in this volume (Chapter 5.3), which details open source research that uncovers corruption in the formal arms trade.

were detained for months without any charges, although the law prohibits arbitrary arrest and detention without a just cause. These occurrences are concerning for many reasons, not least because we know that any day one of us could be targeted.

The country's culture of impunity compounds these hazards. It is risky for monitors to expose and hold accountable members of the armed forces and politicians, who largely remain exempt from reprisals. There is always a chance that monitors' findings can be traced back to the work of individuals or their organizations, which could put their lives at risk and compromise the trusted networks and funding avenues we have developed over time. This issue is exacerbated by the fact that some government officials are threatening to make the laws around NGOs more draconian, citing examples from African countries including Eritrea, Ethiopia, Rwanda and Uganda as justification.

The overlapping range and extent of issues in South Sudan means that SSANSA and its partners are stretched across numerous pressing needs. On top of its core tasks, SSANSA needs to dedicate significant time to accessing funding. We have no sustained income stream. Our work is financed by short-term grants, which can be difficult to access despite the proven need for accurate information about armaments in South Sudan, and the fact that local observers are a very cost-effective way to get this information. We have found that arms control, disarmament and non-proliferation do not attract the same levels of funding as humanitarian projects, even though the mechanisms of violence drive the humanitarian issues. Because of this, it can be hard to obtain funding to pay our monitors, despite their invaluable work and the risks they face. In turn, this contributes to the problems of staff retention – it can be hard to keep trained monitors, build a stable community of monitors, and develop a cumulative body of expertise.

Managing risks and ethics

SSANSA has a number of approaches to managing the risks it faces. In the first instance, we aim to protect our monitors through training, emphasizing that their safety comes first, and advising them against forcing their way into dangerous situations where they might get hurt. We encourage them instead to build and maintain trust within their neighbourhood.

On top of this, we protect our monitors by refusing to reveal information about them or what they have observed.[33] Although at times such information might be necessary to authenticate the provenance of information, divulging certain details puts our trusted contacts in danger. For instance, we have monitors who collect information about black market prices of arms and ammunition. We use such information to analyze demand-and-supply relationships and how these relate to conflict and violence. Government agencies may be interested in the individuals collecting such information and the people they have consulted in their research, but if disclosed, this information could put our monitors and wider network at risk.

Local communal violence in South Sudan is linked to national politics, and it is common for our monitors to find political and military actors at the highest levels involved in arming their communities or fuelling intercommunal violence. To protect our observers, we avoid making public judgements about who is responsible for fuelling conflicts, for fear that named individuals could come after our team and their associates. Given the culture of impunity in the country, powerful generals and politicians often easily get away with murder.

While we do not identify perpetrators ourselves, wherever possible, we transmit the evidence we have collected of arms misuse and illicit diversion etc. to regional and international networks who can act on behalf of local actors. For example, SSANSA is part of the networks associated with the Control Arms Coalition, International Campaign to Ban Landmines and the Cluster Munitions Convention, and we also maintain good working contacts with other like-minded organizations in the field of humanitarian disarmament and arms control. Such partnerships can help address some safety issues, as they are often able to make use of information with less risk. This is where local verification meets international solidarity and advocacy. On-the-ground, verified observations can be used by international partners to conduct follow-up investigations, including into the companies that make and supply the weapons circulating in South Sudan, and the governments of countries where these companies are based.

---

[33] Other chapters in this volume detail the ethical dilemmas of open source research and how practitioners approach these. See, for example, the chapters by Wilson, Samuel & Plesch, Freeman & Koenig, Ahmad, L. Wilson *et al.*, Michie *et al.*, and Bedenko & Bellish (Chapters 1, 2.5, 3.1, 5.1, 5.3 and 5.4).

On top of the physical risks of violence that they face, as noted above, local observers also frequently have to depend on unreliable short-term funding, even though effective monitoring requires attention over sustained periods of time. When potential monitors do not have enough money, their primary focus will be on meeting their basic needs, even if they are well placed to help monitoring efforts. Such situations could reinforce perceptions that those collecting hard evidence of wrongdoing are undervalued and that the international community is content that they remain impoverished, despite the fundamental importance of their work to national, regional and international security. Because of this, SSANSA recognizes that it must maintain a meaningful support system for its network. Further, it argues that North–South resource gaps and inequalities should be tackled to build a robust international verification system that includes deliberate and meaningful plans to support and protect local monitors in the Global South.

As well as mitigating individual risks, our work involves uncomfortable ethical quandaries. In particular, decisions about if, when and how to publish our findings often involve complex multidimensional considerations. For example, some liberation movements can be perceived as having just cause in resisting repressive government actions. If we expose the illegal arms of such movements, and they are then disarmed, this could leave their communities vulnerable to punitive and unjust government forces. Such situations force us to face important but difficult questions about how best to do our work whilst being careful to comply with ethical and legal frameworks. What lenses and indicators should we use to consider who to support, and what we can do to end human suffering at the hands of dictators? How can we collect evidence while ensuring that it is not inadvertently highjacked by national intelligence agencies and used by governments to pursue their own interests, rather than contributing to safety and security in South Sudan and its region? There are no easy answers to these problems; we review dilemmas on a case-by-case basis, consulting our partners when necessary.

Beyond Verification

A good deal of effort is spent in conducting open source research, but it is also important to ask what happens after such work? Investigations are not an end in itself. Just as when a weapon delivery system needs to be assembled and launched, so verified information can be used to hold political and military actors accountable, but only if it is deployed effectively.

Different monitoring organizations have different approaches to this. Some stop when they have collected interesting information, sometimes also disseminating it in a general way. While useful, this is unlikely to achieve maximum possible impact. The success of investigations should be assessed in terms of their ability to achieve desired outcomes, which usually involves a complete cycle that includes deliberate actions to push for relevant stakeholders to act on findings, including through targeted advocacy efforts.

Creating links with global and regional networks focused on arms control, disarmament and non-proliferation is one way of operationalizing the findings of open source verification, as these groups can employ our research findings within their advocacy actions. For greatest effect, this might also entail including these wider networks in the initial design of open source verification projects, to ensure that the evidence collected is adequate for their advocacy needs. When it is safe to do so, SSANSA also seeks to impact domestic policy by informing relevant stakeholders in South Sudan about the weapons flows causing harm in the country, and advising them on what needs to be done to strengthen controls. For example, we have engaged with the government in its work drafting policy and legal frameworks to establish a robust system for domestic controls preventing the illegal diversion of weapons.

We also inform governments when we find that weapons they have supplied are causing harm in South Sudan. We do this directly and indirectly, e.g. through judicious naming and shaming, or by involving partners who can alert the governments through less public channels. As mentioned, we have worked hard to establish networks with other international actors such as the Small Arms Survey and Conflict Armament Research who can authoritatively take our findings to relevant governments when we do not have access to them or cannot travel due to funding constraints.

Conclusion

Despite the formal end of South Sudan's civil war in 2018, and the accompanying disarmament commitments, significant quantities of SALW remain in the country, often in the hands of civilians and youths, many of whom feel they need weapons to protect themselves from warlords and government forces as well as fellow armed civilians who are often from neighbouring communities. On top of this, weapons continue to be supplied to the country, despite a UN Security Council embargo, and in contravention of several international treaties including the Arms Trade Treaty.[34] The increasing number of weapons in South Sudan builds on, and reinforces, legacies of violence deriving from the civil war (2013–2018) and from the events leading up to its independence from Sudan in 2011. The consequences of these events include high levels of armed violence, alongside threats of armed violence, that result in innocent civilians being killed and harmed. They also result in the distortion of the peaceful progress of communities, while the financing of weapons detracts from spending on health and development.

There are multiple challenges in seeking to address and reverse the illegal weapons in South Sudan, not least the difficulties of finding out who has what weapons and where they are. In this context, remote open source monitoring via the internet has limited use. Local practitioner-led efforts are indispensable in establishing the truth about weapons in South Sudan, such as the work of the South Sudan Action Network on Small Arms (SSANSA). However, there are considerable challenges to such monitoring, including the difficulties of keeping local monitors safe in a volatile context, and making sure that findings are noticed and used by people that can act on them, such as international organizations and partners, and governments around the world.

The growth of open source research suggests a potential for increased transparency, which could help empower citizens to keep track, and contribute to the success, of arms control and disarmament initiatives, including the full implementation of the UN Security Council arms embargo imposed on South Sudan, and international agreements, such as the Arms Trade Treaty. To realize the possibilities of this exciting new field, and minimize its risks, open source research could benefit from greater solidarity between local and remote monitors, and between civil society researchers in the Global North and Global South.

---

[34] Although South Sudan is not a state party to the Arms Trade Treaty, many people in the country support it. The country's diplomats and civil society representatives actively participated in negotiations and made substantive contributions towards adoption of the Treaty.

Chapter 2.3

Monitoring Nuclear Weapons Developments with Open Source Intelligence

Hans M. Kristensen and Matt Korda

Abstract

This chapter demonstrates how open source research can be used to establish the details of global nuclear weapons stockpiles. It starts by overviewing the patterns of secrecy that surround nuclear weapons, and argues that in contrast to these practices, greater transparency can help stabilize insecurities and reduce the risks of nuclear weapons. It then presents the authors' work for the Federation of American Scientists, showing how they produce accurate estimates of the world's nuclear arsenals by outlining their overall methods and the open sources that they use, as well as highlighting inherent challenges to their work and how they address these. The chapter also assesses ways in which new digital tools and data are transforming opportunities for open source research, and concludes by demonstrating that non-governmental open source research focused on enhancing transparency benefits societies and their security.

Introduction

Nuclear weapons are supposed to be secret. Many people think that they are the foundation of national security, as well as uniquely dangerous weapon systems, and that too much information about them could potentially aid adversaries and proliferators. Consequently, all nine nuclear-armed states[1] try to keep details about their nuclear arsenals and operations hidden from public view.

---

[1] China, France, India, Israel, Pakistan, North Korea, Russia, the United Kingdom and the United States.

This is an open access article published by World Scientific Publishing Europe Ltd. and distributed under the terms of the Creative Commons Attribution-NonCommercial 4.0 International (CC BY-NC 4.0) License.

Yet there are significant differences in the way nuclear-armed states manage information about nuclear weapons. Some of them release next to nothing, others occasionally showcase general information, while yet others publish detailed budget information and planning documents, and in some cases even publicize the number and history of their nuclear warhead stockpile. This broad range of nuclear secrecy standards is the result of a variety of factors: history, governance, rule of law and public discourse. It takes a long time for any nuclear-armed state to develop a culture of responsible transparency, and there are notable differences in how countries approach this. Democratic states with rule of law and accountability tend to be more open and have structures in place that require some transparency. Authoritarian states tend to be more secretive but may provide some information from time to time.

Even in the most open countries, officials sometimes overclassify or withhold information due to excessive secrecy. This trend has worsened in recent years, as several countries that had previously become more transparent have begun to revert to Cold War-era levels of nuclear opacity. In both 2019 and 2020, the Trump administration reversed nearly a decade of normative nuclear transparency practices and refused to declassify the size of the US nuclear stockpile and the number of dismantled warheads.[2] Similarly, in 2021, the United Kingdom announced its intention to 'no longer give public figures for our operational stockpile, deployed warhead or deployed missile numbers'.[3] With the exception of the United States and France, no other nuclear-armed state has ever made public statements about the exact size of its nuclear arsenal, and one country – Israel – does not even publicly acknowledge that it possesses nuclear weapons.[4]

Given the importance of nuclear weapons and the catastrophic consequences of their use, there are many reasons why it is reasonable – even

---

[2] Kristensen H. M. Trump Administration Again Refuses To Disclose Nuclear Weapons Stockpile Size. *FAS Strategic Security Blog*. 3 December 2020. Available from: https://fas.org/blogs/security/2020/12/nuclear-stockpile-denial-2020/ [Accessed 17 May 2023].

[3] British Government. *Global Britain in a Competitive Age: Integrated Review of Security, Defence, Development and Foreign Policy*. CP 403. HM Stationery Office: London. March 2021. p. 77. Available from: https://assets.publishing.service.gov.uk/government/uploads/system/uploads/attachment_data/file/975077/Global_Britain_in_a_Competitive_Age-_the_Integrated_Review_of_Security__Defence__Development_and_Foreign_Policy.pdf [Accessed 17 May 2023].

[4] The United States and Russia do exchange information about their nuclear arsenals as part of the bilateral New START treaty, however, only some of this information is made public. The United States' full data exchange is available upon request from its State Department, but Russia's data are only available in aggregate form.

essential – that the public has access to information about nuclear weapons. Excessive nuclear secrecy can have significant negative consequences both internationally and domestically.

First, uncertainty or exaggerations about nuclear arsenals and the role they play can lead to mistrust and worst-case assumptions that cause countries to increase their arsenals and readiness levels. This can lead to an arms race or miscalculation during times of heightened nuclear tensions.

Second, nuclear opacity reduces the ability of diplomats to participate in multilateral negotiations on arms control and risk reduction. Burdened by excessive secrecy, officials will be less effective in pushing a proactive and progressive arms control agenda to reduce nuclear dangers.[5] In a similar vein, although being transparent may not guarantee that others will increase their transparency, excessive secrecy will certainly offer adversaries the cover to dismiss calls to do so.

Third, overclassification reduces the abilities of academics, subject matter experts, the media and the public to monitor, comprehend and communicate shifts in policy, thus suppressing public debate. An argument often heard from defence hawks in democratic countries is that there is no point in declassifying nuclear stockpile numbers because adversaries will not do the same. But that misses the point that responsible declassification is as important for domestic democratic needs as it is for attempting to influence adversaries – it is about who *we* are, not who *they* are. Indeed, a lack of transparency regarding such a consequential subject exacerbates existing democratic deficits between governments and their constituents.

The Nuclear Information Project

For these reasons, the Federation of American Scientists' Nuclear Information Project[6] seeks to pull back the curtain on excessive nuclear secrecy (see Fig. 1). We do this to empower the public debate with factual information

---

[5] Several chapters in this volume demonstrate ways in which non-governmental open source research can inform national and international policy-making on weapons of mass destruction (WMD), and how it could interface with international WMD treaties in the future. See the chapters in this volume by Wilson, Samuel & Plesch, Duke, H. Wilson *et al.*, Mathews, Revill & Garzón Maceda, and Liu & Gwadera (Chapters 1, 2.2, 4.1, 4.2, 4.3, 4.4).

[6] For information about the Federation of American Scientists' Nuclear Information Project, see https://fas.org/issues/nuclear-weapons/ [Accessed 17 May 2023].

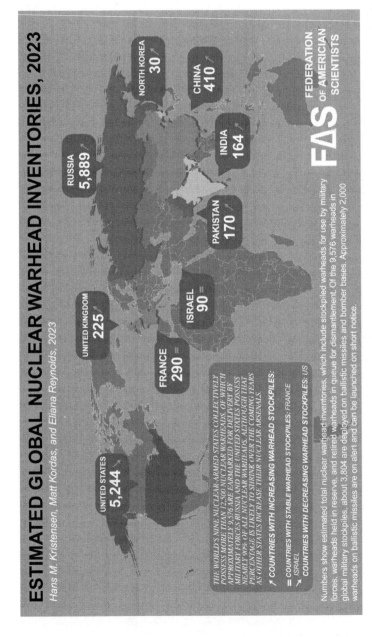

Figure 1: The Federation of American Scientists' Nuclear Information Project seeks to provide the public with the best non-classified estimates for world nuclear forces.[7]

---

[7] Image source: https://fas.org/issues/nuclear-weapons/status-world-nuclear-forces/ [Accessed 17 May 2023]. This resource also provides more information about the status of world nuclear arsenals.

about nuclear weapons policy and operations, challenge false assumptions and improve accountability. The Project aims to produce the best non-classified estimates of global nuclear arsenals and trends by collecting and analyzing information from a variety of open sources.[8]

We collect information about nuclear weapons from several types of open sources, including primary sources from government programme documents, declassified documents, secondary sources from independent experts or media sources, and surveillance tools such as commercial satellite imagery.

Occasionally, official declassifications have provided opportunities to validate our estimates. In 2010, for example, when the US government for the first time declassified the entire history of the size of the US nuclear weapons stockpile, our estimate (5,100 warheads) was only 13 warheads off the official number (5,113). Likewise, in 2018, when the US Department of Defense published the *Nuclear Posture Review*, its estimate for Russian non-strategic nuclear weapons was 'up to 2,000', close to our estimate of 1,830 warheads.

As described further below, each type of open source has advantages and disadvantages, as well as varying degrees of reliability. Therefore, whenever possible, we use multiple sources to corroborate each data point in order to improve confidence. Several other organizations and individuals also conduct analyses of nuclear forces, which are useful for making comparisons and collegial information sharing.

Primary sources

Primary sources of nuclear weapons-related information generally originate from national governments, and can therefore include parliamentary testimonies, intelligence estimates, declassified documents, programme and budgetary documents, military parades, weapon system tests and disclosures about treaty compliance.

While primary sources can be reliable providers of factual information about nuclear weapons, there is always a risk that they may include deliberate or inadvertent bias that could be politically motivated and influenced

---

[8]This chapter uses the terms open source research, open source intelligence and open source investigations interchangeably to refer to analyses based on publicly available tools and information.

by bureaucratic or domestic political pressures. Additionally, official documents may represent the views of a specific government agency or military service, rather than those of an entire country's armed forces and national intelligence community. Some agencies are known to make more hawkish or worst-case assumptions than others. It is also possible that a country might make statements about another country's nuclear forces in order to signal a particular deterrence message.

The size and nature of China's nuclear arsenal, for example, has been subject to much debate over the years, and estimates are not always accurate. Several projections from the US intelligence community about Chinese nuclear weapons during the 1980s and 1990s were exaggerated or simply incorrect although it is important to note that this phenomenon may be related to the questions that these agencies are asked to consider – some are asked to estimate the worst-case scenarios, while others are asked to estimate the most likely scenarios. A US Defense Intelligence Agency (DIA) study from 1984 estimated that China had 150–360 nuclear warheads and projected that this could increase to more than 800 by 1994; however, that prediction did not transpire.[9] Another DIA study from 1999 anticipated that China might have over 460 nuclear weapons by 2020 – which also did not happen[10] (see Fig. 2).

We were therefore sceptical when the DIA in 2019 announced that 'over the next decade, China will at least double the size of its nuclear stockpile'.[11] Even more so when US Strategic Command (USSTRATCOM) in early 2021 stated that 'China's nuclear weapons stockpile is expected to double (if not triple or quadruple) over the next decade'.[12] Neither the DIA nor USSTRATCOM offered any factual information to back up their claims and there was no public information at the time that could support such a

---

[9] Kristensen H. M. DIA assessment of Chinese nuclear forces. *Nuclear Information Project*. 2006. Available from: http://www.nukestrat.com/china/diachina.htm [Accessed 17 May 2023].

[10] US Defense Intelligence Agency. *The Decades Ahead: 1999–2020*. July 1999. p. 38. Classified document reproduced in Scarborough, R. *Rumsfeld's War: The Untold Story of America's Anti-Terrorist Commander*. Washington, D.C.: Regnery Publishing. 2004. p. 197.

[11] Hudson Institute. The Arms Control Landscape: Featuring DIA Lt. Gen. Robert P. Ashley, Jr. On Russian and Chinese Nuclear Weapons. 29 May 2019 [video online and speech transcript]. Available from: https://www.hudson.org/events/1694-the-arms-control-landscape52019 [Accessed 17 May 2023].

[12] Admiral Richard C. A. Commander, US Strategic Command. Forging 21st-Century Strategic Deterrence, *US Naval Institute Proceedings*. February 2021. Available from: https://www.usni.org/magazines/proceedings/2021/february/forging-21st-century-strategic-deterrence [Accessed 17 May 2023].

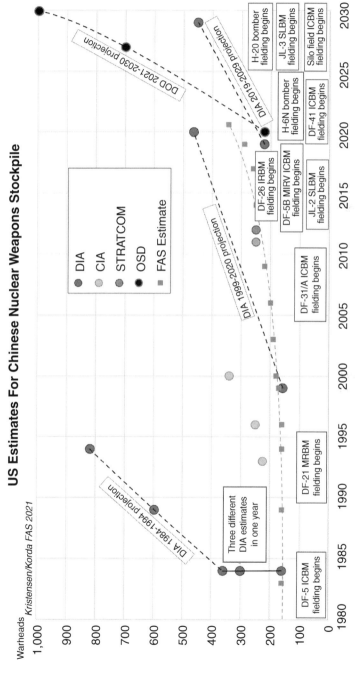

Figure 2: US government projections for Chinese nuclear weapons historically have promised too much too soon. The construction of more than 300 new silos now indicates a significant expansion over the next decade.

dramatic prediction. However, later in 2021, non-governmental researchers (including us) were able to confirm that China was building hundreds of missile silos by using open source research involving satellite imagery, as discussed further below.

Similarly, we have also scrutinized official US announcements about Russian nuclear forces. Russia's arsenal of non-strategic nuclear weapons gained prominence in 2018, when the Trump administration's *Nuclear Posture Review* highlighted these weapons as part of what the *Review* described as Russia's 'escalate to de-escalate' strategy to use nuclear weapons first in a conventional conflict that Russia was losing. The *Review* claimed that Russia had 'up to 2,000' non-strategic nuclear weapons and was building more.[13] This number, which was close to our estimate of Russian non-strategic nuclear weapons at the time, was the first substantial official US public statement on the status and composition of the Russian non-strategic nuclear arsenal in more than two decades. The statement unsurprisingly raised questions about the assumptions and counting rules that underpinned the estimate. Most of Russia's non-strategic weapon systems are dual capable, which means that not all platforms may be assigned nuclear missions and not all operations are nuclear. Moreover, many of the delivery platforms are in various stages of overhaul and would therefore not be able to launch nuclear weapons.

The public statement was important because it formed part of the public narrative that the Trump administration was trying to build: that Russia was a growing nuclear threat and that its non-strategic nuclear arsenal was particularly dangerous and growing both in numbers and diversity. Some officials even suggested Russia might have more than 2,000 non-strategic nuclear weapons.

It was therefore a surprise when the US DIA in 2021 published a lower estimate of 1,000–2,000 non-strategic nuclear weapons.[14] US officials later

---

[13] US Department of Defense, Office of the Secretary of Defense. *Nuclear Posture Review*. 2 February 2018. p. 53. Available from: https://media.defense.gov/2018/Feb/02/2001872886/-1/-1/1/2018-NUCLEAR-POSTURE-REVIEW-FINAL-REPORT.PDF [Accessed 17 May 2023].

[14] Berrier S., Lt. Gen., Director, US Defense Intelligence Agency. *Statement for the Record: Worldwide Threat Assessment*. 26 April 2021. Available from: https://www.armed-services.senate.gov/imo/media/doc/2021%20DIA%20Annual%20Threat%20Assessment%20Statement%20for%20the%20Record.pdf [Accessed 17 May 2023].

told us that the new estimate reflected a range of views within the US intelligence community,[15] and that the Pentagon and USSTRATCOM used the high number. Even so, in testimony to Congress in 2022, USSTRATCOM used the estimate of 1,000–2,000 instead of 'up to 2,000' or approximately 2,000 non-strategic warheads.[16] Moreover, the State Department's annual treaty compliance report in 2022 added to the confusion by revealing that the 1,000–2,000 estimate included retired warheads awaiting dismantlement.[17] Since retired warheads are not part of the useable arsenal, the actual number of warheads that is assigned to Russian non-strategic forces might even be lower.

The narrative that Russia has increased its non-strategic nuclear warheads has been used repeatedly by officials and opponents of reductions and arms control. One senior former official, who is believed to have played an important role in the 2018 *Nuclear Posture Review*, recently claimed that Russia, since the signing of the New START treaty in 2010, 'has deployed between 2,000 and 2,500 modern shorter-range nuclear systems', and that '[b]ecause of the growth of Russian shorter-range nuclear forces in the past 10 years, New Start no longer serves US security interests even in a bilateral US–Russian context'.[18]

But the public record shows that although Russia is modernizing its dual-capable non-strategic nuclear forces, the number of nuclear warheads that the US intelligence community estimates are assigned to those forces has not increased over the past ten years; instead, it has actually declined significantly. Shortly before the 2010 New START treaty was signed, the US Defense Department briefed NATO that Russia had an estimated

---

[15] For information on the US intelligence community, and its use of OSINT, see the chapter by Vogel in this volume (Chapter 3.4).
[16] Richard C. A, Commander, US Strategic Command. *Prepared Statement before the Senate Armed Services Committee*. 8 March 2022. p. 6. Available from: https://www.armed-services.senate.gov/download/richard-statement-03/08/2022 [Accessed 17 May 2023].
[17] US Department of State. Adherence and Compliance with Arms Control, Nonproliferation, and Disarmament Agreements and Commitments. April 2022. p. 11. Available from: https://www.state.gov/wp-content/uploads/2022/04/2022-Adherence-to-and-Compliance-with-Arms-Control-Nonproliferation-and-Disarmament-Agreements-and-Commitments-1.pdf [Accessed 17 May 2023].
[18] Miller F. Outdated Nuclear Treaties Heighten the Risk of Nuclear War. *Wall Street Journal*. 21 April 2022. Available from: https://www.wsj.com/articles/outdated-nuclear-treaties-new-start-treaty-russia-putin-china-xi-heighten-risk-nuclear-war-missile-test-ukraine-deterrence-11650575490 [Accessed 17 May 2023].

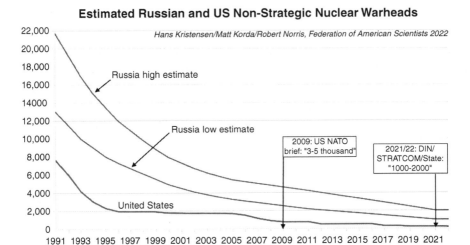

Figure 3: Contrary to claims that Russia has been increasing its non-strategic nuclear warheads over the past decade, official records indicate that the number has declined significantly.

3,000–5,000 non-strategic nuclear weapons,[19] which implies a reduction of 2,000–3,000 non-strategic nuclear warheads over the past decade (see Fig. 3).

Detailed information about particular weapon systems – such as the number of units produced, their components and subcomponents, their production and deployment locations, and their projected deployment dates – can often be found in budgetary and programmatic documents. The information included in these documents is usually highly reliable, given that they are often used to explain and justify the details and costs of these programmes to lawmakers. The United States is the most consistent publisher of this kind of data, followed by the United Kingdom, France and Russia – although Russia publishes considerably less than the others. China, India and Pakistan publish very little information, while Israel and North Korea generally do not publish any detailed information. Typically, countries with more responsive checks and balances, such as parliaments, congresses or opposition political parties, are more prone to releasing this kind of data in

---

[19] PDUSDP Miller Consults with Allies on Nuclear Posture Review. USNATO Cable 378_a. 4 September 2009. Available from: https://wikileaks.org/plusd/cables/09USNATO378_a.html [Accessed 8 August 2023].

order to satisfy requests for information from the legislative branch to the executive branch of government.

Large swaths of valuable primary source information about the history and status of nuclear forces can also be found in treaty documents and declassified intelligence assessments. In particular, US documents related to the 2010 New START treaty provide helpful disaggregated strategic forces deployment data relating to Russian and US nuclear forces.[20] Additionally, certain documents related to the first START treaty and the 1987 Intermediate-Range Nuclear Forces Treaty provide overviews of nuclear arsenals and deployment locations that, in many cases, are still valid today. Some of these documents are automatically declassified and made public by the US government after a certain number of years. In countries with favourable freedom of information laws, such as the United States, large inventories of documents have been declassified and released to the public, and many primary documents have been published in open access libraries like the National Security Archive.[21]

Information about Russian and Chinese arsenals is more sporadic and not available in comprehensive form from official sources. Nonetheless, Russian military commanders often provide statements to Russian military and news media outlets, and the Chinese military frequently publishes articles and videos that describe exercises in vague terms and occasionally reveals locations of missile launchers (see Fig. 4). Whenever possible, it is best for research to be conducted in the language of primary sources. However, if that is not possible, then translation services or colleagues who speak different languages can be tapped as invaluable resources.

Some US agencies – such as the Central Intelligence Agency Freedom of Information Act Reading Room[22] – publish declassified documents on their websites that include their own descriptions of Soviet and Chinese nuclear force developments during the Cold War. Although these documents are

---

[20] For US State Department resources on the New START treaty, see https://www.state.gov/new-start/ [Accessed 8 August 2023]. For analysis of the most recent New START aggregate data see Kristensen H. M. Amidst Nuclear Saber Rattling, New START Treaty Demonstrates Importance. *FAS Strategic Security Blog*. 6 April 2022. Available from: https://fas.org/blogs/security/2022/04/new_start_treaty_importance/ [Accessed 8 August 2023].

[21] For the unique National Security Archive collection of declassified documents relating to nuclear weapons, see https://nsarchive.gwu.edu/project/nuclear-vault [Accessed 17 May 2023].

[22] Freedom of Information Act Reading Room. *US Central Intelligence Agency*. https://www.cia.gov/readingroom/ [Accessed 17 May 2023].

Figure 4: Chinese military videos sometimes allow geolocation of military exercises or new missile brigades, like this deployment of the DF-26 near Jilantai in 2019. This image led to the discovery of the Jilantai training area in 2019, which led to the discovery of new silos with inflatable domes in 2020, which led to the discovery of China's three large missile silos fields in 2021.[25]

over 25 years old and often still have redacted sections, they can nonetheless provide important reference points for understanding the structure and organization of Russian and Chinese nuclear forces today. For more recent information, the US Defense Department's annual report to Congress on Chinese military developments[23] and the US Air Force National Air and Space Intelligence Center (NASIC) report on ballistic and cruise missile threats[24] are important sources.

---

[23] US Department of Defense. *Military and Security Developments Involving the People's Republic of China*. 3 November 2021. Available from: https://media.defense.gov/2021/Nov/03/2002885874/-1/-1/0/2021-CMPR-FINAL.PDF.

[24] US Air Force National Air and Space Intelligence Center (NASIC). *Ballistic and Cruise Missile Threat*. July 2020. Available from: https://media.defense.gov/2021/Jan/11/2002563190/-1/-1/1/2020%20BALLISTIC%20AND%20CRUISE%20MISSILE%%2020THREAT_FINAL_2OCT_REDUCEDFILE.PDF.

[25] Image Source: Kristensen H. Chinese DF-26 Missile Launchers Deploy To New Missile Training Area. *FAS Strategic Security Blog*. 21 January 2019. https://fas.org/blogs/security/2019/01/df-26/ [Accessed 8 August 2023]. Inlay satellite imagery @ 2023 Maxar Technologies.

Overall, official primary sources generally remain the most useful and reliable sources for collecting information about a country's nuclear forces – particularly when the country in question has a degree of transparency about its military activities. If a country does not publish information about its own nuclear forces, however, then researchers must often turn to secondary sources of information.

Secondary sources

Secondary sources are generally those which report on the status of nuclear weapons developments (in contrast to the first-hand accounts provided by primary sources discussed above); they include news media, think-tanks or open source researchers. These sources all play a valuable role in increasing transparency and policy accountability within nuclear-armed states; however, the quality of reporting varies considerably between outlets, countries and organizations. It is therefore imperative to develop media literacy skills and evaluate secondary sources very carefully, while always trying to trace the origin of stories. This can sometimes be challenging, because media reports about nuclear weapons often quote anonymous contributors, such as 'someone involved in defense planning' or 'an industry source', without giving readers any sense of whether the source spoke in an official capacity or even has specific insight on the weapon system being described.

Furthermore, media embellishment in reporting on nuclear weapons issues is common, particularly in countries where governments do not reveal much information about their own nuclear forces. This can often drive exaggeration, sensationalism and mischaracterization of a country's own nuclear capabilities. For example, several Indian media sources reported in 2020 that one of India's newest short-range ballistic missiles – the Shaurya – is nuclear capable.[26] However, this has not been publicly confirmed by the Indian government or by other states in their public assessments of India's

---

[26] Press Trust of India (PTI). India successfully test-fires nuclear capable hypersonic missile Shaurya. *Hindustan Times*. 3 October 2020. Available from: https://www.hindustantimes.com/india-news/india-successfully-test-fires-nuclear-capable-hypersonic-missile-shaurya/story-6OVLkT6uXueovpkKniuxGK.html [Accessed 8 August 2023]. Gupta S. Govt okays induction of nuke-capable Shaurya missile amid Ladakh standoff. *HindustanTimes*. 6 October 2020. Available from: https://www.hindustantimes.com/india-news/shaurya-missile-to-be-inducted-in-strategic-arsenal-agni-5-s-sea-version-by-2022/story-bS1100SkwoGLEXW5ANFQuO.html [Accessed 8 August 2023].

missile arsenal. Likewise, Indian and international media,[27] as well as many private institute websites,[28] frequently report that India's BrahMos missile is nuclear capable, even though there are no known public official reports that credit the weapon with nuclear capability, and US intelligence explicitly lists the missile as conventional.

Satellite imagery

Some aspects of nuclear weapons programmes are large enough, and have sufficient identifiable features, to be visible on satellite imagery, and so commercially available satellite imagery has become a particularly valuable resource for analyzing nuclear deployments, construction of nuclear facilities and changes to force structures. Freely available lower-resolution imagery can be useful for scanning large areas to find evidence of new construction of buildings and bases, while more expensive higher-resolution imagery is useful for identifying specific buildings, features of bases and weapon systems. For example, between 2019 and 2021 the Federation of American Scientists used a variety of satellite imagery sources to track the expansion of China's missile training area near Jilantai in Inner Mongolia (see Fig. 5). Lower-resolution imagery providers like the European Sentinel Hub Playground served as a useful tool in the initial stages to detect new structures, and higher-resolution imagery providers like Planet Labs PBC and Maxar Technologies were then useful in examining particular facilities more closely.

As mentioned above, satellite imagery also enabled non-governmental open source investigations to discover what was behind the DIA and USSTRATCOM projections claiming dramatic increases to the Chinese nuclear stockpile. By scrutinizing satellite imagery, open source researchers

---

[27] See for example: Negi M. India successfully test fires surface to surface BrahMos cruise missile. *India Today*. 23 March 2022. Available from: https://www.indiatoday.in/india/story/india-test-fires-surface-to-surface-brahmos-supersonic-cruise-missile-andaman-nicobar-islands-1928722-2022-03-23 [Accessed 17 May 2023].

[28] See for example: BRAHMOS Cruise Missile. *Military Today*. Available from: http://www.militarytoday.com/missiles/brahmos.htm [Accessed 8 August 2023]. BrahMos. *Wikipedia*. Available from: https://en.wikipedia.org/wiki/BrahMos [Accessed 8 August 2023].

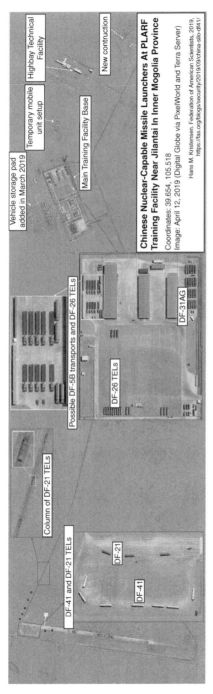

Figure 5: The Federation of American Scientists' Nuclear Information Project used various commercial satellite image services to identify and outline a new missile training facility near Jilantai.[29]

---

[29]Image Source: Kristensen H. New Missile Silo And DF-41 Launchers Seen In Chinese Nuclear Missile Training Area. *FAS Strategic Security Blog*. 3 September 2019. https://fas.org/blogs/security/2019/09/china-silo-df41/ [Accessed 8 August 2023]. Inlay satellite imagery @ 2023 Maxar Technologies. This resource also gives additional information about the FAS investigations, and further details are provided in Kristensen H. M. China's expanding missile training area: More silos, tunnels, and support facilities. *FAS Strategic Security Blog*. 24 February 2021. Available from: https://fas.org/blogs/security/2021/02/plarf-jilantai-expansion/ [Accessed 8 August 2023].

(including us) found indications of three large missile silo fields in central China near Yumen, Hami and Ordos (the Pentagon calls this area Yulin) (see Fig. 6).[30] We are currently tracking approximately 320 silos under construction at these three sites, as well as new silos for liquid-fuel missiles in eastern China and the PLA Rocket Force training site near Jilantai.

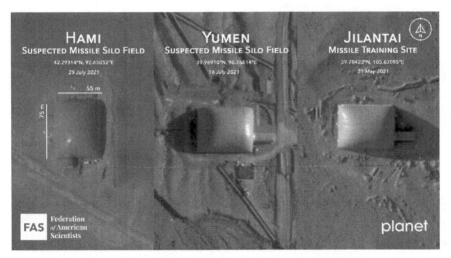

Figure 6: The identification by the Federation of American Scientists' Nuclear Information Project staff of inflatable shelters over silo construction sites at Jilantai allowed discovery of China's three large missile silo fields at Yumen, Hami and Ordos.[31]

---

[30] For the original publications announcing the discovery of the Yumen, Hami and Ordos missile silo fields, see, Warrick J. China is building more than 100 new missile silos in its western desert, analysts say. *Washington Post*. 30 June 2021. Available from: https://www.washingtonpost.com/national-security/china-nuclear-missile-silos/2021/06/30/0fa8debc-d9c2-11eb-bb9e-70fda8c37057_story.html [Accessed 8 August 2023]. Korda M. and Kristensen H. M. China is Building A Second Nuclear Missile Silo Field. *FAS Strategic Security Blog*. 16 July 2021. Available from: https://fas.org/blogs/security/2021/07/china-is-building-a-second-nuclear-missile-silo-field/ [Accessed 8 August 2023]. Lee R. PLA Likely Begins Construction of an Intercontinental Ballistic Missile Silo Site near Hanggin Banner. China Aerospace Studies Institute, US Air Force Air University. 12 August 2021. Available from: https://www.airuniversity.af.edu/CASI/Display/Article/2729781/pla-likely-begins-construction-of-an-intercontinental-ballistic-missile-silo-si/ [Accessed 8 August 2023].

[31] Image Source: Korda M. and Kristensen H. A Closer Look at China's Missile Silo Construction. *FAS Strategic Security Blo.*, 2 November 2021. Available from: https://fas.org/blogs/security/2021/11/a-closer-look-at-chinas-missile-silo-construction/ [Accessed 8 August 2023]. Satellite imagery via Planet Labs PBC. This resource also gives additional details about the underpinning FAS research.

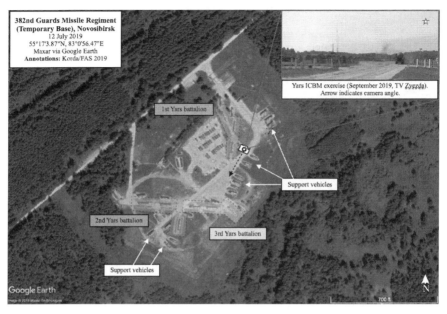

Figure 7: Commercial satellite images have proven invaluable for monitoring and reporting on Russia's modernization of its strategic nuclear forces.[32]

Analyzing satellite imagery can be challenging; features may be difficult to interpret accurately, and states may use camouflage and deceptions to obscure details and confuse adversaries. However, by combining satellite observations with other sources, it is possible to reduce uncertainty and increase confidence in observations. During Russia's modernization of its land-based missile forces, for example, we have gradually improved our understanding of the country's infrastructure, construction and operational patterns. This has allowed us to identify when new launchers arrive at individual garrisons and detect upgrades of missile silos in advance of receiving modern missiles (see Fig. 7).

More recently, we initiated an investigation following President Vladimir Putin's 27 February 2022 announcement ordering the transfer

---

[32] Image Source: Korda M. A Rare Look Inside A Russian ICBM Base. *FAS Strategic Security Blog*. 19 November 2019. Available from: https://fas.org/publication/a-rare-look-inside-a-russian-icbm-base/ [Accessed 8 August 2023]. Satellite imagery @2023 Maxar Technologies. This resource also gives additional details about FAS research.

of Russia's 'deterrence forces' to 'a special regime of combat duty'.[33] This was widely understood to be an order for Russian nuclear forces to increase their alert and staffing levels, but there was little understanding of what this meant on the ground. We used commercial satellite images to check if there were visible changes in the operations of the forces that could indicate an increased nuclear threat. The images showed that the forces continued to operate as normal with occasional small ercises.

A Rapidly Changing Environment for Open Source Research

The open source information landscape is changing rapidly, as emerging technologies and increasingly networked systems allow for new methods of information gathering.

For example, significant improvements in commercial satellite technology now allow independent researchers to analyze some military developments nearly in real time. This has become particularly apparent with analysis of North Korea; over the past few years, researchers have been able to track micro-level activity at the Yongbyon Nuclear Scientific Research Centre, including the presence of smoke or specialized vehicles, in order to determine whether particular facilities are operational.[34] Occasionally, commercial satellites have even managed to capture actual missile test launches as they occurred.[35]

Applying machine learning-powered artificial intelligence to remote sensing is still a relatively nascent practice, but has the potential to yield groundbreaking results.[36] With increased sophistication, such systems could

---

[33] Holloway D. Read the fine print: Russia's nuclear weapon use policy. *Bulletin of the Atomic Scientists*. 10 March 2022. Available from: https://thebulletin.org/2022/03/read-the-fine-print-russias-nuclear-weapon-use-policy/ [Accessed 22 March 2022].

[34] Pabian F., Makowsky P., and Liu J. North Korea's Yongbyon Complex: Activity Picks Up. *38 North*. 30 October 2020. Available from: https://www.38north.org/2020/10/yongbyon201030/ [Accessed 8 August 2023]. Pabian F., Makowsky P., and Liu J. North Korea's Yongbyon Nuclear Complex: Activity Around the UEP Suggests Ongoing Operations. *38 North*. 28 July 2020. Available from: https://www.38north.org/2020/07/yongbyon072820/ [Accessed 8 August 2023].

[35] Cohen Z. and Gaouette N. Exclusive: Images show North Korea missile launch as Pyongyang tests Trump. *CNN*. 5 May 2019. Available from: https://www.cnn.com/2019/05/05/politics/north-korea-missile-launch-image/index.html.

[36] See also the chapter by Withorne in this volume (Chapter 5.2) for a discussion of the possible roles of applying machine learning to open source research.

recognize unique features and patterns across images, thus aiding geolocation.[37] For instance, researchers have begun to develop a process for discriminating between uranium and copper mills using an artificial intelligence that responds to signatures predefined by humans.[38] This could have significant implications for non-proliferation researchers.

Open source information gathering about military matters has also been facilitated by the shift from analog to digital processes. In November 2017, for example, the fitness tracking app Strava released a global heat map encompassing more than three trillion individual GPS data points. Because Strava is popular among several countries' armed forces, the heatmap inadvertently revealed the locations and layouts of military bases across the globe.[39]

Similarly, in May 2021, Bellingcat published an investigation revealing that US Air Force members stationed in Europe were using publicly visible flashcard apps to learn the security procedures relating to nuclear weapons maintenance, security and storage. As the Bellingcat report notes, 'the flashcards studied by soldiers tasked with guarding these devices reveal not just the bases, but even identify the exact shelters with "hot" vaults that likely contain nuclear weapons. They also detail intricate security details and protocols such as the positions of cameras, the frequency of patrols around the vaults, secret duress words that signal when a guard is being threatened and the unique identifiers that a restricted area badge needs to have'.[40]

On the whole, governments have reacted clumsily to these trends, generally falling back on their instinctive preference for excessive secrecy. In response to the Bellingcat investigation, the relevant governments elected

---

[37] Lück N. Machine Learning-Powered Artificial Intelligence in Arms Control. Peace Research Institute Frankfurt. *PRIF Report 8/2019*. 2019. Available from: https://www.hsfk.de/fileadmin/HSFK/hsfk_publikationen/prif0819.pdf [Accessed 8 August 2023].

[38] Sundaresan L., Chandrashekar S., and Jasani B. Discriminating Uranium and Copper mills using satellite imagery. *Remote Sensing Applications: Society and Environment*. January 2017. 5. pp. 27–35. https://doi.org/10.1016/j.rsase.2016.12.002 [Accessed 8 August 2023].

[39] Hsu J. The Strava Heat Map and the End of Secrets. *Wired*. 29 January 2018. Available from: https://www.wired.com/story/strava-heat-map-military-bases-fitness-trackers-privacy/ [Accessed 8 August 2023].

[40] Postma F. US Soldiers Expose Nuclear Weapons Secrets Via Flashcard Apps. *Bellingcat*. 28 May 2021. Available from: https://www.bellingcat.com/news/2021/05/28/us-soldiers-expose-nuclear-weapons-secrets-via-flashcard-apps/ [Accessed 8 August 2023].

to remove the flashcard sets and downplay the issue, instead of acknowledging the widely known presence of nuclear weapons at the bases in question. This was likely done in order to suppress public debate about the issue in the nuclear weapons host countries where support is relatively low.

Similarly, in response to the proliferation of high-resolution commercial satellite imagery, governments have in some cases asked mapping services to censor specific images, leading to the substitution of military facilities with noticeably fake trees, farms and deserts on online mapping platforms.[41] In one instance, a Dutch satellite imagery provider even falsified an image of Volkel Air Base – a storage site for US nuclear weapons – after it was *purchased* by the Federation of American Scientists.[42] In some cases, these types of awkward reactions have inadvertently revealed details about the sensitive facilities that the government in question was attempting to hide. This is a classic example of the phenomenon known as the 'Streisand Effect', named for a 2003 incident when Barbra Streisand sued a photographer for taking a picture of her Malibu mansion, thus inadvertently attracting hundreds of thousands of viewers to the innocuous photograph.

The manipulation of satellite imagery by governments and mapping platforms could open the door for similar actions by malicious actors. In recent years, military officials and independent experts have sounded the alarm over the possible development of 'deep fake geography', in which artificial intelligence could be used to falsify satellite images by introducing landscape features that do not exist in reality.[43]

---

[41] Korda M. Israel's Official Map Replaces Military Bases With Fake Farms And Deserts. *FAS Strategic Security Blog*. 17 December 2018. Available from: https://fas.org/blogs/security/2018/12/israels-official-map-replaces-military-bases-with-fake-farms-and-deserts/ [Accessed 8 August 2023]. Lewis J (@ArmsControlWonk). In The #2020commission, I identified the location of the HQ of South Korea's Army Missile Command in Eumseong-gun... *Twitter*. 11 December 2018. Available from: https://twitter.com/ArmsControlWonk/status/1072583481362927616 [Accessed 8 August 2023].

[42] Kristensen H. M. Nukes in Europe: Secrecy Under Siege. *FAS Strategic Security Blog*. 13 June 2013. Available from: https://fas.org/blogs/security/2013/06/secrecyundersiege/ [Accessed 8 August 2023].

[43] Vincent J. Deepfake satellite imagery poses a not-so-distant threat, warn geographers. *The Verge*. 27 April 2021. Available from: https://www.theverge.com/2021/4/27/22403741/deepfake-geography-satellite-imagery-ai-generated-fakes-threat [Accessed 8 August 2023]. Zhao B., Zhang S., Xu C., Sun Y., and Deng C. Deep fake geography? When geospatial data encounter artificial intelligence. *Cartography and Geographic Information Science*. 19 September 2020, 48, p. 4. https://doi.org/10.1080/15230406.2021.1910075.

The spread of misinformation and disinformation about nuclear weapons can increasingly be amplified through social media platforms like Twitter or Facebook. Although these platforms can beneficially allow for rapid, crowdsourced analysis to respond to breaking news events – such as missile launches or nuclear tests – they also tend to magnify sensational information. For example, when an ammonium nitrate storage site exploded in the port of Beirut in August 2020, the presence of a mushroom cloud prompted conspiracy theorists and uninformed individuals with high-profile accounts to incorrectly tweet that the explosion was caused by a nuclear weapon. Some of the original tweets were deleted; however, not before they had already been retweeted thousands of times and widely shared across the internet.[44]

The most effective way to combat misinformation and disinformation about nuclear weapons is for governments to be more transparent. Of course, it is certainly reasonable to safeguard specific operational details that could pose proliferation or safety risks. However, given that sensitive data are becoming increasingly accessible through open source methods, governments must recognize that true safety is best achieved through effective security, not unnecessary and counterproductive secrecy.

Needlessly withholding fundamental details about one's nuclear programme does not make the world safer; on the contrary, it opens the door to exaggeration, hype and miscalculation. In the absence of government clarity, open source research by groups such as the Federation of American Scientists and others fulfils much-needed transparency and data verification functions, providing robust knowledge about global nuclear stockpiles, correcting false claims and protecting the public from disinformation about the most powerful and dangerous weapons in existence.

---

[44] Gault M. Conspiracy Theorists Adamantly Insist Beirut Explosion Was a Nuke (It Wasn't). *Vice*. 4 August 2020. Available from: https://www.vice.com/en/article/7kpdxz/conspiracy-theorists-adamantly-insist-beirut-explosion-was-a-nuke-it-wasnt [Accessed 8 August 2023].

© 2024 World Scientific Publishing Company
https://doi.org/10.1142/9781800614079_0005

Chapter 2.4

Remote Scrutiny: How Online Information Can Help to Investigate Airstrikes

Christiaan Triebert

Abstract

Numerous countries have conducted airstrikes in Iraq and Syria, resulting in civilian deaths in these countries, as well as the devastation of communities and infrastructure. However, important details about such strikes are often a blind spot for the international community. While there are significant obstacles to conducting on-the-ground investigations at the site of the strikes, online open source research[1] offers possibilities for relatively safe, low-cost and high-impact ways to establish important facts about airstrikes and their ramifications, and can help to bring accountability to violations of international norms. After presenting information on recent airstrikes in Syria and Iraq, this chapter outlines general approaches for conducting open source investigations into airstrikes, and then details how these have been applied in two case studies to reveal the facts about the US bombing of a Syrian mosque and the Russian bombing of a Syrian hospital.

Introduction: Airstrikes in Iraq and Syria

A roar in the cloudy sky was a loud reminder that the war was in full swing at the otherwise eerily quiet Mount Batiwa frontline in Iraq. 'Coalition jets',

---

[1] Many authors choose to use the term open source intelligence (OSINT), defined by the US Federal Bureau of Investigation as research using 'a broad array of information and sources that is generally available'. However, 'intelligence' is a politically loaded term that is often associated with governmental activity or efforts that somehow involve secrecy. When the term is used to describe the activities of, for example, investigative journalists or activists, some may wrongly assume these people are government agents. This chapter favours the use of open source 'investigation' or 'research' over 'intelligence', and uses the terms to mean analyses that are based on publicly available tools and information.

This is an open access article published by World Scientific Publishing Europe Ltd. and distributed under the terms of the Creative Commons Attribution-NonCommercial 4.0 International (CC BY-NC 4.0) License.

said a Peshmerga soldier, looking up: 'They're going to bomb not far from here'. He pointed at the horizon towards Hawija, a town that was then, in December 2016, still held by the so-called Islamic State (IS). Standing at the frontline, we heard two thuds, just faintly, moments later.

The 'Coalition' in this case is the Combined Joint Task Force-Operation Inherent Resolve (CJTF-OIR), which the US established in October 2014 in reaction to IS's rapid territorial gains in northern Iraq and eastern Syria during the first half of that year, as well as reports of atrocities and fear of further conflict spillovers. Its goal was to coordinate efforts 'to militarily defeat [IS] in order to enable whole-of-coalition governmental actions to increase regional stability'.[2] Over the next seven years, no fewer than 14 states conducted over 34,000 air and artillery strikes with the CJTF-OIR in Iraq and Syria.[3] These strikes undeniably contributed to IS being driven out of almost all the territory it once held, but also resulted in widespread destruction and hundreds, if not thousands, of civilian casualties.[4]

In September 2015, roughly a year after the US-led CJTF-OIR began, Russia declared it would also intervene militarily in Syria. Russian President Vladimir Putin defined the goal of the campaign, which came after an official request from the Syrian government for military help against 'rebel and jihadist groups', as 'stabilising the legitimate power in Syria and creating conditions for political compromise'.[5] Russia reported more than 39,000 airstrikes in the first three years of its military intervention. These strikes turned the tide for the Syrian government led by President Bashar al-Assad, helping pro-government forces retake significant parts of the country from IS and other armed groups, but also resulting in wide-scale

---

[2]Combined Joint Task Force – Operation Inherent Resolve Fact Sheet. Nd. Available from: https://web.archive.org/ web/20161105183500/; http://www.inherentresolve.mil/Portals/1/Documents/Mission/Mission.pdf?ver=2016-03-23-091705-717 [Accessed 5 August 2021].

[3]States within the US-led CJTF-OIR that conducted strikes are the US, the United Kingdom, France, Belgium, Netherlands, Canada, Australia, Denmark, Turkey, Saudi Arabia, United Arab Emirates, Bahrain, Jordan, as well as occasional Iraqi strikes in Syria. Airwars. US-led Coalition in Iraq & Syria. *Airwars*. Available from: https://airwars.org/conflict/coalition-in-iraq-and-syria [Accessed 5 August 2021].

[4]The US-led CJTF-OIR itself has confirmed 1,410 civilian deaths due to its actions in Iraq and Syria, originating from 341 separate incidents. The estimate by Airwars is significantly higher: between 8,312 and 13,190. Airwars. Reported civilian deaths from US-led Coalition strikes in Syria. *Airwars*. Available from: https://airwars.org/conflict/coalition-in-iraq-and-syria [Accessed 5 August 2021].

[5]Interfax. Путин назвал основную задачу российских военных в Сирии. 11 October 2015. Available from: http://www.interfax.ru/russia/472593 [Accessed 9 June 2016].

destruction and at least 4,096 locally reported deaths, according to one count.[6]

Together, the US-led CJTF-OIR and Russia self-declared over 70,000 strikes in Syria and Iraq. But even more strikes were conducted by other actors, as well as by these same actors under different banners. The US, for instance, also carried out unilateral strikes in Syria, mostly in the country's opposition-held Idlib governorate. Similarly, Iran, Israel and Turkey all undertook unilateral strikes in Syrian and Iraqi territory. Lastly, the Syrian and Iraqi forces also launched strikes on their own soil.

All in all, no fewer than 19 countries have conducted strikes in Syria and Iraq, resulting in thousands of reported civilian deaths, and often raising questions about which air force was responsible for these casualties. It is important that there is transparency about such instances of civilian harm, not least to ensure that militaries are aware of the full cost of their missions, to enable survivors to know who was responsible for the death of their loved ones, and start the process of bringing accountability to potential violations of the laws of war. Ideally, such claims about civilian deaths would be investigated on the ground by independent observers, however the areas where airstrikes are conducted are often hard to reach and dangerous to access. Even if access is possible, it is costly.

Investigating airstrikes remotely can offer a relatively low-cost and potentially high-impact opportunity to bring accountability to perpetrators of civilian harm – or at least establish the facts about strikes as well as their consequences, and, in cases where ground access is possible, provide some basic understanding of the incident before a visit. In recent years, growing numbers of news organizations and human rights groups alike, alongside individual online open source investigators, have been using publicly available tools and information to investigate airstrikes remotely.[7]

---

[6] Airwars. Russian Military in Syria. *Airwars*. Available from: https://airwars.org/conflict/russian-militaryin-syria [Accessed 5 August 2021].

[7] Examples of organizations working specifically on airstrikes in Iraq and Syria include: Airwars, a non-profit organization that tracks, assesses and archives open source military reports and related civilian harm claims; Bellingcat, an investigative collective that uses open sources to investigate a wide variety of topics; human rights organizations Amnesty International and Human Rights Watch, which have both published detailed reports on airstrikes and their impact on civilians; PAX, a Dutch peace organization that has worked with local partners on the effect of airstrikes on civilians and the environment; and Syrian Archive, a Syrian-led project which aims to preserve, enhance and memorialize documentation of suspected human rights violations and other crimes committed.

This chapter will show how they collect, corroborate and analyze information such as photos and videos uploaded to social media, satellite imagery, witness statements and military reports. First, the chapter will outline open source research tools and methods that can help establish the facts about an alleged airstrike and its aftermath, and some of the challenges involved. Subsequently, two case studies will illustrate how these tools are used in more detail. The case studies derive from investigations I have contributed to: first within a collaborative effort to investigate the US bombing of a Syrian mosque, and second, as part of The New York Times Visual Investigations team's research into the Russian bombing of Syrian hospitals.

The Five Ws

In general, the task of open source researchers investigating remote events is to find and authenticate useful publicly available data, and trace relevant clues from such sources to establish the facts about what has or has not taken place. The investigation process is often directed at answering the five Ws: what, where, when, who and why, described in turn below. It should be noted that there are many overlapping aspects of these processes, and investigators do not always work through them sequentially.

What?

First and foremost, it is important to consider what, if anything, happened. An initial claim that an airstrike occurred can come in many forms. It could be a post on social media from locals on the ground, a statement from a belligerent actor, or perhaps a witness reaching out. Translating initial allegations into confirmed news about a definite event initially requires finding relevant information and confirming that it is genuine, and a first step is often to conduct cross-platform keyword searches on any named locations, ideally in a variety of languages, particularly focusing on scripts local to the areas being searched. For example, if you are investigating an airstrike that reportedly happened in a specific neighbourhood of the Yemeni capital of Sana'a, you would predominantly want to search with a keyword in Arabic characters, not Latin. At this stage, the search can be very broad: Is a location mentioned? Was the event reported on social media? If so, what was the time of the earliest post? Were any weapon remnants found? What was the claimed target? What was allegedly bombed? Any information can be key to further finding out what happened.

An immediate pitfall can be the digital divide. While internet access is widespread in places like Syria, Ukraine and Gaza, it is far lower, and in some cases non-existent, in some rural areas where airstrikes are also being conducted, for example, in Afghanistan, Mozambique and Somalia. In this case, cross-platform searches will often not yield any results. Instead, investigations frequently start with witness accounts from victims reaching out to humanitarian or media organizations. Open source researchers can play a useful role in corroborating these witness accounts, for example, by comparing them with before and after satellite imagery to assess whether an alleged target has been damaged.[8]

When initial cross-platform searches find relevant visuals, it is important to confirm that they are authentic and not mis- or disinformation. An easy and fast way to do this is a reverse image search, which allows researchers to parse through online search engines for images, to make sure the footage is not old or from an unrelated incident. When in April 2018 the US, France and the UK carried out a series of strikes against multiple government sites in Syria in reprisal for the Douma chemical attack, American news channel MSNBC broadcast a video of night airstrikes on a city during their 'breaking news' item – but a quick reverse image search on Yandex revealed that the footage had been taken three years earlier in Ukraine.[9]

While remotely investigating airstrikes opens up cheap and effective possibilities, involving citizens on the ground is often key to investigations – whether they are doctors, local journalists or media activists. Satellite imagery alone can enable researchers to corroborate a military statement about an airstrike, by comparing images from before and after the strike,

---

[8] See for instance, Amnesty International. Somalia: Zero accountability as civilian deaths mount from US air strikes [online]. *Amnesty International*. 1 April 2020. Available from: https://www.amnesty.org/en/latest/news/2020/04/somalia-zero-accountability-as-civilian-deaths-mount-from-us-air-strikes [Accessed 5 August 2021] and Gibbons-Neff., T, Triebert., C, Abed F., and Purkiss, J. Caught Between U.S. and Taliban, a Family Dies and the Survivor Seeks Justice. *The New York Times*. 3 June 2019. Available from: https://www.nytimes.com/2019/06/03/world/asia/ us-taliban-family-dies-justice.html [Accessed 5 August 2021].

[9] Triebert C. Hey @MSNBC, the video you just broadcast as being from today's #SyriaStrikes in Damascus was actually filmed in the Ukrainian city of Luhansk over three years ago. *Twitter*. 14 April 2018. Available from: https://twitter.com/trbrtc/status/985003415079211008 [Accessed 5 August 2021].

but without local footage and witness statements, it is not possible to do much more than this. Some have noted that '[w]hile remote monitoring is an important part of the solution, it needs to be completed by action on the ground'.[10,11]

Even when on-the-ground footage and witness statements are available, investigating airstrikes remotely months or years after they have happened may encounter another obstacle, in that the original online information may have been taken down. Ongoing archiving of content showing alleged airstrikes, and making these archives publicly available, is essential to avoid this problem. If no one has taken the time to archive such material, and the uploader or, often, the social media platform, deletes the content,[12] it will be even harder to find relevant information related to a suspected airstrike.

But if there is reliable information about a strike, such as footage that does not show up on a reverse image search and appears to be authentic, an investigator can be confident that a significant event has occurred. Now, the next W comes into play: Where did the event take place?

Where?

Geolocation is the process of finding the exact location where a photo or video was taken. There are several techniques for doing this. The first step is to look for distinctive landmarks that may help narrow down the search, such as a clock tower, minaret or water tower. Imagine trying to geolocate a video in which you can see the Eiffel Tower, for example – recognizing it would significantly narrow down the area you need to look at. Such landmarks and other topographical features, like rivers, roads and mountain ranges, can then be searched for in satellite imagery, allowing investigators to match the video's exact location to a set of coordinates on a map. Freely

---

[10] Weir D., McQuillan D., and Francis R.A. Civilian science: the potential of participatory environmental monitoring in areas affected by armed conflicts. *Environmental Monitoring and Assessment*. 6 September 2019. 191, p. 618. Available from: https://link.springer.com/article/10.1007/s10661-019-7773-9 [Accessed 5 August 2021].

[11] See also the chapter by Duke in this volume (Chapter 2.2) for details of local monitoring of small arms and light weapons in South Sudan.

[12] Rajagopalan M. The Histories Of Today's Wars Are Being Written On Facebook And YouTube. But What Happens When They Get Taken Down? *Buzzfeed News*. 22 December 2018. Available from: https://www.buzzfeednews.com/article/meghara/facebook-youtube-icc-war-crimes [Accessed 5 August 2021].

available satellite imagery, predominantly via Google Earth, is the most valuable tool for open source investigators trying to geolocate events.

But in certain areas where airstrikes are conducted, high-resolution satellite imagery is not available, or is intentionally downgraded. This happened, for example, in Israel, and by extension the Palestinian Territories. From 1996 to 2020, a US regulation known as the Kyl-Bingaman Amendment limited the quality and availability of satellite imagery produced by US companies covering Israel, as well as the Palestinian Territories and the Syrian territories that Israel occupies.[13] But in June 2020, following sustained pressure from academia and civil society, the amendment was reformed, making higher-resolution satellite imagery legally accessible.[14] Despite this, a year later, in May 2021, when a new war erupted between the Israeli military and armed Palestinian groups, none of the go-to mapping services with freely available high-resolution satellite imagery had updated their imagery. This hampered the work of open source investigators.[15] This same problem has also been encountered in investigations in Afghanistan, Iraq and elsewhere.

Alternatives do pop up, though. For Afghanistan and Iraq, for example, Microsoft's Bing Maps, Apple Maps and HERE WeGo's mapping service did have attainable high-resolution imagery. And in May 2021, the publicly accessible platform *Soar* emerged, which made available high-resolution satellite imagery of Gaza. It can be a challenge for open source researchers to keep on top of the changing legal landscape and technical options.

When?

After establishing that an event has occurred, and where it happened, the next question to pursue is: When did it take place? Answering this question is always about narrowing down the likely timeframe of an event. Using social media to get an earliest estimate of when a suspected airstrike was first reported online is a useful starting point. Several social media, such

---

[13] Aleaziz H. Why Google Earth Can't Show You Israel. *Mother Jones.* 10 June 2011. Available from: https://www.motherjones.com/politics/2011/06/google-israel-us [Accessed 5 August 2021].
[14] Agha Z. Israel Can't Hide Evidence of Its Occupation Anymore. *Foreign Policy.* 3 August 2020. Available from: https://foreignpolicy.com/2020/08/03/israel-cant-hide-evidence-of-its-occupation-anymore [Accessed 5 August 2021].
[15] Giles C. and Goodman J. Israel-Gaza: Why is the region blurry on Google Maps? *BBC News.* 17 May 2021. Available from: https://www.bbc.com/news/57102499 [Accessed 5 August 2021]. Cox J. Google Won't Say If It Will Update Its Blurry Maps of Gaza. *VICE Motherboard.* 17 May 2021. Available from: https://www.vice.com/en/article/m7evkn/google-maps-gaza-israel [Accessed 5 August 2021].

as Twitter, have a search function that can filter down results to a specific timeframe. As explained before, searching in the local language is recommended.

If you are lucky and can obtain the original material from the person who filmed it, you might be able to analyze its metadata. In basic terms, metadata are information associated with a given piece of content, including specific details like the time it was captured. But in many instances, there are no metadata, often because the original videographer cannot be found or contacted, and the footage has been retrieved after being circulated on major social media platforms, which all remove metadata from uploaded content. Analyzing metadata can also be fraught with difficulties – impacted by *ad hoc* complications such as incorrect time settings on a camera.

If footage of an event has been geolocated, it can be possible to chronolocate that footage by using, effectively, a digital sundial. Shadows cast during the day can be analyzed to reveal the position of the sun in the sky, which in turn gives information about the time of the day the image was taken, as well as a rough estimate of the month of the year. Furthermore, some platforms like Google Earth and Living Atlas give access to historical satellite imagery, which can allow researchers to narrow down the time during which an event could have happened.

Sometimes, there are other clues. As detailed below, when the al-Jinah mosque in northern Syria was bombed on 16 March 2017, several eyewitnesses said in videos uploaded to social media that the airstrikes took place during the Isha prayer, one of the five mandatory Islamic prayers, also known as the night prayer. Using a website like *IslamicFinder*, where one can calculate the prayer times by geographic region, this information suggests that the airstrike took place between 7:00 pm and 7:30 pm local time.[16]

Who?

Open source investigators also have techniques for addressing questions about the people involved in an event: Who conducted the airstrike? Who are the victims?

---

[16] Triebert C. CONFIRMED: US Responsible for 'Aleppo Mosque Bombing'. *Bellingcat*. 16 March 2017. Available from: https://www.bellingcat.com/news/mena/2017/03/16/us-missile-remains-reportedly-recovered-from-site-of-aleppo-mosque-bombing [Accessed 5 August 2021].

Sometimes, perpetrators publish this information themselves, e.g. through airstrike videos filmed from an aircraft, which can leave little to no doubt about who is responsible. At the start of its air campaign against IS in Syria and Iraq in 2014, the CJTF-OIR began publishing videos of some of its airstrikes on YouTube and other platforms.[17] A year later, as Russia launched its air campaign in Syria, their Ministry of Defence also started uploading airstrike videos to YouTube. However, in an age of misinformation and disinformation, the claims accompanying these videos cannot be taken at face value, and need authenticating. The Russian Ministry of Defence, for instance, published videos purporting to show their airstrikes in Syria's Raqqa province, but geolocation showed these were in fact in the Idlib area.

Even when the location claim is correct, it may still be hard to find out who specifically conducted the airstrike. CJTF-OIR, for example, published a video that they said showed their targeting of a facility for vehicle-borne improvised explosive devices in the Iraqi city of Mosul, but reporters found out it was a civilian's house without any militant activity.[18] Since CJTF-OIR is a coalition of states, it only became clear that a Dutch F-16 fighter jet had dropped the bombs when the pilot, who said he felt 'sick' of the 'mistake bomb', came forward to journalists after having read about the airstrike in *The New York Times Magazine*.[19]

Why?

Last but certainly not least are questions about why an event happened. Why was this location targeted in this way and at this time? This may be the hardest question of all to answer through openly available information. But, as the following case studies show, whether or not digital investigations can find conclusive evidence about why an event happened, they have proved effective at putting pressure on perpetrators of airstrikes to acknowledge

---

[17] The US deleted most, if not all, of those videos several years later, exemplifying the need to archive online information.
[18] Khan A. and Gopal A. The Uncounted. *The New York Times Magazine*. 16 November 2017. Available from: https://www.nytimes.com/interactive/2017/11/16/magazine/uncounted-civilian-casualties-iraq-airstrikes.html [Accessed 5 August 2021].
[19] Van Joolen O. and Schoonhoven S. F-16 vlieger ziek van vergisbom. *De Telegraaf*. 5 November 2019. Available from: https://www.telegraaf.nl/nieuws/1399298716/f-16-vlieger-ziek-van-vergisbom [Accessed 3 August 2023].

their responsibility, or at least enable people to compare the claims of aerial belligerents with verified evidence from local and remote sources.

Case Study 1: Investigating the US Bombing of the Omar ibn al-Khatab Mosque

'At least 42 dead in Russian raids on Aleppo mosque' reads the headline of an article published by international news channel Al Arabiya on 16 March 2017.[20] In the body of the text, the claim is attributed to the Syrian Observatory for Human Rights, 'virtually a one-man band',[21] which also states that more than one hundred people were wounded by the strike in opposition-held village 'Al-Jineh' in Syria's northern Aleppo governorate. This triggers open source researchers at Bellingcat, including myself, to investigate. Other organizations also start to look into it, including Airwars, Forensic Architecture and Human Rights Watch.

The ten words in the headline contain five claims that are worth fact-checking, roughly along the lines of the five Ws:

- What happened? Was there an airstrike? Were at least 42 people killed?
- Where did it take place? Was it in Aleppo? Was the bombed site a mosque?
- When did it happen?
- Was Russia responsible?
- Why did it occur?

To try and answer these questions, the first step is to gather more open source information. Conducting a keyword search using the name of the place where the incident allegedly took place ('Al-Jineh') across social media platforms, hundreds of posts show up within seconds. As mentioned, it is important to conduct these searches primarily in the language and script used locally ('الجينة'), because those close to the incident are unlikely to post in English, and since there is no standardized way to transliterate Arabic to

---

[20] AFP Beirut. At least 42 dead in Russian raids on Aleppo mosque. *Alarabiya News*. 16 March 2017 (updated 20 May 2020). Available from: https://english.alarabiya.net/News/middle-east/2017/03/16/42-dead-dozens-wounded-in-raids-on-north-Syria-mosque [Accessed 6 August 2021].

[21] MacFarquhar N. A Very Busy Man Behind the Syrian Civil War's Casualty Count. *New York Times*. 9 April 2013. Available from: https://www.nytimes.com/2013/04/10/world/middleeast/the-man-behind-the-casualty-figures-in-syria.html [Accessed 15 October 2021].

Latin script there are many spelling variations for the village in Latin script: 'Al-Jineh', 'Jineh', 'Al-Jinah', 'Jannah', 'al-Jina', 'Jina', etc.

What happened, and when?

A search with the Arabic keyword 'الجينة' on Twitter, filtered by time, shows that the first tweet mentioning an airstrike was at 6:57 pm local time from an account named @AhmadAboAlmagd9, stating that 'warplanes' had targeted the town.[22] A quick scan of the account's timeline shows that it mainly tweets information related to Syrian opposition groups. A minute later, Step News Agency, a local news outlet operating in opposition-held Syria, tweets the same information,[23] quickly followed by other local news outlets Baladi Network and RFS North. None of these first reports on social media suggest who conducted the alleged airstrike. Ten minutes after the first tweet, at 7:07 pm, a first social media post accuses Russia of being responsible, followed by dozens more, some also pointing towards the Syrian Arab Air Force, Russia's ally.[24] At 7:09 pm, a pro-revolution Facebook page gives more specific information about the alleged strike, stating that a first strike targeted the site with four rockets, and a second strike involved two missiles.[25] Instead of Russia, this post accuses the US-led CJTF-OIR.

The first photos and video of the incident are posted roughly an hour later, at, respectively, 8:05 pm and 8:25 pm, by Syria Civil Defence, a volunteer rescue organization also known as the 'White Helmets' that operates in opposition-held areas. A reverse image search on the visuals suggests they are not old, and that they appear to show several buildings, and indeed that part of a larger building has been completely destroyed. A post on Facebook by the 'Free Police of Al-Jinah' gives more specific information, writing that the damaged building is a mosque known as the 'Omar ibn al-Khatab mosque' (Arabic: الخطاب مسجد عمر بن).

---

[22] @AboAlmagd9. *Twitter*. 16 March 2017. Available from: https://twitter.com/AhmadAboAlmagd9/status/842419581004193793 [Accessed 6 August 2021].

[23] Step News Agency. وكالة ستيب الإخبا. *Twitter*. 16 March 2017. Available from: https://twitter.com/Step_Agency/status/842419848462376960 [Accessed 6 August 2021].

[24] @sunnews1000. *Twitter*. 16 March 2017. Available from: https://twitter.com/sunnews1000/status/842422149818269698 [Accessed 6 August 2021].

[25] Triebert C. The Al-Jinah Mosque Complex Bombing – New Information and Timeline. *Bellingcat*. 18 April 2018. Available from: https://www.bellingcat.com/news/mena/2017/04/18/al-jinah-new-info-and-timeline [Accessed 6 August 2021].

Alongside the Syria Civil Defence video, two more videos are uploaded to YouTube. While all three videos are filmed during the night of the strike, they offer important visual indications. Two large craters are visible, which suggest that there had been two large explosions and which several weapons experts say are consistent with a 2,000-pound bomb explosion. The footage also shows two smaller buildings near the craters: a one-story building with two apparent minarets and a small dome, as well as a two-story building. These are all clues that can be used to try to geolocate the incident.

Where did the airstrike happen?

On mapping services like Google Maps, Google Earth Pro and Bing Maps, the village of Al-Jinah is quickly found with both the original Arabic as well as several English transliterations.[26] GeoNames, a geographical database that contains over 11 million place names, suggests there is only one location with the name in Syria, which increases our confidence that we can geolocate the footage within that specific location.[27] Typing in 'mosque' on Google Maps shows three in the vicinity, labelled as the 'Abdul Rahman bin Auf mosque', the 'Othman Bin Affan Mosque', and the 'Musab Bin Omair mosque'. However, none of the ground-level photos of these mosques match the building seen in the footage. Further, the top-down view of the satellite images does not correlate with the nighttime aftermath footage of the mosque, and these names do not match the name mentioned in the Facebook post about the airstrike: the Omar ibn al-Khatab mosque.

Asked about where the mosque was located, local activists say that it was a relatively new construction southwest of their town.[28] Scrolling down the road on satellite imagery, we could indeed geolocate the footage of the

---

[26] However, double-checking across platforms is always recommended. Typing in 'Al-Jinah' into Google Maps, for example, sends you to an unrelated location in the Hama governorate.
[27] GeoNames [online]. Available from: https://www.geonames.org/search.html?q=%D8%A7%D9%84%D8%AC%D9%8A%D9%86%D8%A9&country=SY [Accessed 6 August 2021].
[28] Forensic Architecture. Airstrikes on the Al-Jinah Mosque. *Forensic Architecture*. 17 April 2017. Available from: https://forensic-architecture.org/investigation/airstrikes-on-the-al-jinah-mosque [Accessed 18 October 2021]. Human Rights Watch. *Attack on the Omar Ibn al-Khatab Mosque: US Authorities' Failure to Take Adequate Precautions* [online]. Human Rights Watch. 18 April 2017. Available from: https://www.hrw.org/report/2017/04/18/attack-omar-ibn-al-khatab-mosque/us-authorities-failure-take-adequate-precautions [Accessed 18 October 2021]; Triebert C. The Al-Jinah Mosque Complex Bombing – New Information and Timeline. *Bellingcat*. 18 April 2017. Available from: https://www.bellingcat.com/news/mena/2017/04/18/al-jinah-new-info-and-timeline [Accessed 18 October 2021].

airstrike aftermath to a site southwest of Al-Jinah that Google Maps had not yet labelled as a mosque.[29]

Half a dozen new videos that drip in during the hours after the airstrike allow us to map out the incident site. To the north, closest to the road towards Al-Jinah, there is a small mosque with two minarets and a one-storey building under construction. Historical satellite imagery of the site shows that south of these structures there was a larger building, which has now been partly reduced to rubble – leaving two large craters behind.

In response to a now-deleted tweet that a Hay'at Tahrir al-Sham meeting place had been targeted,[30] the website verify.sy claims that the damaged building was a mosque and posts a picture from the Thiqa Agency showing the mosque sign at the western side of the building, which reads that this is the Omar ibn al-Khatab mosque and a religious school (Arabic: مدرسة شرعية), and displays information about people financing the mosque's construction.

Who conducted the airstrike?

One tweet that claims to show a weapon remnant found at the incident location stands out. The photo was uploaded by a Dutch journalist who said he received it from local contacts.[31] About 50 centimetres of a black piece of metal is visible, with a label on it apparently reading 'WT: 52.0 kg'. Generally, the Russian Air Force uses weapons with inscriptions in the Cyrillic script, not Latin, so this immediately casts doubt on allegations of Russian responsibility. Furthermore, the font type and design of the label strongly resemble those seen on stock photos of the AGM-144 Hellfire, an air-to-surface missile used not by Russia, but by many countries that are part of the US-led CJTF-OIR, including the US itself as well as France, the Netherlands and the United Kingdom, to name a few.[32] While most of

---

[29] Triebert C. Geolocation of mosque bombed by the US is CONFIRMED: southeast of Al-Jīnah, w-Aleppo... *Twitter*. 17 March 2017. Available from: https://twitter.com/trbrtc/status/842529777202487297?s=20 [Accessed 6 August 2021].

[30] Triebert C. The Al-Jinah Mosque Complex Bombing – New Information and Timeline. *Bellingcat*. 18 April 2018. Available from: https://www.bellingcat.com/news/mena/2017/04/18/al-jinah-new-info-and-timeline [Accessed 6 August 2021].

[31] @sakirkhader. Photo shows the remnants of a bomb used in the airstrike on the 'Umar ibn Al-Khaṭṭāb mosque... *Twitter*. 16 March 2017. Available from: https://twitter.com/sakirkhader/status/842480710606864384 [Accessed 6 August 2021].

[32] Other countries which are known to use the AGM-114 Hellfire are Australia, Croatia, Egypt, Greece, India, Indonesia, Iraq, Israel, Italy, Jordan, Japan, Kuwait, Lebanon, Norway, Pakistan, Qatar, South

the stock photos show Hellfire-variants labelled '49.0 kg', a 52-kg variant remnant had been found in a strike in Idlib half a year earlier.[33] Although the photo suggests possible CJTF-OIR involvement, it does not contain metadata or visual clues to determine whether it had actually been taken at the site and could be linked to the suspected airstrike. More photos of weapon remnants appear later, including on Getty Images, one of which mentions US company Woodward, which supplies parts for guidance kits that convert unguided or 'dumb' bombs into guided 'smart' munitions.

On the day of the strike, 16 March 2017, the US Department of Defense (DoD) released a statement, stating that 'US forces conducted an airstrike on an Al Qaeda in Syria meeting location'. They claim the strike had taken place in 'Idlib, Syria' and killed 'several terrorists'. Both the city of Idlib as well as the governorate with that name are at a different place to the Aleppo governorate Al-Jinah location, suggesting the US statement was referring to a different strike, since the geolocation of the incident footage had shown that it was indeed in Al-Jinah.

Questions about culpability continue to arise as the estimates of casualties – from 24 to over 50[34] – make it 'one of the biggest massacres that happened in Syria since 2011', according to Hadi Alabdallah, a Syrian journalist who visits the site soon after the incident.[35] Apparently in response to accusations directed their way, the Russian Ministry of Defence (MoD) say they were not responsible for the strike and urge the US for a comment. 'A photo showing a fragment of an air-to-surface AGM-114 Hellfire missile has emerged', Russian Major-General Igor Konashenkov is cited as saying.

Korea, Saudi Arabia, Singapore, Spain, Sweden, Taiwan (Republic of China), Tunisia, Turkey and United Arab Emirates.

[33] Triebert C. Also h/t to @omar646111, @JakeGodin, @Aswed_Flags + all other digital sherlocks for finding the Idlib drone strike photos... *Twitter*. 16 March 2017. Available from: https://twitter.com/trbrtc/status/842494127711371264 [Accessed 6 August 2021].

[34] The Syrian Network for Human Rights mentioned 29, see SNHR. Massacre in Syrian regime shelling on a mosque in al Jeina village in Aleppo governorate on March 16. *SNHR*. 16 March 2017. Available from: https://news.sn4hr.org/2017/03/16/massacre-syrian-regime-shelling-mosque-al-jeina-village-aleppo-governorate-march-16/ [Accessed 6 August 2021]. The Syria Civil Defence said 35. Available from: https://www.facebook.com/SCDaleppo/posts/1285988564814132:0 [Accessed 4 August 2023], others said over 50.

[35] Available from: https://www.youtube.com/watch?v=29UptxVQwL8 [Accessed 4 August 2023].

'It leaves no chance for the US-led coalition to remain silent as usual and for diplomats to spout anti-Russian rhetoric'.[36]

Hours later, in what *The New York Times* calls 'an unusual defense of an American airstrike',[37] the US DoD publishes an aerial image of the site they said they had targeted, alongside a text stating that it was 'taken after a 16 March 2017, US strike in Jinah, Syria'. US military officials believed the strike had killed 'dozens of al-Qaeda terrorist leaders' (see Fig. 1).[38]

Figure 1: The US Department of Defense released this aerial photograph taken after a 16 March 2017 US airstrike on the building, stating they believed dozens of 'terrorist leaders' were killed in the strike. They explicitly mentioned that they had not targeted the mosque on the left edge of the photo, but had to admit later that the larger building at the centre of the photo was also a mosque.[39]

---

[36] RT. Russia urges US comment on reports of fatal Syria mosque strike. *RT.* 17 March 2017. Available from: https://www.rt.com/news/381144-syria-airstrike-usa-russia [Accessed 6 August 2021].

[37] Gordon M. R. and Saad H. Pentagon Releases Photo to Rebut Contention It Bombed a Mosque. *New York Times*. 17 March 2017. https://www.nytimes.com/2017/03/17/us/politics/pentagon-syria-bombing-mosque.html [Accessed 4 August 2023].

[38] Gordon M. R. and Saad H. Pentagon Releases Photo to Rebut Contention It Bombed a Mosque. *New York Times*. 17 March 2017. Available from: https://web.archive.org/web/20170419183921/; https://www.defense.gov/Photos/Photo-Gallery/igphoto/2001718389 [Accessed 6 August 2021].

[39] DoD endorsement disclaimer: The appearance of US Department of Defense (DoD) visual information does not imply or constitute DoD endorsement.

Speaking to reporters and in a later written statement, a US DoD spokesman emphasizes that a mosque visible on the left edge of the photo was not targeted. 'I wanted to draw your attention to it, because I think there are a lot of reports suggesting we had targeted a mosque', he says. 'We did not. Of course, you know we never would'.[40] Instead, they had targeted a 'partially constructed community meeting hall'.

Filling the gaps: Mosque or meeting hall?

In the face of the initial allegations, evidence and denials, it was important for us to collect more clues to find out what actually happened. Using the dozens of ground-perspective visuals of the aftermath uploaded to social media by local reporters, it was possible to match the aerial image published by the US with the site which several local journalists said was a mosque. This, first of all, suggested that the earlier statement by the US that it had conducted a strike on a site in Idlib was incorrect. Indeed, in an e-mailed reply to Bellingcat, the US DoD acknowledged that they believed the strike they referred to was the same as the one we had identified. 'We do not mean to cause any confusion. Different internal reports may have listed this differently'.[41]

By this stage, it was clear from the remote investigations and official statements that the US – not Russia – had conducted the airstrike in question. But there was a strong discrepancy between the statements of locals and eyewitnesses on the ground, which all said the targeted building was a mosque, and the US, which stressed its forces did not bomb a mosque. What were the facts?

---

[40]Fernando L. Pentagon Spokesman: Dozens of Terrorists Believed Killed in US Strike in Syria. US Department of Defense. 17 March 2017. Available from: https://www.defense.gov/Explore/News/Article/Article/1122791/pentagon-spokesman-dozens-of-terrorists-believed-killed-in-us-strike-in-syria [Accessed 6 August 2021].

[41]This is not the first time the US has mislabelled its own airstrike footage. Bellingcat ran a project trying to geolocate official US-led CJTF-OIR airstrike videos from Iraq and Syria. All of these videos came with a rough description of a location, e.g. 'near Raqqa'. Open source investigator @obretix mapped the geolocated videos and used a Voronoi diagram to get an impression of the region labels the Coalition – which is led by CENTCOM – uses. See https://sami-r.carto.com/viz/dc7a04e6-f284-11e5-8e3d-0ea31932ec1d/embed_map [Accessed 4 August 2023], which shows that these labels were not always accurate, and that governorate borders may well overlap each other: Triebert C. 1000 days of war: The geolocation challenge. *Airwars*. 5 May 2017. Available from: https://airwars.org/news-and-investigations/1000day-geolocations [Accessed 6 August 2021].

Three different organizations – Bellingcat, Forensic Architecture and Human Rights Watch – as well as open source investigators on Twitter, were investigating the strike, some of whom joined efforts and exchanged information to establish whether the damaged building was indeed a mosque or not. Bellingcat, which specializes in finding, verifying and archiving open source information, exchanged information with Human Rights Watch, which spoke to eyewitnesses and local sources. One video, uploaded to YouTube before the strike, turned out to be important. In it, a person starts filming the outside of the building that would later be bombed. Albeit small, it showed the building had at least one speaker on the roof, used for the call to prayer, and that there was also a sign next to the entrance saying this was the Omar ibn al-Khatab mosque. This sign was also visible in aftermath footage, but some suggested that it had been placed there after the strike, to make it seem that the building was a mosque. The pre-strike video confirmed that the sign was already in place at the time of the strike.

The videographer then enters the building and films the interior, which reveals more indications that the building was in use as a mosque. There is a place for worshippers' shoes and a large prayer hall to the south with a *mihrab*, a niche in the wall that indicates the direction of the Kaaba in Mecca and therewith the direction that Muslims should face when praying. These clues built the case that the bombed building was a functioning mosque. The same prayer hall was also seen in post-strike footage from local media.[42]

Forensic Architecture modelled the building based on this and other videos and the architect's blueprints. The southern side was a large prayer hall, described above, and remained largely intact, while the northern side was completely destroyed. That part of the building, Forensic Architecture's 3-D reconstruction showed, housed the imam's flat, where his wife was allegedly killed by the strike, as well as a ritual washing room, toilets, a kitchen and a winter prayer hall that were captured in the pre-strike video. Forensic Architecture noted that except for the kitchen, none of the rooms on the northern side had a door, making them unlikely to be useful for top Al-Qaeda meetings.

Eyewitnesses said that, as the two big bombs were dropped, everyone in the main prayer hall of the larger mosque tried to flee but were targeted

---

[42] Available from: https://www.facebook.com/moaz.Alshami.shada/videos/1836671799918423 [Accessed 6 August 2021].

outside by more missiles. A US official would later confirm the use of these missiles to a *Washington Post* reporter, clarifying the presence of the weapon remnant discussed above.[43] The fleeing survivors rushing out of the mosque may have looked identical to Al-Qaeda militants to US drone operators, Human Rights Watch argued, but noted 'that mistaken impression suggests that their intelligence on the targeted area was woefully inadequate' and that US intelligence had 'inadequately understood the pattern of life in the area'.[44]

Even though they denied the damaged building was a mosque, a spokesperson for the US DoD claimed that they had avoided prayer times. They explained that their surveillance of the target had indicated that prayers had concluded at the small mosque (seen on the left of Fig. 1), and civilians had left the building before the attack, which happened at 6:55 pm – but it is unclear which prayers the spokesperson referred to. The most likely is the Maghrib or sunset prayer, which started at 5:39 pm that day. However, the Isha or night prayer was due to start at 7:09 pm. The airstrike happened 15 minutes before that, meaning the mosque was filling up again – or perhaps had never been empty: 'Usually people move from the prayer hall to the kitchen area after sunset prayer to eat and rest before the night prayer'.[45] Further, local media outlet Step News Agency reported that the building hosted 'a meeting in one of their centres every Thursday which is attended by dozens of students of religious studies, sheikhs, sharia experts and fighters in the Islamic factions and civilians from the region'.[46] If the US had made 'any attempt' to get a pattern of life understanding from people with local knowledge, Human Rights Watch argued, they would have been alerted to the existence of these religious seminars.

---

[43] Gibbons-Neff T. *Twitter*. Nd. captured by *The Wayback Machine*. Available from: https://web.archive.org/web/20170317221503/; https://twitter.com/Tmgneff/status/842740011099459585 [Accessed 6 August 2021].

[44] For information on the US Intelligence Community, and its use of OSINT, see the chapter by Vogel in this volume (Chapter 3.4).

[45] Human Rights Watch. *Attack on the Omar Ibn al-Khatab Mosque: US Authorities' Failure to Take Adequate Precautions*. Human Rights Watch. 18 April 2017. Available from: https://www.hrw.org/report/2017/04/18/attack-omar-ibn-al-khatab-mosque/us-authorities-failure-take-adequate-precautions [Accessed 18 October 2021].

[46] Airwars. Exclusive: US says it carried out deadly strike that hit Aleppo mosque. *Airwars*. 16 March 2016. Available from: https://airwars.org/news/unilateral-strike/ [Accessed 4 August 2023].

In response to the Human Rights Watch report, the US said that they 'carefully review every allegation of civilian casualties that may have been caused by a Coalition airstrike'. However, their preliminary conclusion was that the strike was lawful. 'I acknowledge that the draft Human Rights Watch report could not have taken into account the classified information available to the US authorities. This may help explain why the US investigation reached a different conclusion'. They respectfully requested that Human Rights Watch provide any relevant information to assist their investigations, writing 'Nevertheless, we always welcome additional information to assist our investigations', and, 'we will continue to carefully review the incident in light of your report'.[47]

'A preventable error': The US admits they bombed a mosque

12 weeks later, on 7 June 2017, the US conceded that in a 'preventable error', targeters and pilots had inadvertently conducted airstrikes on part of a mosque complex. In a briefing to invited reporters, recorded and published by Airwars, officials said that F-15 fighter jets dropped ten bombs and MQ-9 drones fired two missiles to strike a target that emerged outside the building. 'None of the buildings were annotated on our no-strike list as category one facilities, which is a register of entities that must be carefully evaluated before an approval to strike'.

'We have a responsibility to identify and characterize no-strike entities as accurately as possible and provide this information to decision-makers in a timely manner'.[48] Their investigation found that irregularities in shift changeovers had 'contributed to a lack of situational awareness, knowledge and understanding among the strike cell individuals. Specifically, important information was not adequately communicated during personnel changeover to the incoming shift'.[49]

---

[47] United States Central Command, Office of the Staff Judge Advocate. Letter to Human Rights Watch. 14 April 2017. Available from: https://www.hrw.org/sites/default/files/supporting_resources/redacted_centcom_response_to_hrw_4-14-17_1.pdf [Accessed 6 August 2021].
[48] Transcript of Pentagon's Al Jinah Investigation media briefing, 16 March 2017. *Airwars*. 27 June 2017. Available from: https://airwars.org/news-and-investigations/transcript-of-al-jinah-investigation-briefing [Accessed 6 March 2021].
[49] *ibid.*

The US said that the damaged building was a religious building under construction, the Omar ibn al-Khatab mosque. As such, US Army Brigadier General Paul Bontrager said that it did not technically have to be on a no-strike list, although he believed it would be advisable to change this practice (see footnote 48). However, the Human Rights Watch, Forensic Architecture and Bellingcat investigations all suggested the mosque was fully operational at the time of the strike. Locals told Human Rights Watch that the mosque only appeared unfinished because it had insufficient funding.

In the days immediately after the attack, the US had insisted in both spoken and written statements that it purposefully had avoided a mosque they knew to be in the area, that is, the smaller building on the left edge of the photo they originally shared (see Fig. 1). However, Mr. Bontrager now acknowledged that the 'target engagement authority' – the people authorizing the strike – did not know the smaller building was a mosque. 'This failure to identify the religious purpose of these buildings led the target engagement authority to make the final determination to strike without knowing all he should have known, and that is something we need to make sure does not happen in the future', he said. If the mosques had been on the list, the process would have gone through more rigorous vetting. Nevertheless, the strike would still have been permitted, Mr. Bontrager said. US military investigators concluded that despite a series of errors, the 16 March strike was legal and had achieved its objective of disrupting a gathering of 'al Qaeda leaders' (see footnote 48). The US military investigators did not mention which Al-Qaeda 'leaders' were present or killed during the attack, something they have done before with unilateral US airstrikes in Syria, Airwars noted.[50]

Human Rights Watch spoke with 14 people with close knowledge of the airstrike, including four eyewitnesses, as well as first responders, who said civilians were lingering around the mosque at the time of the strike. A local activist told *The New York Times* that the people who had been

---

[50] Oakford S. America's shadow war in Syria. *Airwars*. 4 April 2017. Available from: https://airwars.org/news-and-investigations/shadow-american-war-syria [Accessed 6 August 2021].

struck had 'no affiliation with any military faction or any political side'.[51] In comparison, the US said they had not spoken to any eyewitnesses, first responders or anyone else affected by the airstrike.

It is estimated that the US airstrikes killed between 37 and 62 civilians – at least 29 of whom were named by the White Helmets – and injured many more.[52] Footage showed how a 14-year-old boy, later identified as Mohamed al-Orabi, was pulled out of the rubble, alive. He later died of his injuries. However, the US's own assessment was that there was likely only one civilian casualty, which they assessed to be a civilian 'due solely to the individual's stature relative to other fighters'.[53]

Meanwhile, over a year later, on 18 May 2018, Hayat Tahrir al-Sham was said to have executed a man they say was responsible for sharing the location of the Omar ibn al-Khatab mosque with the US-led CJTF-OIR, according to Syrian Observatory for Human Rights.

Case Study 2: Investigating the Russian Bombing of the Kafr Nabl Surgical Hospital

In 2017, the Visual Investigations team at *The New York Times*, which I am part of, began tracking the repeated bombing of medical facilities in Syria. Most of the blame for these was directed towards the Syrian Arab Air Force (SyAAF) and the Russian Aerospace Forces (Russian: Воздушно-космические силы, or VKS). Between April and October 2019, when a government offensive started to reclaim the Idlib governorate from militants opposed to Syria's President Bashar al-Assad, more than 50 health facilities were reportedly attacked, according to the United Nations Office of the High Commissioner for Human Rights.

---

[51] Gordon M. R. and Saad H. US Military Denies Reports It Bombed Mosque in Syria. *The New York Times*. Available from: https://www.nytimes.com/2017/03/16/world/middleeast/us-military-denies-reports-it-bombed-mosque-in-syria.html [Accessed 4 August 2023].

[52] Airwars. CS578. *Airwars*. Available from: https://airwars.org/civilian-casualties/cs578-march-16-2017/ [Accessed 20 October 2021].

[53] Transcript of Pentagon's Al Jinah Investigation media briefing, 16 March 2017. *Airwars*. 27 June 2017. Available from: https://airwars.org/news-and-investigations/transcript-of-al-jinah-investigation-briefing [Accessed 6 March 2021].

Similar to the above case, finding footage of the Syrian hospitals that were badly damaged was straightforward. Hundreds of photos and videos were uploaded by Syrian journalists and citizens to Telegram channels, Facebook groups and Twitter timelines. Furthermore, medical and relief organizations associated with the health facilities, as well as users on those social media platforms, provided more documentation, including internal reports and unpublished videos. While Russia, and in some instances Syria, had long been suspected of conducting the hospital bombings,[54] it was difficult to find direct evidence of their involvement, and Russian officials denied responsibility.

Because our team had successfully investigated airstrikes in Syria for years, closed sources trusted us with tens of thousands of previously unpublished audio recordings between VKS pilots and ground control officers in Syria.[55] Each audio file came with the exact time it was recorded. Furthermore, we obtained months of flight data logged by a network of Syrian observers that had been tracking military aircraft to warn civilians of impending airstrikes. These observations included the exact time, rough location and general type of aircraft spotted.

The question was whether the audio recordings, each only a few seconds long and riddled with seemingly indecipherable military jargon and code words, could provide direct evidence of Russia violating one of the oldest rules of war, which specifies that combatants should not target medical facilities. To verify that the Russian pilot communications and flight logs were authentic and related to the strikes, we corroborated them through comparisons with other airstrike information: geolocations of the targeted health facilities, exact times of the strikes from surveillance footage and metadata from videos filmed by locals, and doctors' witness statements.

There were months of data ... So where to start? We began with 5 and 6 May 2019, as four hospitals were reportedly bombed on those two days. Those hospitals were also on a United Nations-sponsored 'deconfliction

---

[54] There has been at least one strike, possibly two, on a hospital that was conducted by Syria, and some accusations towards the US-led CJTF-OIR, but by far the majority of accusations are directed towards Russia, who sometimes even publish footage themselves showing how they bombed a known hospital.
[55] Several other chapters in this volume discuss hybrid investigations that make use of closed as well as open sources. See for example the chapters by Wilson, Samuel & Plesch, Strick, H. Wilson *et al.* and Michie *et al.* (Chapters 1, 2.1, 4.1 and 5.3).

list' meant to spare them from attack, according to the World Health Organization (WHO). We organized and merged all of our information into a database of spreadsheets. For each airstrike, we examined the evidence recorded at the time of the attack: Were Russian Air Force aircraft in the air? Were they spotted near hospitals? What were they talking about on the intercepted audio?

In the case of Kafr Nabl Surgical Hospital, which had been bombed repeatedly, and restored with help from the WHO in March 2019,[56] local news coverage and incident reports placed the time of the attack at about 5:30 pm on 5 May. In combination with social media posts and news reports, witnesses are often central to estimating timings – and we spoke to a doctor who was working at Kafr Nabl Surgical Hospital when it was hit. He said the hospital was first struck at 5:30 pm, with three more airstrikes following five minutes apart.

Unlike the above case of Omar ibn al-Khatab mosque, which happened at night, these strikes happened during the day. Local journalist Hadi Abdallah, who was also present at the mosque strike, as well as local media outlets Halab Today TV and Euphrates Post, started filming after the first strike, and captured what they said were projectiles hitting what may have been the hospital in subsequent strikes. Did they all show the same airstrike? Or multiple ones – perhaps even three more, as the doctor had described?

We managed to geolocate all of the videos and determined that the explosions all happened at Kafr Nabl Surgical Hospital. We then analyzed the explosions and smoke patterns. After going through each video frame by frame and synchronizing several videos next to each other, it was evident that there was footage of three different strikes on the Kafr Nabl Surgical Hospital taken from multiple angles.

We estimated the times of the strikes using chronolocation. But to get the exact time, we asked local journalists and news agencies to send us their original footage, so we could analyze the files' metadata to see when each strike hit the hospital. Date and time settings on recording devices are not always set to real time, and we often ask journalists to take a photo

---

[56] WHO. Resuming services after an attack on health in Syria [YouTube video]. 15 March 2019. Available from: https://www.youtube.com/watch?v=RgT8z1PU8vM [Accessed 6 August 2021].

of a correct clock with their recording device so that we can compare the metadata from that photo with the real time on the clock and double check the time calibrations. Once we received the original files, we could establish when each of the subsequent strikes happened, down to the second: 5:36:12, 5:41:14 and 5:49:17 pm.

There was visual evidence of three airstrikes on Kafr Nabl Surgical Hospital, and there were reliable witness statements of the first strike. Now the question of *who* conducted those strikes arose. The flight logs and videos of the aircraft above Kafr Nabl that day were not conclusive; both the Russian and Syrian air forces had been active. However, once we had the exact time of four explosions from the video metadata, the VKS communications provided clear evidence of Russia's responsibility.

We had spent weeks translating and deciphering code words: 'Package received' meant a pilot had received coordinates for a target; 'Correction is on' suggested the target had been locked; 'Calculating 15:30' referred to the minute and second the pilot would strike; 'Three 7s' was an approval by the dispatcher to strike; and 'Srabotal', the Russian phrase which directly translates as 'It's worked', was confirmation that the pilot had released his weapon. The audio files revealed that a Russian-speaking pilot released a weapon before each of the explosions at the hospital. The pilot, who identified himself as '72', also said 'Srabotal' at 5:30 pm, when the doctor as well as other eyewitnesses said the first airstrike happened. Five minutes later, at 5:35 pm, as well as at 5:40 and 5:48 pm, the pilot repeated this word. Four weapon releases in all, each about five minutes apart and about some 40 seconds before the time of impact we had calculated from the metadata.

Because the hospital was dug deep under its original building after repeated bombings, only one person was killed. Many others were injured. We found three other instances, over a period of 12 hours in early May, when the Russian Air Force 'worked' on hospitals: the Nabad al-Hayat Surgical Hospital, the Kafr Zita Cave Hospital and the Al-Amal Hospital. The evidence was clear in each case. Our findings were cited at the UN Security Council, although the Russian authorities dismissed our investigation as 'fake news'.

Concluding Remarks

While the airstrikes on Omar ibn al-Khatab mosque and Kafr Nabl Surgical Hospital are just a tiny portion of the tens of thousands of strikes that have been conducted in Syria and Iraq, the two cases exemplify some key methodologies and tools that can be used to investigate airstrikes in conflict zones around the world, as well as some of the challenges of doing so. The cases also show how open source research has the potential to bring about enhanced accountability to those responsible for harming civilians through airstrikes. Although it is hard to establish intent or purpose through open source research, the case studies show that remote investigations can generate clear conclusions about who is responsible for conducting airstrikes that harm civilians. In some cases, including the first study presented here, these findings can lead to admissions of culpability. While remote open source investigations can be painstaking and difficult, and do not always produce such categorical answers or outcomes, the two case studies presented here show that they can be invaluable in shining a light on some of the most complex and opaque combat operations, and their toll on civilians, in the world.

© 2024 World Scientific Publishing Company
https://doi.org/10.1142/9781800614079_0006

Chapter 2.5

Links in the Chain: How The Berkeley Protocol is Strengthening Digital Investigation Standards in International Justice

Lindsay Freeman and Alexa Koenig

Abstract

This chapter discusses how digital open source investigations present a unique opportunity to strengthen coordination between justice actors and improve the quality of information used for decision-making purposes, as well as achieve accountability for wrongdoing. The international justice community comprises a complex ecosystem of actors with differing interests and end goals – from humanitarian efforts aimed at predicting and preventing mass atrocities, to advocacy efforts designed to pressure governments to respond to violations of international law, to legal efforts targeted at ensuring judicial accountability for the perpetrators of international crimes. Increasingly, however, these end goals can only be achieved if the diverse actors work together. Cooperation and coordination between first responders, civil society groups, intergovernmental organizations and judicial institutions are essential to ensuring that those most responsible for the world's gravest crimes are identified and held to account. Depending on the degree and quality of cooperation, the diversity of actors involved in international justice and security can be beneficial or detrimental. In this chapter, we discuss these issues, illustrating them with examples from active war zones, and highlight how the further development of international standards for open source investigations is essential to ensure these efforts positively impact human security and justice worldwide. We also introduce the *Berkeley Protocol on Digital Open Source Investigations*, a recently launched UN manual providing common standards and ethical principles for conducting digital investigations.

This is an open access article published by World Scientific Publishing Europe Ltd. and distributed under the terms of the Creative Commons Attribution-NonCommercial 4.0 International (CC BY-NC 4.0) License.

Introduction

Humanitarian aid workers rush towards a smoking pile of rubble where a hospital once stood. Minutes earlier, the medical facility was fully operational and filled with civilians receiving health services. Now, the bodies of the dead lie prostrate, while the injured are scattered and await assistance. The rubble is surrounded by fragments from some sort of explosive device.

The scene is nothing new. Attacks on hospitals during armed conflict can be traced back to World War I.[1] What is new, however, is that this scene is captured on video – shot by a bystander with a camera phone, uploaded to the internet and viewed by thousands of people across the world. The video now resides in a database on the internet with many just like it, documenting the myriad attacks against medical facilities in Syria, and waiting for the day they will be shown in court.[2,3]

When videos captured during armed conflicts appear online, investigators must act fast to preserve them before they disappear from the internet. The graphic nature of war photographs and videos often make them short-lived on social media platforms, which regulate and moderate user-generated content.[4,5] Imagery depicting violence and other graphic material violates most websites' terms of service and, therefore, can be removed at any time without warning.[6] The brief window for digital evidence collection poses huge challenges for investigators at international legal institutions, who rarely have the ability to react or the authority to investigate in the immediate aftermath of mass atrocities. Rather, these investigators are

---

[1] McLean D. Medical care in armed conflict: Perpetrator discourse in historical perspective. *International Review of the Red Cross*. August 2019. 101 (911), pp. 771–803.

[2] Syrian Archive. *Targeting Health: Attacks Against Medical Facilities in Syria* [online]. Syrian Archive. Available from: https://medical.syrianarchive.org/ [Accessed 29 July 2021].

[3] See also the chapter by Triebert in this volume (Chapter 2.4) for details of his work investigating airstrikes against Syrian hospitals.

[4] Koenig A. *et al. Digital Lockers: Archiving Social Media Evidence of Atrocity Crimes*. Human Rights Center. 2021.

[5] Human Rights Watch. *"Video Unavailable" Social Media Platforms Remove Evidence of War Crimes*. Human Rights Watch. 2020.

[6] Asher-Schapiro A. and Barkawi B. *'Lost memories': War crimes evidence threatened by AI moderation*. Reuters. 19 June 2020. Available from: https://www.reuters.com/article/us-global-socialmedia-rights-trfn/lost-memories-war-crimes-evidence-threatened-by-ai-moderation-idUSKBN23Q2TO [Accessed 29 July 2021].

unavoidably dependent on the work of digital first responders who are not bound by the same political and procedural restrictions.

Holding perpetrators accountable for international crimes requires a diverse ecosystem of actors, each playing unique and indispensable roles in atrocity documentation, evidence collection and case building. When it comes to investigating violations of international criminal, humanitarian and human rights law, this ecosystem consists of the media, citizen journalists, civil society, governments, non-governmental organizations (NGOs), intergovernmental organizations (IOs) and judicial institutions.[7] All of these actors may participate, in one way or another, in the evidentiary chain of custody from the crime scene to the courtroom. All of these actors have a stake in the outcome.

The diversity of the 'international justice community' – a broad term comprising these many stakeholders – can be highly beneficial or extremely detrimental, depending on several factors. In particular, the degree and quality of cooperation and collaboration between the parties can have a profound impact on outcomes. Historically, differing approaches to fact-finding have created tension, with actors at times working competitively or even at cross-purposes to each other. For example, interviews by journalists and human rights investigators tend to be shorter and less formal than the investigative interviews conducted by law enforcement and prosecutors. Individuals interviewed by the former may inadvertently diminish their value for the latter, since improperly worded questions can contaminate witness accounts, and prior witness statements shared across media can be used to impeach those witnesses' testimony at trial. Ambassador Stephen Rapp has termed this gap between criminal investigations and human rights investigations "the Hague–Geneva divide," reflecting ideological and operational differences in the professional communities associated with each locale.

To counter these challenges, the international justice community has embarked on several initiatives to improve cooperation and coordination between international criminal investigators and the various groups that support their work through evidence documentation, collection and preservation. As the international justice community has grown and professionalized

---

[7] Koenig A., Cody S., Lampros A., and Raynor J. *First Responders: Collecting and Analyzing Evidence of Digital Crimes*. UC Berkeley Human Rights Center. 2014.

over time, common principles and practices have been developed that set minimum standards for investigations. In 2001, the United Nations Office of the High Commissioner for Human Rights (UN OHCHR) published the *Istanbul Protocol* – a manual that is now regarded as the principal guide on torture investigations.[8] Similarly, the *Minnesota Protocol,* released in 2017, is a UN manual on the effective investigation of extra-legal, arbitrary and summary executions, which is used as the benchmark for assessing the quality of such investigations.[9] The UK Foreign and Commonwealth Office has released an *International Protocol on the Documentation and Investigation of Sexual Violence in Conflict*, now in its second edition.[10] These texts provide much-needed guidance on their respective areas of practice, so that forensic examiners all over the world understand and work to the same minimum standards – facilitating better information sharing as well as improving the quality of investigations, and increasing the chances that they can effectively support legal processes.

The most recent addition to the international justice canon – one designed to help meet the demand for guidance around the handling of *digital* information and evidence – is the *Berkeley Protocol on Digital Open Source Investigations*.[11] This manual, co-published by the UN OHCHR and Berkeley Law's Human Rights Center, underscores the importance of standardization, professionalization, legal compliance and establishing ethical norms

---

[8] *Manual on the Effective Investigation and Documentation of Torture and Other Cruel, Inhuman or Degrading Treatment or Punishment ("Istanbul Protocol")*. UN Office of the High Commissioner for Human Rights. Report number: HR/P/PT/8/Rev.1. 2004. Available from: https://www.refworld.org/docid/4638aca62.html [Accessed 29 July 2021].

[9] *The Minnesota Protocol on the Investigation of Potentially Unlawful Death (2016): The Revised United Nations Manual on the Effective Prevention and Investigation of Extra-Legal, Arbitrary and Summary Executions*. United Nations. Office of the High Commissioner for Human Rights. 2017. Available from: https://www.ohchr.org/Documents/Publications/MinnesotaProtocol.pdf [Accessed 29 July 2021].

[10] Ribeiro S. F. and van der Straten Ponthoz D. *International Protocol on the Documentation and Investigation of Sexual Violence in Conflict: Best Practice on the Documentation of Sexual Violence as a Crime or Violation of International Law*. UK Foreign & Commonwealth Office. 2nd ed. March 2017. Available from: https://www.un.org/sexualviolenceinconflict/wp-content/uploads/2019/06/report/international-protocol-on-the-documentation-and-investigation-of-sexual-violence-in-conflict/International_Protocol_2017_2nd_Edition.pdf [Accessed 29 July 2021].

[11] *Berkeley Protocol on Digital Open Source Investigations* ('Berkeley Protocol'). Human Rights Center UC Berkeley School of Law and UN Office of the High Commissioner for Human Rights. 2020. Available from: https://www.ohchr.org/sites/default/files/2022-04/OHCHR_BerkeleyProtocol.pdf [Accessed 14 May 2023].

for digital investigations. Early adoption of the *Berkeley Protocol* by several NGOs reflects how a common standard for identifying, collecting, preserving and analyzing digital information from open sources can save precious time and resources, facilitate inter-organizational coordination, improve the quality of investigations, minimize the risk of biases and offset disclosure challenges.

Focusing on the need that gave rise to the creation, adoption and implementation of the *Berkeley Protocol*, this chapter examines how digital investigations present a unique opportunity for the international justice community to align its work and improve the pursuit of justice and accountability by strengthening every link in the evidentiary chain. It starts by outlining the diversity of efforts focused on collecting digital evidence, before providing an overview of how these connect with the international justice community, using work on the Syrian conflict as a case study. The chapter also describes the process of establishing the *Berkeley Protocol*, and how it can be used to address the challenges, and maximize the opportunities, of online open source research.

Links in the Digital Evidence Chain

The digital evidentiary chain starts with those at the scene of the crime – victims, witnesses and even perpetrators – who document events as they unfold in real time. This initial link also includes those who arrive in the immediate aftermath of the events, such as medics, humanitarian workers, local reporters and other first responders. Their digital documentation of international crimes has steadily increased with the proliferation of smartphones, which can be used to take photographs, record videos and post observations online.

When it comes to digital open source investigations, those involved in on-the-ground documentation are often referred to as 'content creators' or 'social media users'. Once uploaded to the internet, their videos, images and posts are referred to as 'user-generated content'.[12] This initial documentation has tremendous potential value for intelligence gathering and legal

---

[12]Lutkefend T. and Schneider T. *Methodology*. Global Public Policy Institute. September 2020. Available from: https://chemicalweapons.gppi.net/methodology/ [Accessed 29 July 2021].

process, contemporaneously capturing important elements about the crime scene and casualties from a witness perspective and sharing that information with stakeholders outside the region. However, despite the sometimes prolific coverage, such content needs to be collected, processed and analyzed before it can be used within subsequent accountability efforts, as, for example, 'working with data from an active war zone almost inevitably means dealing with gaps and inconsistencies in documentation, some of which may be driven by political interests or individual agendas that underpin reporting on the topic'.[13] Such work also involves dealing with the ephemeral nature of digital data and the dynamic information environment in which it may be stored or shared.

The immediate aftermath of a crime is often called 'the golden hour', referring to the period in which evidence can be properly preserved before it degrades or disappears. On the ground, this equates to a time period when others might join the initial witnesses documenting the unfolding scene – for example, by photographing destroyed buildings and dead bodies, taking witness statements, or collecting debris and documents. In the case of ongoing atrocities that develop over a longer time, this golden period can persist over days, weeks, months or even years.

For digital investigations, the golden hour is the period after user-generated content is uploaded to the internet and made public, and before it is removed – either by the original poster (who may come to regret the posting) or by the platform (which may find the content violates its standards). To take advantage of this time window, digital first responders, often from outside the conflict-affected country, have the task of quickly identifying relevant content and preserving it before it disappears or becomes decontextualized.

Prioritization and selection of relevant information is paramount, because of the enormous volume of potentially relevant information.[14] The contemporaneous capture of digital content by online investigators serves several important purposes. One is simply securing data about an event

---

[13] Burton N. *What is Forensic Triage?* ADF News. 28 December 2018. Available from: https://www.adfsolutions.com/news/what-is-forensic-triage [Accessed 29 July 2021].

[14] McDermott Y., Koenig A., and Murray D. Open Source Information's Blind Spots: Human and Machine Bias in International Criminal Investigations. *Journal of International Criminal Justice*. 7 April 2021. 11 (3).

before the moment is lost. In addition, swift capture can be important for later work to authenticate content. Since it takes time to digitally manufacture or manipulate content, the closer the time between harvesting data and the event they record, the less likely that data are to be fake.

However, despite the importance of data collection in real time, few organizations have the capacity to capture everything, nor would they want to, given numerous security, privacy, data management, cost and disclosure concerns. Thus, technology companies, particularly social media service providers that house user-generated content, are becoming important links in the evidence chain, since their platforms serve as popular repositories for digital data generated by civilians (see footnote 4). While not the intent of social media companies, their servers have become important digital evidence archives and historical records of war (see footnote 4).

There will be gaps and inconsistencies in the information that comes out of an active war zone. In addition, the information that gets prioritized and preserved by digital first responders – such as journalists and NGOs – has its own biases. Information deemed critical for collection can vary significantly based on the identity and needs of the collector. For example, there can be pressure on journalists to report on the aspects of a conflict that are likely to generate the most interest as measured in eyeballs and clicks, for reasons related to both impact and revenue. While all fact-finding is meant to be objective, objectivity can mean different things in journalistic and legal contexts. Journalists tend to collect information relatively selectively, concentrating on what they consider to be the most compelling and relevant to the wider public interest. They also often operate in competitive environments under enormous time pressure, which can make it difficult for them to thoroughly verify that digital information is genuine, which is especially the case for journalists working in relatively small teams. Further, war reporters, particularly those who are working from outside a conflict, often republish user-generated content along with other information collected from open and closed sources.[15] Ideally, they should authenticate this material before using it, although they do not always have the capacity to do so.

The digital content produced by social media users and the news articles produced by traditional media are also consumed by human rights

---

[15] See also the chapter by Ahmad in this volume (Chapter 3.1) for discussion of the connections between open source research and investigative journalism.

researchers and investigators, who frequently use this information as the basis for their own reports. Working on a slightly slower but nevertheless pressured timeline are the human rights advocates who seek to inform a more selective audience of decision-makers with the aim of influencing national and international legislation and policy.[16] This group primarily includes human rights advocates working for NGOs, as well as some state actors. The purpose of advocacy is often to push for policy change or a shift in practice, and it is generally focused on promoting specific actions by governments or intergovernmental organizations like the UN Security Council. Again, advocates' information collection may be selective, designed to identify the most culpable actors, in order to support particular narratives or policy goals.

The next link in the chain is frequently human rights investigators working for UN Commissions of Inquiry (COIs) or Fact-Finding Missions (FFMs), who have a similar or slightly more robust evidentiary standard to human rights advocates and investigators. The main difference between these two types of UN activities is their intent: COIs focus on discovering atrocities and then advocate for a position, while FFMs aim to objectively inform. UN investigators often have a clearer mandate with a more defined scope of investigation than other links in the chain. Moreover, they work within a specific legal framework, and follow a common methodology established by the OHCHR's Methodology, Education and Training Section (METS). However, in line with their nature and mandate, COIs and FFMs are not required to establish guilt in the way courts do and as such they do not apply the criminal law standard of proof 'beyond reasonable doubt'. They have instead most commonly adopted 'reasonable suspicion' or 'reasonable grounds to believe', as their evidentiary standard.[17]

The final link in the international legal accountability chain comprises the international criminal prosecutors and investigators working in national

---

[16] See also the chapters by H. Wilson *et al.* and Mathews in this volume (Chapters 4.1 and 4.2) for consideration of how open source research has contributed to national and international policy-making to outlaw chemical and biological warfare.

[17] *Commissions of Inquiry and Fact-Finding Missions on International Human Rights and Humanitarian Law: Guidance and Practice.* United Nations. Office of the High Commissioner for Human Rights. 2015. Available from: https://www.ohchr.org/documents/publications/coi_guidance_and_practice.pdf [Accessed 29 July 2021].

and international judicial systems that are focused on legal accountability. In criminal cases, they must meet the highest burden of proof – beyond reasonable doubt – and follow the most rigorous procedures in order to ensure the fairness of proceedings. Vested with varying degrees of investigative authority or police powers, their work is subject to substantial oversight – it must be transparent and auditable. Therefore, they handle evidence, including digital open source evidence, in compliance with well-defined rules of procedure to ensure that it is admissible at trial and given the proper weight. The goal of this group is to identify and punish the perpetrators of crimes and deter future wrong-doing, as well as incapacitate and rehabilitate proven culprits.[18] Lawyers also aim to deliver justice to victims by achieving retribution, restoration and reparations.

Unregulated practices of the parties at the beginning of the evidentiary chain can cause serious damage downstream, thwarting the success of subsequent accountability processes through the inadvertent mishandling of evidence or by embedding biases within the information ecosystem that distort the factual record.[19] These diffuse and conflicting roles can only work together well if the various parties first identify some common ground.

Different Approaches, Same Aims

Despite the different practices of journalists, human rights advocates, human rights investigators and criminal investigators, they all share a desire for some type of justice and accountability, although those terms mean different things to different people. Justice can be found in the street, in the court of public opinion or in a court of law – this may include 'naming and shaming', official admissions of guilt, truth and reconciliation processes, indigenous justice processes, resignations, financial penalties or convictions that lead to the jailing of perpetrators.

In other words, while the broader aim of justice may be shared, the end goals of these various actors often differ – journalists seek to bring attention

---

[18] Koenig A., Stover E., O'Donnell P., and Crittenden C. *Beyond Reasonable Doubt: Using Scientific Evidence to Advance Prosecutions at the International Criminal Court*. UC Berkeley Human Rights Center. 2021.

[19] Richardson A. V. The Coming Archival Crisis: How Ephemeral Video Disappears Protest Journalism and Threatens Newsreels of Tomorrow. *Digital Journalism*. 25 November 2020. 8 (10), pp. 1338–1346.

to issues of relatively wide public interest, human rights advocates seek to influence policy-makers to act in the face of human rights violations and prosecutors seek to hold perpetrators legally accountable for their crimes. These different goals – and, more consequentially, the different evidentiary standards that these groups work to and the types of information needed to meet those standards – make it difficult to identify a clear workflow for information sharing related to international crimes.

At the same time, since the establishment of the International Criminal Court (ICC), lawyers have struggled to secure convictions due to inadequate evidence[20] – not a lack of evidence *per se*, but a lack of *reliable* evidence.[21] The Rome Statute, the founding instrument of the ICC, entered into force in 2002, providing the Court jurisdiction over core international crimes – war crimes, crimes against humanity and genocide – in the territories of member states. The ICC was modelled on two *ad hoc* tribunals that pre-dated it – the International Criminal Tribunal for the former Yugoslavia (ICTY) and International Criminal Tribunal for Rwanda (ICTR), which were created as temporary institutions to address specific conflicts. Unlike the International Court of Justice (ICJ), which settles legal disputes between states, the ICC is mandated to hold individual perpetrators accountable for criminal violations of the law. The ICC Office of the Prosecutor is charged with investigating cases within the Court's jurisdiction based on specific criteria.

Judges at the ICC have generally given little weight to the findings of journalists and human rights groups, whose work is often out of sync with the high evidentiary threshold, stringent procedures and due process safeguards required by criminal proceedings. As a result, journalists' and human rights groups' findings usually function as 'lead information' – that is, information that leads criminal investigators to potential witnesses and other relevant sources – but not as primary evidence.

In their decisions, ICC judges have provided several reasons for not relying on findings of journalists and human rights investigators. The general rationale is the chasm between journalistic standards, human rights investigation standards and criminal investigation standards. The judges'

---

[20] Spyer J. Assad or We Burn the Country: How One Family's Lust for Power Destroyed Syria. *Middle East Quarterly*. 2021. 27 (5), p. 2.

[21] Van Schaack B. *Imagining Justice for Syria*. Oxford: Oxford University Press. 26 October 2020.

reluctance to rely on traditional open sources such as news articles, NGO reports and UN reports is justifiable given that they are secondary or even tertiary sources, and often contain significant amounts of rumour or anonymous hearsay. However, as a result of discounting such material, international criminal investigators have historically found themselves having to start an investigation from scratch years after events have occurred, once they finally have been granted the authority to investigate. Often, they have to redo the work of others in a manner that complies with the rules of procedure and evidence to which they are bound. By the time this process starts, however, much of the evidence may have been lost, destroyed or altered.

International criminal judges have yet to fully grapple with the reliability of newer forms of open source information such as user-generated content, which are frequently primary sources, but nevertheless lack many of the traditional indicators of reliability – such as an identifiable author or provenance. While some lawyers and investigators automatically lump user-generated content together with news articles and NGO reports found online, assuming that it should only be used as lead information, others advocate that it be admitted as direct evidence, recognizing the potential value of digital videos and photographs to establish the details of a crime or the linkages between high-level perpetrators and the crimes committed by their subordinates.

The introduction of digital technologies in investigations – and the near impossibility of any one sector mastering the full range of available material in a timely manner, especially given the scale and ephemerality of online information[22] – is quickly changing the dynamic between the various actors traditionally involved in investigating and prosecuting human rights abuses. One reason for this change is the democratization of access to information and communications generated through digital technologies, which have greatly improved the ability of different groups to obtain online information and work together to deploy that information across a range of uses. With more than 6,000 tweets posted every second,

---

[22] Rapp S. J. Bridging The Hague-Geneva divide: Harmonizing Multiple Investigations of International Crimes. *Intersections*. 2016. 7 (11). See also footnote 6.

500 hours of video uploaded to YouTube every minute, a rapidly increasing array of platforms emerging online and an information environment replete with mis- and disinformation, the digital information landscape in which the international justice community is working is both massive and complex.

While UN-mandated COIs and FFMs have long relied on open source information for intelligence and lead information, their main source of evidence has traditionally been human sources. However, because of increasing difficulty in accessing locations they need to investigate – for financial, political, security and, most recently, health reasons – UN investigators are having to look for alternative sources of information and remote investigation techniques, and have found that open source digital investigations could meet some of the needs. This turn towards the digital domain has been given added urgency in light of a global pandemic, climate concerns and often-insufficient budgets that have further limited travel and in-person investigative activities.

The rise in relevant and probative digital information about armed conflicts that is equally accessible to public and private actors presents an opportunity to narrow and possibly even close the Hague–Geneva divide. While it is difficult to change well-established and engrained investigation practices, the newness of digital open source investigations provides a unique opportunity to get the international justice community to operate to a common standard. Since digital open source information is available at the same time and in the same format to all parties discussed above, and the techniques required to exploit this information can be relatively easily taught, digital investigations can serve as common ground for building standardization and strengthening collaboration. Digital investigations present an exciting opportunity to align procedures and practices from the start, so that evidence is properly handled at every link in the chain.

A Networked Approach to Syria

There is no better example of both the drawbacks and benefits of the multitude of actors operating in the international justice arena than Syria's armed conflict and the related efforts aimed at bringing accountability to the perpetrators of war crimes and crimes against humanity. In March 2011, civil war erupted in Syria.²³ As violence against the civilian population grew in the wake of President Bashar al-Assad's violent crackdown on Arab Spring protestors, so too did calls for justice. Syria, however, is not a State Party to the Rome Statute, and therefore is not subject to ICC jurisdiction without a unanimous referral from the UN Security Council. Two permanent members of the Security Council, Russia and China, have consistently blocked any resolutions calling for accountability mechanisms to address the situation in Syria.²⁴ Thus, the ICC Prosecutor does not have jurisdiction to investigate crimes there. In the absence of this clear path to justice, however, other actors have stepped up.

At the start of the war, journalists, NGOs and civil society groups began to fill the investigatory gap by documenting, collecting and preserving any information that could serve as future evidence,²⁵ hoping that a pathway to justice would eventually be forged that would make use of this information. In 2011, the Syrian Center for Media and Freedom of Expression established the Violations Documentation Center. Around the same time, a non-profit news organization, the Syrian Free Press, was created to support and amplify the 2011 uprising. A humanitarian group – the Syrian Civil Defence, also referred to as the White Helmets – strapped go-pro cameras to their helmets during rescue efforts to record the aftermath of bombings and other attacks. Numerous NGOs formed, including foundation-funded groups like the Syrian Archive (now Mnemonic), and state-funded groups like the Syrian Justice and Accountability Centre and Commission for International Justice and Accountability, which began systematically archiving digital and analogue documentation of atrocities that was at acute risk of destruction from both inside and outside the country.

In addition to a burgeoning civil society effort to preserve potential evidence, the UN Human Rights Office established the *Independent International Commission of Inquiry on the Syrian Arab Republic* (COI-Syria)

---

[23] D'Alessandra F. and Sutherland K. The Promise and Challenges of New Actors and New Technologies in International Justice. *Journal of International Criminal Justice*. 7 June 2021.

[24] Radeva E. The Potential for Computer Vision to Advance Accountability in the Syrian Crisis. *Journal of International Criminal Justice*. 17 May 2021.

[25] Anwar R. and Eyad A. At the Higher Regional Court in Koblenz on 23 April 2020. Available from: https://trialinternational.org/latest-post/anwar-r-and-eyad-a/.

on 22 August 2011,[26] with a mandate to investigate all alleged violations of international human rights law since March 2011 in Syria. In December 2016, the UN General Assembly adopted a resolution to establish an *International, Impartial, Independent Mechanism to Assist in the Investigation and Prosecution of Those Responsible for the Most Serious Crimes under International Law Committed in the Syrian Arab Republic since March 2011* (IIIM-Syria) to collect, aggregate and process potential evidence, much of which had already been preserved by NGOs (see footnote 22). While the IIIM-Syria does not have the prosecutorial powers of the ICC or *ad hoc* tribunals (such as the above-mentioned International Criminal Tribunals for Yugoslavia and Rwanda), it does have a mandate to conduct investigations to a criminal evidence standard, distinguishing it from all prior COIs and FFMs.

Working in coordination with the IIIM, and with support from private and public lawyers from international firms and NGOs, national war crimes prosecutors have built viable criminal cases against Syrian regime officials.[27] Several states have developed the national capacity to investigate and prosecute international crimes under the principle of universal jurisdiction, which is based on the theory that certain crimes are so horrendous that they are crimes against all of humanity and therefore all courts should have jurisdiction. In practice, universal jurisdiction is nowhere near that expansive, with some countries rejecting the notion and other countries adopting it with limitations, for example, by requiring that the victim be a national of that state. As of this writing (2021–2022), many of these cases have been filed, several have been litigated and at least one has completed, resulting in a conviction.[28] Others are waiting in the wings. In order for these cases to exist, digital information has had to travel many miles – from the cell phone of a witness, to the internet, to digital archives, to the forensic lab,

---

[26] *Independent International Commission of Inquiry on the Syrian Arab Republic*. United Nations Human Rights Council. Available from: https://www.ohchr.org/en/hr-bodies/hrc/iici-syria/independent-international-commission [Accessed 14 August 2023].

[27] Aksamitowska K. Digital Evidence in Domestic Core International Crimes Prosecutions Lessons Learned from Germany, Sweden, Finland and The Netherlands. *Journal of International Criminal Justice*. 16 May 2021.

[28] Syrian Archive. Methods and Tools: Open Source Tools and Methods for Open Source Investigations [online]. *Syrian Archive*. Available from: https://syrianarchive.org/en/about/methods-tools [Accessed 29 July 2021].

to the courtroom. The digital information has also passed through many hands – usually transmitted from documenters, to digital first responders, to NGOs, to COIs, to a UN-appointed Investigative Mechanism and finally to a prosecuting authority such as a national war crimes unit.

This information sharing shows positive movement towards collaboration between different parties. However, it took nearly a decade to get here. The long road to justice for Syria, while slowed by political opposition, is due in part to the lack of common standards and practices used by all parties in the evidentiary chain, many of which had to reformat or re-verify digital information as it came to them. The multitude of actors pursuing justice and accountability for Syria has played an important role in providing much-needed capacity to collect the volume of relevant digital information available and the flexibility to react and preserve it in a timely manner. At the same time, poor coordination, inconsistent practices and the lack of a clear workflow have led to inefficiencies. The Syria case illustrates the positive and negative impacts of having such a large and diverse ecosystem of actors operating in the same space, and demonstrates why cooperation and coordination – made possible through common terms and standards – are key to making justice work.

Increasing Acceptance for a Common Standard

While digital open source information has begun to enter the evidentiary record, the challenge of ensuring the reliability and validity of such malleable material remains. As a result, the UC Berkeley Human Rights Center led a team of multi-disciplinary practitioners and legal experts to develop the *Berkeley Protocol*, which includes shared methodologies for verification of online content and sources,[29] as well as guidance on ethics,[30] legal compliance, security, forensic collection and digital preservation, to help standardize practices engaged in at each link in the chain from a conflict to

---

[29] Koenig A. "Half the Truth is Often a Great Lie": Deep Fakes, Open Source Information, and International Criminal Law. *AJIL Unbound*. 2019. 113, pp. 250–255.

[30] Many other chapters in this volume detail ways in which open source research practitioners approach the ethics of their work. See, for example, the chapters by Duke, Ahmad, Toler, L. Wilson *et al.*, and Bedenko & Bellish (Chapters 2.2, 3.1, 3.2, 5.1, and 5.4).

the courtroom. Establishing common practice and handling of digital evidence will increase the likelihood that lawyers can establish its authenticity at trial and, in doing so, increase judicial confidence in relying on these newer forms of evidence.

Given recent efforts to enhance the reliability of digital information for court purposes, 'Open sources such as newspapers and other publications, news agencies, television stations, websites, NGO reports, government reports, social media and United Nations reports (have become) invaluable for gathering background information' (see footnote 17). The purposes for which online open source information is used are broad and diverse. 'Open source material [can] be mined for information on events relevant to the mandate of the commission/mission, which will assist in identifying key incidents, help to define the priorities for investigations, provide leads for investigations and identify sources' (see footnote 17).

Ultimately, the development and adoption of common professional standards for international investigations is critical for the success of such efforts – as they optimally enhance efficacies, efficiencies and ethics. Adherence to common standards will help minimize bias in the identification and collection processes and ensure that collected information is relevant, probative and can be authenticated.

On this last point, the coordination of diverse actors with expertise on digital open source information collection can prove especially helpful. Keeping mass information collection outside of the courts can help with timely acquisition. In addition, it can relieve the burden on under-resourced prosecution teams. But perhaps, most importantly, it can aid with disclosure obligations. Instead of investigators and prosecutors siphoning up enormous quantities of digital information and then not being able to comply with disclosure obligations because they don't know what they have, they can come to third-party actors with specific, targeted requests for information – ultimately increasing accessibility to relevant and manageable information by both the prosecution and defence.

In order to harness the possibilities of digital open source investigations to contribute in these ways, the *Berkeley Protocol* is a guide for every link in the digital evidentiary chain. It contains eight chapters that span a range of areas, including foundational principles, relevant legal frameworks, security considerations, preparation and investigation minimum standards and best practices, and options for reporting on findings. The *Protocol* also includes a series of annexes designed to help with everything from digital open source investigation planning to how to conduct a digital landscape assessment, to ascertain which online sites may be most relevant to an investigation and whose perspectives and information may be represented at those sites.

Importantly, the *Protocol* is tool-agnostic, i.e. it does not recommend or discourage the use of specific applications or software for the identification, collection, verification and preservation of digital content. This is to ensure that the *Protocol* will remain useful as a guide for standardization despite rapid changes in social media platforms and the technologies needed to mine those platforms. Thus, while the *Protocol* provides a solid foundation for practice, most investigation teams will want and/or need to create their own internal-facing standard operating practices (or 'SOPs') to bridge guidance provided by the *Protocol* with different legal and operational frameworks. For example, during the development of the *Berkeley Protocol*, the Berkeley Human Rights Center collaborated with an internal working group in the ICC Office of the Prosecutor to create their own procedures and practices. Similarly, various UN FFMs and COIs that use the *Berkeley Protocol* for reference are likely to adapt it to the specific context in which they are working.

Conclusion

The pursuit of justice is often a long game and it inevitably involves a multitude of individuals and entities in documentation and investigation efforts. However, the chain of actors, and the information they handle and process, will only be as strong as the weakest links, which means attention needs to be paid to the quality and overall efficacy of the work done at each link along the chain.

The *Berkeley Protocol* was created to support this process. These standards were developed with input from a professionally diverse and global array of actors, all with the shared purpose of strengthening the quality of online investigations as international criminal courts and tribunals operate in an increasingly digital landscape. The *Berkeley Protocol* is targeted at a broad audience of actors – ranging from witnesses to journalists to researchers to lawyers – and is focused on minimum standards that would prove feasible for most, while increasing consistency and quality for later use in court.

By establishing a common lexicon, the *Berkeley Protocol* provides courts with a better understanding of how to measure the reliability of digital open source information, and guides the diverse ecosystem of documenters, analysts and archivists on courts' expectations. In doing so, it represents a first step towards unifying the international justice community. The best way to advance accountability and justice is to improve communication and coordination across the entire sector – and establish a common understanding of how to maximize the strength of each link in the evidentiary chain.

Part 3
Information and Societies

© 2024 World Scientific Publishing Company
https://doi.org/10.1142/9781800614079_0007

Chapter 3.1

Open Source Journalism, Misinformation and the War for Truth in Syria

Muhammad Idrees Ahmad

Abstract

Open source research has reinvigorated investigative journalism, enabling it to exploit the increased visibility brought to world events by new technologies, and creating robust methodologies to collect and analyze data about them. This chapter details these developments and shows how they are addressing the challenges facing contemporary journalism, including reduced access to conflict regions, cutbacks in funding and an increasingly contested information landscape marked by misinformation and organized disinformation campaigns. Demonstrating that digital open source research is rigorous, collaborative and ethical, this chapter shows that it is helping investigative journalism rebuild credibility and trust, answer its critics and enhance global transparency and accountability.

Introduction: A Digital Panopticon

On 4 April 2017, a suspected chemical weapons attack on the Syrian town of Khan Shaykhun killed 92 people. The country's ruling regime claimed that the deaths were staged while its ally Russia blamed rebels for the atrocity. On 7 April, the US military launched 59 Tomahawk missiles on the airbase from which the attack reportedly originated. The US action was symbolic and had little effect on the Assad regime's military capability.[1] But it quickly

---

[1] Ahmad M. I. The Trump Administration Responds to Syria's Assad with Missiles. *The Progressive*. 7 April 2017. Available from: https://progressive.org/latest/the-trump-administration-responds-to-syria%E2%80%99s-assad-with-miss/ [Accessed 22 June 2023].

This is an open access article published by World Scientific Publishing Europe Ltd. and distributed under the terms of the Creative Commons Attribution-NonCommercial 4.0 International (CC BY-NC 4.0) License.

mobilized elements of the western left and right into protesting the airstrikes and suggesting that the chemical attack was staged to create a rationale for 'regime change'. These voices included the noted linguist Noam Chomsky, who in a speech at the University of Massachusetts Amherst cast doubt on the regime's responsibility, stating that 'actually we don't [know what happened]'.[2] They also included the celebrated journalist Seymour Hersh, who in an article for the German daily *Die Welt* claimed that the deaths in Khan Shaykhun had resulted from a conventional attack on a jihadi facility, rather than from chemical weapons.[3]

Both Chomsky and Hersh have a reputation for defying orthodoxies in the pursuit of truth and are revered by millions. They have a record of exposing the corruptions of power, and appeared – once again – to be demolishing official narratives with support from what they claimed were unimpeachable sources. Their interventions raised doubts, making the US claims appear no more valid than the Syrian or Russian ones. Was the US too hasty in retaliating? Could we know anything at all about the incident in the fog of war?

As it happened, within days of the attack – and before Chomsky and Hersh ever spoke – enough evidence had accumulated from multiple independent sources to leave little doubt about the nature of the attack and its perpetrator. Virtually every significant detail of the incident had been captured digitally, in social media postings, images, videos, sounds, maps and witness testimonies. Contrary to Chomsky's claims, we did know what had happened.

On 4 April, 6:26 am local time, as General Mohammed Hasouri of Syria's Air Force Brigade 50 took off from the Shayrat airbase in his Sukhoi Su-22, call-sign 'Quds-1', his communications had been intercepted by Syria Sentry – a network of spotters who monitor air traffic and warn Syrian citizens of incoming airstrikes.[4] The jet's flight path on its bombing run over

---

[2] Chomsky N. The Prospects for Survival [recorded speech]. *YouTube*. 13 April 2017. Available from: https:// www.youtube.com/watch?v=1uSwEqyJhGI [Accessed 22 June 2023].

[3] Hersh S. Syria: Trump's Red Line. *Die Welt*. 25 June 2017. Available from: https://www.welt.de/politik/ausland/article165905578/Trump-s-Red-Line.html [Accessed 7 January 2023].

[4] Smith H. L. Pilot of sarin gas jet flew in previous chemical attack. *The Times*. 10 April 2017. Available from: https://www.thetimes.co.uk/article/pilot-of-sarin-gas-jet-flew-in-previous-chemical-attack-3pn62d3xw [Accessed 22 June 2023].

Idlib had been recorded by the US Central Command and posted online. Twelve minutes later, when Hasouri delivered his lethal payload on the town of Khan Shaykhun, multiple witnesses had reported the strike on social media, some capturing it on cellphone videos, which they posted online. The videos had been verified and geolocated by journalists.[5] Doctors Without Borders (MSF) medics who treated the survivors and the World Health Organization (WHO) had found the symptoms – dilated pupils, muscle spasms, foaming mouths, breathing difficulties, violent convulsions and involuntary defecation – 'consistent with exposure to neurotoxic agents such as sarin' (see footnote 1).

Subsequent reports provided additional evidence. By 19 April 2017, the Organisation for the Prohibition of Chemical Weapons (OPCW) had collected bio-medical samples and four separate labs had analyzed them, concluding that the evidence of sarin exposure was 'incontrovertible'.[6] On 30 June, OPCW's Fact Finding Mission (FFM) published a comprehensive report confirming that the nerve agent used was sarin.[7] These findings were corroborated by the UN-OPCW Joint Investigative Mechanism after interviews with 17 witnesses and analysis of other evidence, as detailed in its 26 October 2017 report.[8] The conclusion was unequivocal: The sarin had been delivered by a Syrian Air Force jet. In a separate investigation in

---

[5]Triebert C. The Khan Sheikhoun Chemical Attack – Who Bombed What and When? *Bellingcat*. 10 April 2017. Available from: https://www.bellingcat.com/news/mena/2017/04/10/khan-sheikhoun-chemical-attack-bombed/ [Accessed 22 June 2023]. Browne M., Reneau N., and Scheffler M. How Syria Spun a Chemical Strike [video online]. *New York Times*. 26 April 2017. Available from: https://www.nytimes.com/video/world/middleeast/100000005063944/syria-chemical-attack-russia.html; https://www.youtube.com/watch?v=MYOMEDK_uVs [Accessed 22 June 2023].

[6]OPCW. OPCW Director-General Shares Incontrovertible Laboratory Results Concluding Exposure to Sarin. *OPCW*. 19 April 2017. Available from: https://www.opcw.org/media-centre/news/2017/04/opcw-director-general-shares-incontrovertible-laboratory-results [Accessed 3 July 2023].

[7]OPCW. OPCW Fact-Finding Mission Confirms Use of Chemical Weapons in Khan Shaykhun on 4 April 2017. *OPCW*. 30 June 2017. Available from: https://www.opcw.org/media-centre/news/2017/06/opcw-fact-finding-mission-confirms-use-chemical-weapons-khan-shaykhun-4 [Accessed 22 June 2023].

[8]Seventh report of the Organisation for the Prohibition of Chemical Weapons-United Nations Joint Investigative Mechanism. 26 October 2017. Available from: https://reliefweb.int/report/syrian-arab-republic/seventh-report-organisation-prohibition-chemical-weapons-united-nations [Accessed 22 June 2023].

May, Human Rights Watch had reached the same conclusion.⁹ The doubts that Chomsky and Hersh had raised were refuted by multiple independent analyses.

The episode is instructive in showing that new communications technologies have changed the practice of journalism, creating new investigative possibilities when traditional methods aren't viable. It demonstrates that in conflicts, where the motivation to lie or mislead is high, one needn't rely on the self-serving claims of belligerents or the obfuscations of poorly informed commentators and ideologues, since audio-visual data produced by victims, witnesses or perpetrators can now be used for independent scrutiny. The ubiquity of smartphones and the advent of social media have ensured that wherever there is access to the internet or mobile data, most human activities are caught in a panopticon, potentially in sight of an active or passive digital witness.¹⁰

This chapter reviews developments in digital open source research¹¹ and their significance for journalism. It starts by outlining how user-generated content (UGC) from digital technologies has made global activities visible, and shows how this addresses challenges facing contemporary journalism, as underscored by reporting on the war in Syria. It then goes on to show how citizen journalists pioneered new approaches that use publicly accessible digital data for a robust new form of journalism, notable for its transparency and replicability. While some journalists have tried to disparage open source journalism as an inadequate substitute for traditional reporting, such arguments are disingenuous, since open source journalism supplements rather than replaces boots-on-the-ground reportage. The chapter demonstrates that open source research often relies on and complements traditional journalism; it is inherently collaborative and its practitioners are acutely conscious of their ethical obligations.

---

⁹Human Rights Watch. Death by Chemicals: The Syrian Government's Widespread and Systematic Use of Chemical Weapons. *Human Rights Watch*. 1 May 2017. Available from: https://www.hrw.org/report/2017/05/01/death-chemicals/syrian-governments-widespread-and-systematic-use-chemical-weapons [Accessed 22 June 2023].

¹⁰English philosopher Jeremy Bentham used the word 'panopticon' in the late 1700s to describe a theoretical prison in which inmates were constantly observed. In the 1970s, Michel Foucault expanded the idea to explain how citizens internalize social controls through considering states' capacities to observe their actions.

¹¹This chapter defines open source research as research that uses publicly available tools and information.

Investigative Journalism: Crises and New Hopes

Journalism has always relied on human and documentary sources for information. But the combination of smartphones and social media has dramatically increased the speed, access, and reach of this reliance. It has become common practice for news organizations to solicit photos or videos from witnesses to major incidents as stories develop. During the 7 July 2005, terrorist attack on the London underground, for example, much of the initial reporting was based on UGC. Likewise, UGC has been invaluable in situations which were previously beyond the reach of journalistic scrutiny, whether it is cell phone videos of police brutality in the US, Israeli repression of protests in Gaza, China's mass incarceration of the Uyghurs, the execution of civilians by Cameroonian soldiers,[12] accidents, natural disasters or terrorist attacks.

While human sources were often seen as a helpful aid to traditional reporting, several developments have increased journalism's dependency on UGC. Financial constraints have led many news organizations to downsize, and the burden of cost-cutting has fallen mainly on foreign coverage and investigative reporting. Both are notoriously expensive to produce and have uncertain rewards, since investigative journalism carries the risk of legal retaliation while a costly foreign bureau can be scooped by a Twitter user who isn't bound by professional journalists' commitment to verification and accuracy. The pace and volume of news have convinced some editors that sending journalists abroad isn't worth the cost. At the same time, challenges from new media and reductions in resources and reach have contributed towards a loss of authority for the entire sector.

Meanwhile, there has been a decrease in safe access to places of interest. State and non-state actors that used to court foreign correspondents in the hopes of favourable coverage have harnessed the power of social media and digital video to control their own narratives. Journalists – who are often deemed a nuisance or a threat – are now seen as dispensable. They no longer enjoy the qualified immunity they once had when combatants tolerated journalists in attempts to generate positive press (though reporting

---

[12] See the chapter by Strick in this volume (Chapter 2.1) for details of the BBC Africa Eye research into the murder of women and young children in Cameroon, and BBC Africa Eye. *Anatomy of a Killing* [video online]. 24 September 2018. Available from: https://www.youtube.com/watch?v=4G9S-eoLgX4 [Accessed 14 May 2023].

was never risk-free). Increasingly, however, state and non-state actors are making it more dangerous for journalists to report from warzones without explicit authorization and the watchful presence of minders.

In Syria, the Assad regime, the Islamic State and Al Qaeda affiliates have all targeted reporters with threatened or actual violence. The Assad regime impeded reporting by controlling access to locations and targeting those that tried to report without its authorization. After the killing of *Sunday Times* correspondent Marie Colvin and the death of *New York Times*' Anthony Shadid in Syria, both papers faced criticism and, in the case of the latter, a lawsuit from Shadid's family.[13] This made news organizations doubly reluctant to send journalists to Syria without the regime's consent. But while such authorization gives journalists access and some protection, it limits their mobility and independence.

Even without these constraints, however, journalism faces a crisis of credibility. Distrust in the profession is not a new phenomenon; according to the Ipsos MORI Veracity Index, journalists remain among the five least trusted professions in the UK.[14] It doesn't help that serious reporters have to share the label of 'journalist' with tabloid hacks and social media figures who have no commitment to fairness or accuracy. The integrity of even reputable journalism was greatly damaged in the prelude to the 2003 Iraq War and the 2007–2008 financial crisis, where much mainstream media published inaccurate reports. Added to this, many newspapers often blur the distinction between fact and opinion. The British daily *The Independent* for example publishes some reportages under the 'Voices' section; and journalists and editors at the *Wall Street Journal* were so troubled by similar trends at their own paper that in July 2020, 280 of them signed a letter demanding that the publisher enforce clearer boundaries between news and opinion.[15] Similarly, people have started ignoring the division between professional and amateur journalists as the former have often shown themselves

---

[13] Abramson J. *Merchants of Truth: The Business of News and the Fight for Facts*. London: Simon & Schuster. 2019.

[14] Ipsos MORI Veracity Index 2021 – Trust in Professions Survey. Available from: https://www.ipsos.com/sites/default/files/ct/news/documents/2021-12/Veracity%20index%202021_v2_PUBLIC.pdf [Accessed 22 June 2023].

[15] Trachtenberg J. A. WSJ Journalists Ask Publisher for Clearer Distinction Between News and Opinion Content. *Wall Street Journal*. 12 July 2020.

willing to bend truth in service of ideology in ways usually associated with the latter. With public trust in facts receding, news coverage has devolved into a contest of narratives where audiences pick and choose according to their predilections. The sources of this epistemic crisis are institutional,[16] but it has been exacerbated by the weaponization of disinformation by malicious – often state-backed – actors. Information warfare is nothing new and many states engage in it – western and non-western – but the nature and scale of recent campaigns are unprecedented,[17] even if their impact is often overstated.[18]

Open source journalism is providing the means to address several of these crises by restoring the primacy of facts and emphasizing the importance of verifiability. The catalyst for many of these innovations was the war in Syria. Thanks to the wide availability of smartphones and the rise of social media, this became one of the best documented conflicts in history (that is, until the war in Ukraine started). Indeed, former war crime prosecutor Stephen Rapp claims that the evidence massed against the Syrian Assad regime is more extensive than that used to convict Nazis at Nuremberg.[19]

But the war also occasioned an unprecedented disinformation campaign. As noted above, the Assad regime initially tried to control the narrative by denying visas to journalists it deemed unsympathetic to its aims and threatening those that entered the country without authorization, making independent newsgathering dangerous. Consequently, more news organizations came to rely on UGC. Such material is useful, but it carries the risk of manipulation. With help from Russia, the Syrian regime has exploited this by mobilizing armies of trolls to create digital noise that diminishes trust in UGC. Individuals affiliated with the opposition, too, have manipulated or exaggerated data at times, though this is not comparable to the Assad regime's efforts which are organized and systematic. Given the balance of

---

[16] Roberts H., Faris R., and Benkler Y. *Network Propaganda: Manipulation, Disinformation, and Radicalization in American Politics*. Oxford: Oxford University Press. 2018.

[17] Online open source research can help uncover influence campaigns (see Strick's chapter in this volume, Chapter 2.1). Thomas Rid documents Russia's ongoing disinformation campaigns and how these build on the Soviet Union's activities. Rid T. *Active Measures: The Secret History of Disinformation and Political Warfare*. London: Profile. 2020.

[18] Roberts H., Faris R., and Benkler Y. 2018. *op. cit.*

[19] CBS News. Former prosecutor: More evidence of war crimes against Syrian President Assad than there was against Nazis [online video]. *CBS 60 Minutes*. 18 February 2021. Available from: https://www.cbsnews.com/news/bashar-al-assad-syria-60-minutes-2021-02-18/ [Accessed 22 June 2023].

responsibility for atrocities, the regime has greater motivation for distortion. Open source research has proved essential, generating tools that can establish the authenticity of audio-visual material and weed out disinformation.

Without citizen journalists and UGC, Syria would be a black hole from where the state could control the narrative. For all the Assad regime's efforts to limit journalists' movements and deter them from reporting freely, there has been no dearth of material coming out of the country. From Aleppo to Douma, millions of tweets, images and videos have documented the regime's war crimes, providing rich material for open source investigations. And open source analysis of this material has accumulated a record of such consistent accuracy that more and more human rights organizations and war crimes investigators are incorporating it into their research.[20]

These innovations have helped the international community bypass the obstructions to justice that most perpetrators inevitably create. Indeed, in 2017, the International Criminal Court issued its first indictment based primarily on open source evidence against the Libyan warlord Mahmoud al-Werfalli for a series of extra-judicial killings.[21] There is also a salutary effect on the journalism profession. The transparency and robustness of open source methods are encouraging greater rigour and resourcefulness even among traditional journalists. Moreover, they have exposed the limitations of traditional human sources, who are not without agenda and biases, and can sometimes turn journalists into inadvertent vessels of disinformation.

OSINT and Investigative Journalism

Along with HUMINT (human intelligence), SIGINT (signal intelligence) and IMINT (image intelligence), OSINT (Open Source Intelligence) has long been a part of national intelligence and law enforcement toolkits.[22] In the US in 2004, the 9/11 Commission recommended the creation of a

---

[20] For more information about open source investigations, the war in Syria and the international justice system, see the chapter by Freeman & Koenig in this volume (Chapter 2.5).

[21] Irving E. And So It Begins… Social Media Evidence In An ICC Arrest Warrant. *OpinioJuris*. 2017. Available from: http://opiniojuris.org/2017/08/17/and-so-it-begins-social-media-evidence-in-an-icc-arrest-warrant/ [Accessed 15 December 2021].

[22] See the chapter by Vogel in this volume (Chapter 3.4) for more information about the use of open source intelligence within the US intelligence community.

dedicated OSINT unit, a proposal that was reinforced a year later by the Iraq Intelligence Commission. The potential efficacy of OSINT, however, is limited by the secretiveness and hierarchy of national security organizations. It was in the hands of citizen journalists, who combined community with distributed expertise, that open source research found its most dynamic and effective use.

Though open source research has a longer history, digital open source investigations really took off in the first decade of the 21st century. Perhaps the earliest triumph of this form of journalism was when networks of plane spotters around the world were able to unravel the mystery of the US Central Intelligence Agency's (CIA's) 'extraordinary rendition' programme by observing flight patterns of planes that were ferrying suspected terrorists for torture to places like Syria, Egypt, Libya and Jordan.[23] Beginning in 2010, the open newsroom tool Storyful became a platform for collaborative investigation, laying the ground for this new branch of journalism. One resourceful member of the Storyful collective was Leicester-based blogger Eliot Higgins, who started using creative new methods to crack intractable cases, such as a suspected August 2013 chemical weapons attack in Syria (described below). In 2014, Higgins built on his successes to found Bellingcat, an international collective that conducts research using techniques he pioneered and introducing many new ones. For much of its existence, Bellingcat operated on a shoe-string budget, relying on the commitment and motivation of volunteers. Initially, its main source of income was the training sessions it organized for journalists and researchers (I attended one of these in December 2017). Major grants from the Dutch Postcode Lottery in 2019 and 2021 gave Bellingcat more financial stability, allowing it to hire full-time staff. Since its founding, the organization has chalked up an impressive record of breakthroughs, and its alums lead, participate in or support every notable open source enterprise currently in operation.

Many of the most ingenious open source investigators have diverse backgrounds. Some emerge from gaming subcultures, while others are experts from various fields (including architecture, medicine, chemistry, finance and

---

[23] Johnson C. Otherwise Dealt With. *London Review of Books*. 8 February 2007. Available from: https://www.lrb.co.uk/the-paper/v29/n03/chalmers-johnson/otherwise-dealt-with [Accessed 22 June 2023].

law) and have found new uses for their specialist knowledge. For example, British-Israeli architect Eyal Weizman has pioneered the field of forensic architecture, using open source data for spatial investigations into human rights violations; chemical weapons expert Dan Kaszeta has contributed to several Bellingcat investigations; and UC Berkeley's Human Rights Investigations Lab recruits from over a dozen disciplines.

The central pursuit in open source investigations is finding publicly accessible data on an incident, verifying the authenticity of the data, establishing the temporal and spatial dimensions of the incident, and cross-referencing details with other digital records and witness testimonies. Open source analysts are acutely aware of the risk of data manipulation and thus take a foundationalist approach, authenticating audio-visual data *before* drawing any conclusions from them. This is the closest that journalism has to a scientific method: gathering data systematically, establishing their validity and corroborating them, while being transparent about the process so anyone can replicate their research, examine the underlying data and test the conclusions.

Recent achievements – such as Bellingcat's investigations into the Skripal and Navalny poisonings; the *New York Times'* investigations into the killing of Gaza medic Rouzan al-Najjar[24] and the murder of Saudi dissident Jamal Khashoggi;[25] BBC Africa Eye's award-winning work exposing the killers of women and children in Cameroon;[26] Digital Forensic Research Lab's work on Twitter trolls; and UC Berkeley Human Rights Center's contribution to Reuters's Pulitzer Prize-winning investigation in Myanmar[27] – are compelling not just for their multi-disciplinary approach and findings,

---

[24] Al-Hloou Y., Browne M., Woo J., and Halbfinger D. M. An Israeli Soldier Killed a Medic in Gaza. We Investigated the Fatal Shot [video online]. *New York Times*. 2018. Available from: https://www.nytimes.com/video/world/middleeast/100000005933727/israel-gaza-medic-killed-rouzan-najjar.html [Accessed 16 December 2021].

[25] Botti D., Browne M., Jordan D., Singhvi A., Kirkpatrick D. D., Gail C., and Hubbard B. Killing Kashoggi: How a Brutal Saudi Hit Job Unfolded [video online]. *New York Times*. 2018. Available from: https://www.nytimes.com/video/world/middleeast/100000006154117/khashoggi-istanbul-death-saudi-consulate .html [Accessed 16 December 2021].

[26] See the chapter by Strick in this volume (Chapter 2.1).

[27] Stecklow S. Why Facebook is losing the war on hate speech in Myanmar. *Reuters Investigates*. 15 August 2018. Available from: https://www.reuters.com/investigates/special-report/myanmar-facebook-hate/ [Accessed 16 December 2021].

but for their methodological transparency. Such successes have encouraged investment in open source research capability by mainstream media, human rights organizations, think-tanks and academic institutions. These are part of a larger effort focused on information integrity called for by emerging threats to democracy and public discourse from weaponized disinformation.

Traditional Reporting vs. New Methods

Most human rights organizations, journalists and news consumers have welcomed these developments. But some traditional journalists remain sceptical. Veteran investigative journalist Seymour Hersh, for example, has disparaged Eliot Higgins and open source investigations.[28] His criticism, however, inadvertently confirms the value of open source journalism.

In August 2013, two suburbs in Damascus were targeted with the nerve agent sarin, killing over 1,400 civilians.[29] On an obscure blog named Brown Moses, Eliot Higgins had quickly gathered data from YouTube videos, satellite imagery and UN reports to verify the dimensions of the rockets used in the attack, identify their make and establish their trajectory. The rockets matched a model in the Assad regime's arsenal and the trajectory could be traced back to territory held by the regime. Two months later, however, Seymour Hersh published a long essay in the *London Review of Books* (LRB)[30] claiming that the Obama administration had manipulated evidence and colluded in a false-flag operation to blame the Assad regime for the attack. Hersh based his case on testimony from an unnamed 'former senior intelligence official'. Though a wealth of evidence contradicted this story, and his claims soon fell apart, Hersh doubled down and published an even longer story with more elaborate claims from the unnamed former intelligence official. 'We now know it was a covert action planned by [Turkish

---

[28] Is the Obama Admin Ignoring the Role of Turkey & Saudi Arabia in Syria's 2013 Sarin Gas Attacks? [video online and transcript]. *Democracy Now*. 25 April 2016. Available from: https://www.democracynow.org/2016/4/25/is_the_obama_admin_ignoring_the [Accessed 23 June 2023].

[29] See also the chapter by Revill & Garzón Maceda in this volume (Chapter 4.3).

[30] Hersh S. M. Whose sarin? *London Review of Books*. 19 December 2013, 35 (24). Available from: https://www.lrb.co.uk/the-paper/v35/n24/seymour-m.-hersh/whose-sarin [Accessed 17 December 2021].

President Recep] Erdoğan's people to push Obama over the red line', the contact apparently told Hersh.[31]

Hersh was demanding the reader's trust based on a single anonymous source whose credibility he could not confirm, citing documents he hadn't seen and making allegations he could not substantiate. By contrast, Higgins's case relied on authenticated data, verifiable results and a robust method. Higgins's conclusions were corroborated by investigations from a range of other governmental and non-governmental groups. For Hersh's story to be true, these groups had to be not just wrong but also colluding with each other. Higgins's analysis, on the other hand, was based on accessible information and supported by physical evidence, witnesses on the ground and numerous international observers and institutions, including the UN, human rights groups, and the US, British, German and French governments, who had all independently reached the same conclusion about the attack.

The cycle repeated in 2017, after the chemical weapons attack on the town of Khan Shaykhun. While Bellingcat conducted rigorous and transparent open source analysis that demonstrated that the Assad regime was responsible for the attack, Hersh presented an alternative narrative that relied on an unnamed 'senior adviser to the US intelligence community'. On this occasion, the LRB declined to publish his story,[32] and Hersh turned instead to the German conservative daily *Die Welt*. The story had errors and omissions: He got the time of the attack wrong, could not identify its location and ignored the fact that the impact site had been filmed and bore no resemblance to the scene he described. A subsequent comprehensive investigation by the Joint Investigative Mechanism (JIM) conducted by the UN and the OPCW corroborated Bellingcat's findings,[33] leaving Hersh and his publisher humiliated.

---

[31] Hersh S. M. The Red Line and the Rat Line. *London Review of Books*. 17 April 2014, 36 (8). Available from: https://www.lrb.co.uk/the-paper/v36/n08/seymour-m.-hersh/the-red-line-and-the-rat-line [Accessed 17 December 2021].

[32] Ahmad M. I. Syria and the case for editorial accountability. *Aljazeera*. 12 July 2017. Available from: https://www.aljazeera.com/opinions/2017/7/12/syria-and-the-case-for-editorial-accountability/ [Accessed 17 December 2021].

[33] UN Security Council. Letter dated 26 October 2017 from the Secretary-General addressed to the President of the Security Council. S/2017/904. 2017. Available from: https://www.securitycouncilreport.org/atf/cf/%7B65BFCF9B-6D27-4E9C-8CD3-CF6E4FF96FF9%7D/s_2017_904.pdf [Accessed 17 June 2022].

Digital open source journalism shows that distance is not always a barrier to a robust investigation, just as for traditional journalism, proximity is no guarantee of accuracy. What matters in both cases is the reliability of sources and the verifiability of claims. The aim of this discussion is not to pit foreign correspondents against open source journalists, since they both fulfil irreplaceable functions. Instead, it is to address a common response from some traditional journalists who dismiss open source journalism as something deficient. Open source journalists are not vying for foreign correspondents' throne; they are merely adding new layers of scrutiny. Traditional reporters can forget that foreign correspondents have their own limitations – from the compromises of access, the presence of minders, to the reliance on self-interested sources. Their methods may be different, but they are complementary and both are bound by the same ethic – a commitment to accuracy, fairness and verifiability.

Traditional journalists have been hobbled in recent years by the emergence of social media, and the speed of its interactions. Before a reporter can file a report, or even reach a news event, images, videos and claims are often already on social media. Many reporters are adapting to this reality by changing their reporting habits. More and more, journalists have come to either integrate information from social media into their reporting, or at least use it to provide context to their work. In recent years, some journalists have got their best stories from communicating with sources in combat zones over encrypted apps like WhatsApp, Signal or Telegram rather than by interviewing them in the presence of minders. But they don't take such interactions on trust: Just as investigative journalists in the past had to corroborate interview data with documents, letters, financial records, etc., they can now do this by accessing online databases and public records.

Critics suggest that the distance between open source analysts and the places they investigate is a problem, but this misunderstands the nature of the work. Much of the data used in open source analysis come from people on the ground. The pervasiveness of smartphones with high-quality cameras means that many newsworthy incidents are documented by local witnesses,[34] and even people living under siege or authoritarian regimes

---

[34] Some 5 billion people worldwide own mobile phones, half of which are equipped with cameras. Silver L. Smartphone Ownership is Growing Rapidly Around the World, but Not Always Equally. *Pew Research Center*. 5 February 2019. Available from: https://www.pewresearch.org/global/2019/02/05/

are electronically accessible. There are certainly risks involved in capturing and uploading on-the-ground digital records in many places,[35] but nevertheless citizen journalists in Syria were able to upload texts, images and videos not just from rebel areas but also from territory under the control of the Assad regime and ISIS. Though powerful states have tried to restrict electronic communications, information has so far generally found a way to escape.

In this new global panopticon, few significant events go unrecorded. Victims, witnesses and even perpetrators can all document crimes. Individual experiences are thus added to an objective world of factuality, available for any researcher to verify and analyze. All of this is particularly welcome for human rights and war crimes monitors, especially as the obsessive commitment of open source investigators means that they remain focused on a story long after it has dropped out of news headlines.

To be sure, open source analysis has its limitations. It works best when it confines itself to addressing factual questions, and can falter if it starts making judgements based on available data without taking account of information that is inaccessible. The New America Foundation, for example, produced widely cited statistics on drone strikes during the Obama era that were based on media reports. However, these estimates ignored the fact that the reporting on drone strikes was sporadic and casualty figures were drawn from official claims that had not been subject to any on-the-ground verification. Predictably, this led to undercounting civilian casualties.[36,37] A similar issue was revealed in a different theatre when Azmat Khan and Anand Gopal conducted a year-long investigation for *The New York Times*

---

smartphone-ownership-is-growing-rapidly-around-the-world-but-not-always-equally/ [Accessed 15 April 2022].

[35] See also the chapter by Duke in this volume (Chapter 2.2) for discussion of the difficulties and dangers local monitors can face.

[36] Ahmad M. I. The magical realism of body counts: How media credulity and flawed statistics sustain a controversial policy. *Journalism*. 4 August 2015, 17 (1). Available from: https://journals.sagepub.com/doi/pdf/10.1177/1464884915593237?casa_token=u5xFZ8ljRAgAAAAA:-egA6sxUH6 l1urb-Qg6ljVPBbvvqjj QEpNJ6C9VdGtRdpnP3z2PdHU2IkSx48upb4uIYiOcmCR7YXg [Accessed 17 December 2021].

[37] Carboni & Raleigh (Chapter 3.4) document similar issues with official estimates of casualties in Yemen.

into the US-led coalition's anti-ISIS campaign in Iraq, revealing that civilian casualties occurred in 20% of airstrikes, a rate over 31 times higher than the Pentagon was reporting.[38]

A more systematic method for monitoring airstrikes was eventually developed by the Bureau of Investigative Journalism's Chris Woods, who combined media reports with independent corroboration to produce more reliable casualty figures.[39] Woods now runs the independent Airwars.org, which gathers open source data to monitor the US-led coalition's airstrikes against ISIS operations in Iraq and Syria.

In years to come, responsible publishers will have to invest in greater capacity for fact-checking and digital verification. At the moment, only human rights organizations and media giants like the *New York Times* or the BBC have the resources to maintain fully staffed open source investigations units. Meanwhile, dedicated organizations like Bellingcat will continue to produce the bulk of such analyses. However, as *Bellingcat: Truth in a Post-Truth World* (2018), the Emmy-winning documentary by the Dutch broadcaster VPRO, reveals, this model of small organizations and independent researchers operating without large institutional backing can leave practitioners exposed when taking on the interests of state actors as ruthless as the Kremlin or the Saudi regime.

Community and Cognition

Along with its precision and transparency, open source research is notable for its collaborative nature. Open source investigations are inherently collective efforts, usually requiring teams of people working together to harvest, authenticate and analyze data. It is worth noting that many traditional

---

[38] Khan A. and Gopal A. The Uncounted. *New York Times*. 16 November 2017. Available from: https://www.nytimes.com/interactive/2017/11/16/magazine/uncounted-civilian-casualties-iraq-airstrikes.html [Accessed 22 June 2023].

[39] Woods C. Why White House civilian casualty figures on civilian are a wild underestimate. *The Bureau of Investigative Journalism*. 2016. Available from: https://www.thebureauinvestigates.com/opinion/2016-07-01/comment-official-estimates-show-civilians-more-likely-to-be-killed-by-cia-drones-than-by-us-air-force-actions-the-reality-is-likely-far-worse [Accessed 17 December 2021]. See also the chapter by Triebert in this volume (Chapter 2.4) for detailed analysis of investigating airstrikes through open source research.

journalists also rely on collaborations, working with others to facilitate their reportage, including fixers, stringers, witnesses and experts. Indeed, with the increasing risks and shrinking investment in foreign news, freelancers and stringers now carry much of the burden of foreign reporting. But unlike in the open source research community, such collaborations are rarely acknowledged. To the extent that they are, a hierarchy persists in which staff reporters get top billing, regardless of their actual contribution. It is common in the mainstream press for stories to be bylined by the paper's own correspondent even when the reporting and the actual risks have been taken by a stringer, who is only acknowledged in a footnote.

By contrast, open source researchers readily credit each other and their greatest asset is the goodwill of the community, which in turn rewards research efforts with cognitive surplus. Open source culture combines public spiritedness with the rigor of investigative journalism, bringing together professionals and non-professionals in collaborative projects which emphasize transparency and credibility. This hybrid environment also serves as a form of instant peer review to either confirm or invalidate a hypothesis.

Cognitive scientists Steven Sloman and Philip Fernbach explore the benefits of collaborative work, pointing out that, 'When multiple cognitive systems work together, group intelligence can emerge that goes beyond what each individual is capable of'.[40] They note the increasing tendency for scientists to work collaboratively, and cite the work of educational psychologist Ann Brown, who finds that cultivating teams which embody distributed expertise and interdependence encourages 'an atmosphere of joint responsibility, mutual respect, and a sense of personal and group identity'.[41] In the open source research community, one finds a similar culture organically emerging, with people voluntarily offering their expertise and specializations to create deeper knowledge and sophisticated methods. This balance of expertise also serves as a useful check on the limitations of human cognition, including against 'groupthink'.

According to Yale psychologist Irving Janis, 'groupthink' happens when members in a group fail to scrutinize each other's positions and consider

---

[40] Sloman S. and Fernbach P. *The Knowledge Illusion: Why We Never Think Alone*. London: Penguin. 2017.

[41] Brown A. L. Transforming schools into communities of thinking and learning about serious matters. *American Psychologist*. 1997, 52 (4), pp. 399–413.

alternatives, thus reinforcing their beliefs, and making the group more polarized, inflexible and prone to error.[42] Collaboration does not guarantee accurate results. Sloman and Fernbach caution, 'crowdsourcing works only when it provides access to expertise. Without expertise, it can be useless and even detrimental'. An example of crowdsourcing going wrong comes from the aftermath of the April 2013 Boston marathon bombing when sleuths on a Reddit forum worked collaboratively to identify the culprits and ended up wrongly identifying an innocent man as one of the guilty parties.[43]

Collectives like Bellingcat have avoided these problems by emphasizing the importance of verifiability in their work. Even when open source journalists benefit from 'closed' material such as tip-offs or confidential sources, like all good investigative journalists, they seek a verifiable way to corroborate their material and findings, as can be seen in Bellingcat's investigation into the assassination attempt on Sergei and Yulia Skripal in Salisbury UK, or BBC Africa Eye work revealing the people responsible for murdering two women and two young children in Cameroon.[44]

Standards and ethics

Ethical principles are at the heart of many open source investigators' work. For example, Bellingcat has published a six-page 'Editorial Standards and Practices'[45] document, which is in line with the Ethical Journalism Network's five principles: truth and accuracy, independence, fairness and impartiality, humanity, and accountability.[46] These are also the principles of the Global Investigative Journalism Network, of which Bellingcat is a member.

In a separate document titled 'Principles for Data Collection',[47] Bellingcat lays out the ethical questions it considers when using online data, including that which is publicly available. These questions relate to the public interest value of investigation, potential for harm, availability of alternative

---

[42] Janis I. L. Groupthink. *Psychology Today*. 1971, 5 (6), pp. 43–46, 74–76.
[43] See also the chapter by Toler in this volume (Chapter 3.2) for examples of crowdsourced research being carelessly conducted, leading to erroneous findings as well as unlawful and harmful actions.
[44] See the chapter by Strick in this volume (Chapter 2.1).
[45] Available from: https://www.bellingcat.com/app/uploads/2020/09/Editorial-Standards-Practices.pdf [Accessed 19 December 2021].
[46] Available from: https://ethicaljournalismnetwork.org/who-we-are [Accessed 19 December 2021].
[47] https://www.bellingcat.com/app/uploads/2020/09/Principles-for-Data-Collection.pdf [Accessed 19 December 2021].

means of investigation and verifiability of data. They form the basis of a set of working guidelines that include a commitment to protecting the identities of victims and sources, protecting children and removing them from images, and sharing investigation datasets externally only when doing so directly serves the interest of justice. Bellingcat is careful in managing its collaborations, and ensures that none of its datasets are used for commercial purposes or sold to third parties.

A case study illustrates how these principles guide Bellingcat's work. Bana al-Abed, then a seven-year-old girl, was live-tweeting from besieged Aleppo in 2016 with the help of her mother.[48] Her snapshots of the horrors of life under siege and bombardment drew attention to the plight of the people trapped in Aleppo. The Assad regime, the Russian media and their online supporters responded by threatening, trolling, mocking and harassing the child, alternately claiming that she didn't exist or that she was a fabricated avatar for a jihadist-friendly PR operation run out of Turkey. Nick Waters, a former British Army infantry officer working with Bellingcat, used images and videos Bana had posted online to establish who she was, where she lived and how she accessed the internet.[49] Knowing the threat Bana was under, though, Waters and Bellingcat withheld their findings until she and her family were safely evacuated by the Red Crescent. Instead of pursuing a scoop, Bellingcat recognized the obligation to protect the subject of its investigation.

Conclusion

Over the past decade, the business of newsgathering has been struggling to assert its legitimacy amid a broader epistemic crisis. By combining the goodwill of community with a commitment to accuracy and transparency, open source journalism has alleviated some of the distrust that has come

---

[48] Specia M. Bana al-Abed on Twitter: Proof of Life in a War Zone. *New York Times*. 14 December 2016. Available from: https://www.nytimes.com/2016/12/14/insider/bana-al-abed-on-twitter-proof-of-life-in-a-war-zone.html [Accessed 19 December 2021].

[49] Waters N. and Allen T. Finding Bana – Proving the Existence of a 7-Year-Old Girl in Eastern Aleppo. Bellingcat. 14 December 2016. Available from: https://www.bellingcat.com/news/mena/2016/12/14/bana-alabed-verification-using-open-source-information/ [Accessed 19 December 2021].

to surround the profession. In contrast to the competitive ethos of traditional journalism, the open source approach is cooperative, which allows it to tap the cognitive surplus of the community and draw expertise from a host of relevant disciplines. Professional journalists have in turn adapted by introducing greater rigour into their own reporting, placing a premium on accuracy and verifiability. A symbiotic relationship has developed between some professional journalists and open source researchers, allowing both to complement and strengthen each other's work, providing journalism with a badly needed infusion of vitality and credibility.

© 2024 World Scientific Publishing Company
https://doi.org/10.1142/9781800614079_0008

Chapter 3.2

Saviour or Menace? Crowdsourcing Open Source Research and the Rise of QAnon

Aric Toler

Abstract

Crowdsourcing volunteer research can enable open source investigations to proceed more quickly, cheaply and effectively. Public contributions to larger research projects have proven able to provide positive outcomes in achieving transparency and justice to crimes and wrongdoing. However, they can also be the route to inaccurate findings and subsequent destructive mob justice. This chapter explores both the benefits of crowdsourcing and its dark side. After considering the elements of a productive crowdsourcing effort, it will examine the rise of the QAnon movement and how it was able to thrive, culminating in the 6 January 2021 US Capitol Hill riot. The movement used many techniques nearly identical to benign open source research projects. While there are limits to how far damaging applications can be restrained, methodological differences provide lessons about how best to conduct crowdsourcing so that it generates reliable findings while also guarding against harmful trends.

Introduction

Aliaume Leroy and Benjamin Strick sent out tweets[1,2] in July 2018 asking their followers to help determine the location of a video of Cameroonian

---

[1] Leroy A. With @EmmanuelFreuden, we are trying to geolocate that video. We want to find the exact village... *Twitter*. 11 July 2018. Available from: https://twitter.com/Yaolri/status/1017034469121908737 [Accessed 12 June 2021].

[2] Strick B. The video of #Cameroonian executions of mothers and children by alleged Military forces has evidence that will lead to the exact location... *Twitter*. 14 July 2018. Available from: https://twitter.com/BenDoBrown/status/1018042303783620608 [Accessed 12 June 2021].

This is an open access article published by World Scientific Publishing Europe Ltd. and distributed under the terms of the Creative Commons Attribution-NonCommercial 4.0 International (CC BY-NC 4.0) License.

soldiers leading two women and two young children to their executions. Aliaume was with the BBC Africa Eye team, an investigative unit that heavily relied upon digital open source materials for their research,[3] and Ben would soon be hired to join him. Following the tips gathered through crowdsourced efforts, alongside other systematic analyses, the videos were located as coming from a village in northern Cameroon and the soldiers were identified in large part because of their publicly visible Facebook pages. The collective research was synthesized into the BBC Africa Eye's Peabody-winning documentary *Anatomy of a Killing*.[4]

While much of the legwork of this investigation was handled by professional journalists, human rights investigators and local sources, there were also significant contributions from anonymous amateur enthusiasts, as demonstrated in the film's closing credits, which list four people based on their online handles: @Sector035, @JHarris_UK, @MFlumf, and 'Samir' (@obretix). For proper analysis of the blurry execution video, expertise and professionalism were not enough. It also required dozens of hours of decentralized labour to conduct rote tasks, such as matching backgrounds and trawling through Facebook profiles. Ultimately, thanks largely to the findings of the *Anatomy of a Killing* investigation[5] and the international attention it brought, the men who carried out this execution were arrested and charged[6] for murder in Cameroon.

The crowdsourced research harnessed by the *Anatomy of a Killing* team led to as close as one can get to unequivocally positive results, generating clear findings about an unambiguous atrocity, and triggering a formal process of accountability and justice. However, there are questions about the extent to which this case is an outlier. Most people who can name an instance of crowdsourced research would point to a far different and more irresponsible effort: the misidentification of suspects

---

[3]This chapter defines open source materials as those that are publicly available.
[4]Chapter 2.1 of this volume (by Benjamin Strick) details the BBC Africa Eye investigation into the murders.
[5]Human Rights Watch. Cameroon: Soldiers Get 10 Years for Murder of Civilians. *Human Rights Watch*. 23 September 2020. Available from: https://www.hrw.org/news/2020/09/23/cameroon-soldiers-get-10-years-murder-civilians [Accessed 12 June 2021].
[6]BBC Africa Eye. *Anatomy of a Killing* [video online]. 2018. Available from: https://www.youtube.com/watch?v=XbnLkc6r3yc [Accessed 14 May 2023].

in the 2013 Boston Marathon bombing, largely organized on Reddit at r/FindBostonBombers.[7]

The line between digital mob vigilantes and responsible investigation can be almost invisible. Even the most well-intentioned crowdsourcing campaigns can incorrectly identify a person as guilty of some misdemeanour, and thereby bring about irreparable reputational harm to them, or worse. Two recent events that have mobilized crowdsourcing relate to the 2017 Unite the Right protest in Charlottesville US and the 6 January 2021 US Capitol Hill insurrection. Along with non-governmental and self-organized crowdsourced digital research, the Federal Bureau of Investigation (FBI) and other law enforcement bodies responded to these events with specific requests to the public to help identify those suspected of wrongdoing. Much of the online community involved in these efforts acted responsibly and self-moderated, but for events that have as wide-ranging interest and emotional responses as these, both intentional and unintentional harm is possible and perhaps inevitable.

For a lesson in how crowdsourced digital investigation can be highly organized and deeply irresponsible, we look to the evolution of QAnon. This movement began on the anonymized social media platform 4chan, where a member participating in the popular genre of 'larping' (live action role playing) pretended to be a high-level government insider with exclusive information. It then grew into a 'crowdsourced conspiracy' with millions of adherents[8,9] who were motivated by cryptic posts, or 'Q drops', to uncover 'hidden truths' embedded within publicly available information. Many of the fundamental techniques and elements from the *Anatomy of a Killing* crowdsourcing effort were used in the QAnon movement, but with far different results. This chapter details aspects of QAnon's rise. After identifying

---

[7]Lee D. Boston bombing: How internet detectives got it very wrong. *BBC*. 19 April 2013. Available from: https://www.bbc.co.uk/news/technology-22214511 [Accessed 12 June 2021].

[8]Bellingcat: The Q Origins Project. The Making of QAnon: A Crowdsourced Conspiracy. *Bellingcat*. 7 January 2021. Available from: https://www.bellingcat.com/news/americas/2021/01/07/the-making-of-qanon-a-crowdsourced-conspiracy/ [Accessed 12 June 2021].

[9]PRRI Staff. Understanding QAnon's Connection to American Politics, Religion, and Media Consumption. *PRRI*. 27 May 2021. Available from: https://www.prri.org/research/qanon-conspiracy-american-politics-report/ [Accessed 12 June 2021].

attributes of ethical crowdsourcing , it examines QAnon's methods and how these depart from the principled approaches.

Ethical Institutional Crowdsourcing

Successful and responsible investigative crowdsourcing campaigns are often set up with concrete goals and tasks, allowing contributors to approach a problem with a realistic scope and framework. Specifying project goals and tasks is half of the requirements for constructive digital investigation crowdsourcing. The other half is having access to contributors who bring at least one of two competencies: local and immediate knowledge, and/or enthusiasm. The local and immediate knowledge element provides simple shortcuts – if someone quickly recognizes a location, person or object, then an investigative task can be quickly solved. For many campaigns, including something as ubiquitous as a 'most wanted' poster calling for people to simply identify the face of a person, this type of local and immediate knowledge is the only thing necessary and desired from contributors. Meanwhile, the second element, enthusiasm, is often needed for larger problems, and allows volunteers to sort through large amounts of information and work far faster and cheaper than is possible for a small, salaried newsroom or investigative unit.[10]

Outside of journalism, calls for help from the public to solve difficult investigations[11] is far from new, with a notable example being American law enforcement asking for, and finding success in, crowdsourcing tips with television programmes such as *America's Most Wanted* and *Unsolved Mysteries*, which dramatize real-life crimes and ask for assistance in identifying or locating the suspects. In the case of *America's Most Wanted,* a 2013 study[12] showed that a fugitive's appearance on the television programme 'substantially' increases the rate of apprehension of criminals, and

---

[10] Other chapters in this volume consider the advantages, challenges and practicalities of working across diffuse collaborative networks. See, for example, chapters by Wilson, Samuel & Plesch, Freeman & Koenig, Ahmad, and Bedenko & Bellish (Chapters 1, 2.5, 3.1 and 5.4).

[11] Velez M. See Something, Say Something, Send Something: Everyone Is a Cyber Detective. *Police Chief Magazine*. 2018. Available from: https://www.policechiefmagazine.org/see-something-say-something-send-something/ [Accessed 12 June 2021].

[12] Miles T. J. Estimating the Effect of America's Most Wanted: A Duration Analysis of Wanted Fugitives. *The Journal of Law and Economics*. 2005, 48 (1), pp. 281–306.

decreases their time on the run. Local and immediate knowledge is clearly important here – neither the police nor the television programme is asking for viewers to go out, play detective and find suspects; rather, the task is for viewers to just call in tips if they recognize somebody on their screen.

A modern evolution of the *America's Most Wanted* model of public intelligence gathering can be seen in Europol's 'Stop Child Abuse – Trace an Object' campaign, launched in 2017. This online project requests public assistance to identify specific objects visible in images depicting child abuse and exploitation. The objects are completely isolated and edited to be devoid of all indications of the original harmful and explicit content, and then shared on Europol's Trace an Object website (for example, see Fig. 1). Such objects include shopping bags, shirts and toys, and identifying them can lead researchers to a better understanding of when and where the original abuse was likely to have taken place, and thus can lead to the rescue of the children and apprehension of the suspects. Volunteers can submit their tips about the objects directly on Europol's site, as seen below, or through various social media channels where people can follow up on each other's ideas. Europol has stated that, as of March 2021, this programme has led to 'over

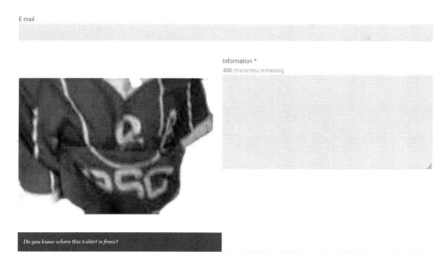

Figure 1: Europol tip submission form on their website (europol.europa.eu).[13]

---

[13] Note from the editors. We are very grateful to Europol for its kind permission to use the images from 'Europol's Stop Child Abuse – Trace an Object' campaign. The low resolution of the images follows that of the originals, which were cropped from sources to omit harmful content.

26,000' tips, the rescue of ten children victims, and the identification and prosecution of three suspects.

Dedicated online communities of amateur sleuths have emerged to meticulously study and identify the listed objects, organizing independently of Europol. On Reddit, by June 2021, the r/TraceAnObject community[14] had garnered over 75,000 members, where new threads emerge for each object shared by Europol, attracting dozens of comments within days. After Reddit, the second-most popular arena for public exchanges on these objects is Twitter, where discussion is organized either in replies and quotes of Europol's tweets or with the #TraceAnObject hashtag.

For example, on 19 May 2021, Europol shared a photograph of a wristband, with the caption 'Do you have any idea where this wristband is from?' (see Fig. 2). On Twitter, the official @Europol account with over 100,000 followers tweeted the image, with the caption 'Are you regular [sic] surfing the net? If so, we need you!'[15] On Reddit, a moderator of the r/TraceAnObject community with the username I_Me_Mine, posted a thread with just the image and the original description provided on the Trace an Object site.[16]

On the same day of the tweet and Reddit thread, users unearthed a huge amount of information related to the object. The wristband, as the user

Figure 2: Wristband from Europol's Stop Child Abuse – Trace an Object Campaign.

---

[14]Trace An Object & FBI Endangered Child Alert Program. *Reddit*. Available from: https://www.reddit.com/r/TraceAnObject/ [Accessed 12 June 2021].

[15]Europol. Are you regular surfing the net? If so, we need you!... *Twitter*. 14 May 2021. Available from: https://twitter.com/Europol/status/1393175530120388611 [Accessed 12 June 2021].

[16]r/TraceAnObject – [TAO: 17578] 19-MAY-2021 Do you have any idea where this wristband is from? *Reddit*. Available from: https://www.reddit.com/r/TraceAnObject/comments/ng2qm3/tao_17578_19may2021_do_you_have_any_idea_where/ [Accessed 16 June 2021].

Saviour or Menace? Crowdsourcing Open Source Research and the Rise of QAnon   153

communities detailed, is from the American grocery store Kroger, that gives the bands to children at either their in-house daycare, or at public events they sponsor. One Reddit user wrote that they 'worked at Kroger during high school'[17] and recognized the wristband, while others found an online image album showing children wearing similar wristbands at a public event in Michigan.[18] On Twitter, one person found Facebook photographs of the Michigan state fair with children wearing these same wristbands,[19] while another pulled a map of a number of Kroger's grocery stores.[20] All of this information was gathered through a combination of personal experience and/or intense online sleuthing.

Trying to find obscure objects can seem like a fairly boring task – after all, how can identifying a wristband in Michigan or a grocery bag from central Europe be fun? But for many, it has become something like a game, or elaborate puzzle, or treasure hunt. Outside of praise and respect from others conducting the investigation, finding a solution for the Europol investigations in particular offers volunteers the potential to contribute to as close to an objectively good cause as one can imagine, in the rescue of abused children. In one thread in the r/TraceAnObject subreddit, a user noted how they were 'challenged' by the images, as if they were a puzzle or game to master: 'How do we get more images to trace? I'm obsessive over these images. I feel challenged to try and figure one out. Haven't even come close yet'.[21]

---

[17] u/mouseblouse on r/TraceAnObject – [TAO: 17578] 19-MAY-2021 Do you have any idea where this wristband is from? *Reddit*. Available from: https://www.reddit.com/r/TraceAnObject/comments/ng2qm3/tao_17578_19may2021_do_you_have_any_idea_where/gyq88s0/?utm_source=reddit&utm_medium=web2x&context=3 [Accessed 16 June 2021].

[18] u/paroles on r/TraceAnObject – [TAO: 17578] 19-MAY-2021 Do you have any idea where this wristband is from? *Reddit*. Available from: https://www.reddit.com/r/TraceAnObject/comments/ng2qm3/tao_17578_19may2021_do_you_have_any_idea_where/gz3rnvk/?utm_source=reddit&utm_medium=web2x&context=3 [Accessed 16 June 2021].

[19] @DaniScotchIrish. Kroger used to have child care while you shopped... *Twitter*. 20 May 2021. Available from: https://twitter.com/DaniScotchIrish/status/1395302153141596163 [Accessed 12 June 2021].

[20] @ZeDh4rm. The middle branding/logo closely resembles a grocery store chain called Krogers... *Twitter*. 15 May 2021. Available from: https://twitter.com/ZeDh4rm4/status/1393449752549859231 [Accessed 16 June 2021].

[21] u/8moves on r/TraceAnObject – bellingcat – Creating Impact: A Year On Stop Child Abuse – Trace An Object. *Reddit*. Available from: https://www.reddit.com/r/TraceAnObject/comments/g6073o/bellingcat_creating_impact_a_year_on_stop_child/fq51t93/?utm_source=reddit&utm_medium=web2x&context=3 [Accessed 12 June 2021].

However, as seen in some less well-intentioned investigations, there are darker elements that can arise, even in an institutionally grounded and well-organized research campaign such as Trace an Object. The emotional intensity of the subject at hand acts as a tremendous force motivating volunteers to make useful contributions, but along with this we can also find these communities discussing revenge fantasies against the perpetrators of child abuse, and even attempting to identify suspects. Europol has created something like guard rails in its campaigns, with careful and robust redactions of images, clear instructions about not sharing personal information related to the objects, and has fostered an online community that self-moderates and quickly reports new tips up the chain to Europol. If we were to create a blueprint of a crowdsourced investigation effort without any of these guard rails, but with the emotional intensity and enthusiasm of its volunteer efforts, it could look a lot like the QAnon movement.

Introduction to QAnon

The 4chan user 'Q' made their first post on 28 October 2017 to the popular /pol/ section of the platform's image board, reporting that the extradition of Hillary Clinton was 'already in motion', and stating that 'massive riots (will take place)' in the aftermath of the former Secretary of State's arrest (see Fig. 3).[22]

This, obviously, did not happen, but this anonymous poster has since gained millions of followers, helped inspire the US Capitol Hill insurrection of 6 January 2021, and been cited as a motivating force for numerous

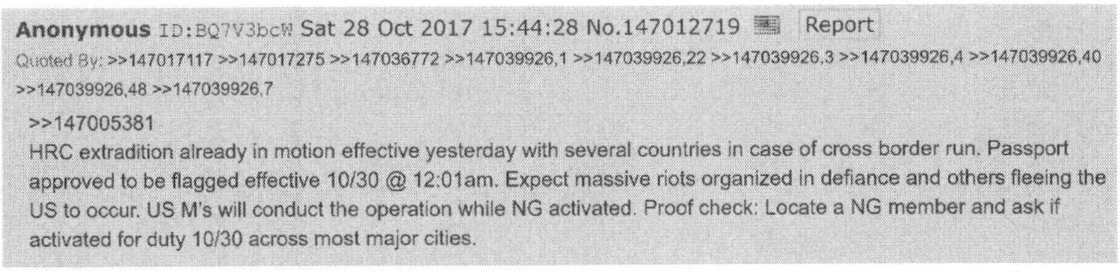
Anonymous ID:BQ7V3bcW Sat 28 Oct 2017 15:44:28 No.147012719 Report
Quoted By: >>147017117 >>147017275 >>147036772 >>147039926,1 >>147039926,22 >>147039926,3 >>147039926,4 >>147039926,40 >>147039926,48 >>147039926,7

>>147005381
HRC extradition already in motion effective yesterday with several countries in case of cross border run. Passport approved to be flagged effective 10/30 @ 12:01am. Expect massive riots organized in defiance and others fleeing the US to occur. US M's will conduct the operation while NG activated. Proof check: Locate a NG member and ask if activated for duty 10/30 across most major cities.

Figure 3: The first 'Q drop' from 2017, posted on 4chan.

[22] 4Plebs.org [online]. Available from: https://archive.4plebs.org/pol/thread/146981635/#q147012719 [Accessed 16 June 2021].

violent crimes ranging from murder to kidnapping.[23] With themes and baseless assertions carried over from the Pizzagate conspiracy community that emerged in 2016, in which unfounded accusations were made about a fictitious paedophilia ring related to a pizzeria associated with Hillary Clinton and the Democratic Party, QAnon became an all-encompassing conspiracy movement that was preoccupied with allegations of children being kidnapped and abused, and claims that then-President Trump was leading a secret war against the political, economic and media elite conducting these fantasy crimes.

Despite the first QAnon Q drop proving to be a failed prophecy, the movement has grown from a single obscure 4chan member to having millions of adherents, many of whom had never heard of 4chan before joining. How did this happen? A relatively straightforward way to answer this may be to consider the differences between the promises of presidential candidate Trump, and the reality of President Trump. On the campaign trail, Trump repeatedly promised to 'lock her up', referring to Hillary Clinton. All through Trump's presidency, Clinton still walked free, so an alternate reality was sought, in which she was either on the verge of being extradited or had already been secretly arrested, to assuage this cognitive dissonance. Some have pointed to the religious aspects of the movement – as one author put it, it is 'A New American Religion'[24] – as the QAnon community heavily relies on Christian evangelical language and themes. Others have pointed out[25] that QAnon resembles an ARG (alternate reality game), where players piece together 'clues' that have been incorporated into the real world, which acts as the setting of a large, narrative-driven mystery or challenge.

All of these elements feed into one of the most powerful appeals of QAnon: It seemingly offers a perspective into a secret world operating in plain sight. Adherents to QAnon frequently refer to their 'awakening'

---

[23]Beckett L. QAnon: A timeline of violence linked to the conspiracy theory. *The Guardian*. 16 October 2020. Available from: http://www.theguardian.com/us-news/2020/oct/15/qanon-violence-crimes-timeline [Accessed 12 June 2021].

[24]Nyce C. M. The Atlantic Daily: QAnon Is a New American Religion. *The Atlantic*. 14 May 2020. Available from: https://www.theatlantic.com/newsletters/archive/2020/05/qanon-q-pro-trump-conspiracy/611722/ [Accessed 12 June 2021].

[25]Rabbit Rabbit. Berkowitz R. A Game Designer's Analysis of QAnon: Playing with Reality. *Medium; Curiouser Institute*. 30 September 2020. Available from: https://medium.com/curiouserinstitute/a-game-designers-analysis-of-qanon-580972548be5 [Accessed 12 June 2021].

and directly invoke *Alice in Wonderland* ('going down the rabbit hole' and 'following the white rabbit') and *The Matrix* ('taking the red pill'), reflecting how QAnon provides its followers with a fundamental rearrangement of perspectives on politics, economics and even the nature of reality itself.

QAnon is not a static ideology or set of canonical texts that require strict adherence; rather, it is a malleable collection of loose assertions and frayed connections that centre on the concrete tenets that present Trump as a force for good and his enemies as evil powers involved in kidnapping and abusing children. Exactly who these evil people are and how Trump is fighting them is, by design, open to extreme interpretation, and QAnon supporters are encouraged to figure these things out by analyzing 'clues' scattered across the internet and on our television screens. Thus, QAnon becomes an à la carte ideology where a person can pick and choose the elements that they prefer, ranging from a relatively tame domestic political intrigue of Trump versus the Democrats, to anti-Semitic tropes regarding child sacrifice, and even the incorporation of other long-running irrational conspiracy theories such as the earth being flat, or that vaccination programmes will lead to the mass extermination of populations.

Crowdsourced Analysis of Q Drops

A hallmark feature of QAnon's posts, or Q drops, is their obfuscation of clear meaning. In some cases, this is done quite superficially, with easily decipherable acronyms and code words, while in other cases the language is too vague to have any obvious referent, allowing for especially creative interpretation.

At first glance, the 'research' being done around Q drops resembles the online discussion and fan theories about television shows that incorporate complex mysteries in their plotlines. Popular online communities for dissecting TV programmes have emerged with each evolution of the internet, apparent in Usenet's discussions in the 1990s of *The X-Files*, and message boards obsessing over *Lost* in the mid-2000s, with more recent social platforms analyzing shows like *Westworld* and *Game of Thrones*. Two of the many differences between QAnon research and TV fan speculation are that the latter is low stakes, and it is conducted within a closed system of

Saviour or Menace? Crowdsourcing Open Source Research and the Rise of QAnon   157

Figure 4: 'Q drop' #95, posted on 4chan in 2017.

interpretation. Fans of *The X-Files*[26] can vigorously search for clues in the script about who Fox Mulder's dad really is,[27] but ultimately the answers to this question have no actual effect on the world, and discussions stay within the parameters of the fictional world created by the show's writers and producers. By contrast, with QAnon, delusions about conspiracies encompass all aspects of life, and speculation into who is involved can, and often does, lead to real-world harassment, death threats and even violence.

Q drop #95 (see Fig. 4), posted on 5 November 2017,[28] encapsulates the QAnon formula quite well: short, punctuated lines with vague references, and invitations for readers to participate, either via leading questions or direct requests from the author:

> What happened in SA will happen here, Asia, and EU.
> Keep digging and keep organizing the info into graphics (critical).
> God bless.
> Hillary & Saudi Arabia
> Snow White
> Godfather III
> Q

---

[26] Fanlore. *alt.tv.x-files* [online]. Available from: https://fanlore.org/wiki/Alt.tv.x-files [Accessed 12 June 2021].

[27] Cancerman is Fox's Dad: it all works!!! [Google group]. Available from: https://groups.google.com/g/alt.tv.x-files/c/Z7ksjnAO3yo/m/L6KlrGctYmUJ [Accessed 12 June 2021].

[28] Intel Drop #95 [online]. Qalerts.app. Available from: https://qalerts.app/?n=95 [Accessed 16 June 2021].

The first line is relatively straightforward, as a massive purge of Saudi leadership, organized by Mohammed bin Salman, had been reported the day before the post.[29] The second line is a direct call for action through collective research ('Keep digging') and distribution of findings through easily shareable infographics. The fourth, fifth and sixth lines are much more vague – the mention of 'Hillary & Saudi Arabia' may encourage some readers to infer some corrupt relationship between the two, but 'Snow White' and 'Godfather III' invite literary interpretation rather than intelligence analysis, and are still debated years after their first mentions in Q drops.

A summary of interpretations of the cryptic reference to 'Godfather III' illustrates how problematic such posts are, as, for QAnon followers, anyone linked to this reference is assumed to be, at best, corrupt and worthy of expulsion from public life, and at worst, a murderer or child abuser. One QAnon personality who hosts a digital livestreamed show wrote[30] on Twitter that the movie reference points to CNN anchor Chris Cuomo, with the 'evidence' for this association being how Trump has referred to him as 'Fredo', which is the name of a character from the *Godfather* trilogy[31] (the fact that Fredo Corleone only appeared in *Godfather III* once in a flashback, and is more heavily featured in the two previous movies, is not considered especially relevant by this QAnon sleuth). Many others interpret 'Godfather III' as a reference to the Pope and the Catholic Church, as they feature heavily in the film. For yet others, the frequently invoked George Soros is also seen as a referent for 'Godfather III', by virtue of an anti-Semitic conspiracy that he and other financiers are the true powers running the Catholic Church.[32]

---

[29] Beauchamp Z. The purge in Saudi Arabia, explained. *Vox*. 6 November 2017. Available from: https://www.vox.com/world/2017/11/6/16613088/saudi-arabia-princes-arrested-mohammed-bin-salman [Accessed 12 June 2021].

[30] A thread written by @SeesInPixels. *Archive.org*. Available from: http://web.archive.org/web/20210602163218/https://threader.app/thread/1161697442024296449 [Accessed 12 June 2021].

[31] Clark D. "Fredo": Trump mocks CNNs Chris Cuomo with "Godfather" name. *NBC News*. 23 September 2019. Available from: https://www.nbcnews.com/politics/politics-news/giuliani-took-fredo-cleaners-trump-trashes-cnn-s-cuomo-during-n1057871 [Accessed 12 June 2021].

[32] Caffier J. A Guide to QAnon, the New King of Right-Wing Conspiracy Theories. *Vice*. 12 June 2018. Available from: https://www.vice.com/en/article/ywex8v/what-is-qanon-conspiracytheory [Accessed 16 June 2021].

All of these associations and pseudo-logical threads arose from cryptic, uncontextualized references to a movie, with Q and the mythmakers in the movement encouraging the 'digital soldiers' to keep digging and propagating their findings. This scavenging for loosely connected data points does not stop with direct requests from Q or with their specific references, as the secret world that QAnon reveals to its followers is not restricted to the 'canonical' drops hosted on 4chan, and later 8kun (formerly known as 8chan), another image board to which Q migrated in 2018.

In multiple drops, Q has asked his readers to 'Follow Sen Grassley' and 'TRUST GRASSLEY',[33] referring to the 87-year-old senator from Iowa. This focus has led to QAnon adherents latching on to every social media post from Senator Grassley, trying to interpret his tweets as part of the QAnon mythos. A sample of the Senator's tweets shows that they are messy and strange, enabling wishful QAnon advocates to look for and find hidden meaning and coded details in them. For example, 'Work on farm Fri. Burning piles of brush WindyFire got out of control. Thank God for good naber He help get undr control PantsBurnLegWound',[34] and, 'If u lost ur pet pidgin/ it's dead in front yard my Iowa farm JUST DISCOVERED here r identifiers Right leg Blue 2020/3089/AU2020/SHE ///LEFT LEG GREEN BAND NO PRINTED INFO. Sorry for bad news'.[35]

In a December 2020 Instagram post, Grassley shared a photograph of his vacuum cleaner, with the caption, 'Bc of coronavirus I wasn't home w my family for Thanksgiving. I have to help around the house for Christmas so 2day my chore is w my vacuum, Beth. She's 38+ yrs old'.[36] This post is a bit odd, but probably not deserving of exegesis. However, QAnon self-styled researchers treat Grassley's posts like passages from James Joyce's *Finnegan's Wake*, noting that the vacuum cleaner was made by Hoover, so Grassley may be leaving a hidden reference to the FBI, as the first director

---

[33] Intel Drop #2445 [online]. Qalerts.app. Available from: https://qalerts.app/?n=2445 [Accessed 12 June 2021].
[34] Grassley C. Work on farm Fri... *Twitter*. 11 April 2009. Available from: https://twitter.com/chuckgrassley/status/1494816858 [Accessed 12 June 2021].
[35] Grassley C. If u lost ur pet pidgin... *Twitter*. 19 September 2020. Available from: https://twitter.com/ChuckGrassley/status/1307421592411156482 [Accessed 12 June 2021].
[36] Grassley C. Bc of coronavirus I wasn't home w my family for Thanksgiving... *Instagram*. Available from: https://www.instagram.com/p/CJMl2tgjyax/?igshid=1nyap781g3r21&hl=en [Accessed 12 June 2021].

of the FBI was J. Edgar Hoover.[37] For QAnon participants, there must be some coded meaning in this post beyond a middle-aged vacuum cleaner and Christmas Eve chores; as one QAnon believer put it, 'Grassley's bizarre tweets always have meaning'.[38]

As noted above, Europol's Trace an Object campaign sets clear objectives and carefully constructed guard rails that motivate the average internet user to contribute to research that could help save children from abuse. QAnon offered the same end goal – saving children from abuse – but was built on a bedrock of disinformation, and deliberately avoided implementing guard rails. Sometimes, this leads to fairly harmless crowdsourced research, such as creative interpretations about Grassley's vacuum cleaner, but more often the investigations are malicious, accusing anyone perceived to oppose Trump, such as Chris Cuomo and other journalists, of being a member of an elite cabal of child abusers. This QAnon research is not done in isolated pockets, but rather is highly organized and boosted with resources and platforms similar to those used by investigative journalists. This is no accident. Ron Watkins, one of the key figures in QAnon and the administrator of Q's new home of 8kun, explained how he worked to provide QAnon adherents with guidance in conducting crowdsourced research: 'It was basically three years of intelligence training, teaching normies how to do intelligence work'.[39]

---

[37] Jones C. Grassley posted an old Hoover on his IG yesterday… *Twitter*. 25 December 2020. Available from: https://twitter.com/MyMorningDew07/status/1342541710602215425 [Accessed 12 June 2021].

[38] qanon.news: Q drops, POTUS Tweets and offsite archive [online]. Archive.org. Available from: https://web.archive.org/web/20210601164531/https://qanon.news/Archives/clone/12159101?__cf_chl_managed_tk__=9f2466a2ea5c74ed1fe22cd7d5e2b16c6896f1d1-1622565900-0-Ae91GY udamlTj-cpknRadWH4qF89riwHHS2diUMlm7AJ7TM5FgSVyc89nGAq_b9VuGBRpdn8jtAjHu VtOcyiqU0FvThxAWNkBfGuPDjkAA-a3Hx3LEKsCHY6Q7lPYuMKfOWaxH2JxgT1K_Pzn5A aowOHvK8LQTO7WLviF5VbTI5OMX3pozdKNkFIz_EwtildyUoUyh2rkfWSB0DWZG1Z-LKX RtkjXqighedzykRkQ6vZTOabaocy7EP87Rw9SX34YWHuQQ3670AIpFeHaQKcLfNvYLw4xBg aYcVG17dLuIOcJotk5Qlleig4fultNcI1fSHCcJsgICO4b5LAjH3--APdDjxXrgCdRCCc6BuxOFoF kXL5Dow3en-nAY7_uSguOgnLlQPgjpOn2IToq4up2JQr0OF0rz1Bk1j68M4WoQoDCAArhxQ54 62_Y-bhixhzCuc0WG2--BSRZaEBnHeXnLkSki03DjJC61FM00pMM9ozS91l62yY3I_rIKPZZ-I AlJAFsk1bWQfSv2Ap4jtNeLE0P-ibewcQsEU5bMVR0C3gZ_ycEgadmT29lCDH98qR8GxkuV_ aPZLiiPBkIoNxSc0EULDC4R_xax_WRMy3k0sqi2jkIS5NMRR36oPYvkQOvSDXkeeFHNV2xy TfYHpWkpU [Accessed 5 June 2023].

[39] Harwell D., and Timberg C. A QAnon revelation suggests the truth of Q's identity was right there all along. *Washington Post*. 5 April 2021. Available from: https://www.washingtonpost.com/technology/2021/04/05/ron-watkins-qanon-hbo/ [Accessed 12 June 2021].

QAnon Collective Interpretation

Where and how does QAnon's research and organization take place? The largest arenas for collective research and interpretation around QAnon are as follows:

- Major social media platforms (Twitter, Telegram, YouTube, etc.);
- 'Alt-tech' social media platforms (Gab, Parler, etc.);
- QAnon-related podcasts and livestreaming shows;[40]
- 8kun's QResearch channels;[41]
- The QResear.ch website.[42]

In 2020, most mainstream Western social media platforms banned QAnon content by suspending influential QAnon accounts and reducing the visibility of QAnon-related terms and slogans. However, before these actions, QAnon content was almost completely unmoderated, allowing its rapid growth from an obscure 4chan member to a worldwide movement. By using social networks like Twitter and Instagram, QAnon communities have been able to easily coordinate their investigations and subsequently harass their 'research subjects' – most often journalists, celebrities and politicians – in the same place.[43,44] Following the 6 January 2021 Capitol Hill insurrection, the messaging application Telegram is the only major platform that has little to no moderation of large QAnon accounts.

For QAnon followers who have been banned or chose to leave popular social platforms, 'alt-tech' sites – which include Gab and Parler – have offered a safe haven, along with others on the far right.[45] At the time of

---

[40] Arbel T. Extremists exploit a loophole in social moderation: Podcasts on Apple, Google. *USA Today*. 16 January 2021. Available from: https://www.usatoday.com/story/tech/2021/01/15/apple-google-podcasts-qanon-extremist-loophole-capitol-riot/4184444001/ [Accessed 12 June 2021].

[41] /qresearch/ – Q Research [online]. 8Kun.top. Available from: https://8kun.top/qresearch/index.html [Accessed 12 June 2021].

[42] QResear.ch. *QResear.ch – The 8chan/8kun QResearch Board Search* [online]. Available from: https://qresear.ch [Accessed 12 June 2021].

[43] Ryan M. QAnon Came For Me. *Medium: CtrlAltRightDelete*. 20 September 2020. Available from: https://medium.com/ctrlaltrightdelete/qanon-came-for-me-5627eac57e10 [Accessed 12 June 2021].

[44] Dickson E. J. Did QAnon Drive Chrissy Teigen from Twitter? *Rolling Stone*. 25 March 2021. Available from: https://www.rollingstone.com/culture/culture-news/chrissy-teigen-deletes-twitter-qanon-1143259/ [Accessed 12 June 2021].

[45] Bond S. Unwelcome On Facebook And Twitter, QAnon Followers Flock To Fringe Sites. *NPR*. 31 January 2021. Available from: https://www.npr.org/2021/01/31/962104747/unwelcome-on-facebook-twitter-qanon-followers-flock-to-fringe-sites [Accessed 12 June 2021].

writing (2021–2022), Gab in particular is the new home for the largest number of QAnon 'prophets', whose interpretations of Q drops trickle down to the rest of the community. Many of these figures host podcasts, regularly livestream broadcasts and produce other programmes that discuss world events through the lens of QAnon. A number of mainstream figures, such as General Michael Flynn, have appeared on these QAnon-focused shows, which boast tens of thousands of viewers.[46]

The QResearch channels hosted on 8kun and other platforms provide a space for organized user communities that behave somewhat similarly to the Europol-inspired Trace an Object groups on Reddit and Twitter, but without any hint of responsibility or caution in their research processes. There are fewer participants on these channels than on other platforms, as 8kun is not easily accessible to average internet users, but the community is as active as it is passionate in researching the 'crumbs' left behind by Q.

Some QAnon sites include investigative resources such as databases and links to external sites that list business registrations, flight records and personal information made searchable to assist in QAnon 'research'. In particular, the QResear.ch website hosts what it claims are nearly 20 million data points, ranging from QAnon-specific resources (archived Q drops, posts from other QAnon research channels, etc.) to mainstream, legitimate investigative databases, such as the Panama Papers and a list of hundreds of helicopter crashes (see Fig. 5).

Superficially, this site is not dissimilar to portals used by investigative journalists who collect and index many of the same databases to assist researchers uncovering corruption and financial crimes. In fact, QResear.ch pulls from many of the databases listed on the Organized Crime and Corruption Reporting Project (OCCRP) Investigative Dashboard,[47] which has catalogued and made searchable hundreds of databases, leaks and other sources of information used by investigative journalists worldwide. However, unlike the OCCRT, all the platforms used for crowdsourced QAnon research were mobilized to generate a string of conspiracies around baseless

---

[46]Greenspan R. E. After his pardon, Michael Flynn appears to be deepening his ties to the QAnon conspiracy theory. *Insider*. 10 December 2020. Available from: https://www.insider.com/michael-flynn-trump-pardon-qanon-2020-12?render-embed=video [Accessed 12 June 2021].

[47]OCCRP [online]. Available from: https://id.occrp.org/ [Accessed 16 June 2021].

Saviour or Menace? Crowdsourcing Open Source Research and the Rise of QAnon

```
     110  Mass Shootings (events - since 1982) from "Mother Jones - Mass Shootings Database, 1982 - 2019"-list
   1,096  Executive Orders (since 1994) from federalregister.gov
  33,709  Hillary Clinton Emails from WikiLeaks
  59,148  Podesta Emails from WikiLeaks
  44,041  DNC Emails from WikiLeaks
 138,185  Bahamas Leaks (Names and Companies) from ICIJ Offshore Leaks Database
 168,758  Offshore Leaks (Names and Companies) from ICIJ Offshore Leaks Database
 212,321  Panama Papers (Names and Companies) from ICIJ Offshore Leaks Database
 171,376  Paradise Papers (Names and Companies) from ICIJ Offshore Leaks Database
3,727,246 White House Visitors (2009-2014) from archives.gov
```

Figure 5: Some of the databases hosted on the QResear.ch site, which allow users to search a single resource that combines and indexes all of these information sources.

accusations, including those incorrectly claiming voter fraud in the 2020 US presidential election.

How QAnon Crowdsourced Disinformation and Harassment

The two months following the November 2020 US presidential election were likely the high water mark of the QAnon movement. Trump's electoral defeat struck a blow at the cornerstone of the QAnon mythos, where the voting result was not seen as just a standard flip between Republican and Democratic presidents, but rather as an existential crisis in which QAnon adherents reasoned massive fraud must have occurred to displace the man who had always been portrayed as destined to be inevitably victorious over a secret cabal of child abusers. QAnon is a participatory conspiracy at its core, in which Q would ask their followers to research and propagate their creative writing exercises masquerading as intelligence leaks. Thus, it fell upon this community to find the implied wrongdoing that led to Trump's defeat and take action to reverse it, and these efforts ultimately culminated in the 6 January 2021 Capitol Hill insurrection.

In this case, crowdsourced QAnon 'research' largely focused on baseless disinformation about Dominion Voting Systems, the organization that provided much of the infrastructure for many of the voting arrangements used in the election. The conspiracies that emerged in the weeks after the election held that Dominion had deleted or modified legitimate votes to prevent Trump's victory, and that it had left behind traces of its actions that could be discovered by QAnon enthusiasts and other Trump supporters. These conspiracies were boosted by then-President Trump and many of those close to him, including his lawyers Rudy Guiliani and Sydney Powell, and Fox News host Jeanine Pirro.[48]

Ron Watkins was one of the organizers of the campaign around Dominion, trying to mobilize QAnon 'digital soldiers' to find evidence of voter fraud. He asked his QAnon followers to go to the voting counting sites in Georgia that had Dominion staffers, and film the tabulation process from various angles.[49] Some of his followers did make it to the sites, and Watkins shared a video filmed in Gwinnett County supposedly showing a Dominion staffer using a USB drive to commit voter fraud.[50] On the QResearch channel, anonymous users identified this Dominion staffer by finding his LinkedIn page. From there, the QResearch users found his old college assignments hosted online, his Facebook, his Instagram, his address, his sister's Facebook and other personal details.[51] As one user replied in the thread doxxing[52] the Dominion staffer, 'Thanks CodeMonkeyZ [Ron Watkins]. Took 4chan 20 minutes!' The next day, a noose was left outside the Dominion staffer's house.[53] In the months following these unfounded conspiracy theories that cast doubt on the electoral process, a number of states have passed laws that restrict voting access in order to create 'electoral integrity'.[54]

---

[48] Atlantic Council's DFRLab. #StopTheSteal: Timeline of Social Media and Extremist Activities Leading to 1/6 Insurrection. *Just Security*. 17 February 2021. Available from: https://www.justsecurity.org/74622/stopthesteal-timeline-of-social-media-and-extremist-activities-leading-to-1-6-insurrection/ [Accessed 12 June 2021].

[49] Ron. The public addresses of the Georgia Dominion Voting Machine delivery points. #DominionWatch. *Twitter*. 30 November 2020. Available from: *Archive.org*. http://web.archive.org/web/20201130100705/https://twitter.com/CodeMonkeyZ/status/1333351626371866625 [Accessed 12 June 2021].

[50] (We) Are The News [online]. *Archive.org*. Available from: http://web.archive.org/web/20210604150910/https://wearethene.ws/notable/175188 [Accessed 12 June 2021].

[51] /qresearch/ – Q Research [online]. Archive.org. Available from: http://web.archive.org/web/20210604160233/https://8kun.top/qresearch/res/11851518.html [Accessed 12 June 2021].

[52] Revealing the personal details and identity of individuals online.

[53] Greenspan R. E. A QAnon harassment campaign led to a noose being left at the home of a young Dominion contractor, according to a Georgia official. *Insider*. 3 December 2020. Available from: https://www.insider.com/dominion-voting-qanon-harassment-campaign-noose-georgia-fraud-2020-12 [Accessed 16 June 2021].

[54] Benner K. Meadows Pressed Justice Dept. to Investigate Election Fraud Claims. *The New York Times*. 5 June 2021. Available from: https://www.nytimes.com/2021/06/05/us/politics/mark-meadows-justice-department-election.html [Accessed 12 June 2021].

Pandora's Box Opened

The rise of QAnon shows the sinister possibilities of crowdsourced digital investigations, and where these can lead – including the threatened and actual harm to people and property seen in the 6 January 2021 Capitol Hill insurrection. Due to the very nature of digital, open source investigations, the requisite tools and methodologies are widespread, accessible and either free or very inexpensive to use. Coordinated harassment and disinformation using these techniques may be inevitable, even with strict and attentive content moderation from major platforms and services, which history shows can't be relied on.

Many of the processes that led QAnon to misidentify an innocent Dominion staffer are identical to those used by open source researchers to correctly identify the guilty perpetrators of human rights abuses. Without all-encompassing, repressive censorship, it is impossible to completely mitigate irresponsible speech and research online, whether it be the doxxing of an innocent person or the propagation of disinformation on vaccines. This tenet should be reflected in how organizers of responsible and fruitful crowdsourcing campaigns construct a path for their volunteer contributors. Irresponsible research efforts lead with open questions that invite the open identification of individuals, as seen in collective research around the Boston Bombing and, most egregiously, the activities of QAnon communities.

More responsible campaigns avoid open-ended queries and focus on specific tasks – can you identify *this object*, can you *submit information* on a specific individual, can you *identify the time and location* of a photograph or video? Surrounding these tasks are guard rails that, ideally, contain the more wild and speculative elements of a research effort. These guard rails can comprise limiting the submission of identities to a restricted form, or heavily censoring an image to isolate just an object or location to protect and respect victims' privacy.

Volunteers in crowdsourcing campaigns are motivated by a range of factors, but a common one is the desire to right what feels wrong, and participate in seemingly remote world events. When this passion is directed irresponsibly, the consequences are all too clear; however, responsible crowdsourcing is possible. As we see in Europol's 'Trace an Object' campaign and the *Anatomy of a Killing* documentary, with care, passionate volunteers can positively steer the world through digital sleuthing.

© 2024 World Scientific Publishing Company
https://doi.org/10.1142/9781800614079_0009

Chapter 3.3

Collecting Conflict Data Worldwide: ACLED's Contribution

Andrea Carboni and Clionadh Raleigh

Abstract

The Armed Conflict Location & Event Data Project (ACLED) compiles and curates a dataset of individual political disorder events across the world. Its focus is on political violence and protest, and it monitors the activity of a variety of conflict actors and armed groups, as well as multiple forms of unrest. Unlike other datasets that use machine-led coding, ACLED relies on a researcher-led data collection process that allows for the incorporation of conflict and protest events from a wide range of sources, including local-language media, conflict observatories and other situation reports, which mitigates overreliance on international news agencies. This chapter provides an overview of ACLED's contribution to the open source research community, discussing its methodology, coding and sourcing strategies in relation to other conflict datasets, using case study examples to explore and demonstrate ACLED's unique approach.

Introduction

Disaggregated conflict datasets have advanced the understanding of the contexts and mechanisms of violence onset, diffusion and escalation within and across states. By breaking down data about conflict, micro-level event catalogues have provided important insights into the agents and geographies of violence. Most datasets have typically been based on country-level studies, drawing upon historical or archival research. While useful,

---

This is an open access article published by World Scientific Publishing Europe Ltd. and distributed under the terms of the Creative Commons Attribution-NonCommercial 4.0 International (CC BY-NC 4.0) License.

these raise methodological questions about the extent to which conclusions from such within-country studies can be generalized to other contexts. Over the past two decades, however, the greater availability of open source data – including online access to traditional and new media – has allowed for large-scale, georeferenced data collection efforts spanning multiple countries.

The Armed Conflict Location & Event Data Project (ACLED) has a unique role in this space, as it monitors a very wide set of events, and because it has developed and implemented robust tracking methodologies involving a global network of researchers and partner organizations. As part of this, it has built up, and supports, an international group of associates, who work to common standards to collect multiple data points and develop clearer understanding of global events.[1] It disseminates its research by publishing weekly reports and has full transparency about its sources of information and research methods, providing its end users with reliable, near real-time insights into patterns of political violence.

Formally launched as an academic project to record political violence in African countries,[2] ACLED has since evolved into a global organization that monitors different forms of political disorder across the world. It applies a broad definition of disorder, which incorporates international wars and large-scale civil conflicts, as well as unrest in countries that are typically not included in conflict datasets, such as situations in which conflict actors engage in violent or destabilizing behaviour that does not fall within traditional conceptualizations of conflict. Unlike other datasets that use fully automated processes to gather data on conflict events, ACLED relies on researcher-led collection and categorization of contemporaneous media coverage and situation reports, along with accounts from local partners, conflict observatories and local-language media. This reliance on local sources is crucial to achieving accurate and thorough coverage,[3] especially

---

[1] Several other chapters in this volume present examples of distributed networks of people collaborating on open source investigations. See, for example, the chapters by Freeman & Koenig, Ahmad, H. Wilson *et al.*, and Bedenko & Bellish (Chapters 2.5, 3.1, 4.1 and 5.4). Meanwhile, Toler (Chapter 3.2) warns against the dangers of crowdsourced research that is poorly designed and conducted.
[2] Raleigh C., Linke A., Hegre H., and Karlsen J. Introducing ACLED: An Armed Conflict Location and Event Dataset. *Journal of Peace Research*. 2010, 47 (5), pp. 651–660.
[3] See also the chapter by Duke in this volume (Chapter 2.2) for details of local monitors that track small arms and light weapons in South Sudan.

in areas around the world where violence rarely gets reported by international news agencies.

Over the years, ACLED has thus become an invaluable open source information repository that is available to, and relied on by, other open source research practitioners. Whether ACLED's findings are used to independently scrutinize claims by public officials or as an early warning tool to monitor the escalation of violence in volatile contexts, they demonstrate how conflict occurs in a multitude of countries. Importantly, ACLED is transparent about its methodology; its users can find out how its data were collected and reproduce its work. This benefits both data developers and user communities, lending credibility to ACLED's research and building confidence in its findings.

This chapter outlines ACLED's contribution to the open source research community. First, it details what the group monitors and how it does its work, discussing how ACLED sources events and addresses reporting biases. It then compares ACLED's inclusion criteria, methodology and sourcing to those of other conflict datasets to show how diverse approaches can result in significantly different results about political violence and protest. Finally, examples from Yemen and the United States are presented to show how ACLED data have contributed to the coverage of political disorder in those countries.

ACLED's Process and Methodology

Data collection and processing

ACLED collects evidence about multiple forms of political disorder, including both political violence and demonstrations. It is important to clarify ACLED's definitions of these terms, as they are the sole basis for determining what events are included in the ACLED dataset. ACLED characterizes 'political violence' as the use of force by a group with political motivations or objectives, which can include the following: attempts to replace a particular agent or system of government; the protection, harassment or repression of identity groups, the wider population or political organizations; the destruction of safe, secure, public spaces; contestation over territorial control; and mob violence. Meanwhile, it classifies 'demonstrations' as any reported violent riot or peaceful protest of more than three

Table 1. ACLED event types.

General	Event Type	Sub-Event Type
Violent events	Battles	Armed clash
		Government (re)gains territory
		Non-state actor takes over territory
	Explosions/Remote violence	Chemical weapon
		Air/drone strike
		Suicide bomb
		Shelling/artillery/missile attack
		Remote explosive/landmine/IED
		Grenade
	Violence against civilians	Sexual violence
		Attack
		Abduction/forced disappearance
Demonstrations	Protests	Peaceful protest
		Protest with intervention
		Excessive force against protesters
	Riots	Violent demonstration
		Mob violence
Other	Strategic developments	Agreement
		Arrests
		Change to group/activity
		Disrupted weapons use
		Headquarters or base established
		Looting/property destruction
		Non-violent transfer of territory
		Other

people, regardless of the reported cause of the action. It includes these events because, while demonstrations are typically not considered to be 'political violence', they are forms of political disorder. Additionally, ACLED collects information on specific non-violent events or 'strategic developments', to capture contextually important events and developments which may trigger future unrest. Table 1 summarizes the event categories that ACLED captures.[4]

ACLED's broad inclusion criteria reflect an assumption that contemporary political disorder is best viewed as a spectrum of active mobilization. At one end of this, a state or international military body with an

---

[4] ACLED. *Codebook.* January 2019. Available from: https://acleddata.com/download/2827/ [Accessed 30 September 2021].

armed, hierarchical order can engage with other conflict agents and be present across a territory. In these cases, the types, intensity and frequency of the associated violence are expected to be extensive. At the other end of the spectrum are unarmed protesters engaging in occasional contestation, often with little organization, funding and capabilities. Between these two extremes are a range of different expressions of violence and disorder, such as rebel groups attempting to replace an incumbent government; militias who are 'hired' and whose objectives are closely tied to a political patron; community armed groups who provide specific security services to identity-based constituencies; cartels who require territorial and population control to engage in extensive economic rackets; violent mobs who respond to community threats with targeted violence before disbanding, that often emerge in areas with poor police presence and trust; and rioters who emerge to quickly create disorder before reconstituting or swiftly fading away. The underlying common theme of these groups and forms of disorder is that they are all organized to varying degrees in a defined time and space to pursue political objectives, and many resort to violence to achieve their aims.

Different forms of political disorder often occur simultaneously, blurring the lines between 'civil wars', 'terrorism', 'election violence' and 'communal violence'. This is one reason why, while ACLED has developed extensive classifications for different actors and events as shown in Table 1, it does not designate particular sorts of 'conflict', nor silo 'types' of conflict by assigning specific conflict categories. Problems and inaccuracies can be introduced when making these sorts of grand distinctions and aggregations, and data collection projects that make arbitrary designations and cutoffs to fit their research theme can distort findings about how violence occurs within countries by ignoring some forms while promoting others. A second reason that ACLED avoids categorizing particular conflict types is that countries that experience violence often also have concurrent activity that has little to do with the classification cleavage within a single research question. For example, to designate all violence occurring in a state within a specific time period as 'election violence', or to decide that the dozens of armed groups operating in a state are doing so within a 'civil war', could misrepresent how and why political violence occurs within states, and could instead only serve narrow research agendas. Such analytical decisions in research have stifled inquiries into how modern political violence develops, and are ultimately unnecessary. ACLED has designed its research with the aim of avoiding simplistic and misleading classifications.

Information sources

ACLED systematically collects information from a wide selection of secondary sources to capture evidence of political disorder. It does not independently verify each piece of information that it collects, but instead it regularly scans a selection of credible media outlets, partners and organizations that provide information throughout a country, and it then triangulates the information from these to develop an understanding of what is happening on the ground in given areas. The breadth and depth of sourcing are the most important factors determining a project's findings. In other words, the combination of sources that are consulted, and how these sources are used, are critical for accurate and comprehensive data collection.

Several studies of traditional and new media suggest that, together, these cover most actively reported events in conflict environments.[5] However, smaller, peripheral, nascent, complicated or less deadly conflicts are not exhaustively covered by national or international media. Further, the ways in which political violence manifests, levels of press freedom, penetration of new media and domestic politics, amongst other factors, can all impact the extent of conflict coverage. Given this, ACLED tailors its selection of information sources to specific countries or contexts. For example, national media may be integral in one context where there is a robust and free press, yet in a more closed press environment, local conflict observatories and new media sources might play a more important role. Meanwhile, ACLED has also found that extensive and accurate information collection also usually requires a robust network of local partners and local-language media.

ACLED has developed several practices to deepen its country-specific data collection, such as integrating a very wide variety of sources in its routine media scanning, and including local information. ACLED collects reports from thousands of sources in over 75 distinct languages, ranging

---

[5]Dowd C., Justino P., Kishi R., and Marchais G. Comparing 'New' and 'Old' Media for Violence Monitoring and Crisis Response: Evidence from Kenya. *Research & Politics*. July 2020, pp. 1–9.

from national newspapers to local radio. Select new forms of media are also monitored to address the limitations of traditional outlets. These include the Twitter accounts of vetted journalists and activists, as well as trusted Telegram channels or WhatsApp groups. Reports from international and non-governmental organizations are also reviewed to corroborate or challenge information, for example, from state-sanctioned sources. Overall, this extensive effort results in the weekly review of over 1,500 local and subnational sources worldwide. ACLED researchers often live and work in the environments they monitor, and hence benefit from understanding local context, language and bias.

ACLED's greatest area of advancement is in its partnerships with local conflict observatories, human rights organizations and media outlets reporting from violent spaces. ACLED has supported and extended the capacity of monitors from Thailand to Yemen, to Zimbabwe and many others. It has become a platform for groups in conflict-affected states to share resources and publicize their information, and it currently has over 60 local partners across Latin America, South Asia, Africa and more. ACLED has built this infrastructure over the past 10 years, and is the first event-based conflict data collection project to bring together such deep and established networks across the world.

Dealing with biases

Relying on secondary sources to record political disorder events entails confronting their reporting biases. ACLED has developed several approaches to minimize its own research biases and avoid perpetuating those of other sources. It is extremely careful in how it deals with the aspects of reporting that tend to be more susceptible to bias. For instance, ACLED does not record who initiated a violent encounter, because reporting sources often differ in their assessments or allegations of whose 'fault' an event might be. Further, ACLED does not publish information on the cause of particular events, neither does it predetermine which groups it will include in its assessments of cumulative fatalities, nor does it use fixed demarcations of how different groups interact. Doing so would risk introducing an external bias into event classification, based on the intentions of the researcher. It could also exacerbate the many biases within the sources it consults.

Fatality numbers are frequently the most biased and poorly reported component of conflict data.[6] Estimates are often debated and can vary widely. Conflict actors may overstate or underreport fatalities to appear strong or to avert international backlash. While ACLED identifies and uses the most conservative reports of fatality figures to minimize the chance of overcounting, this does not mitigate biases that exist around fatality figures at large, and this information cannot reliably be used to distinguish between larger conflicts or to differentiate conflict agents from each other.

The provenance of information is critical when assessing source bias.[7] Conflict parties have incentives to exaggerate their own achievements, while playing down those of their opponents. At the same time, they are often important sources of information about small-scale skirmishes or assaults in remote areas where more reputable sources lack access. In Afghanistan, for example, Taliban-affiliated media may be the only sources reporting on events within their area of control. ACLED follows the same process for all its sources, testing whether information is credible enough before including it within the profile for a specific context.

There are inherent biases involved in choosing one piece of information over another. Incorporating local partner information can sometimes involve a trade-off between detail and regular access to information; for example, these organizations often have detailed verification processes and are usually less prone to conflict biases, yet these procedures may not allow for real-time data releases. On the other hand, the broader 'narrative' of conflict emphasized by international media is biased in many other ways: These media often track large-scale events that are popular to a broad audience, rather than providing full and thorough accounts of a more representative set of activities. International sources are heavily skewed towards reports that are in English and that are written by foreign correspondents, which distorts

---

[6]Raleigh C., Kishi R., Russell O., Siegle J., and Williams W. *The Washington Post*. 2 October 2017. Available from: https://www.washingtonpost.com/news/monkey-cage/wp/2017/10/02/boko-haram-vs-al-shabaab-what-do-we-know-about-their-patterns-of-violence/ [Accessed 30 September 2021].

[7]Barranco J. and Wisler D. Validity and Systematicity of Newspaper Data in Event Analysis. *European Sociological Review*. 1999, 15 (3), pp. 301–322.

their coverage. For example, foreign and English-language correspondents may not be able to access all parts of a country, and are often based in capital cities, which can result in introducing an urban bias to their reporting.[8] English-language media may frame conflicts in a certain way, inadvertently or deliberately using different filters based on the primary audience for their reporting – for example, portraying a context that reproduces and perpetuates audience prejudices or reflects editorial interventions.[9]

Transparency

Transparency is essential when dealing with conflict data. Datasets must be valuable and practical if they are to be relied upon for analysis, and their end users should be able to access the details of how conflict data are coded and collected. To this end, it is important for a dataset's methodology to be clear and transparent. Conversely, projects that are not transparent risk spreading inaccurate interpretations of the data which may influence policy decisions, mislead public opinion and negatively affect human security. In addition to publicly available codebooks (see footnote 4), and user guides detailing the methodology of data collection and categorization, open, continual and transparent reviews and discussions of collection processes benefit both data developers and user communities.

Decisions made by research teams about what events to monitor and how to categorize these, must be consistent with the rules of the wider organization, and such rules should be explained in terms of how they create clear, consistent, relevant and robust conflict data. Not every end user will require fine-grained details about how decisions are made, but anyone should be able to find or ask for those details if they need or want them. This allows users to know exactly what assumptions and caveats are necessary when working with the data, which in turn impacts how findings from the data should be interpreted. In other words, methodological transparency is the key to trust between users and data providers, and to robust understanding about events. ACLED is designed to fulfil these principles.

---

[8]Kalyvas S. The Urban Bias in Research on Civil Wars. *Security Studies*. 2004, 13 (3), pp. 160–190.
[9]Zaheer L. War or Peace Journalism: Comparative analysis of Pakistan's English and Urdu media coverage of Kashmir conflict. *South Asian Studies*. 2020, 31 (2), pp. 713–722.

ACLED Compared to Other Conflict Datasets

Today, there are many conflict datasets that people can choose from. These datasets purport to provide unambiguous and precise evidence of political violence and aim to catalogue the constituent events of larger episodes. Yet, it is often noted that these datasets present extremely different depictions of conflict, raising questions about their individual accuracy or mutual compatibility.[10] Although there is some overlap between datasets – in other words, they aim to capture information about similar happenings – variations in how events are defined and how information is sourced can lead to substantial differences in their findings.[11]

How projects access information and where they get it from are possibly the most important factors in explaining these discrepancies. A data project can only ever be as reliable and accurate as its methodology and information sourcing allow. And while no data collection can claim to represent the 'Truth' about conflicts, as there will always be differences in information access and interpretation, some methods and sources are likely to get you closer to more reliable and robust results. To this end, as discussed above, ACLED privileges a wide and deep net of sourcing when gathering information, which comes from traditional media, select new media, public and private reporting, and partnerships with local conflict observatories. Information from these different sources is then processed using a standardized methodology. While following the same general principles, the information for each unique context is therefore a particular combination of these sourcing types, suited to the specific reporting environment in each state.[12]

Other conflict datasets use different information sources. The Uppsala Conflict Data Programme Georeferenced Event Dataset (UCDP GED) primarily uses news aggregators – which are useful in bringing together disparate sources over longer periods of time – and a selection of additional sources if the former do not generate sufficient information. However,

---

[10]Eck K. In data we trust? A comparison of UCDP GED and ACLED conflict events datasets. *Cooperation and Conflict*. 2012, 47 (1), pp. 124–141.
[11]Raleigh C., Kishi R., and Linke A. Political instability patterns are obscured by conflict dataset scope conditions, sources, and coding choices. *Humanities and Social Sciences Communications*. 2023, 10 (1), pp. 1–17.
[12]Raleigh C., Batten-Carew M., and Carboni A. Conflict Environments and Coverage. *Clingendael Netherlands Institute of International Relations*. 22 January 2018. Available from: https://www.clingendael.org/publication/conflict-environments-and-coverage [Accessed 30 September 2021].

news aggregators have in-built biases as they tend to privilege national and international news sources, and especially English-language reports. In the absence of a systematic review of local source materials, relying primarily on international sources may produce a partial representation of conflict, tilted towards the most publicized or accessible accounts. The Global Terrorism Database (GTD) also relies on online aggregators, as it reviews media articles and electronic news archives, as well as other secondary sources. Meanwhile, machine-based data collection projects – such as the Integrated Crisis Early Warning System (ICEWS) dataset and the Global Database of Events, Language, and Tone (GDELT) – use a different range of sources and monitor sources in several languages, which expands the range of information they can review.

Data collection methodologies are also key to explaining differences between conflict datasets. Rules about what events to monitor, and how to code them, determine which information is selected, how that information is categorized and what types of conflict are included. Researcher-led datasets rely on teams of people who individually review reports and digitally record relevant information according to a set methodology. In ACLED, information goes through three rounds of review before it is released, to check for cross-context consistency and to make sure events are not double counted or duplicated (which can be a regular occurrence when reviewing multiple reports on the same incident).

Unlike researcher-led datasets, machine-based coding platforms are collections of events based entirely on automated data collection and analysis,[13] without any intervening researchers. Machine-based data projects including GDELT, ICEWS and Phoenix typically allow for wider internet searches than researcher-led information collection. Relevant reports are pulled from distinct sets of sources and isolated using a selection of relevant keywords, building datasets according to a wide remit, with little to no oversight. Thus, rather than creating a potential set of events that are then reviewed according to a methodology and scrutiny schedule (as happens with most human-led projects), the inclusion criteria become the de facto methodology of the set

---

[13] Several chapters in this volume present examples of automated data collection and processing. See, for example, the chapters by L. Wilson *et al.* and Withorne (Chapters 5.1 and 5.2).

for machine-led projects. In other words, these boundaries determine the follow-on machine commands for what events to include. This often leads to inflated reporting due the inclusion of false positives – that is, events that have been included incorrectly due to duplicates or incorrect identifications which have not been spotted and rectified by a human reviewer. For example, 'sports battles' can be misinterpreted as actual violent incidents (see footnote 11). Further, such approaches could introduce an additional layer of opacity, as end-users may not have access to or understand the algorithms used to collect data.

On the other hand, for researcher-led projects, there is variation in the criteria determining the events monitored, and this can account for considerable disparities across datasets. As noted above, ACLED has a wide definition of disorder which allows it to capture reported acts of political violence and demonstrations, regardless of whether they are committed by governments, rebels, militias or others, or upon other armed groups, the government, civilians or demonstrators. Other data projects have alternative inclusion criteria. GTD, for instance, is concerned exclusively with acts of 'terrorism' carried out by non-state actors. Yet, an act of terrorism by a non-state actor is not identical to the activity of a terrorist group. Accordingly, GTD would track events involving the Islamic State that conform to its definition of terrorism, but not all acts of violence by the Islamic State are necessarily included because GTD does not categorize them all as terrorist acts.

The UCDP GED has twofold inclusion criteria. To begin with, an event must involve armed force used by one organized actor against another, or against civilians. Second, events resulting in at least one direct death at a specific location-date are only included once a threshold has been crossed of 25 battle-related deaths in a given year in a given conflict. While these criteria have been developed with the intention of identifying the most relevant conflicts in a designated space, the arbitrary cutoff of at least 25 deaths tends to obscure the activity of several armed groups operating across states, and thereby distorts the depiction of conflict. As such, some countries experiencing persistent, yet low-level, conflict may be missing from the dataset's coverage, while others may only be partially represented.

These variations in definitions and scope are important to recognize, as a dataset will only include and categorize an event of political violence if it falls within its specified inclusion criteria. Who is considered a relevant and legitimate actor in conflict is pre-determined by the mandate of the dataset; the definitions, designated sources and categorizations are critical, as they tell a user who and what is likely to be included, as well as what is missing. In turn, the rules of inclusion determine how, and to what level of detail, we understand 'violence'. This can be as simple as the number of events each dataset includes for the same conflict, to the composition of those events and the resulting interpretation of conflicts by the wider community. Inclusion criteria should therefore allow for accurate representations of political violence, while being flexible in responding to how political violence changes.

The Use of ACLED Data in Open Source Investigations

ACLED's weekly data releases seek to capture the most accurate and available information and enable near-real-time monitoring by its end users. In order to do this, ACLED has developed the ability to capture low-level events, seek accurate sources of triangulation and corroboration, work within a robust checking and updating system, and do these things at speed. Because of these characteristics, ACLED data are valued around the world, and have recently contributed to a variety of open source research projects. Thanks to their georeferenced and timely nature, ACLED data have helped inform media reporting of political violence and demonstrations across the world, assessments of humanitarian access, monitoring weapons use in conflict-affected contexts and the design of early warning systems.

For example, ACLED data have been used to strengthen analysis and reporting on the conflict in Yemen and protest policing in the United States. ACLED's open source data have provided significant insights into the evolution of violent conduct in both cases, sparking calls for greater accountability of police and military forces engaging in domestic repression or international interventions.

The case of Yemen

Since 2014, Yemen has been engulfed in a civil war that has caused what the United Nations (UN) has termed 'the single largest humanitarian crisis in the world'. In September that year, Ansarallah – an armed group hailing from Yemen's northern highlands – overran the capital Sana'a and took control of most government institutions. A few months later, Ansarallah placed the Yemeni President Abdrabbuh Mansur Hadi under arrest, and threatened to close in on the southern port city of Aden. A coalition of Arab countries spearheaded by Saudi Arabia responded to calls by Hadi – who had meanwhile fled Ansarallah-controlled areas to Aden – and launched a military intervention to restore the authority of the government and prevent Aden from falling to Ansarallah. The conflict in Yemen has gone on since then, and no permanent political or military solution has yet materialized as of early 2023.

The war in Yemen has long been overshadowed by other conflicts across the region, most notably those in Libya and Syria. Few foreign journalists covered Yemen prior to 2014, and even fewer were present in the country at the outbreak of the war. Those who continued to report from Yemen often faced movement restrictions and intimidation threats. Unlike the war in Syria, probably the most documented conflict in modern history (at least until the war against Ukraine started in 2022),[14] the events in Yemen have struggled to garner international attention.

Until 2018, both the media and aid organizations cited a figure – 10,000 people – to refer to the number of victims in the conflict. The figure, which started to circulate in 2016, was based upon estimates provided by hospitals and health centres across the country. From the very beginning, however, it was considered a significant underestimate, as many casualties – mostly combatants – are unlikely to be recorded by health clinics and therefore would not appear in their official counts.[15–17] Yet, due to the lack of reliable

---

[14] Roca C. Long read: How the Syrian War Changed How War Crimes Are Documented. *The New Humanitarian*. 1 June 2017. Available from: https://deeply.thenewhumanitarian.org/syria/articles/2017/06/01/long-read-how-the-syrian-war-changed-how-war-crimes-are-documented [Accessed 30 September 2021].

[15] Fahim K. The deadly war in Yemen rages on. So why does the death toll stand still? *The Washington Post*. 3 August 2018. Available from: https://www.washingtonpost.com/world/the-deadly-war-in-yemen-rages-on-so-why-does-the-death-toll-stand-still-/2018/08/02/e6d9ebca-9022-11e8-ae59-01880eac5f1d_story.html?noredirect=on [Accessed 30 September 2021].

[16] Ahmad (Chapter 3.1 in this volume) documents similar issues with official estimates of airstrikes.

[17] Cockburn P. The Yemen war death toll is five times higher than we think – we can't shrug off our responsibilities any longer. *The Independent*. 26 October 2018. Available from: https://www.independent.co.uk/voices/yemen-war-death-toll-saudi-arabia-allies-how-many-killed-responsibility-a8603326.html [Accessed 30 September 2021].

data, the figure remained unchanged for over two years, reinforcing a perception that the conflict in Yemen did not constitute a priority internationally.

ACLED released its first data on Yemen in 2018. To this end, it collaborated with an existing data collection project, the Yemen Data Project, which had tallied airstrikes conducted by the Saudi-led coalition since 2015. Fatality estimates provided by ACLED and the Yemen Data Project, which were limited to the numbers of victims (including both civilians and combatants) of the conflict, were five to seven times higher than official death counts. Subsequent updates to the dataset put the total reported fatalities from 2015 as being over 100,000, and these new estimates are now cited by the UN.[18]

It is important to remember that open source fatality estimates like those recorded by ACLED should not be treated as an exact count. Reporting is often imprecise or highly biased, and an accurate verification of casualties arising from each event is nearly impossible. Even so, ACLED's assessments, generated from its transparent and robust methods, have contributed to building awareness of the true scale of the conflict, although admittedly many details remain somewhat obscured by the shortage of data and absence of international reporting.

ACLED also contributed to open source investigations tracking the use of weapons in Yemen. In 2019, investigative journalism organization 'Disclose' published leaked documents showing the use of French-made weapons in the conflict, including CAESAR howitzers and tanks used for offensive purposes.[19] The French government had repeatedly denied that the weapons it sold to Saudi Arabia were used for offensive purposes, claiming instead that they were only for defence. After confirming the position of French-made weapons along the Saudi–Yemeni border and the western coast revealed in the exposed confidential documents, the journalists compared this information with open source data from ACLED showing that artillery fire killed dozens of civilians in areas situated within the range of the

---

[18] Disclose. *Made In France*. 15 April 2019. Available from: https://made-in-france.disclose.ngo/en [Accessed 30 September 2021].

[19] McCarthy T. Police criticized over heavy-handed response to peaceful protests across US. 2 June 2020. Available from: https://www.theguardian.com/us-news/2020/jun/02/police-criticized-heavy-handed-response-peaceful-protests-across-us [Accessed 30 September 2021].

CAESARs and the tanks. This investigation, which combined leaked classified material with open source data, led to calls for greater accountability of the French government into its involvement in the war in Yemen.[20]

The case of the United States

On 25 May 2020, Minneapolis police officers killed George Floyd, an unarmed Black man they suspected of using counterfeit bills. His murder sparked a wave of demonstrations across the United States (US) and the world. The largely peaceful protest movement, named Black Lives Matter (BLM), called for racial justice, and was met with violence by supremacist groups and heavy-handed crackdowns by law enforcement.[21] During the 2020 US presidential campaign, the Republican Party and then-President Donald Trump also described the racial justice movement as consisting of rioters, anarchists or violent left-wing activists.

Together with the Bridging Divides Initiative at Princeton University, ACLED began to track political violence and demonstrations in June 2020, the first data collection effort of its kind in the US.[21] The project involved monitoring hundreds of national, state and local media outlets, along with selected social media accounts that provided real-time coverage of both demonstrations and violent events. This data collection effort has resulted in the documentation of tens of thousands of events countrywide, including coverage of BLM demonstrations, law enforcement responses, and armed militia activity.

These data have contributed to corroborating or refuting the competing narratives over the perceived violence of BLM and law enforcement. For example, perceptions that the BLM movement resulted in widespread violence were discredited as the data showed that close to 95% of all demonstrations associated with the movement were peaceful. In fact, law enforcement was more likely to forcefully disperse demonstrations that were pro-BLM

---

[20] Several other chapters discuss hybrid approaches in which open source investigations involve an element of closed material. See e.g. the chapters by Wilson, Samuel & Plesch, Strick, Triebert, H. Wilson *et al.*, and Michie *et al.* (Chapters 1, 2.1, 2.4, 4.1 and 5.3).
[21] ACLED.
Introducing the US Crisis Monitor. *ACLED*. 9 July 2020. Available from: https://acleddata.com/2020/07/09/introducing-the-us-crisis-monitor/ [Accessed 30 September 2021].

than any other protest rallies. These findings have been noticed and have had a large echo in the media, and across the political spectrum.[22]

Open source data were also used in public hearings conducted in state legislatures. In February 2021, ACLED, for example, was invited to submit public testimony to the Oregon House Judiciary Committee, to provide evidence on how law enforcement responded to pro-BLM demonstrators in the state.[23] In particular, data revealed that law enforcement authorities in Oregon were significantly more likely to use force against peaceful protesters than the national average. Importantly, state- and city-level bans on tear gas did not prevent federal agents from using it to disperse protesters, with local police occasionally resorting to other forms of coercion.

Conclusion

Open source event data have transformed conflict analysis. Granular, geo-referenced data have overturned typical explanations and expected modalities of political violence across the world, allowing researchers and users to identify escalation patterns, monitor changes in the behaviour of armed groups and improve predictive scenarios for early-warning tools. While no dataset can return absolute 'Truth' about violence or conflicts, open source data can build reliable understanding of patterns of behaviour, which can in turn inform public opinion and policy-makers and allow for more transparent discussions and actions. This is what ACLED sets out to do in its monitoring of political disorder and violence, using a researcher-led coding strategy, a transparent methodology and a broad coverage of sources. The examples from Yemen and the United States, among many others, show how ACLED's open source research and data can have a considerable impact on public debate and policy decisions.

---

[22] Koerth M. The Police's Tepid Response To The Capitol Breach Wasn't An Aberration. *FiveThirty Eight*. 7 January 2021. Available from: https://fivethirtyeight.com/features/the-polices-tepid-response-to-the-capitol-breach-wasnt-an-aberration/ [Accessed 30 September 2021].
[23] ACLED. *Written Testimony*. Oregon State Legislature, House Judiciary Subcommittee on Equitable Policing. 3 February 2021. Available from: https://olis.oregonlegislature.gov/liz/2021R1/Downloads/PublicTestimonyDocument/1707 [Accessed 30 September 2021].

© 2024 World Scientific Publishing Company
https://doi.org/10.1142/9781800614079_0010

Chapter 3.4

OSINT and the US Intelligence Community: Is the Past Prologue?

Kathleen M. Vogel

Abstract

This chapter will discuss the definition and history of open source intelligence (OSINT) within the US intelligence community, and the various cultural factors that have shaped its acceptance there. It reviews the US intelligence community's use of and attitudes to OSINT, and demonstrates that despite stating a commitment to OSINT, and setting up institutional arrangements for this, the sector has often been less enthusiastic about it than might be expected, with intelligence practitioners frequently preferring intelligence derived from classified sources. Finally, the chapter considers how the growth of digital technologies and publicly available information is putting pressure on the US intelligence community to change its working relationship with OSINT, and details ways in which it might do this.

Introduction

As the various chapters in this book reflect, there is a growing interest in and demand for open source information and open source intelligence (OSINT) to understand different national and international security concerns. There are also a variety of government and non-government entities that have entered the OSINT arena. In light of these developments, it is useful to ask the following question: What role does OSINT have and what role should it

---

This is an open access article published by World Scientific Publishing Europe Ltd. and distributed under the terms of the Creative Commons Attribution-NonCommercial 4.0 International (CC BY-NC 4.0) License.

play within the US Intelligence Community (IC)?[1] This chapter looks at the historical development and use of OSINT within the IC, how cultural factors have shaped the incorporation of OSINT within intelligence practice, and how OSINT intersects with the growing information and communications revolution. It will also discuss particular challenges and opportunities OSINT poses to the IC now and in the future.

OSINT

At the outset, it is important to clarify the distinction between open source information in general and OSINT as used within US intelligence.

Definitions and use

The IC defines open source information (either in verbal, written or electronic form)[2] as that which can be obtained legally, for instance, from the internet, a human source or physical locations that US or allied forces have taken control of.[3,4] Open source information[5,6] can include, in electronic or non-electronic form, various categories, such as the following: (1) traditional media (e.g. foreign and domestic television, radio and print media); (2) information obtained via the internet which includes online publications, online reviews, blogs, discussion groups, citizen media and user-generated content (e.g. people taking pictures with their cell phones and posting them), YouTube, and social media and networking sites (e.g.

---

[1] The US Intelligence Community comprises numerous organizations and activities spanning national intelligence, military intelligence, civilian intelligence and more. See https://www.intelligence.gov/ for more information about it.

[2] Richelson J. T. Open Sources, Site Exploitation, and Foreign Materiel Acquisition, in Richelson J. T. (ed.), *The US Intelligence Community,* 7th ed. New York: Routledge. 2015. pp. 346–369.

[3] *ibid.*

[4] By contrast, see e.g. the US Congress in the 2006 Defense Authorization Act, which defines OSINT as, 'intelligence that is produced from publicly available information collected, exploited, and disseminated in a timely manner to an appropriate audience'. See: 109th Congress, *Public Law* 109–163–6 January 2006, National defense authorization act for fiscal year 2006, Subtitle D — Intelligence-Related Matters, Sec. 931. Department of Defense Strategy for Open-Source Intelligence. Available from: https://www.congress.gov/109/plaws/publ163/PLAW-109publ163.pdf [Accessed 28 July 2023].

[5] Hulnick A. The Dilemma of Open Sources Intelligence: Is OSINT Really Intelligence? In: Johnson L. K. (ed.), *The Oxford Handbook of National Security Intelligence*. Oxford: Oxford University Press. 2010. pp. 229, 230–241. doi:10.1093/oxfordhb/9780195375886.003.0014.

[6] Henricks S. C. Social Media, Publicly Available Information, and the Intelligence Community. *American Intelligence Journal*. 2017. 34 (1), pp. 21–31.

Facebook, LinkedIn, Instagram and Twitter), online discussion groups such as Reddit, bookmarking sites such as Pinterest, and E-Commerce such as Amazon; (3) public government data (e.g. government reports, budgets, hearings, telephone directories, press conferences, websites and speeches); (4) professional/industry/academic publications and commercial data (e.g. commercial imagery, financial and industrial assessments, and databases); (5) seized foreign material; (6) grey literature,[7] including foreign or domestic open source material that is usually only available through specialized outlets and may not enter normal channels or systems of publication, distribution, bibliographic control or acquisition by booksellers or subscription agents (e.g. technical reports, patents and business documents).[8]

It is important to note that open source information is not considered OSINT until 'it is analysed by an intelligence analyst in the context of national security requirements'.[9] Intelligence agencies can create OSINT either by having intelligence analysts do this work in-house, or by contracting it to outside entities (e.g. private companies, defence contractors, non-governmental organizations (NGOs) and academia).

Within the US IC, the use and importance of OSINT has varied. During the Cold War, it is thought that at times approximately 20% of US intelligence about the Soviet Union came from open sources.[10] Contemporary practitioners have arrived at higher estimates – that about 80–95% of US intelligence now comes from open sources (the 80% figure is most frequently mentioned).[11] It is not always clear how these percentages are arrived at, although some have noted that the higher figures are often cited for economic intelligence or information operations for which there is a

---

[7] National Grey Literature Collection. US Interagency Gray Literature Working Group Definition, 1995. Available from: http://allcatsrgrey.org.uk/wp/knowledgebase/u-s-interagency-gray-literature-working-group-definition-1995/ [Accessed 03 January 2022].

[8] For further discussion of categories of open sources, and how these relate to closed material, see also the chapter by H. Wilson *et al.* (Chapter 4.1).

[9] Saunders K. *Open Source Information – A True Collection Discipline*. MA thesis. Royal Military College of Canada. 2000. pp. 5, 26, 50, 105, 120, 108–116. Available from: https://docplayer.net/42068921-Open-source-information-a-true-collection-discipline.html [Accessed 03 January 2022].

[10] Lowenthal M. M. *Intelligence: From Secrets to Policy*. 4th ed. Washington, DC: CQ Press. 2009. p. 103.

[11] Mercado S. C. Reexamining the Distinction Between Open Information and Secrets. *Studies in Intelligence*. 2005. 49 (2). Available from: https://www.cia.gov/static/5d8a8df615f1bb014e49bb1452991991/Difference-Open-Info-Secrets.pdf [Accessed 28 July 2023].

large quantity of publicly available information.[12] Regardless, there is a widespread acknowledgement among intelligence experts that a sizeable amount of intelligence information now comes from open sources.

The US history of OSINT

Kimberly Saunders traced the first modern, institutionalized OSINT effort to the establishment in 1941 of the Office of the Coordinator of Information (COI). Launched before the United States joined the Second World War, this was the first peacetime, civilian, intelligence agency in the US (see footnote 9). A section called Research and Analysis (R&A) was set up within COI, which employed experts from several elite American universities and other subject matter specialists, who produced a variety of OSINT on enemy and allied countries. In 1942, the Office of Strategic Services (OSS) was created, which replaced the COI and provided a new base for the R&A branch (see footnote 9). Within the OSS, the R&A's main task was to provide strategic intelligence; to do this, its experts sought out and analyzed a wide variety of publicly available information from around the world. The R&A staff drew on their extensive expertise, experience and skills with open source research in academia to do their work, and developed a reputation among some that, 'R&A was the most important unit in the OSS'(see footnote 9). After the war, the OSS was abolished by Executive Order, and most of the researchers from the R&A unit returned to their universities.

In a distinct, parallel effort, the Foreign Broadcast Monitoring Service (FBMS) was created in 1941 under the Federal Communication Commission.[13] The mandate of the FBMS was to record, translate, transcribe and analyze propaganda radio programmes by the Axis powers – particularly those from Germany and Japan. After the Japanese attack on Pearl Harbor, and the US entry into the Second World War, FBMS changed its name to the Foreign Broadcast Intelligence Service, and the OSS relied on its work

---

[12] Saunders K. *Open Source Information – A True Collection Discipline*. MA thesis. Royal Military College of Canada. 2000. p. 50. Available from: https://docplayer.net/42068921-Open-source-information-a-true-collection-discipline.html [Accessed 03 January 2022].

[13] Mercado S. C. FBIS Against the Axis, 1941–1945: Open–Source Intelligence From the Airwaves. *Studies in Intelligence*. 2001. 11, pp. 33–43. Available from: https://www.cia.gov/static/96048eae9f1b9aa309a24c4b5582ea62/fbis-against-the-axis.pdf [Accessed 03 January 2022].

for various wartime assessments.[14] At the end of World War II, the Foreign Broadcast Intelligence Service was transferred to the War Department,[15] and then to the Central Intelligence Agency (CIA) where it was renamed the Foreign Broadcast Information Service (FBIS), and from where it monitored foreign media outputs.[16] FBIS became the central arm of the CIA's OSINT efforts during the Cold War. From the creation of the OSS until the 1990s, the bulk of open source analysis within the IC was scrutinizing and translating foreign press sources.

During the Cold War, the access to and use of open source information in the US declined, as the lowering of the Iron Curtain meant that many countries became closed to the West. This led the IC to depend more on information obtained through clandestine means, e.g. human sources (via spies) or classified technological systems. Because of this, the IC became increasingly structured around the collection and analysis of classified information, and OSINT was correspondingly de-emphasized. Analysts progressively relied upon (and became more trusting of) classified information for their assessments (see footnote 9).

Between the late 1980s and mid-1990s, with the advent of new information and communications technologies, the opening of previously closed Soviet bloc countries and the rise of various transnational threats, US intelligence began to recognize the growing availability of open source information and how it could be beneficial for intelligence assessments (see footnote 9, p. 5). In 1994, the CIA created the Community Open Source Program Office (COSPO)[17] to enable open source information to be more widely used within US intelligence. COSPO, however, failed to significantly

---

[14] Mercado S. C. FBIS Against the Axis, 1941–1945: Open-Source Intelligence From the Airwaves. *Studies in Intelligence*. 2001. 11, pp. 33–43. Available from: https://www.cia.gov/static/96048eae9f1b9aa309a24c4b5582ea62/fbis-against-the-axis.pdf [Accessed 03 January 2022].

[15] Roop J. E. *Foreign Broadcast Information Service: History, Part I: 1941–1947*. Foreign Broadcast Information Service. April 1969 (Approved for Release 10 August 2009). pp. 110, 277–282, 298–307. Available from: https://worldradiohistory.com/Archive-FBIS/FBIS-History-First-Five-Years.pdf [Accessed 04 January 2022].

[16] *ibid.* p. 298–307.

[17] Director of Central Intelligence Directive 2/12: Community Open Source Program (Effective 1 March 1994). Available from: https://irp.fas.org/offdocs/dcid212.htm [Accessed 04 January 2022]. See also footnote 9, p. 4.

change the existing reluctance to use, and overcome barriers to including, open source information within US intelligence.[18] From 1994–1996, the Aspin/Brown Commission on Intelligence Reform emphasized the need for the IC to increase its efforts to collect and use open sources, and to build more connections with outside subject matter experts.[19] In spite of this and other calls, by the end of the 20th century, the IC had failed to develop a meaningful capacity for OSINT.

The 11 September 2001 terrorist attacks on the United States led to a renewed focus on increasing OSINT by several legislators and intelligence managers. The Intelligence Reform and Terrorist Prevention Act of 2004[20] mandated the foundation of an Open Source Center (OSC), under the direction of the newly created post of Director of National Intelligence, to be managed by the CIA. In 2005, the Commission on the Intelligence Capabilities of the United States Regarding Weapons of Mass Destruction (WMD Commission),[21] which was set up to examine the intelligence failures leading up to the 2003 Iraq War, also recommended creating an OSC within the CIA to ensure that the IC maximized the use of open source information.[22] Soon after, the Director of National Intelligence followed these suggestions and established the OSC within the CIA to be the centre of expertise on open source information for the entire US government. The CIA's previous open source research centre, FBIS, was subsumed within this.[23] However, despite this renewed focus on OSINT, former intelligence officer Arthur Hulnick writes, 'policy officials, the ultimate recipients of finished intelligence, were not quite as enthusiastic about OSINT as those who created the new system' (see footnote 5). In spite of the intelligence reform

---

[18]Lowenthal M. Open source intelligence: New Myths, New Realities. *Intelligencer*. 1999. 10 (1), pp. 7–9.

[19]Best R. A. Jr. *Open Source Intelligence (OSINT): Issues for Congress*. CRS Report for Congress. 28 January 2008. pp. 2–3, 9, 12. Available from: https://apps.dtic.mil/sti/pdfs/ADA488690.pdf [Accessed 04 January 2022]. See also footnote 10.

[20]Public Law 108-458—Dec. 17, 2004. *Intelligence Reform and Terrorism Prevention Act of 2004*. Available from: https://www.archives.gov/files/declassification/pidb/legislation/pdfs/public-law-1 08-458.pdf [Accessed 04 January 2022].

[21]Commission on the Intelligence Capabilities of the United States Regarding Weapons of Mass Destruction. *Report to the President*. 31 March 2005. p. 45. Available from: https://irp.fas.org/off docs/wmd_report.pdf.

[22]Bean H. The DNI's Open Source Center: An Organizational Communication Perspective. *International Journal of Intelligence and CounterIntelligence*. 2007. 20 (2), pp. 240–257.

[23]Best R. A. 2008. *op. cit.*

efforts post 9/11, OSINT continued to suffer, often being perceived as a lesser intelligence discipline by the IC. To attempt to address this, in 2015, the OSC was redesignated the Open Source Enterprise and incorporated into the CIA's new Directorate of Digital Innovation, which is responsible for increasing the adoption of new digital tools and techniques across the CIA, to include cyber operations and OSINT.[24] The jury is still out as to how this reorganization has affected the status and use of OSINT within the IC.

The former Director of the OSC noted that although intelligence officials have increased their respect for and understanding of OSINT, financial constraints and competition among classified sources and platforms have hindered its uptake and progress.[25] As a result, over the years, eighteen IC members[26] have developed their own disparate OSINT operations, rather than engaging in a coherent, overarching OSINT policy and programme across the IC (see footnote 18). This has led to some concluding that OSINT is plagued by its 'persistent status as a subordinate intelligence discipline'.[27] This does not mean that OSINT has not garnered more representation and distinction over the years, but as one intelligence official has usefully commented on the state of play,

> I'd make a distinction between 'operationalized' and 'institutionalized.' 'Institutionalize' is very easy. Every agency has received a number of open source positions and resources. So, from an institutional standpoint, you can now identify open source officers in every agency in the intelligence community. ... In terms of structure, I would say that this is first time in the history of the United States intelligence community that there are dedicated open source positions across the board. ... But in terms of operationalizing [open source intelligence], that's very different. We are still a long way from people looking at their business processes and saying, 'Ok, how do we inject open source in here?'[28]

---

[24] Aftergood S. Open Source Center (OSC) Becomes Open Source Enterprise (OSE). *Secrecy News*. 28 October 2015. Available from: https://fas.org/blogs/secrecy/2015/10/osc-ose/ [Accessed 04 January 2022].

[25] Bean H. The Paradox of Open Source: An Interview with Douglas J. Naquin. *International Journal of Intelligence and CounterIntelligence*. 2014. 27 (1), pp. 42–57. doi: 10.1080/08850607.2014.842797.

[26] US Department of Defense. USSF Becomes 18th Member of Intel Community. 8 January 2021. https://www.defense.gov/News/Releases/Release/Article/2466657/ussf-becomes-18th-member-of-intel-community/ [Accessed 04 January 2022].

[27] Bean H. 2014. *op. cit.*

[28] Bean H. *Constructing 'open source': Institutional discourse, cultural change & the post-9/11 reshaping of US intelligence*. PhD thesis. Boulder: University of Colorado. 2009. pp. 136–137, 192–193, 231.

Another OSINT proponent has surmised that 'The real sign that open source [intelligence] has arrived is when an independent agency is created to pursue open source, to train open-source disciples, to promote it within the different agencies of the intelligence community. We're not there yet'.[29] Other intelligence scholars and practitioners have also called for this reorganization.[30] To date, OSINT and its various roles, scope and authorities have been repeatedly deprioritized and under-resourced within the IC.

Intelligence Culture and OSINT

Many intelligence scholars and practitioners have noted that the problems with increasing the role, practice and prominence of OSINT within the IC stem from the culture among intelligence officials, managers and analysts, which – since the Cold War – has valued and prioritized classified information and classified collection systems.[31] In part, this is because the collection and use of classified information has been what makes the US intelligence community special and distinct from other government and non-government entities. Former Assistant Deputy Director of National Intelligence for Open Source Eliot Jardines sums this up, saying, 'Let's keep in mind that we in the intelligence community take pride in knowing things or having the ability to know things that others don't, and so there's just the natural tendency that if the document's got a fancy cover sheet that says Top Secret and all sorts of fancy code words on it, that we tend to view that as more important than, say, something that's taken just from open sources'

---

[29] Bean H. *Constructing 'open source': Institutional discourse, cultural change & the post-9/11 reshaping of US intelligence.* PhD thesis. Boulder: University of Colorado. 2009, pp. 192–193.

[30] Zegert A. and Morell M. Spies, Lies, and Algorithms: Why U.S. Intelligence Agencies Must Adapt or Fail. *Foreign Affairs.* May–June 2019. 98(3), pp. 85–96. Available from: https://fsi-live.s3.us-west-1.amazonaws.com/s3fs-public/zegartmorell.pdf [Accessed 4 January 2023].

[31] Lowenthal M. Open Source Intelligence: New Myths, New Realities. *Intelligencer.* February 1999. 10(1). pp. 7–9.

(see footnote 29, p. 136). Some argue that there is also competition within the IC between proponents of classified documentation and OSINT advocates, with the latter maintaining 'that there is no question that the secret side has interfered with the development of a full and complete open source capability' (see footnote 29, pp. 136–137). Others have noted a less sinister reason; the IC responds to the collection priorities laid out in the National Intelligence Priorities Framework (NIPF)[32] – and the IC's solutions for addressing this mostly consist of using classified technological systems that result from decades of large investments.[33] As one former Director of Central Intelligence (DCI) stated, 'I only have money to pay for secrets'.[34] Thus, funding priorities continue to focus on classified platforms and investments in new classified collection technologies.

Persistent challenges

This prioritization has also been shaped by policy-officials and other intelligence customers who tend to want 'material from spies, intercepts, or any of the other more exotic material available to intelligence analysts' (see footnote 19, pp. 2–3). Otherwise, they claim, reading intelligence analysis is no different from reading the daily newspapers (see footnote 5, p. 230). As noted above, the intelligence failures leading up to 9/11 created an opening for OSINT, but the IC has still failed to overcome its inherent preference for classified information (see footnote 29, pp. 136–137). Intelligence scholars Tore Pedersen and Pia Therese Jansen recently conducted a randomized controlled trial in which they found that, in certain instances (detailed below), intelligence analysts significantly assign more credibility to secret information, even when the secret and open sources are identical.[35]

---

[32] Office of the Director of National Intelligence. *Intelligence Community Directive 204: National Intelligence Priorities Framework*, 7 January 2021. Available from: https://www.dni.gov/files/documents/ICD/ICD_204_National_Intelligence_Priorities_Framework_U_FINAL-SIGNED.pdf.

[33] Weinbaum C. The Intelligence Community's Deadly Bias Toward Classified Sources. *The RAND Blog*. 12 April 2021. Available from: https://www.rand.org/blog/2021/04/the-intelligence-communitys-deadly-bias-toward-classified.html [Accessed 4 January 2022].

[34] Marks R. A. Spying and the Internet. *The Washington Times*. 25 April 2005. p. A–21. Available from: https://www.washingtontimes.com/news/2005/apr/24/20050424-101721-8924r/.

[35] Pedersen T. and Jansen P. T. Seduced by secrecy — perplexed by complexity: effects of secret vs open-source on intelligence credibility and analytic confidence. *Intelligence and National Security*. 2019. 34(6), pp. 881–898. https://doi.org/10.1080/02684527.2019.1628453.

Similarly, they found that intelligence analysts are considerably more confident in assessments when they are based on classified information versus identical analysis based on open source information. Interestingly, Pedersen and Jansen found that these results only applied to cases when the intelligence estimate corresponded to a 'complex' problem characterized by a high degree of uncertainty, and not when the estimate addressed a 'simple' problem characterized by a low degree of uncertainty. They surmise that these results could be explained by the fact that intelligence analysts have tended to work more with classified information than with open source information (see footnote 33), or because they do not have the time or resources to carefully vet the open source information. This can lead to what Luis Garciano and Richard Posner call the 'herding problem' in intelligence, in which analysts can tend to focus on the same limited, classified information when making their assessments. This herding problem often gets 'locked in' because of the privileging of classified collection systems and information.[36]

However, despite this apparent resistance to OSINT in the IC, there are internal advocates promoting its importance and use. Some argue that open source information can be instrumental in helping analysts to narrow and define the scope of classified collection and analysis, and can provide important contextual understanding of classified data.[37] One useful case in point comes from the work of Professor Flagg Miller, a linguistics anthropologist and religious studies scholar, who analyzed over 1,500 cassette tapes from Osama bin Laden's former home in Kandahar, Afghanistan, after the fall of the Taliban in 2001 (the FBI had vetted the cassettes, deemed them insignificant, and then donated them to Williams College, thereby making them open sources).[38] Through careful study of these tapes, underpinned by his expertise in public domain literature, Miller worked to understand why bin Laden and his followers engaged in terrorist activities. His analysis of these tapes revealed a fundamental misunderstanding in the West's characterizations

---

[36] Garciano L. and Posner R. A. Intelligence failures: An Organizational Economics Perspective. *Journal of Economic Perspectives*. 2005. 19 (4), pp. 151–170.
[37] Davitch J. M. Open Sources for the Information Age: Or How I Learned to Stop Worrying and Love Unclassified Data. *Joint Force Quarterly*. 2017. 87, pp. 18–25. Available from: https://ndupress.ndu.edu/Publications/Article/1325926/open-sources-for-the-information-age-or-how-i-learned-to-stop-worrying-and-love/ [Accessed 04 January 2022].
[38] Miller F. *The Audacious Ascetic: What the Bin Laden Tapes Reveal About Al-Qa'ida*. Oxford: Oxford University Press. 2015.

of bin Laden's activities as being a transnational, anti-American terrorist network. Rather, Miller found that in the 1990s bin Laden and his Al Qaeda organization were focused on what they saw as apostates of the Muslim world, and on winning religious and political battles within Muslim-majority societies. Bin Laden's later targeting of America was built on western security discourse and narratives that he exploited when he understood there was political capital in doing so. This kind of nuanced understanding of bin Laden and his affiliates, based on open source information and analysis of these audio cassettes, could have led to a very different kind of intelligence assessment and set of policy responses towards Al Qaeda's activities during the 1990s and early 2000s.

Beyond these kinds of contextual studies, others say that open source information, and OSINT, has value as an intelligence discipline in and of itself. Former OSC analyst Stephen Mercado argues that OSINT beats classified information in terms of speed, quantity, quality, clarity, ease of use and cost, and that it 'often equals or surpasses secrets in addressing such intelligence challenges of our day as proliferation, terrorism, and counterintelligence' (see footnote 13). He and his fellow OSINT advocates, however, have not managed to penetrate the IC's longstanding preference for classified information and classified systems.

Some intelligence practitioners have pointed out that intelligence managers can play an important role in overcoming these internal barriers to OSINT.[39] Former IC practitioner John Gentry describes analytic managers as 'barons' who are the key decision-makers on a given analytic product/project and thus decide 'who and what gets to play' on a given issue.[40] Therefore, if IC managers are vested in OSINT. This can translate to analysts working more with open source information and producing OSINT. This could work separately from, or in tandem with, ongoing calls for structural changes and reforms within the IC to promote OSINT.

New challenges

While the IC has been slow to fully incorporate open source information and OSINT into its practices, the rise of private companies and non-government

---

[39] Gentry J. A. Managers of Analysts: The Other Half of Intelligence Analysis. *Intelligence and National Security*. 2016. 31 (2), pp. 154–177. See also footnote 27.
[40] *ibid.*

entities, and the creation of an OSINT market, may force it to reconsider its longstanding preference for classified sources and systems. Over time, because of dissatisfaction with IC assessments, policy-makers and other intelligence customers have turned to OSINT from outside groups.[41] This was noted particularly during the George W. Bush Administration, in which then Under Secretary for Defense Policy, Douglas Feith, set up intelligence gathering and analytic entities within the Department of Defense to gather information and conduct assessments to rival the IC's assessments on the Iraq–Al Qaeda relationship.[42] In addition, others would point out that the ongoing digital technology revolution is putting more and more information about the outside world directly into policy-makers' hands in near real time, giving them the feeling that they do not have to depend on the IC to acquire and understand information on important world and security developments.[43] Over the past few decades, the IC has had to compete for policy-makers' attention with 24-hour news media and instantaneous communication via social media, as well as other online platforms. Some have raised concerns that this may encourage policy-officials to rely on raw data (that has not been authenticated and assessed), and may tempt some officials to conduct their own analysis (see footnote 30). In this world of instant information, intelligence analysts will need to provide added value and context, beyond what is easily available to policy-makers, and the value of OSINT will be in the analysis of such raw data.[44] Marcos Degaut argues that now and in the years to come, the IC is and will be competing with a complex and diverse group of domestic and foreign information collectors, brokers and analysts providing information almost instantaneously as events happen,[45] the veracity of which must be

---

[41] Sands A. Integrating Open Sources into Transnational Threat Assessments, in Sims J. E. and Gerber B. (eds). *Transforming U.S. Intelligence*. Washington, DC: Georgetown University Press. 2005. pp. 63–78.
[42] Pincus W. and Smith R. J. Official's Key Report on Iraq is Faulted. *The Washington Post*. 8 February 2007. Available from: https://www.washingtonpost.com/wp-dyn/content/article/2007/02/08/AR2007020802387.html [Accessed 9 August 2023].
[43] Degaut M. Spies and Policy-makers: Intelligence in the Information Age. *Intelligence and National Security*. 2016. 31 (4), pp. 509–531. doi: 10.1080/02684527.2015.1017931.
[44] Duvenage M. *Intelligence Analysis in the Knowledge Age: An Analysis of the Challenges Facing the Practice of Intelligence Analysis*. Stellenbosch, South Africa: Stellenbosch University. 2010.
[45] ibid.

vetted and may need to be challenged. This information environment is far different to that operating during the Cold War and immediate post-Cold War period, in which the IC had essentially a monopoly of policy-makers' attention on security developments.

In light of this changing environment, some have suggested that the IC must devote more internal human and technical resources to OSINT (see footnotes 11, 43). Others would argue that – given the recent rise in non-governmental OSINT – it is already too late for this, and that instead, the IC must create new external partnerships with industry, academia, and other groups and individuals that already have the expertise needed to conduct OSINT. Since the late 1990s, several OSINT businesses and consultants, often former intelligence practitioners, have set up shop as 'information middlemen'(see footnote 43) to provide this kind of service to the IC (see footnotes 5, p. 231, 22, p. 247, 28, p. 4). These entities have grown with the proliferation of information from the internet and various social media and online sources, as well as with the reduction of the IC workforce in the post-Cold War 'peace dividend' period.[46] Contracting with and/or outsourcing to private-sector companies to collect and analyze open source information has become a way for the IC to manage the growing big data/information burden. Tim Shorrock has called the rise of these arrangements the 'Intelligence-Industrial Complex'.[47] There are concerns about these developments, with some arguing that the IC should not outsource work that it has no competency to evaluate (see footnote 25, p. 51). It should be noted that as the number of these non-governmental entities and their capabilities grow, they will have a growing financial stake in how OSINT is defined and managed, and they will increasingly shape the ongoing debate on the IC's relationship with OSINT now and into the future.

Regardless of whether and how the IC handles OSINT now or later, there are additional challenges that arise with a move towards more OSINT. The use of commercially available datasets by the IC has raised questions about

---

[46]Shorrock T. *Spies for Hire: The Secret World of Intelligence Outsourcing*. New York: Simon & Schuster. 2008.
[47]*ibid.*

privacy protections of US citizens. In one example, the IC collected and analyzed location data from smartphone apps from a commercial, third-party information broker, to scrutinize the movements of US citizens without a warrant.[48] According to a 2018 Supreme Court ruling, the IC is required to obtain a warrant in order to compel phone companies to turn over location data about their customers.[49] However, the IC and other government agencies can purchase similar data from commercial information brokers, and the law is unclear about whether a warrant is needed for this. The proliferation of third-party, commercial information brokers across various communication technologies, as well as through online and social media platforms, raises continued questions about the IC, OSINT and privacy protections in the digital age.

The proliferation of online open source information also raises analytic challenges in terms of sorting through misinformation, disinformation and algorithmic biases.[50] In this context, Nicole Softness raises the issue of 'context collapse',[51] whereby social media messages or posts originally meant for a small, specific audience might be misconstrued once accessed by a larger audience. She and others[52] further point out that analyzing these kinds of online posts cannot reveal the intentions or motivations of an actor

---

[48] Savage C. Intelligence analysts use U.S. smartphone Location Data without Warrants, Memo Says. *The New York Times*. 22 January 2021; updated 25 January 2021. Available from: https://www.nytimes.com/2021/01/22/us/politics/dia-surveillance-data.html#:~:text=Intelligence%20Analysts%20Use%20U.S.%20Smartphone%20Location%20Data%20Without,coronavirus%20testing%20site%20last%20year%20in%20San%20Francisco [Accessed 9 August 2023].

[49] Liptak A. In Ruling on Cellphone Location Data, Supreme Court Makes Statement on Digital Privacy. *The New York Times*. 22 June 2018. Available from: https://www.nytimes.com/2018/06/22/us/politics/supreme-court-warrants-cell-phone-privacy.html [Accessed 9 August 2023].

[50] Rønn K. V. and Søe S. O. Is social media intelligence private? Privacy in public and the nature of social media intelligence. *Intelligence and National Security*. 2019. 34(3), pp. 362–378. Søe S. O. Misleadingness in the Algorithm Society: Misinformation and Disinformation. *Medium*. 6 March 2017. Available from: https://medium.com/big-data-small-meaning-and-global-discourses/misleadingness-in-the-algorithm-society-misinformation-and-disinformation-28f78f14e78f [Accessed 9 August 2023]. Søe S. O. Algorithmic Detection of Misinformation and Disinformation: Gricean Perspectives. *Journal of Documentation*. 2018. 74(2), pp. 309–332. doi:10.1108/JD-05-2017-0075, https://www.emerald.com/insight/content/doi/10.1108/JD-05-2017-0075/full/pdf?title=algorithmic-detection-of-misinformation-and-disinformation-gricean-perspectives.

[51] Softness N. A. Social Media and Intelligence: The Precedent and Future for Regulations. *American Intelligence Journal*. 2017. 34 (1), pp. 32–37.

[52] Rønn K. V. and Søe S. O. Is social media intelligence private? Privacy in public and the nature of social media intelligence. *Intelligence and National Security*. 2019. 34 (3), pp. 33, 362–378.

or group (some of whom may deliberately try to mislead), yet some OSINT attempts to make just such a determination. Therefore, expertise and quality control are needed to sort through the veracity of open source information, as well as the analytic methods used to process it and make sense of it.[53]

Finally, the increasing algorithmic mining of open source information also raises questions of how to think about the role of the intelligence analyst vis-à-vis these digital technologies, regardless of whether OSINT is conducted in-house or outsourced. Typically, assessments of the potential of OSINT have tended to have a technocratic focus, for example, examining new technological capabilities which many hope will enable the mining of more diverse open source information and larger datasets.[54] Instead, some argue that it would be better for the IC to start by asking precisely what intelligence questions need to be answered, and then considering which resources and methods are best suited to answering these, which could include a combination of different sources of information, analytic techniques, analyst expertise and skill sets, as well as software and technologies. Former Director of the Open Source Center Douglas Naquin argues that 'Technology and statistical analysis should allow us to organize haystacks better, but I believe we will still depend on substantive – and Open Source – experts to derive insight from those haystacks, let alone find any needles' (see footnote 25). Some intelligence scholars and practitioners argue that in this context, rather than focusing on the technology, the IC should focus on hiring more subject matter experts, creating partnerships with outside experts, and developing more analytic standards and methods in the use of human judgment, to help inform and interrogate OSINT collection and analysis.[55,56] Others have also pointed to how intelligence analysts need more training, as well as access to unclassified sources, tools and platforms, in

---

[53] Haggerty K. D. and Ericson R. V. The Surveillant Assemblage. *The British Journal of Sociology*. 2000. 51(4), pp. 605–622. See also footnote 25, p. 50.

[54] Eldridge C., Hobbs C., and Moran M. Fusing algorithms and analysts: open-source intelligence in the age of 'Big Data'. *Intelligence and National Security*. 2018, 33 (3), pp. 391–406. https://doi.org/10.1080/02684527.2017.1406677 [Accessed 04 January 2022]. See also footnote 18 and 25, p. 49.

[55] Several chapters in this volume consider non-governmental research that uses hybrid approaches, that span both open and closed sources, and provide examples of non-governmental open source research correcting official accounts. For example, see chapters by Wilson, Samuel & Plesch, Strick, Kristensen & Korda, Triebert, and Carboni & Raleigh (Chapters 1, 2.1, 2.3, 2.4 and 3.3).

[56] Eldridge C., Hobbs C. and Moran M. Fusing algorithms and analysts: open-source intelligence in the age of 'Big Data'. *Intelligence and National Security*. 2018. 33(3), pp. 391–406. Lim K. Big Data and

order to better understand how to effectively collect and analyze open source information[57] (see footnote 19, pp. 8–9).

Conclusion

OSINT has had a long and varied history within the US IC. For much of this time, however, OSINT has been subjugated within intelligence practices. Rather than having a focused, coherent policy and programme, OSINT has tended to be scattered across different intelligence organizations, and the community has been inclined to underfund OSINT and instead favour intelligence that originates from classified sources.

However, the ongoing information revolution has started to challenge this, by giving rise to external information brokers and private OSINT entities that are putting pressure on the IC to consider how to best integrate open source information and intelligence into its structures and practices. OSINT is challenging traditional notions of what constitutes 'intelligence', and what makes the 'intelligence community' distinct from other government or non-government analytic bodies. Meanwhile, OSINT conducted by non-governmental groups is demonstrating that it can achieve results quickly, cheaply and accurately, and that it can complement and enhance intelligence based solely on classified sources.

The US IC's traditional resistance to OSINT has 'deep roots' (see footnote 5), and it is likely that a paradigm shift will be needed to change this (see footnote 25, p. 46). This will require strong, sustained, high-level internal advocates across IC management levels, as well as larger cadres of analysts who have expertise in how to use OSINT effectively. It remains to be seen how various social factors internal and external to the IC will shape the influence of OSINT in the years to come. This will be a space that is interesting to watch.

Strategic Intelligence. *Intelligence and National Security*. 2016. 31(4), pp. 619–635. See also footnote 25, p. 48, and footnote 51, p. 37.

[57] Weinbaum C., Parachini J. V., Girven R. S., Decker M. H., and Baffa R. C. "Perspectives and Opportunities in Intelligence for U.S. Leader". September 2018. Avaialable from: https://www.rand.org/content/dam/rand/pubs/perspectives/PE200/PE287/RAND_PE287.pdf.

Part 4
Global Governance

Chapter 4.1

Open Source Investigations before the Age of Google: The Harvard Sussex Program*

Henrietta Wilson, Richard Guthrie and Brian Balmer[†]

Where is the wisdom we have lost in knowledge?
Where is the knowledge we have lost in information?
T.S. Eliot, *The Rock*, 1934, quoted by Chris Freeman (Founder of the University of Sussex Science Policy Research Unit)[1]

Abstract

This chapter shows how open source research can be used to inform national and international policy-making. It takes as a case study an open source research

---

*This chapter is based on research conversations between Henrietta Wilson and: Mary Kaldor (Professor Emeritus of Global Governance and Director of the Conflict Research Programme at The London School of Economics and Political Science, and HSP co-Founding Director Julian Perry Robinson's life partner and widow); Matthew Meselson (Thomas Dudley Cabot Professor of the Natural Sciences at Harvard University and co-Founding Director of the Harvard Sussex Program); Peter Pringle (former foreign correspondent for *The Sunday Times*, *The Observer* and *The Independent* and close friend to Julian Perry Robinson and Matthew Meselson); and James Revill (Head of the Weapons of Mass Destruction and Space Security Programmes at UNIDIR, former Research Fellow at the Harvard Sussex Program and co-author of this book's Chapter 4.3). It was written with warm thanks to them.

[†] The three co-authors worked for the Harvard Sussex Program at different junctures.

[1] Christopher Freeman was colleague to HSP's co-Director Julian Perry Robinson. With thanks to Mary Kaldor for signposting this quote, which is also reported in: Sutz J. The contribution of Christopher Freeman to the study of National Systems of Innovation and beyond: Some words from Latin America. *Innovation and Development*. 2011, 1 (1), pp. 5–8.

This is an open access article published by World Scientific Publishing Europe Ltd. and distributed under the terms of the Creative Commons Attribution-NonCommercial 4.0 International (CC BY-NC 4.0) License.

project that predates the current generation of digital online investigations – that is, the Harvard Sussex Program on Chemical and Biological Weapons (HSP). Starting in 1990, HSP formalized the collaboration between Professor Matthew Meselson (Harvard) and Professor Julian Perry Robinson (Sussex), and institutionalized their work strengthening global prohibitions against chemical and biological warfare. The chapter overviews HSP's open source research, and shows how it underpinned the group's efforts to inform and impact policy. It also considers wider insights that derive from HSP's experiences, including how the distinction between 'closed' and 'open' sources is not always fixed or clear, and broad lessons about best practice in open source research and its applications.

Introduction: The Harvard Sussex Program, Its Directors, and Their Impact

Reflections on open source research can quickly lead to questions about its nature and purpose, for example, what difference can it really make?[2] And how truly 'open' is it? This chapter considers such matters by examining an example of open source research that precedes the current growth in digital open source investigations – the work of the Harvard Sussex Program (HSP)[3] in the 1990s. HSP has useful lessons for contemporary online investigations, demonstrating how open source research can support effective national and international policy-making, and highlighting fundamental challenges facing open source research, such as the difficulty of managing large amounts of information and the complexities involved in using these to arrive at strong conclusions about events.

From 1990 until 2020, HSP conducted specialist research and dissemination with the aim of informing public policy on chemical and biological warfare (CBW), and reinforcing and extending global prohibitions against CBW weapons. It was founded by co-Directors Matthew Meselson from Harvard University, USA, and Julian Perry Robinson from the University of Sussex, UK, consolidating and enhancing two decades of

---

[2]This chapter defines open source research and open source investigations as analyses that rely on publicly available tools and information.

[3]HSP's formal name was originally the Harvard Sussex Program on CBW Armament and Arms Limitation, but over time this was simplified to the Harvard Sussex Program on Chemical and Biological Weapons.

their earlier collaborations. They remained co-Directors until Robinson's untimely death from COVID-19 in April 2020.

The Directors' backgrounds, attributes and commitment were central to HSP's working methods and achievements. Meselson had established himself as an eminent biologist by his late 20s,[4] and joined Harvard as a tenured professor in 1960. He began thinking about CBW policy in 1963 during a summer placement at the newly formed US Arms Control and Disarmament Agency (ACDA). Here, he gained a high-level security clearance, and developed an understanding of policy-making processes through working on contemporary issues alongside influential and talented people, including Freeman Dyson and Henry Kissinger. Working at ACDA also triggered a lifelong commitment to understanding CBW and finding ways to strengthen global bans against it, for example, by encouraging US support for the international negotiations that led to the 1972 Biological Weapons Convention (BWC), understanding herbicide use in Vietnam (1970), uncovering and discrediting US allegations of Soviet-supported chemical weapons use in Asia in so-called 'Yellow Rain' incidents (1983),[5] and, with his wife Professor Jeanne Guillemin, investigating the 1979 anthrax outbreak in Sverdlovsk (1992–1999).[6,7]

In parallel, Robinson studied chemistry at Oxford University (1960–1964) and then trained as a patent lawyer, before joining the research staff of

---

[4]Matthew Meselson invented the equilibrium density-gradient centrifugation method for analyzing the densities of large molecules, which he applied in the Meselson-Stahl experiment (1958) that demonstrated the semi-conservative nature of DNA replication, and in 1961, with Sydney Brenner and Francois Jacob, used the method in experiments confirming the existence of mRNA (1961). Meselson M. and Stahl F. The replication of DNA in Escherichia Coli. *Proceedings of the National Academy of Sciences*. 1958, 44 (7), pp. 671–682. Available from: https://www.ncbi.nlm.nih.gov/pmc/articles/PMC528642/ [Accessed 27 May 2022]; https://scholar.harvard.edu/meselsonlab/biocv; Brenner S., Jacob F., and Meselson M. An unstable intermediate carrying information from genes to ribosomes for protein synthesis. *Nature*. 1961, 190, pp. 576–581. Available from: https://www.nature.com/articles/190576a0 [Accessed 27 May 2022].

[5]Meselson M. S. Curriculum Vitae. Available from: https://scholar.harvard.edu/meselsonlab/biocv [Accessed 18 September 2021].

[6]Shaw J. He Has Made the World a Safer Place. *Harvard Magazine*. 1 June 2018. Available from: https://www.harvardmagazine.com/2018/06/meselson-celebration [Accessed 8 October 2021].

[7]Guillemin J. *Anthrax: The Investigation of a Deadly Outbreak*. California: University of California Press. 1999.

the Stockholm International Peace Research Institute (SIPRI) where he was based between 1968 and 1971. During this period, he contributed to a series of foundational books on CBW for SIPRI,[8] and coordinated the production of influential reports for the UN Secretary General and the World Health Organization (WHO).[9] These are credited as facilitating the development of international prohibitions against CBW, including through informing the BWC negotiations.[10] From 1968 onwards, Robinson developed his reputation as a world-leading authority on CBW,[11] valued for his work conceptualizing the difficulties of outlawing CBW[12] and devising new approaches to address these problems.

Throughout this time, Robinson was consulted by international policymakers; for example, as Peter Pringle writes:

> In the early 1980s, a frustrated mandarin in the [UK] Foreign Office complained to his colleagues about his American counterpart. The US official had flown over to Britain to talk to chemical weapons experts, but had returned home without having a meeting in Whitehall. When asked for an explanation, the American had said he had simply contacted Professor Julian Perry Robinson at the University of Sussex instead and had found out all he needed to know. "I do not want to be too stiff-necked about this," the mandarin harrumphed, "but I think you'll agree that we are entitled to raise an eyebrow."[13]

---

[8] SIPRI. *The Problem of Chemical and Biological Warfare* (6 volumes). Stockholm: Almqvist & Wiksell. 1971–1975. Published in digital format April 2000. Available from: https://www.sipri.org/publications/2000/problem-chemical-and-biological-warfare [Accessed 19 September 2021].

[9] World Health Organization. *Health Aspects of CBW*. 1970. Reissued and updated as *Public Health Response to Biological and Chemical Weapons*, 2003. Available from: https://www.who.int/csr/delibepidemics/en/allchapspreliminaries_may03.pdf [Accessed 19 September 2021].

[10] SIPRI. April 2000. *op. cit.*

[11] Sims N. A. Julian Perry Robinson, top chemical and biological arms control expert, dies of coronavirus. *Bulletin of the Atomic Scientists*. 30 April 2020. Available from: https://thebulletin.org/2020/04/julian-perry-robinson-top-chemical-and-biological-arms-control-expert-dies-of-coronavirus/ [Accessed 19 September 2021].

[12] For example, Robinson outlined a framework distinguishing between verifying that CBW stocks had been eliminated and verifying efforts to prevent proliferation. Before this, there had been a tendency to consider all CBW verification as one homogeneous challenge. Robinson J. P. The Negotiations on Chemical-warfare Arms Control. *Arms Control* (London). May 1980, 1 (1), pp. 30–52.

[13] Pringle P. Professor Julian Perry Robinson obituary. *The Sunday Times*. 19 May 2020. Available from: https://www.thetimes.co.uk/article/professor-julian-perry-robinson-obituary-5d7gtgg9j [Accessed 19 September 2021].

Robinson and Meselson met in 1963, and began to build their friendship and working partnership the following year.[14] They each embodied scientific expertise, intellectual rigour and political understanding, and both cultivated specialist knowledge of CBW weapons and regulation. Establishing HSP enabled them to grow and amplify their independent and joint anti-CBW work, allowing them to access funding for shared endeavours, set up advisory and staffing structures to support their overall mission, and extend the visibility of their work, e.g. through producing and publishing a quarterly in-house journal – originally called *The Chemical Weapons Convention Bulletin* and renamed *The CBW Conventions Bulletin* in June 1997 (issue 36) – hereafter referred to as *The Bulletin* in this chapter.[15]

Individually and together, Meselson and Robinson undertook scholarly research, while also engaging with and impacting on national and international political debates and decision-making. As detailed below, they developed working methods which leveraged expert knowledge to gain access to policy-making spaces and officials, and used such interactions to improve their collection and comprehension of open sources. During the 1990s, for example, the pair are credited with promoting and informing the international negotiations that led to the 1993 Chemical Weapons Convention (CWC)[16] – the global treaty that outlaws chemical weapons and regulates the destruction of all declared stocks, including by successfully advocating that the Convention should define chemical weapons through a robust 'General Purpose Criterion',[17] and supporting effective national implementation of the treaty.[18] HSP also evaluated accusations of CBW weapons use – for example, assessing allegations of US use of *Thrips palmi* in Cuba,[19] extending Meselson's studies discrediting US allegations

---

[14] Note from Matthew Meselson to Henrietta Wilson. 12 November 2021.

[15] The first issue of *The Chemical Weapons Conventions Bulletin* was published in 1988, before HSP was formalized. Note from Matthew Meselson to Henrietta Wilson. 12 November 2021.

[16] Triumph of a long campaign. *New Scientist*. 23 January 1993. Available from: https://www.newscientist.com/long-campaign/article/mg13718571-200-triumph-of-a-long-campaign/ [Accessed 19 September 2021].

[17] McLeish C. Obituary Julian Perry Robinson. *Nature*. 21 May 2020. Available from: https://www.nature.com/articles/d41586-020-01450-1 [Accessed 11 August 2021].

[18] Guthrie R. Julian Perry Robinson obituary. *The Guardian*. 8 May 2020. Available from: https://www.theguardian.com/world/2020/may/08/julian-perry-robinson-obituary [Accessed 11 August 2021].

[19] For example, see HSP News Chronology entries for 6 May 1997 and 30 June 1997. *The CBW Conventions Bulletin*. p. 37, September 1997, Available from: http://www.sussex.ac.uk/Units/spru/hsp/documents/cbwcb37.pdf [Accessed 21 September 2021].

of chemical warfare in 'Yellow Rain' incidents[20] and helping to uncover facts about the 1995 sarin attack on the Tokyo underground.[21]

Declassified documents demonstrate that HSP was taken seriously by policy-makers in Washington and London government agencies. One example involves a short commentary that Robinson wrote for *New Scientist* in 1975 in response to press reports revealing that the UK government patent on VX nerve agent had been found in a public library. Robinson's article pointed out that while the disclosure of the VX formula was not entirely new – 'all that has been available [before] is a set of chemical equations devoid of those essential practical details which only a chemist of exceptional experience and courage could provide for himself' – the patent had now provided step-by-step instructions for making VX.[22] The article was definitely noted by the UK government; it can be found in the file DEFE 13/233 in the UK National Archives (a governmental repository of declassified documents), and in the same file there is an excerpt from the SIPRI volumes containing a table of V-agents that had been described in the open literature.

HSP's Open Source Research

HSP's open source research is reflected in, and was driven by, two of HSP's cornerstone activities: its archive of open CBW-relevant information – the Sussex Harvard Information Bank (SHIB) – and its News Chronology on global events related to CBW.[23]

SHIB (which still exists at its Harvard and Sussex sites) is HSP's paper-based repository of open source materials on CBW and related issues, developed from the co-Directors' earlier archives. Wide-ranging

---

[20] Meselson M. and Robinson J. The Yellow Rain Affair: Lessons from a Discredited Allegation. In Clunan A. L., Lavoy P. R., and Martin S. B. (eds). *Terrorism, War, or Disease? Unraveling the Use of Biological Weapons*. Redwood City CA: Stanford University Press. 2008. Available from: https://www.belfercenter.org/sites/default/files/files/publication/Meselsonchapter.pdf [Accessed 19 September 2021].

[21] See for example HSP News Chronology entry for 24 August 1998. *The CBW Conventions Bulletin*. December 1998, p 42. Available from: http://www.sussex.ac.uk/Units/spru/hsp/documents/cbwcb42.pdf [Accessed 19 September 2021].

[22] Perry-Robinson J. Behind the VX Disclosure. *New Scientist*. 9 January 1975, 65 (931), p. 50.

[23] *The CBW Conventions Bulletin* was published regularly between 1988 and 2011. PDF copies are available from: http://www.sussex.ac.uk/Units/spru/hsp/pdfbulletin.html [Accessed 20 July 2023].

and multidimensional, SHIB is perhaps the largest archive of its kind in the world.[24] It has a unique coverage, containing papers from scientific journals, newspaper cuttings, industry publications, army pamphlets, textbook excerpts, popular writings, Congressional testimonies, parliamentary records, declassified documents accessed through government archives, the answers to Freedom of Information Act requests, rare documents, ephemera, and many more.

SHIB is stored within an interconnected, hierarchical and cross-referenced filing system, so that researchers and visitors can easily find relevant sources, and discover unexpected synergies and perspectives. The sites at Harvard and Sussex contain different sets of information, although they partially duplicate each other. The University of Sussex holdings occupy about 230 metres of shelving, span a very large number of subject areas, and are usually open to visitors on request. The Harvard collection is smaller, and reflects Meselson's research interests. For example, it includes specialist holdings on the 1979 anthrax outbreak in Sverdlovsk, the US military BW programme, the military use of herbicides and the 'Yellow Rain' allegations.

Meanwhile, the News Chronology captured a sense of CBW-relevant events as they unfolded, compiled from open sources. Extracts of it were published in HSP's quarterly journal *The CBW Conventions Bulletin*,[25] and was valued for the way it integrated diverse information and perspectives. SHIB and the News Chronology were tightly interconnected, and Julian Perry Robinson was central to both. He oversaw HSP's open source information collection, read the incoming material, decided on its end location/s within SHIB, and undertook the bulk of work scrutinizing and synthesizing important details for the News Chronology.

While open source research underpinned SHIB and the News Chronology, HSP never regarded these efforts as discrete end goals. Instead, they were seen as a means to impact on the development and implementation of effective policies and actions, and it is important to recognize their role

---

[24]Feakes D. Julian Perry Robinson (1941–2020): Dedicated to Eradicating Chemical and Biological Weapons. *Arms Control Today*. June 2020. Available from: https://www.armscontrol.org/act/2020-06/features/julian-perry-robinson-1941-2020-martin-b-malin-1961-2020 [Accessed 8 October 2021].

[25]A total of 87 issues of *The CBW Conventions Bulletin* were published between 1988 and 2011. Pdf copies are available from: http://www.sussex.ac.uk/Units/spru/hsp/pdfbulletin.html.

within this wider cycle. In the first instance, open source research enabled the co-Directors, and their teams, to build their knowledge across an extremely wide range of CBW-related areas. The nature of CBW is complex and intricate, not least because the capacity to develop, weaponize, use, protect against and prevent chemical and biological weapons overlaps heavily with a very wide range of non-military uses, including the pharmaceutical, agricultural and food industries, and many aspects are surrounded by layers of extreme secrecy. Accordingly, attempts to fully grasp the proliferation risks and other problems posed by CBW weapons, and possible solutions to these, require integrating a broad variety of expert knowledge. HSP's co-Directors achieved this through immersing themselves in open source materials over many years, and they thereby developed in-depth understanding of, amongst other things, chemical and biological armaments, proliferation, protective equipment, CBW health effects and risks, as well as the technical and legal aspects of controlling and eliminating these weapons. This cumulative and multifaceted expertise underpinned HSP's research outputs, which included academic and popular publications, meetings, presentations and policy papers.

On top of constructing in-house anti-CBW specialisms, HSP's open source research also enhanced its reputation, credibility and visibility within global communities of scholars, advocates and government officials focused on CBW disarmament and non-proliferation. The fact that HSP based its knowledge and research on open sources added to its authority; everything in its research outputs could be traced, which generated confidence in the accuracy and independence of its analyses. This credibility supported HSP's work building global networks, which in turn enabled the group to better understand the needs of different agencies and organizations and to circulate information specific to them. Notably, it facilitated HSP's access to relevant policy-making and policy-shaping spaces, helping the group to connect with the people and processes responsible for devising and implementing national and international policies against CBW. It also enabled them to connect with civil society groups active in promoting CBW disarmament.

These connections were important in accelerating HSP's grasp of topical policy challenges, and its development of workable solutions to these. At any moment, some issues are ripe for a policy change, and HSP's networks assisted it in establishing which decision points were currently under deliberation. Further, through their ongoing interactions, HSP co-Directors became increasingly skilled at presenting information to policy-makers in ways that maximized the chances that it would be considered,[26] recognizing that policy papers should be short, elucidate different components of a problem and its possible solutions, and written in a style and language directly accessible to intended audiences.

Overall then, there was a reciprocal dynamic between SHIB, the News Chronology and HSP's policy research: The contents of SHIB reflected and extended the team's collective expertise, allowing staff to write the Chronology,[27] which was circulated to and read by journalists, scholars, government officials and policy-makers worldwide. This boosted HSP's reputation, and attracted policy-makers and scholars to engage with HSP. Simultaneously, the increased access to these people enhanced the coverage and accuracy of SHIB and the Chronology, better enabling HSP to connect with policy-making spaces, and impact policy development.

In other words, the different strands to HSP's work were a virtuous circle. Its open source research helped it to create and consolidate links with global networks of researchers and officials, and these global networks contributed to the quality of its open source information collection and dissemination. Interactions with government officials and others provided useful checks on the veracity of HSP's research, confirmed that the group was addressing relevant issues and 'live' decision points, and ensured that HSP's recommendations could be understood and acted on.

HSP's Open Source Information Collection Methods

HSP collected open sources through overlapping systems. The basic level was that paid staff regularly scanned designated newspapers and academic, government and trade publications, identifying relevant information, and assessing it to decide on its final destinations in SHIB and whether it contained material that was useful for the News Chronology. Through these

---

[26] Other chapters in this volume consider ways that open source research can be used to inform policy, including those by Duke, Kristensen & Korda, and Mathews (Chapters 2.1, 2.3 and 4.2).

[27] Initially, Robinson wrote all the News Chronologies, and later he was assisted by HSP project staff. Meselson proof-read the Chronologies.

activities, they could detect discrepancies or gaps in the incoming material, which often triggered follow-up investigations.

In other words, routine information collection identified 'red flags' that prompted further research.[28] The process of detecting anomalies, and distinguishing whether they signified genuine concerns, rested on researchers' abilities to recognize events that were out of the ordinary. And in turn, this required them to have baseline information about what constituted a 'normal' context or set of behaviours. For example, to be able to evaluate the likelihood that an outbreak of illness was the result of a biological weapon use, researchers would need to know the incidence of relevant naturally occurring diseases in the location, whereas to gauge the possibility of CBW proliferation, they might need to know standard patterns of trade in equipment or materials that could be used in either legitimate activities or in an illicit CBW programme.[29]

Once the team found areas that needed further investigation, they often had to think creatively about how to resolve the resulting questions and ambiguities. SHIB's multidisciplinary characteristics and organization could be extremely useful here. As mentioned, its diverse material was arranged within a tiered and interlinked system, and all documents were carefully indexed and cross-referenced. This enabled researchers to quickly retrieve the information they needed, and it also helped them to interpret it, recognize valuable context, spot useful symbioses and overlaps, and infer likely gaps in the records. From this perspective, SHIB's utility did not just lie in its contents – it was invaluable that these had been sorted and stored according to expert understandings, in anticipation of being comprehensible and accessible from a range of starting points.

HSP's iterative information collection processes – routine scanning, identifying red flags, and investigating anomalies – were supported by its extensive networks, which were useful to both its information collection and dissemination. HSP had a series of informal partnerships within its home institutions at Harvard and Sussex Universities, including with those organizations' general and specialist libraries. HSP's co-Directors were also

---

[28] For discussion of 'red-flag' monitoring in different contexts, see also the chapters by Liu & Gwadera and Michie *et al.* in this volume (Chapters 4.4 and 5.3).

[29] See also the chapter by Mathews in this volume (Chapter 4.2).

central to several global networks. Particularly important was their work with SIPRI and the Pugwash Conferences on Science and World Affairs. Having worked at SIPRI before joining the University of Sussex, Robinson developed connections and information exchanges between HSP and SIPRI through the 1990s. Additionally, Meselson and Robinson were key players in the Pugwash Conferences on Science and World Affairs,[30] coordinating the Pugwash Study Group on CBW, which in the 1990s organized biannual meetings of global scholars, policy-makers and other experts to consider global policy on CBW.[31]

In addition, the co-Directors cultivated links with scientists working on CBW defence science and technology and officials in governments around the world, as well as old-timers who had left government and a range of private individuals. Moreover, HSP staff often continued as a source of information and analysis after they left the group, as many went on to work with national polities and international organizations.

These networks reveal a complementarity between open and closed sources. Although SHIB and the News Chronology were compiled from open sources, they reflected and were shaped by closed material, not least because HSP's networks included people with security clearances and access to classified material. There is no sense that any of these people betrayed secrets or disclosed classified information. Nevertheless, interactions with insiders were useful in informing HSP's research directions and confirming the accuracy of its findings, and it is clear that they inadvertently or deliberately steered aspects of HSP's work, for example, by alerting HSP to particular areas of interest, or providing 'behind the scenes' checks to HSP's hypotheses. Indeed, many officials wanted to hear what conclusions

---

[30] The Pugwash Conferences on Science and World Affairs was set up to facilitate scientists' efforts to ban nuclear weapons, following the Russell-Einstein Manifesto. See "About Pugwash", Available from: https://pugwash.org/about-pugwash/ [Accessed 2 September 2021] and "Russell-Einstein Manifesto, 1955", Atomic Heritage Foundation, Available from: https://www.atomicheritage.org/key-documents/russell-einstein-manifesto [Accessed 2 September 2021].

[31] Robinson J. P. The impact of Pugwash on the debates over chemical and biological weapons. *Annals of the New York Academy of Sciences*. 1998, 877 (1), pp. 224–252. An earlier version is available at Robinson J. P. Contribution of the Pugwash Movement to the International Regime Against Chemical and Biological Weapons. *Pugwash Meeting No 242. 10th Workshop of the Pugwash Study Group on the Implementation of the Chemical and Biological Weapons Conventions: The BWC Protocol Negotiation: Unresolved Issues, 28–29 November 1998*. Available from: http://www.sussex.ac.uk/Units/spru/hsp/documents/pugwash-hist.pdf [Accessed 2 September 2021].

HSP had drawn from open source material. Meselson and Robinson treated conversations with officials as pointers to other sources; rather than taking such information on trust, they were careful to corroborate it with other sources before using it in any way, including in their written publications.[32]

Open vs. Closed: Types of Information

The large number of different types of open source materials employed by HSP reveals important features of the practicalities and dynamics of open source research. First, it emphasizes that being 'open' does not necessarily mean that sources are universally accessible. While most material in SHIB was collected from open sources, a lot of its contents cannot be easily obtained elsewhere. Further, SHIB demonstrates that the distinction between open and closed is not always clear or fixed. It suggests that, instead of thinking in terms of a binary between 'open' and 'closed' sources, it would be useful to think about four different categories of information: open-available, open-obscure, open-response and closed-protected.

The simplest of these categories – open-available – encompasses information that is both open and relatively easy to obtain, for example, mainstream publications such as newspapers that are either free or relatively cheap. As well as being accessible, these sources are usually straightforward to decode, comprehend and evaluate. By contrast, open-obscure sources – sometimes called 'grey literature' – are publicly available but difficult to obtain. They include policy reports by NGOs or think-tanks, and industry reports. Finding and acquiring open-obscure sources is complicated by their tending to be niche publications; they are often only produced in small quantities and are not widely disseminated. Further, they are frequently inscrutable and can be easily overlooked, as when governments put useful information in a footnote of an open but dense report. Meanwhile, open-response sources are those which can be accessed if researchers ask the right people the right questions, and include information retrieved via freedom of information legislation requests and parliamentary questions (in places where these options are available). Finally, closed-protected sources are

---

[32] Note from Mary Kaldor to Henrietta Wilson, 1 February 2022.

actively restricted, for example, information that governments have classified as secret.

While HSP worked with all forms of public-domain information, it specialized in tracking down and understanding open-obscure sources. It was extremely careful in how it managed these sources: carefully assessing whether they contained information, misinformation or disinformation, and considering why they had been released, by whom and how reliable they were. This process was reflected in the full News Chronology entries, which made clear the provenance of the source information used to compile different entries.

The distinctions between the four information categories are not static or permanent; information can move between them. For instance, if a mainstream newspaper gains access to an open-obscure source and publishes it, the information in it may become open-available, even if the source itself remains obscure. Similarly, classified information that is leaked may become open-available if it is published online in a widely read blog, or may remain open-obscure if it ends up in a remote archive. Once declassified, closed-protected sources become open. It is rare for open materials to become closed, although this is not unknown. For example, shortly after the 9/11 terrorist attacks in New York 2001, US President Bush reclassified many documents that had previously been declassified.

The four categories of information remain relevant to understanding today's online investigations. The wide reach of the internet connects open source researchers to a wealth of open-available information, suggesting that information may now be tracked down to a far greater extent than has been typical for practitioners working within traditional sectors or disciplines. However, despite the internet's power and breadth, it does not give enhanced visibility to all open source data. Many sources remain open-obscure or may continue to be open-response sources that can only be unlocked with assistance from knowledgeable third parties.[33]

In practice, there are constraints to who can do online open source research, and limits on what they are able to find. Digital research requires

---

[33] It should be noted that, while HSP's manual compilation of newspaper cuttings involved more work than many simple internet searches today, sophisticated internet searches often require time, expertise and technical resources.

time, patience and specialist search skills, as well as the resources required to access necessary equipment and information that is kept behind paywalls.[34] Further, the accessibility of sources is determined by a researcher's geographical location, since some parts of the world are less connected than others, and different countries place different restrictions on internet usage. And even when researchers are, in principle, able to access relevant information, they may still find it difficult to identify and retrieve it from the wider pool of irrelevant information within which it is located – some information might go unnoticed unless searched for precisely (which may depend on researchers already knowing that it exists and being able to use exact search terms), while some information is in effect hidden by the way internet search engines find and rank their results.

Cautionary Lessons, and Best Practice, for Contemporary Open Source Research

HSP provides lessons regarding how to work with large amounts of information, and what conclusions can be drawn from such work. HSP's project team and global networks collected and managed information manually, while most current open source research relies on the huge growth in the availability of and access to digital data afforded by the internet. In both cases, it is often necessary to sift through numerous sources to find the right sorts of information needed to answer a particular question and understand its wider context. However, HSP's experiences suggest that having more information does not inevitably lead to researchers having more clarity or arriving at better conclusions – in fact, acquiring information from multiple sources can sometimes magnify uncertainties rather than resolve them.

Many open source research projects often operate in contested information environments, in which there are competing claims and narratives. These contexts can make it harder to reach accurate and objective conclusions; for example, while wading through different accounts, researchers can intentionally or unconsciously 'pick a side', and then approach their

---

[34] Like other open source research, HSP mostly comprised educated white people located in Western countries.

work in a way that confirms their initial bias. For example, it has proven difficult to categorically resolve the US allegations that 'Yellow Rain' incidents were caused by chemical weapons, despite evidence from Meselson and other experts that they were most likely caused by bee faeces (at the time of writing – 2021–2023 – the US had still not retracted their accusations).[35,36]

Some investigations would appear to be fundamentally more amenable to achieving clear results. For example, an assessment of evidence for a ballistic missile capability can focus on tangible, identifiable objects. However, other investigations can find it harder to ascertain necessary details. For instance, it has been difficult for the international community to arrive at a definitive account about the use of chemical weapons in Ghouta in August 2013, despite the considerable level of information about the events and interest in understanding them.[37–39] Moreover, in the future, as perpetrators become more familiar with open source research capabilities, they may become better at hiding their work. Consequently, open source research is best regarded as a process of building a picture of likely occurrences and trends, rather than an exercise in categorically proving full particulars about events.

The difficulty in reaching conclusions can exacerbate political tensions, as the inherent ambiguities can allow adversaries to twist findings and narratives about events. As Robinson said, 'Accusations of association with them [CBW] have for centuries, even millennia, been used by well intentioned as well as unscrupulous people to vilify enemies and to calumniate rivals'.[40]

---

[35] Tucker J. B. The "Yellow Rain" Controversy: Lessons for Arms Control Compliance. *The Nonproliferation Review*. Spring 2001, pp. 25–42. Available from: https://www.nonproliferation.org/wp-content/uploads/npr/81tucker.pdf [Accessed 22 May 2022].

[36] In 2005 the US appeared to water down its position in a factsheet. US Department of State, Bureau of Verification, Compliance, and Implementation Fact Sheet, Case Study: Yellow Rain. 1 October 2005. Available from: https://2001-2009.state.gov/t/vci/rls/prsrl/57321.htm [Accessed 11 January 2023].

[37] Revill J., McLeish C., Johnson S., Ghionis A., and Edwards B. Workshop Summary. HSPOP Syria Collection. June 2016. Available from: http://sro.sussex.ac.uk/id/eprint/62217/1/SYRIA%20WORKSHOP%20FINAL%20.pdf [Accessed 22 May 2022].

[38] Hart J. and Trapp R. Collateral Damage? The Chemical Weapons Convention in the Wake of the Syrian Civil War. *Arms Control Today*, April 2018. Available from: https://www.armscontrol.org/act/2018-04/features/collateral-damage-chemical-weapons-convention-wake-syrian-civil-war [Accessed 27 September 2021].

[39] See also the chapters by Ahmad and Revill & Garzón Maceda (Chapters 3.1 and 4.3) in this volume.

[40] Robinson J. P. Alleged Use of Chemical Weapons in Syria. *HSPOP 04*. Available from: http://www.sussex.ac.uk/Units/spru/hsp/occasional%20papers/HSPOP_4.pdf [Accessed 27 September 2021].

In crisis situations, open source research findings are likely to be subject to increased scrutiny and cynicism – particularly by people or agencies that are under investigation – and it is unclear whether or how different national and international governance systems will deal with inevitable uncertainties or controversies.[41]

HSP's News Chronology sidestepped these issues by presenting its analyses as an unfolding picture of what was known about events, rather claiming that they were setting down definitive conclusions about them. Similarly, the best current open source research practitioners actively avoid making absolute claims prematurely. Further, HSP was transparent about its working methods and sources, so that others (including national and international bodies, and non-governmental organizations) could replicate its research and build confidence in its findings. As part of this, it was aware of, and clear about, the provenance of sources, and closely examined incoming open sources to understand their context as well as their content. Likewise, best practice in current open source research also emphasizes the importance of transparency about working methods and sources, and checks the origin of sources. While the growth of the internet has complicated these tasks by enabling a huge proliferation of open sources as well as widespread manipulation of information, the chapters of this book showcase awareness of, and possible approaches to, addressing these challenges.

Conclusion

One principle governing HSP was that good information is essential to good policy; policy-makers cannot make good decisions if they do not understand what they are dealing with, and outsiders cannot hold decision-makers to account if they do not fully know or comprehend information relevant to the policy landscape. Accordingly, HSP dedicated time and effort to collecting and analyzing open source information, and facilitating its dissemination, including through developing its open access research archive, SHIB, and

---

[41] For discussion of the possibilities and challenges of using open source research to strengthen international treaties prohibiting weapons of mass destruction, see also the chapters in this volume by Revill & Garzón Maceda and Liu & Gwadera (Chapters 4.3 and 4.4).

writing and publishing its News Chronology, as well as through generating other research outputs.

While open source information was important to HSP, it was never the ultimate goal. Rather, its open source research was one aspect of a set of complementary activities, ultimately enabling it to connect with the world where policy decisions are made. In contrast to groups that focus on generating publicity or media coverage, HSP orientated its work to understanding and engaging directly with policy-making. As a result, HSP's open source research went beyond expertise building. Rather, it was at the heart of the network building that enabled it to better understand policy challenges, devise possible solutions, and have those solutions inform government officials and policy-makers. By building intimate familiarity with open source literatures, HSP was able to help global policy-makers arrive at better decisions to prevent CBW.

© 2024 World Scientific Publishing Company
https://doi.org/10.1142/9781800614079_0012

Chapter 4.2

The Verification of Dual-Use Chemicals under the Chemical Weapons Convention through Open Source Research: The Pugwash-SIPRI Thiodiglycol Project

Robert J. Mathews

Abstract

Can non-governmental open source research help meet the information requirements of international weapons treaties? This chapter explores this question by considering the Pugwash-SIPRI Thiodiglycol Project, a non-governmental study conducted between 1989 and 1991 that supported the final stages of the Chemical Weapons Convention (CWC) negotiations. The project worked to elucidate aspects of the dual-use chemical thiodiglycol (TDG), such as the nature of the global industry using TDG as well as its potential military uses. It also assessed different verification options for the CWC, including by evaluating whether various measures would be able to detect the diversion of TDG from legitimate to illicit uses. The project took place before recent developments in digital open source research, and the chapter finishes by considering the degree to which new technologies may enable more effective verification of the CWC.

Introduction

International arms control and disarmament treaties require substantial amounts of information in their design and implementation. When they are under negotiation, information is needed about the weapons systems which

---

This is an open access article published by World Scientific Publishing Europe Ltd. and distributed under the terms of the Creative Commons Attribution-NonCommercial 4.0 International (CC BY-NC 4.0) License.

are to be regulated, such as how they and their components are produced, and options for practical and cost-effective verification provisions to monitor treaty compliance. Once negotiations have concluded, and a treaty has entered into force, information is also needed for its implementation, including establishing and operating the verification systems.

This chapter examines the extent to which information available from open sources can support international weapons treaties, both in their negotiation and implementation. It takes as a case study a non-governmental research project that used open sources to elucidate challenges facing the developing Chemical Weapons Convention (CWC).[1] The Pugwash-SIPRI Thiodiglycol Project was conducted between 1989 and 1991, during the concluding phase of the CWC negotiations, and aimed to examine what provisions the CWC would need to verify that thiodiglycol (TDG) was not diverted to military uses. TDG was of particular concern as it is a dual-use chemical that presents major risks – it can be used to make the sulphur mustard chemical warfare agent[2] and also has a wide range of legitimate uses. Emphasizing the realities of these risks, Iraq had used TDG to produce the sulphur mustard chemical warfare agent, which it deployed extensively between 1983 and 1988 in the Iran-Iraq war.

The Pugwash-SIPRI TDG Project was conducted using open source information – that is, information that was publicly available. Accordingly, as well as fulfilling its core objectives, the project provides an example of how open sources can support the development of international arms control and disarmament treaties. The chapter commences by describing the CWC negotiations in the late 1980s, and then details the project and how its work informed the negotiations. Following this, it then reviews the experiences of CWC verification since the treaty entered into force and became operational in 1997, and considers how new digital open source research might contribute to CWC verification in the future.

---

[1] The 1993 Convention on the Prohibition of the Development, Production, Stockpiling and Use of Chemical Weapons and on Their Destruction ('Chemical Weapons Convention') opened for signature on 13 January 1993, and entered into force on 29 April 1997.

[2] Nowadays, the chemical warfare agent bis(2-chloroethyl)sulphide is generally referred to as sulphur mustard. Historically, it was often referred to as 'mustard gas', even though it exists as an oily liquid in typical climatic conditions, as it has sufficient volatility to cause serious vapour injuries, particularly in warmer climates. The Pugwash-SIPRI TDG study group used the name 'mustard gas'.

The Chemical Weapons Convention

When the CWC negotiations concluded in 1992, the treaty was recognized as being a revolution in arms control and disarmament.[3] It was the first comprehensively verifiable multilateral treaty that completely bans an entire class of weapons, and firmly limits and monitors activities that may contribute to producing those weapons. It goes further than any other treaty in terms of the scope of its prohibitions and verification provisions, i.e. the measures by which states parties assess treaty compliance, and the systems for detecting and investigating alleged non-compliance.[4] The CWC's verification measures require states parties to make national declarations about relevant industrial and military activities, and provide for routine inspections of declared industrial and military facilities to confirm the accuracy of the declarations. They also include arrangements for 'challenge inspections', under which a state party can request a short-notice inspection of any site in another state party, and mandate the establishment of an international organization to oversee treaty implementation and manage its verification requirements – the Organisation for the Prohibition of Chemical Weapons (OPCW).

The CWC negotiations commenced in 1969 and took place in various formats between 1969 and 1984, including 'exploratory discussions' within the Geneva Disarmament Committee, and bilateral negotiations between the USA and USSR (1977–1980). At the beginning of 1984, as an early sign of improving superpower relations, the Geneva-based Conference on Disarmament (CD) (as the Disarmament Committee was called from February 1984) agreed that negotiations should now move away from 'exploratory discussions' and start the 'final elaboration' of a chemical weapons ban. The negotiations gradually developed momentum, and from 1984, a 'Rolling Text' was registered in Appendix 1 of the formal end-of-session reports to the CD from its Ad Hoc Committee on Chemical Weapons.[5] In keeping

---

[3] Letts M., Mathews R. J., McCormack T. L., and Moraitis C. The conclusion of the chemical weapons convention: An Australian perspective. *Arms Control*. 1993, 14, p. 311.

[4] For further discussion of weapons treaty verification, and the roles that open source research could play in this, see the chapters in this volume by Duke, Revill & Garzón Maceda, and Liu & Gwadera (Chapters 2.2, 4.3 and 4.4).

[5] Report of the Ad Hoc Working Group on Chemical Weapons. Conference on Disarmament Document CD/539. 28 August 1984, Appendix I.

with common practice in international negotiations, the introduction of a Rolling Text containing draft wording for the treaty generally signified a resolve to reach agreement on a final text.

By the end of 1988, there was a reasonable level of agreement on the general structure of the future treaty, including on the provisions to monitor the production and use of dual-use chemicals, that is, chemicals that have legitimate uses in industry but that could be used as chemical weapons or that are chemical precursors of these weapons. The chemicals to be subject to routine monitoring by the treaty had been divided into three schedules. Those on Schedule I include nerve and blister chemical warfare agents, direct chemical precursors to nerve agents and two toxins. It had been agreed that these chemicals could be produced for permitted purposes in aggregate quantity not to exceed one metric tonne at a single declared facility, or in small quantities at research facilities. Chemicals on Schedule 2 are either toxic chemicals suitable for use as chemical weapons or key precursors of chemical weapons, which are not produced in large commercial quantities. Schedule 3 contains other chemical warfare agents used in World War I as well as other precursors (such as earlier precursors for nerve agents), including some which are produced in large quantities by the chemical industry (some being referred to as 'bulk chemicals').

However, despite this broad agreement, by the end of 1988, many important details remained unresolved, including whether routine inspections should be limited to facilities working with Schedule 1 and Schedule 2 chemicals, or should be extended to include Schedule 3 facilities; whether particular dual-use precursor chemicals (e.g. TDG) should be listed in Schedule 2 or Schedule 3;[6] and whether there should be mandatory declarations and routine inspections of other chemical production facilities (OCPFs)[7] which were deemed capable of producing scheduled chemicals.[8]

As the draft verification procedures were developed and incorporated into the Rolling Text, they were evaluated through more than 60 National

---

[6]The placement of a particular dual-use chemical in either Schedule 2 or Schedule 3 is based on the balance between the risk that the particular chemical poses to the Convention and the practicality of effectively monitoring the chemical using the more intensive verification measures that had been developed for Schedule 2 facilities.

[7]Mathews R. J. The Regime for Other Chemical Production Facilities: A Technical Perspective. *CBW Conventions Bulletin*. July 2009, 83/84.

[8]For clarity, this chapter uses the acronym OCPF throughout, although at times the CWC negotiations used different terms, e.g. 'CW capable facilities'.

Trial Inspections (NTIs) conducted by CD delegations and observers.[9] However, at the end of 1988, uncertainty remained about how effective the different verification provisions would be in practice. Based on the experiences of NTIs, the negotiators recognized that there would need to be adjustment and refinement of the procedures for routine inspection of the chemical industry, including for OCPFs.[10]

The Pugwash-SIPRI Thiodiglycol Project

The uncertainties included questions about how to approach those parts of industry involved with producing, processing, consuming and trading TDG. This prompted the establishment of the Pugwash-SIPRI Thiodiglycol Project, conducted between early 1989 and 1991 by a group of academics, industry representatives and government scientists.[11] Aiming to elucidate the proliferation risks of TDG, and ways that the treaty could address these, the study group considered the following: TDG's military relevance; legitimate applications; verification tools and techniques; and a preliminary assessment of the verification provisions contained in the 1990 CWC Rolling Text.[12] These are described next.

Production and military utility of sulphur mustard

The project generated useful insights into the production and military utility of the sulphur mustard blister agent, through consulting widely available open source information,[13] which presented a broad synthesis of scholarly

---

[9] Trapp R. *Verification under the Chemical Weapons Convention: On-Site Inspections in Chemical Industry Facilities*. SIPRI Chemical and Biological Warfare Studies No. 14. New York: Oxford University Press. 1993.

[10] Mathews R. J. Verification of chemical industry under the Chemical Weapons Convention, in Poole J. B. and Guthrie R. (eds). *Verification 1993: Arms Control, Peacekeeping and the Environment*. London: VERTIC & Brassey's. 1993, pp. 41–54.

[11] A group of fourteen experts from different disciplines – from chemistry and manufacturing to operations research and systems science – was assembled under the auspices of Pugwash and SIPRI. The experts acted in their personal capacities. Lundin S. J. (ed). *Verification of Dual-Use Chemical Weapons under the CWC: The Case of Thiodiglycol*. New York: SIPRI and Oxford University Press. 1991.

[12] Report of the Ad Hoc Committee on Chemical Weapons to the Conference on Disarmament. Document CD/1053. 10 August 1990, Appendix I.

[13] This chapter echoes the information categories introduced by H. Wilson *et al.* in this volume: open-available (articles from peer-reviewed scientific journals and readily available reference documents); open-obscure (publicly available information which is difficult to get hold of); response sources

understanding of chemical and biological warfare, and provided a conduit to information that would otherwise be obscure, including information from World War 1 and World War 2 archives.[14] Understanding how chemical warfare agents can be made and used is crucial to efforts to prevent their development, production, stockpiling and use; without it, regulators are likely to miss details about the activities and materials they seek to ban.

Commercial applications of TDG

Similarly, the project uncovered important details about the commercial aspects of TDG from widely available open sources,[15] including information on research and development of TDG, and the major commercial applications of TDG, such as the production of ballpoint pen inks, fabric dyeing and specialty lubricants. This research was important in establishing the extent of the legitimate uses of TDG, which in turn was useful in considering how the CWC's verification regime could protect legitimate secrets, including commercial proprietary information. The research was also vital in understanding how TDG production could be used in a chemical weapons programme. When this project commenced in 1989, it was clear that Saddam Hussein's Iraq was producing TDG from two widely available bulk chemicals (2-chloroethanol and sodium sulphide).[16] The relative ease of this production method supported CWC negotiating positions that suggested there would be benefits in routinely monitoring OCPFs.

(information from sources which are in theory open, but can only be accessed if researchers ask the right people the right questions); and closed-protected (information that is actively restricted, for example, information that governments have classified as secret).

[14]United Nations Secretary-General. *Chemical and Bacteriological (Biological) Weapons and the Effects of their Possible Use*, Document A/7575/Rev.1. New York. 1969. World Health Organisation, *Health Aspects of Chemical and Biological Weapons*. Geneva. 1970. Perry Robinson J. P. The Rise of CB Weapons, Volume I of *The Problem of Chemical and Biological Warfare*. SIPRI. Stockholm: Almqvist and Wiksell. 1971. Gillis R. G. The Gillis Report: Australian Field Trials with Mustard Gas 1942–1945 (tabled in the Australian Parliament by the Defence Minister in March 1987, and subsequently published by the Australian National University Peace Research Centre, 1992).

[15]For example, we scrutinized scientific journal articles, patents and the Chemical Abstracts Service produced by the American Chemical Society, which collects abstracts of articles from the open source chemical literature.

[16]Mathews R. J. Comparison of the Chemicals on the Australia Group Control List with those in the CWC Schedules. *CBW Conventions Bulletin*. 1993, 21, pp. 1–5.

Lessons from National Trial Inspections (NTIs)

Delegations to the CWC negotiations (including both member and observer delegations) provided significant quantities of open source information via Working Papers that they submitted to the CD, some of which reported on various NTIs, including the US NTI at a TDG production facility.[17] The Pugwash-SIPRI Thiodiglycol Project accessed additional information about NTIs from the authors of these Working Papers during workshops and other Q&A sessions.[18]

From these, the Project concluded that the 1990 Rolling Text[19] Schedule 2 inspection provisions should be able to determine the non-diversion of Schedule 2 chemicals, and the non-production of Schedule 1 chemicals, from an inspected facility. The study group also considered the problems associated with verifying Schedule chemicals in a multi-purpose plant. For example, it examined the verification of OCPFs, and concluded that there may be benefit in linking routine Schedule 2 inspections and routine inspections of OCPFs.

The project considered whether various verification methodologies and tools – including portable detection equipment, and sampling and analysis equipment, which had been used in some of the NTIs – might facilitate the verification of TDG in the chemical industry. The project concluded that the technologies had useful applications, depending upon the objectives of the particular inspection and details of the facility being inspected. It also recognized that other factors required evaluation, including whether confidential business information acquired during an inspection could be securely stored, as well as the cost, reliability and ease of transportation of each system.[20]

---

[17] Eckhaus S. R. US national trial inspection at a thiodiglycol facility. Chapter 11 in Lundin S. J. (ed). *Verification of Dual-Use Chemical Weapons under the CWC: The Case of Thiodiglycol.* New York: SIPRI and Oxford University Press. 1991.

[18] Trapp R. *Verification under the Chemical Weapons Convention: On-site inspections in chemical industry facilities.* SIPRI Chemical and Biological Warfare Studies No. 14. New York: Oxford University Press. 1993.

[19] Report of the Ad Hoc Committee on Chemical Weapons to the Conference on Disarmament. Document CD/1053. 10 August 1990, Appendix I.

[20] Mathews R. J. The Application of Portable Vapour Detectors in Verification of Non-production of Chemical Warfare Agents. Chapter 6 in Lundin S. J. (ed). *Verification of Dual-Use Chemical Weapons under the CWC: The Case of Thiodiglycol.* New York: SIPRI and Oxford University Press. 1991.

It should be noted that the NTIs would have generated other useful information that was kept closed. For example, some information derived from NTIs conducted at military facilities (including practice challenge inspections) was not published in order to protect legitimate defence secrets. The project did not need access to these to arrive at robust findings about the proposed CWC verification systems.

The global survey of thiodiglycol

To achieve its objectives, the project needed to understand the global pattern of TDG production, trade and consumption,[21] which in turn required detailed information on commercial uses of TDG. To obtain this information, it conducted the following surveys:

1. A written questionnaire was sent to the 39 member delegations and 26 observer delegations to the CD, requesting information on the use of TDG in their nation;
2. Various chemical industry databases were scrutinized;
3. Information was requested from chemical industry representatives, including from companies known to produce and use TDG.

These surveys suggested that in 1990 there were fewer than 12 producers of TDG worldwide, and that these were concentrated in Germany, Japan and the United States. There were also estimated to be 100–150 companies processing or consuming more than one tonne of TDG per year, with another 20–30 companies processing or consuming more than ten tonnes of TDG per year. It was clear that the industry was dynamic as different companies entered and exited the TDG market based on demand, and that the number of producers had decreased since the mid-1980s, perhaps as a result of companies not wishing to inadvertently supply TDG for a chemical weapons production programme.[22]

---

[21] Mathews R. J. Global Survey of Thiodiglycol. Chapter 4 in Lundin S. J. (ed). *Verification of Dual-Use Chemical Weapons under the CWC: The Case of Thiodiglycol.* New York: SIPRI and Oxford University Press. 1991.

[22] By 1990, some companies had already taken the decision, sometimes encouraged by government officials, to stop exporting TDG to avoid the possibility of inadvertent involvement in CW proliferation.

The surveys indicated that although TDG is an important commercial chemical with many useful properties, other chemicals with fewer military applications (and that would not be subject to the CWC's routine monitoring) could be used instead of TDG, for example, in textile dyeing, as a printing solvent or in the production of specialty lubricants. At least some TDG producers were already aware that its production would be closely monitored under the future CWC, and some producers had indicated that they might stop producing TDG if they considered the finally agreed CWC verification provisions to be too onerous.

The project recognized that, although the surveys were useful, the information they provided was incomplete. This was partly because, following the introduction of harmonized tariff categories for chemicals, TDG had been grouped with 'other organo-sulphur chemicals' and many of the negotiators reported that their country had difficulty in identifying TDG as an individual chemical from its standardized trade data. Another reason was that TDG is a 'specialty chemical'. Trade in such chemicals is typically highly lucrative and competitive. TDG trade data are generally regarded as confidential business information; for ongoing business success, including to maintain competitive advantage, it is essential to protect commercial secrets such as the details of domestic and export trade, as well as export quantities and destinations. Thus, several companies provided their production, trade and consumption quantities in ranges rather than as exact quantities.

Despite being incomplete, the results from the surveys were sufficient for the project to conclude that TDG is a 'specialty chemical' produced and consumed in comparable quantities to other dual-use chemicals already assigned to Schedule 2 (for example, dimethyl methylphosphonate). This finding was useful to those delegations which considered that TDG should be listed in Schedule 2 rather than Schedule 3, as it enabled those delegations to make a stronger case. Moreover, to be confident that none of the TDG being traded and consumed was subsequently used to produce sulphur mustard, the project recognized that the proposed CWC verification regime would need to be able to check the absence of sulphur mustard production in various diversion scenarios (discussed next), as well as monitoring the non-diversion of TDG.

Considering diversion scenarios

The surveys enabled the project to consider possible diversion scenarios – situations in which TDG could be transferred from legitimate activities to illicit ones. For example, in the hypothetical case of a facility located in a CWC member state which produces TDG and then diverts a portion of this to produce sulphur mustard in the same facility, the project concluded that 1990 Rolling Text Schedule 2 data reporting and on-site inspection provisions were satisfactory, provided that the objectives of routine inspections included confirming the absence of sulphur mustard.

However, the study group concluded that the 1990 Rolling Text provisions would not be able to detect other possible diversion scenarios, including diversion of TDG through distributors (chemical traders). Moreover, the survey results indicated that it would not be feasible to accurately account for all TDG produced, traded and consumed, and that the provisions in the 1990 Rolling Text would not enable CWC member states to establish the life cycle of TDG.

The study group was particularly concerned about possible scenarios in which exported TDG was diverted from its declared commercial purpose, e.g. a theoretical case in which TDG exported to a CWC state party is diverted for use in another country's chemical weapons programme. The project noted that the 1990 Rolling Text verification arrangements (and indeed, those in the final CWC text agreed in August 1992) did not require sufficient information to detect such scenarios. This suggested a need for each state party to declare annually its accurate aggregate national data (AND) on quantities of TDG produced, imported, consumed and exported. Similarly, the project concluded that declarations of Schedule 2 chemical storage facilities, and more detailed declarations on import–export of Schedule 2 chemicals, would be needed to overcome these deficiencies (discussed further below).

The Pugwash-SIPRI Thiodiglycol project – Overall findings

The project generated results that were directly relevant to the CWC negotiators' work solving challenges associated with the routine verification of chemical industry. It was able to achieve the following.

- Confirm the negotiators' decision that sulphur mustard poses a sufficiently high risk to the Convention for it to be listed in Schedule 1.
- Determine that TDG should be listed in Schedule 2, because it poses significant risks to the Convention, and is produced in quantities that would allow it to be effectively monitored using the verification provisions being developed for Schedule 2 chemicals.
- Conclude that TDG can be produced clandestinely with relative ease from two readily available 'bulk chemicals'. This conclusion supported the argument of some delegations that OCPFs should be subject to routine monitoring.
- Conclude that the CWC Rolling Text verification provisions would not be able to detect all potential TDG diversion scenarios, as this would require the establishment of material balances at all stages of the life cycle of TDG, which was deemed impossible given the limited amount of AND required to be declared by states parties for Schedule 2 chemicals.

These findings assisted in the final shaping of the CWC's routine industry verification provisions, including the placement of TDG in Schedule 2,[23] and the agreement that routine verification arrangements should include OCPFs.[24] However, the finally agreed Convention AND provisions did not take fully into account some of the potential diversion scenarios considered by the study group.[25]

---

[23] OPCW. Annex on Chemicals. Available from: https://www.opcw.org/chemical-weapons-convention/annexes/annex-chemicals/annex-chemicals [Accessed 18 April 2022].

[24] Mathews R. J. The Regime for Other Chemical Production Facilities: A Technical Perspective. *CBW Conventions Bulletin*. July 2009, 83/84.

[25] Based on the diversion issues identified by the study group, during informal consultations among Western Group delegations in late 1991 the Australian delegation suggested that the declaration threshold for AND be 10% of the declaration threshold for Schedule 2B facilities (i.e. 100 kg for Schedule 2B chemicals). However, several delegations opposed this, arguing that this level of detail would reveal confidential trade information. During the CWC 'end-game' negotiations, Australia proposed a compromise figure for the AND calculation based on individual export and import thresholds of 500 kg, but this was not agreed upon. See Australia. Proposed Convention on the Prohibition of the Development, Production, Stockpiling and Use of Chemical Weapons and on their Destruction. Document No CD/1043. 12 March 1992.

Verifying Thiodiglycol under the CWC – The OPCW Scorecard so Far

The Pugwash-SIPRI TDG Project's findings informed the final stages of the CWC negotiations, by elucidating how the future Convention could best deal with dual-use chemicals. As noted, this was a topical concern, emphasized by Iraq's use of imported TDG in the 1980s to produce the sulphur mustard chemical warfare agent, which it then used extensively in the Iran-Iraq war. When export controls made it difficult for Iraq to acquire TDG, it produced TDG from two more readily available precursors (2-chloroethanol and sodium sulphide).[26] Some of these activities resulted in criminal convictions[27] and companies being penalized.[28] In 1993, there were also concerns that TDG was being illegally shipped to a country of possible proliferation concern.[29] These examples demonstrate the security and proliferation risks associated with TDG, as well as the limited options for dealing with these risks before the Chemical Weapons Convention became operational in 1997.

The situation since entry into force of the CWC in April 1997 provides a useful and apparently promising contrast. Overall, the Schedule 2 inspections, which commenced shortly after the CWC's entry into force, appear to have worked well. In particular, the OPCW has apparently never had any serious compliance issues in its conduct of routine inspections of declared Schedule 2B facilities, including those facilities that states parties have declared to be producing, processing or consuming TDG at above the inspection threshold of ten tonnes per year. Likewise, there have been no indications from the OCPF inspections that TDG has been produced in

---

[26] Mathews R. J. Comparison of the Chemicals on the Australia Group Control List with those in the CWC Schedules. *CBW Conventions Bulletin.* 1993, 21, pp. 1–5.

[27] For example, Dutch businessman Frans van Anraat was sentenced to 17 years imprisonment for supplying thousands of tonnes of CW precursor chemicals to Iraq between 1984 and 1988. See Harvard Sussex Programme CBW News Chronology. 6 December 2004.

[28] For example, in 1989, US company Alcolac was fined $438,000 for supplying CW precursor chemicals, including 210 tonnes of TDG, to Iraq. See Harvard Sussex Programme CBW News Chronology. 19 January 1989.

[29] In 1993, US officials were concerned that a Chinese cargo ship, the Yin He, was carrying CW precursor chemicals to a destination in the Middle East for CW purposes. The US officials were permitted to inspect the ship's cargo, and subsequently admitted that their intelligence sources had 'proved to be wrong'. See Harvard Sussex Programme CBW News Chronology. 2 September 1993.

quantities above the declaration threshold of one tonne/year.[30] Also, based on informal discussions, there do not appear to have been any clarifications related to TDG that have been sought through Article IX Paragraph 2 procedures.[31] And there have been no challenge inspections (therefore, obviously no challenge inspections related to TDG).

It would also appear that there have been no AND discrepancies associated with exports of TDG that have caused alarm bells to ring.[32] That said, unfortunately, there have been significant inconsistencies in the declarations on aggregate export and import data by matching pairs of states parties. The OPCW has noted that transfer discrepancies are an ongoing problem, as a large proportion of those that are detected are never resolved.[33] As a result, it has been recognized that the practical utility of these declarations for transparency and confidence-building among states parties remains doubtful.[34]

However, these discrepancies do not necessarily indicate, or even suggest, that any exports of Schedule 2 chemicals have been, or are being, diverted for prohibited purposes – instead, it may be a result of different accounting practices in different states parties, which itself is a result of the original design of the reporting system. The CWC does not specify the threshold quantities states parties should use to calculate their AND declarations, and so the calculations are made in different ways. Some states parties use the reporting thresholds for facilities to calculate their AND information (e.g. one tonne for TDG and other Schedule 2B chemicals), while others use a lower declaration threshold, or include all imports and exports, even laboratory quantities.[35] Another reason for the discrepancies is that, particularly in situations in which a Schedule 2 chemical is exported towards the end of a calendar year, the same transaction may be reported in different calendar years (e.g. the export of a shipment from the territory of

---

[30] Based on the author's informal discussions with various members of the OPCW Technical Secretariat, 1997–2022.

[31] Based on the author's informal discussions with CWC states parties' delegates, 1997–2022.

[32] *ibid.*

[33] OPCW. Report of the Scientific Advisory Board at its Thirty-Second Session. SAB-32/1. 17 June 2021, Paragraph 5.11.

[34] Krutzsch W., Myjer E., and Trapp R. (ed). *The Chemical Weapons Convention: A Commentary*. UK: Oxford University Press. 2014, p. 592.

[35] Based on the author's informal discussions with CWC states parties' delegates, 1997–2022.

one state party may be reported towards the end of a calendar year, and the import reported in the following calendar year based on the date when the shipment actually arrives into the territory of the importing state party).

But while there may be innocent explanations for AND discrepancies, there is no room for complacency. The Syrian chemical weapons stockpile was declared following Syria's accession to the CWC in 2013 after widespread use of chemical weapons in the country's civil war;[36] it contained substantial quantities of sulphur mustard, at least some of which may have been produced by the TDG process. We cannot preclude the possibility that at least some TDG exported by a CWC state party, and nominally designated for a permitted purpose, may ultimately have been diverted and used to produce Syrian chemical weapons.

Can CWC Verification be Enhanced in the 'Age of Google'?

During the CWC negotiations, delegates recognized that the treaty's industry verification arrangements would need to be refined over time, because of, *inter alia*, advances in verification technologies, lessons from routine inspections of chemical industry and changes in the chemical industry.[37] Can novel digital technologies support this process, similar to the Pugwash-SIPRI TDG Project's work informing the CWC negotiations?

The project noted that even if all import and export data were made available, the quantities involved in monitoring AND relevant to TDG are so great that very sophisticated data processing algorithms would be needed to detect possible discrepancies.[38] It is unlikely that any member of the project imagined the advances in digital data collection and processing that would take place by 2022, 30 years after their work concluded. Nevertheless, despite these developments, it is not clear whether and how they could be incorporated into the CWC's verification processes – which must be agreed

---

[36] For discussion of open source analyses of the use of chemical weapons in the Syrian civil war, see also chapters by Ahmad and Revill & Maceda (Chapters 3.1 and 4.3).
[37] Mathews R. J. Verification of chemical industry under the Chemical Weapons Convention, in Poole J. B. and Guthrie R. (eds). *Verification 1993: Arms Control, Peacekeeping and the Environment.* London: VERTIC & Brassey's. 1993, pp. 41–54.
[38] Lundin S. J. (ed). *Verification of Dual-Use Chemical Weapons under the CWC: The Case of Thiodiglycol.* New York: SIPRI and Oxford University Press. 1991, p. 135.

upon by states parties before they can be adopted. In 2011, an OPCW Advisory Panel on Future Priorities made the following comment:

> In an era of globalisation with chemical industry spreading around the globe and chemical trade creating global partnerships and dependencies, and where information about chemical activities is available from an ever-expanding pool of authoritative sources on the Internet, it is difficult to comprehend why the [OPCW] Technical Secretariat does not make better use of open-source information, particularly that from company websites and information that is officially provided to other international organizations such as the UN.

The Advisory Panel recommended that the OPCW's policy-making organs should study the matter of using open source information for verification purposes and provide guidance to the organization's Technical Secretariat about this.[39] Unfortunately, several states parties were reluctant to accept this advice,[40] but it is hoped that it will be considered more positively. It seems that there is some momentum building towards this, as it has received further consideration recently. In the meantime, as documented elsewhere in this book, it is clear that new digital tools have much relevance for weapons treaty verification.[41]

The OPCW is currently working with industry associations with the objective of developing practical steps to improve the efficiency of industry inspections, including to optimize, streamline and digitize chemical industry verification. This informal collaboration echoes the working model of the TDG Project, and is considering the potential of new technologies. In particular, it is attempting to develop a better understanding of life cycle assessments of Scheduled chemicals, as well as the use of computing and artificial intelligence in the chemical industry. Further, in recent years, the OPCW has been considering the development of improved data management systems which might help to resolve AND discrepancies. One such approach being considered by the OPCW Scientific Advisory Board is the possibility of using distributed ledger technology (also known as

---

[39] OPCW. *General Report of the Advisory Panel on Future Priorities of the Organisation for the Prohibition of Chemical Weapons*. Office of the Director-General. Document No. S/951/2011. 25 July 2011, Annex 2, p. 13, Paragraph 48.

[40] Based on the author's informal discussions, it appears that some states parties are concerned about the level of accuracy and reliability of some of the information obtained from various websites.

[41] See for example the chapters by Kristensen & Korda, Revill & Garzón Maceda, Liu & Gwadera, Withorne, and Bedenko & Bellish in this volume (Chapters 2.3, 4.3, 4.4, 5.2 and 5.4).

"blockchain technology") to help states parties align their export records with the import records of counterparties and thereby significantly reduce transfer discrepancies.[42] Another recently reported technology that may assist with more accurate AND information being provided by states parties is a functioning prototype of a chemo-informatics tool that automates the task of determining whether a particular chemical being imported or exported is part of a chemical weapons control list, including whether the chemical is contained within a CWC Schedule family of chemicals.[43]

Concluding Comments

The Pugwash-SIPRI Thiodiglycol Project informed the CWC negotiations by generating findings about the nature of the dual-use chemical TDG – including its possible military applications and actual commercial uses – and evaluating methods that could be used to verify its non-diversion (and by extension, that of other Schedule 2 chemicals) from legitimate to illegal activities.

This project used traditional information gathering methods – including scrutinizing scientific and industry publications, and consulting industry representatives – to understand global TDG production, trade and consumption, and to consider how this and other dual-use chemicals could be effectively verified by the CWC. Novel digital technologies have much to offer industry verification, as well as other CWC verification provisions and requirements. But these technologies should be seen as complementing traditional methods, rather than replacing them. The novel technologies will not provide a 'magic wand' or 'silver bullet' when researching particular issues such as the global production of 'specialty chemicals' (including the challenges associated with access to, and adequate protection, of confidential business information obtained from a range of industry sources), and they cannot replace the types of traditional information gathering and analysis methods used by the Pugwash-SIPRI TDG Project (notwithstanding the

---

[42] OPCW. Report of the Scientific Advisory Board at its Thirty-Second Session. SAB-32/1. 17 June 2021, Paragraph 5.3.
[43] Costanzi S., Slavick C. K., Abides J. M., Koblentz G. D., Vecellio M., and Cupitt R. T. Supporting the fight against the proliferation of chemical weapons through cheminformatics. *Pure and Applied Chemistry*. 2022. https://doi.org/10.1515/pac-2021-1107.

fact that the internet facilitates some access to published materials). Thus, when proposals are made to add dual-use chemicals to the CWC Schedules, a similar information gathering exercise on their global production, consumption and trade may be necessary in order to justify their inclusion in Schedule 2 or 3.

The project's use of open sources has paved the way for possible applications from new digital technologies such as, *inter alia*, artificial intelligence, machine learning, metadata analysis and open source satellite imagery to support the treaty in similar CWC verification studies. For example, the new technologies may enhance monitoring certain aspects of the production of Schedule 2 chemicals (e.g. TDG) from earlier precursors. Therefore, these methods should be further developed and refined, and potential applications in CWC verification studies explored. It should be noted that open source research technologies are developing at a rapid rate. Even if applications are not apparent today, it may not be very long until at least some of the tools will be capable of supporting at least some of the challenges currently facing CWC industry verification.

New digital open source research tools will offer advantages when addressing some verification challenges, such as adapting verification measures to reflect inspection experiences and changing industry practices, as well as in investigations of alleged use of chemical weapons and when monitoring the destruction of chemical weapon stockpiles during armed conflict (as happened recently in Syria). It is clear that there will be important roles for appropriately validated open source information, including from novel digital technologies, to achieve more effective and efficient verification of the CWC.

© 2024 World Scientific Publishing Company
https://doi.org/10.1142/9781800614079_0013

Chapter 4.3

The Role of Open Source Data and Methods in Verifying Compliance with Weapons of Mass Destruction Agreements*

James Revill and María Garzón Maceda

Abstract
Open source tools have the potential to contribute to monitoring and verifying compliance with weapons of mass destruction (WMD) related agreements. However, there are constraints on the extent to which open source data and methods can be effectively applied in these politically sensitive areas. This chapter assesses the different functions and users of open source data in WMD treaty verification, as well as the limits of open source tools. It argues that these tools can be useful in monitoring and verifying treaty compliance and could play an increasingly significant role as part of a 'new vision' for arms control and disarmament. However, open source tools cannot supplant existing verification measures and new open source data will bring new challenges to WMD treaty verification.

Introduction

The idea of applying open source data and methods[1] to verifying weapons of mass destruction (WMD) treaties is not new. Similar approaches have been

---

*The authors' views in this chapter do not necessarily reflect those of UNIDIR or the UN. The authors would like to thank Eleanor Krabill for comments on an earlier version of this chapter.
[1] As detailed later, we define open source data and methods as those that are publicly available.

This is an open access article published by World Scientific Publishing Europe Ltd. and distributed under the terms of the Creative Commons Attribution-NonCommercial 4.0 International (CC BY-NC 4.0) License.

considered in the past under the label of 'societal verification',[2] 'citizens reporting' or 'social monitoring'. However, new information technologies are advancing and converging with other technologies and, in the process, expanding the possibilities for accessing and generating information relevant to WMD treaty verification.

The emergence of new open source data streams – such as social media, online databases, commercial satellite imagery or environmental monitoring and sensing systems – presents several exciting and potentially transformative possibilities for verifying compliance with WMD treaties, including the 1968 Treaty on the Non-Proliferation of Nuclear Weapons (NPT), the 1972 Biological Weapons Convention (BWC) and the 1993 Chemical Weapons Convention (CWC). However, in the sensitive area of WMD treaty verification, there remains a yawning gap between what is technically possible with open source data and methods, on the one hand, and what is politically acceptable at the international level, on the other.

To better understand how open source research can be leveraged – or not – in WMD treaty verification, this chapter begins with an outline of the process of verification. It proceeds to look at some of the roles open source information and technology have played, or could theoretically play, in enhancing treaty verification. It then explores how different actors might provide and use – or potentially misuse – open source research in this area. The chapter concludes by looking at what is required to fulfil the potential of open source data and technologies in the realm of WMD treaty verification.[3]

WMD Treaty Verification

In general terms, WMD treaty verification can be understood as the process of collecting and assessing information in order to reach a judgement about member states' compliance or non-compliance with their treaty obligations. This process provides states parties to an agreement with the ability to detect

---

[2] Deiseroth D. Societal verification: Wave of the future? in Findlay T. (ed). *Verification Yearbook 2000*. London, UK: VERTIC. 2000. pp. 265–280. Available from: https://www.vertic.org/media/Archived_Publications/Yearbooks/2000/VY00_Deiseroth.pdf [Accessed 27 July 2023].

[3] See also the chapter by Liu & Gwadera in this volume (Chapter 4.4) for a discussion on how existing open source research could be scaled up and applied to WMD treaty verification.

indicators of significant treaty violations in sufficient time to respond[4] and builds confidence in treaty compliance.

Verification is typically achieved through a process of monitoring, analysis and determination. Monitoring and analysis are largely technical processes involving observations of 'activities of the parties relevant to their obligations under an agreement'.[5] They can be achieved unilaterally through national technical means (i.e. approved national intelligence capabilities including satellites and other remote sensing technologies), cooperatively, or in some cases both. However, verification is never an entirely technical exercise. States will draw from the available evidence to reach a political determination as to whether another state is complying with its treaty obligations and, where deemed necessary, take further actions.

The consequences of a determination of non-compliance with WMD-related treaty obligations can be significant; in some cases, states have undertaken military action on the basis of concerns over WMD treaty non-compliance. As the ramifications are potentially substantial, the process of technical assessment needs to be robust and able to withstand considerable international scrutiny. In addition to such political sensitivities, the design of technical assessments needs to consider ways of protecting confidential information, as these processes sometimes require access to carefully guarded commercial or military secrets.

In practice, the process through which verification is achieved varies across different WMD-related regimes. Some multilateral agreements have developed sophisticated procedures to monitor and assess compliance. For example, the CWC includes an intrusive industry inspection regime administered by the Organisation for the Prohibition of Chemical Weapons (OPCW).[6] In contrast, it is commonly observed that the

---

[4]Podvig P. and Woolf A. *Monitoring, Verification, and Compliance Resolution in US–Russian Arms Control*. WMDCE Series No. 5. Geneva, Switzerland: UNIDIR. 2019. Available from: https://doi.org/10.37559/WMD/ 19/WMDCE5.

[5]Tulliu S. and Schmalberger T. *Coming to Terms with Security: A Lexicon for Arms Control, Disarmament and Confidence-Building*. Geneva, Switzerland: UNIDIR. 2003. Available from: https://www.unidir.org/files/publications/pdfs/coming-to-terms-with-security-a-lexicon-for-arms-control-disarmament-and-confidence-building-en-547.pdf [Accessed 27 July 2023].

[6]Trapp R. *Compliance Management Under the Chemical Weapons Convention*. WMD Compliance and Enforcement Series No. 3. Geneva, Switzerland: UNIDIR. 2019. Available from: https://doi.org/10.37559/WMD/19/WMDCE3.

BWC lacks any substantive verification mechanism, despite a concerted effort in the 1990s to develop an additional treaty protocol which included verification components.[7] As a result, states rely on national technical means and other mechanisms outside of the treaty to verify compliance with the BWC.

Roles of Open Source Research

The responsibility for undertaking treaty verification has traditionally rested on states who, on occasion, have delegated aspects of the verification process to international organizations, such as the OPCW and the International Atomic Energy Agency (IAEA), which is responsible for the nuclear safeguards required by the NPT. However, open source approaches – understood here as activities or information that are publicly accessible, either for free or at a price, as is the case for some materials or services such as commercial satellite data or newspaper subscriptions – have the potential to feed into WMD treaty verification. Specifically, they create scope for non-governmental organizations (NGOs) and individuals to engage in tasks associated with treaty verification, including monitoring compliance and supporting investigations with additional data. In addition, under certain conditions, open source approaches could play a role in alerting the international community to the use of chemical and biological weapons, and nuclear proliferation, and even contribute to holding individuals to account for the development and use of weapons prohibited under international law.

Providing possible indicators of compliance and non-compliance

Monitoring compliance requires collecting and collating different types of data with which to build a picture of states' adherence to their treaty obligations. Some forms of data suggest compliance with treaty regimes – such as details of a state's national legislation or internal regulatory systems, domestic codes of conduct or oversight measures. Other data points may indicate possible non-compliance with treaty obligations – such as the construction of special military facilities or suspicious transfers of dual-use materials

---

[7]Lentzos F. *Compliance and Enforcement in the Biological Weapons Regime*. WMDCE Series No. 4. Geneva, Switzerland: UNIDIR. 2019. Available from: https://doi.org/10.37559/WMD/19/WMDCE4.

or equipment (i.e. materials or equipment that can be used for peaceful or hostile purposes).[8,9]

It is unlikely that any single data point will provide conclusive proof of non-compliance (or compliance). Put otherwise, there is rarely a 'smoking gun' for treaty violations. However, collectively data can allow a clearer view of the activities of any given state to emerge. Tracking sets of data over time can contribute to broader understandings about patterns of behaviour relevant to compliance with any given treaty. In turn, this can facilitate a more informed determination over whether a state is complying with its obligations under such an agreement.

Open source data and methods can play a valuable role in building a picture of treaty compliance. For example, public sources of data, such as the United Nations Resolution 1540 Committee Legislative Database[10] or national government websites, can provide insights into national legislative measures or regulations pertaining to different weapons. Open source trade data, freely accessible through the United Nations Commodity Trade Statistics Database (UN Comtrade) and elsewhere, can and has been used to identify trends in dual-use imports and exports.[11] Further, social media materials, such as photos or videos, can be used to identify new weapons systems or uncover clandestine activities related to weapons of mass destruction; and material released for official purposes can inadvertently provide useful insights into weapons-related activity.[12] Other data collected through various apps can be used to inform assessments

---

[8] Several other chapters in this volume detail open source research focussed on detecting illicit WMD proliferation. See, for example, the chapters by Kristensen & Korda, Liu & Gwadera, and Bedenko & Bellish (Chapters 2.3, 4.4 and 5.4).

[9] United Kingdom of Great Britain and Northern Ireland. We need to talk about compliance: A response to BWC/MSP/2012/WP.11. BWC/MSP/2013/MX/WP.1. Geneva: United Nations. 2 July 2013. Available from: https://digitallibrary.un.org/record/756027?ln=en [Accessed 27 July 2023].

[10] United Nations 1540 Committee. Legislative Database: General Information [online]. Available from: https://www.un.org/en/sc/1540/national-implementation/legislative-database/general-information.shtml [Accessed 27 July 2023].

[11] For analysis on this see: Borrett V., Hanham M., Jeremias G., Forman J., Revill J., Borrie J., *et al. Science and Technology for WMD compliance monitoring and investigations.* Geneva, Switzerland: UNIDIR. 2020. Available from: https://doi.org/10.37559/WMD/20/WMDCE11 [Accessed 27 July 2023].

[12] Podvig P. and Eveleth D. Open-Source Intelligence in Verification. in: Podvig P. (ed). *Exploring Options for Missile Verification.* Geneva, Switzerland: UNIDIR. 2022. Available from: https://doi.org/10.37559/WMD/22/Misver/01 [Accessed 27 July 2023].

of compliance, for example, through determining specific troop or brigade movements or facility locations.[13]

In addition, certain forms of commercially available data can play an informative role in technical assessment of compliance. Hanham highlights the important role that advances in commercial satellite imagery can play, in conjunction with other monitoring efforts, in nuclear verification activities:

> The growing number of space-based sensors is raising confidence in what opensource satellite systems can observe and record. These systems are being combined with local knowledge and technical expertise through social media platforms, resulting in dramatically improved coverage of the Earth's surface. These opensource tools can complement and augment existing treaty verification and monitoring capabilities in the nuclear regime (see footnote 11).

Collectively, open source investigations can therefore play a role in monitoring compliance, particularly when integrated 'with the other tools available in the international treaty monitoring toolkit'.[14]

Alerting to possible uses of chemical or biological weapons

Open source data can provide alerts of the use of certain prohibited weapons. Indeed, early (albeit partial) indications of a possible use of chemical or biological weapons are likely to first emerge in public from decentralized open source channels. The revised International Health Regulations (2005), for example, empower the World Health Organization to use unofficial reports in the identification of possible public health emergencies. This includes open source materials from non-governmental entities such as the Program for Monitoring Emerging Diseases (ProMED), an internet service that identifies unusual health events related to emerging and re-emerging infectious diseases and toxins. ProMED has been the first organization in the world to detect several major disease outbreaks and is often

---

[13] See e.g. Pérez-Peña R. and Rosenberg M. Strava fitness app can reveal military sites, analysts say. *The New York Times*. 29 January 2018. Available from: https://www.nytimes.com/2018/01/29/world/middleeast/strava-heat-map.html [Accessed 27 July 2023].

[14] Renda G., Cojazzi G. G. M., and Kim L. K. Open Source Analysis in Support to Non-Proliferation: A Systems Thinking Perspective, in Niemeyer I., Dreicer M., and Stein G., (eds). *Nuclear Nonproliferation and Arms Control Verification: Innovative Systems Concepts*. Cham: Springer International Publishing. 2020. pp. 309–324. Available from: https://doi.org/10.1007/978-3-030-29537-0_21 [Accessed 27 July 2023].

able to provide indicators of biological events quicker than formal reporting systems.[15]

In other cases, warnings that emerge through informal networks can also contribute to alerting the world to the possible use of certain forms of WMD. Early indicators of the use of chemical weapons in Ghouta, Syria, in August 2013 were broken through the circulation of material on local Facebook and Twitter accounts.[16] This was followed by video material circulated through YouTube. Within hours of the event, which was later confirmed as a chemical attack involving the nerve agent sarin, 'all hell broke loose in the social media'.[17] More traditional media sources, many of which were unable to operate in Syria at the time, drew from this material in their reporting,[18] as did NGOs and other actors seeking to document details pertaining to the use of chemical weapons in Syria.[19]

Supporting investigations of non-compliance

Open source data can also play a role in supporting investigations of alleged non-compliance with WMD-related agreements. For example, in 2014, the OPCW established a Fact Finding Mission (FFM) with the purpose of investigating allegations of chemical weapons attacks in Syria. Notably, the FFM combined more traditional measures, such as interviews and physical evidence collection, with other sources of information, including social media

---

[15] The Program for Monitoring Emerging Diseases (ProMED) is a programme of the International Society for Infectious Diseases (ISID). ProMED was launched in 1994 as an internet service to identify unusual health events related to emerging and re-emerging infectious diseases and toxins. For more on this see Carrion M. and Madoff L. C. ProMED-mail: 22 years of digital surveillance of emerging infectious diseases. *International Health.* May 2017. 9 (3), pp. 177–183. Available from: https://doi.org/10.1093/inthealth/ihx014 [Accessed 4 August 2023].

[16] Crowley M., McLeish C., and Revill J. The Role of Civil Society in Combating the Development, Proliferation and Use of Chemical Weapons in: Crowley M., Dando M., and Shang L. (eds). *Preventing Chemical Weapons: Arms Control and Disarmament as the Sciences Converge.* Cambridge: Royal Society of Chemistry. 2018. pp. 580–618. Available from: https://books.rsc.org/books/edited-volume/1884/chapter-abstract/2471337/The-Role-of-Civil-Society-in-Combating-the?redirectedFrom=fulltext [Accessed 27 July 2023].

[17] United States Secretary of State. *Statement on Syria* [recorded speech and transcript]. Washington DC: Department of State. 30 August 2013. Available from: https://2009-2017.state.gov/secretary/remarks/2013/08/213668.htm [Accessed 27 July 2023].

[18] Ghannam J. *Digital Media in the Arab World One Year After the Revolutions.* Washington DC: Center for International Media Assistance, National Endowment for Democracy. 2012. Available from: https://www.cima.ned.org/publication/digital_media_in_the_arab_world_one_year_after_the_revolutions [Accessed 27 July 2023].

[19] See also the chapter by Ahmad in this volume (Chapter 3.1).

and open source information.[20] More recent OPCW FFMs have used 'information gathered from open-source media' and employed 'an expanded search of open sources' to gather information.[21]

Taking this one step further, in 2018, the OPCW established an attribution mechanism responsible for identifying the perpetrators of chemical attacks in Syria: the Investigation and Identification Team (IIT). The first IIT report indicated that it had 'collected information from open sources', including 'flight data confirmed by open source material'.[22] This helped the IIT establish a connection between aerial bombings implicated in chemical weapons attacks and the aircrafts from which the munitions were dropped, thereby contributing to the attribution of chemical weapons use.

Contributing towards accountability

Finally, open source data and research can potentially contribute to holding treaty violators to account. For example, in 2016, the United Nations General Assembly adopted Resolution 71/248, establishing the International, Impartial and Independent Mechanism (IIIM) to assist in the investigation and prosecution of persons responsible for the most serious crimes under international law committed in the Syrian Arab Republic since March 2011. This Mechanism uses open source data amongst a wider range of evidentiary

---

[20] OPCW. Note by the Technical Secretariat: Summary Report of the Work of the OPCW Fact-Finding Mission in Syria Covering the Period from 3 May to 31 May 2014. S/1191/2014. The Hague: OPCW. 2014. Annex 2, p. 7. Available from: https://www.opcw.org/sites/default/files/documents/Fact_Finding_Mission/s-1191-2014_e_.pdf [Accessed 27 July 2023].

[21] OPCW. Note by the Technical Secretariat: Report of the OPCW Fact-Finding Mission in Syria Regarding an Alleged Incident in Saraqib, Syrian Arab Republic on 4 February 2018. S/1626/2018. The Hague: OPCW. 15 May 2018. Annex 2. Available from https://www.opcw.org/index.php/documents/2018/05/s16262018/note-technical-secretariat-report-opcw-fact-finding-mission-syria [Accessed 27 July 2023].

[22] OPCW. Note by the Technical Secretariat: First Report by the OPCW Investigation and Identification Team Pursuant to Paragraph 10 of Decision C-SS-4/Dec.3 addressing the Threat from Chemical Weapons Use Ltamenah (Syrian Arab Republic) 24, 25, and 30 March 2017. S/1867/2020. The Hague: OPCW. 8 April 2020. p. 17. Available from: https://www.opcw.org/sites/default/files/documents/2020/04/s-1867-2020%28e%29.pdf [Accessed 27 July 2023].

materials that are collected and rigorously assessed for credibility with a view to assisting criminal proceedings in courts.[23]

Notably, some non-state actors have also used open source research findings to support national criminal procedures against individuals responsible for the development and use of prohibited weapons. For example, in October 2020, a collective of civil society actors 'filed a criminal complaint in Germany on behalf of victims of the chemical weapons attacks on Eastern Ghouta on 21 August 2013'.[24] Evidence to support this criminal complaint was based in part on open source investigation methods.

It should be noted, however, that treaty verification and enforcement are *different* from criminal prosecution and the latter goes 'beyond the traditional understanding of how disarmament treaties and their implementing organizations manage cases of non-compliance' (see footnote 6). As Trapp and Cheng have noted, questions remain around 'whether and how compliance enforcement of international arms control laws can interface with legal proceedings related to individual criminal responsibility'.[25]

Users and Producers of Open Source Research

Open source information of relevance to WMD treaty verification is both generated and used by a variety of stakeholders, ranging from civil society actors to international organizations and states. These groups work with open source research findings in various ways and with differing objectives and limitations.

---

[23] United Nations General Assembly. Report of the International, Impartial and Independent Mechanism to Assist in the Investigation and Prosecution of Persons Responsible for the Most Serious Crimes under International Law Committed in the Syrian Arab Republic since March 2011. A/74/699. New York: UN. 13 February 2020. Available from: https://undocs.org/en/A/74/699 [Accessed 27 July 2023].

[24] Human Rights Center, UC Berkeley School of Law. Chemical Weapons Attack in Eastern Ghouta, Syria [online]. 2020. Available from: https://storymaps.arcgis.com/stories/56c19f1dbcbb4054b524cacc5f6a9fa5 [Accessed 21 June 2021].

[25] Trapp R. and Tang C. *Enhancing the Management and Enforcement of Compliance in the Regime Prohibiting Chemical Weapons*. Geneva, Switzerland: UNIDIR. 2021. https://doi.org/10.37559/WMD/21/CWC/01 [Accessed 27 July 2023].

Civil society

Civil society – understood broadly here as including NGOs, academia and other groups of advocates or researchers outside traditional national government or international governance structures – has long contributed to assessments of compliance with WMD-related treaties. Civil society actors are often able to adopt technological innovations more quickly than official government actors and have pioneered many new open source research methods and applications.

Moreover, they are also often able to produce assessments faster (and be more forthright in their assertions) than other actors, certainly compared with international organizations, which tend to be more restricted. Civil society actors have made advances in several areas of treaty verification using open source research. Investigative journalism is one example. The founder of Bellingcat, Eliot Higgins, has pioneered the use of online sources, specifically those found 'in social-media postings, in leaked databases, in free satellite maps' to support investigations into, amongst other things, allegations of chemical weapons use.[26] Another example is the work of think-tanks and NGOs using open source intelligence variously for tracking emerging nuclear threats,[27] nuclear proliferation[28] and the trafficking of nuclear materials,[29,30] or for helping to monitor compliance with international norms surrounding chemical or biological weapons.[31,32]

---

[26] Higgins E. *We are Bellingcat: An intelligence agency for the people*. New York: Bloomsbury Publishing. 2021, p. 2.

[27] One Earth Future Foundation. Open Nuclear Network [online]. Available from: https://www.oneearthfuture.org/open-nuclear-network [Accessed 27 July 2023].

[28] Arterburn J., Dumbacher E., and Stoutland P. *Signals in the Noise: Preventing Nuclear Proliferation with Machine Learning and Publicly Available Information*. C4ADS and Nuclear Threat Initiative. 2021. Available from: https://c4ads.org/s/NTI_C4_Signals-in-the-Noise.pdf [Accessed 27 July 2023].

[29] Nuclear Threat Initiative. *CNS Global Incidents and Trafficking Database* [online]. Available from: https://www.nti.org/analysis/articles/cns-global-incidents-and-trafficking-database [Accessed 27 July 2023].

[30] See also the chapters in this volume by Kristensen & Korda, and Bedenko & Bellish (Chapters 2.3 and 5.4).

[31] See for example: Hunger I. (ed.) *BioWeapons Monitor 2010* [online]. BioWeapons Prevention Project. 2010. Available from: http://www.bwpp.org/documents/BWM2010WEB.pdf [Accessed 27 July 2023].

[32] See also the chapters by H. Wilson *et al.*, and Mathews in this volume (Chapters 4.1 and 4.2).

However, there are limits to the roles non-governmental actors can play in contributing to WMD treaty verification based on open source data. Rapid adoption and application of open source methods can lead to vulnerabilities in methodologies and findings; the race to produce results can lead to errors. Moreover, questions can, and have, arisen over the impartiality of NGOs and other civil society actors when producing open source assessments of WMD treaty compliance. Indeed, some states have contested 'both the authenticity and the basis of open-source data' provided by civil society actors.[33]

There are also constraints on the extent to which civil society actors can effectively feed into discussions around treaty compliance in WMD regimes. Civil society engagement is often restricted to one-way communications with states and international organizations focused on WMD arms control, disarmament and non-proliferation. For example, through presenting or publishing findings and reports for the consideration of state actors, without open dialogue. This contrasts with international humanitarian law treaties which tend to be more flexible. For example, the Mine Ban Treaty and the Convention on Cluster Monitions encourage societal monitoring and a verification system based on the Landmine and Cluster Munition Monitor Report, which is published every year jointly by civil society actors.[34]

International organizations

International organizations – specifically WMD treaty secretariats such as the OPCW Technical Secretariat – are sometimes entrusted with responsibility for aspects of the verification process, typically through undertaking monitoring and technical analysis. Such entities cannot ignore the potential of open source research to contribute to monitoring treaty compliance and are gradually incorporating it into their toolkits.[35]

---

[33] Revill J., Ghionis A., and Zarkan L. *Exploring the Future of WMD Compliance and Enforcement: Workshop Report.* Geneva, Switzerland: UNIDIR. 2020. Available from: https://unidir.org/publication/exploring-future-wmd-compliance-and-enforcement-workshop-report [Accessed 27 July 2023].

[34] See also the chapter by Duke in this volume (Chapter 2.2) for further information about international instruments that allow for NGO participation.

[35] As pointed out by the former Director General of the IAEA, the agency is "responsible for the *technical* work of implementing safeguards. Member States make any *policy* decisions they may consider necessary, based on the factual and impartial reports which we provide." See Amano, Y. Challenges in Nuclear Verification. Statement at CSIS [speech]. Washington DC: IAEA. 5 April 2019. Available from: https://www.iaea.org/newscenter/statements/challenges-in-nuclear-verification [Accessed 27 July 2023].

However, compared to civil society actors, international organizations must exercise more caution both in the methods they use and the statements they produce. International organizations that support treaties, particularly the secretariat-type bodies, are expected to produce authoritative outputs based on carefully considered technical assessments. In doing so, they must maintain independence and impartiality, leaving political determination of compliance to states as part of an established division of work (see footnote 35). Moreover, secretariat bodies within international organizations must operate as far as possible in accordance with the methods and sources that states parties have agreed to accept. Innovative or alternative processes are possible, but they remain more vulnerable to criticism, particularly when such processes have not been validated by states parties to a treaty as part of a collectively agreed treaty procedure.

Accordingly, international organizations are often more cautious in using open source data than civil society groups. Nonetheless, some international organizations have been or are beginning to take advantage of open source data to supplement their verification-related activities. For example, the IAEA draws on a number of open source materials and consults commercially available satellite imagery,[36] and the OPCW has formally adopted open source approaches in investigating allegations of non-compliance with the CWC (as discussed above). Indeed, the OPCW Scientific Advisory Board (SAB) has acknowledged the growing role of open sources and social media information in non-routine missions.

States

States are also producers and users of open source data. For states with advanced capabilities to assess treaty compliance, open source research can usefully be combined with national technical means to augment evidence and judgements about other countries' compliance. For those states with more limited resources, open sources can form a valuable and accessible source of information. This can raise nations' overall knowledge of, or confidence in, the compliance of other countries.

---

[36] IAEA. *Information collection and evaluation* [online]. IAEA. 2016. Available from: https://www.iaea.org/topics/information-collection-and-evaluation [Accessed 4 August 2023].

For state actors, open source research also provides a useful alternative public source to 'classified' information that can be used in support of public statements related to non-compliance. However, open source research findings – like all other forms of data used in treaty verification – are not immune to politicization, particularly in contested information environments in which there are competing analyses linked to different sets of vested interests. In such circumstances, data and methods alike can be easily challenged, and this is particularly true in situations in which open source data challenges the narratives and interests of powerful states.

A Healthy Dose of Realism

New open source research technologies and data streams clearly present exciting opportunities for WMD treaty verification and related activities, and it is likely that open source tools will feature prominently in efforts to develop new arms control and disarmament agreements. However, a healthy dose of realism is required when considering the possibilities. Realizing the potential of open sources and tools requires not just demonstrating their technical advantages but also navigating the politics of WMD treaty verification and facilitating widespread buy-in around the application of new methods and technologies. Some entities, such as the IAEA, have made progress in these areas, but other relevant bodies have yet to do so.

Further progress here will involve developing systems to, *inter alia*, ensure the authenticity of data provided through open source research; corroborate open source information with materials collected through formal agreed procedures where these exist; validate the methods used to extract insights from open source data; carefully manage and securely store data accrued through open source research; and finally diversify expertise in the use of open source methods. These are now discussed in turn.

Data authentication

First, the data used in any open source assessment related to treaty verification need to be authenticated; as the OPCW Temporary Working Group report on Investigative Science and Technology notes, 'before [open source] information can be relied upon, its authenticity needs to be established'.[37] Determining the veracity of materials – that they are genuine and have not been manipulated – could, for example, require the development of the necessary expertise to undertake forensic analysis of metadata associated with photographic or video material. Such expertise is important and may not be immediately available; it may therefore necessitate the development of 'working relationships with sources of such expertise'.[38] In the future, data authentication will become even more significant as developments in technology could be exploited to facilitate data manipulation, including through the use of artificial intelligence to create 'deepfake' data to confuse or mislead verification efforts.[39]

Corroboration

Open source material can also require a wider process of corroboration. Information often needs to be confirmed through several methods and other sources, and analyzed in conjunction with wider sources of expertise. These processes should follow the principle of replicability, which stipulates that for research to be credible, it should reproducible, and that people following the same research methods should arrive at the same findings. However, without context and corroborating information, such as physical samples from the scene or witness testimony,[40] the authenticated open source data cannot provide a complete picture and might be vulnerable to competing interpretations.

---

[37] OPCW Scientific Advisory Board. *Investigative Science and Technology: Report of the Scientific Advisory Board's Temporary Working Group*. SAB/REP/1/19. The Hague: OPCW. December 2019. Available from: https://www.opcw.org/sites/default/files/documents/2020/11/TWG%20Investigative%20Science%20Final%20Report%20-%20January%202020%20%281%29.pdf [Accessed 27 July 2023].

[38] Borrett V., Hanham M., Jeremias G., *et al. Science and Technology for WMD Compliance Monitoring and Investigations* [online]. Geneva, Switzerland; UNIDIR. 2020. Available from: https://doi.org/10.37559/WMD/20/WMDCE11 [Accessed 4 August 2023]. .

[39] For further insights into the potential of AI and Deepfakes see: Anand A. and Bianco B. *The 2021 Innovations Dialogue on Deepfakes, Trust and International Security Conference Report*. Geneva, Switzerland: UNIDIR; 2021. Available from: https://unidir.org/publication/2021-innovations-dialogue-conference-report [Accessed 27 July 2023].

[40] Several chapters in this volume emphasize the importance of local monitors to open source investigations. For example, see the chapters by Wilson, Samuel & Plesch, Strick, Duke, Triebert, and Freeman & Koenig (Chapters 1, 2.1, 2.2, 2.4 and 2.5).

For example, as mentioned before, social media materials, particularly YouTube videos from Ghouta, Syria, in August 2013, strongly suggested that an attack involving chemicals had occurred, and different groups mobilized to collect and analyze social media posts about this. A range of narratives rapidly emerged as to exactly what had happened and who was responsible. To simplify greatly, while most – not all – agreed that chemical weapons had been used, some argued the attacks had been instigated by the forces of the Syrian Arab Republic,[41] while others suggested the chemical attacks were perpetrated by rebel groups.[42]

These positions were neatly woven into wider conflict narratives and were highly politicized. The experience highlights the importance of employing a wide range of methods and corroborating sources, as well as ensuring that methods and findings are replicable and sufficiently robust to withstand considerable scrutiny.

Validation of methods

For open source research to be used in treaty verification, not only does the data need to be authenticated and corroborated but the methods for collecting data need to be 'scientifically sound, validated, and robust for use in the field' (see footnote 6). Open source research often requires multiple contributors and many iterative processes. The findings are more likely to be accepted in circumstances where the providers follow agreed methods (and are transparent about the methods they use). The validation of methods will be particularly important if open source tools are to be accepted in the practice of WMD treaty verification by international organizations, given the political sensitivities that are involved.

Validating research methods entails the development of standards for collecting open source data and measures to ensure their integrity through

---

[41] See for example: Hague W. Foreign Secretary: UN must get access to chemical attack site [online]. Foreign and Commonwealth Office. 23 August 2013. Available from: https://www.gov.uk/government/news/foreign-secretary-un-must-get-access-to-chemical-attack-site [Accessed 27 July 2023].

[42] Putin V. A Plea for Caution From Russia. *The New York Times*. 12 September 2013. Available from: http://www.nytimes.com/2013/09/12/opinion/putin-plea-for-caution-from-russia-on-syria.html [Accessed 27 July 2023].

the chain of custody, in passing from the generator to the consumer without any tampering.[43] For example, maximizing the use of commercially available satellite data 'may further require that satellite data providers share details on calibration of their satellite systems as well as the methods they employed in processing data' (see footnote 11). Notably, in some issue areas, collaborative partnerships are emerging to consider sector-wide approaches; for example, work monitoring human rights violations has led to the development of the *Berkeley Protocol on Digital Open Source Investigations* that provides 'standards and guidelines for the identification, collection, preservation, verification, and analysis of digital open source information with an aim toward improving its effective use in international criminal and human rights investigations'.[44,45] Such guidelines could be useful to further consider in WMD treaty verification, where they could provide robust and reliable processes for conducting open source research, as well as accepted systems for understanding and using open source research findings.

Data management

A fourth area demanding attention is the issue of information management. New open source data streams are creating significant amounts of data. For example, in 2019, the Director General of the IAEA stated that the Agency handled 140 million items of open source data every year.[46] The IAEA has assembled a Collaborative Analysis Platform to manage this information. Such data streams are likely to continue to increase and expand. This raises questions about how international organizations and other stakeholders can identify, store and collate relevant information for use at some point in the future. Notably, significant quantities of open source data may only become relevant sometime after they have been collected, for instance, in

---

[43] Patton T., Lewis J., Hanham M., Dill C., and Vaccaro L. *Emerging Satellites for Non-Proliferation and Disarmament Verification*. Vienna, Austria: Vienna Center for Disarmament and Non-Proliferation. 2016. Available from: https://vcdnp.org/wp-content/uploads/2016/06/160614_copernicus_project_report.pdf [Accessed 27 July 2023].

[44] See also the chapter by Freeman & Koenig in this volume (Chapter 2.5) for more information about the *Berkeley Protocol*.

[45] Amano Y. Challenges in Nuclear Verification. Statement at CSIS [speech]. Washington DC: IAEA. 05 April 2019. Available from: https://www.iaea.org/newscenter/statements/challenges-in-nuclear-verification [Accessed 27 July 2023].

[46] *ibid.*

a subsequent investigation of WMD treaty compliance. However, to be of value, the data will need to have been properly collected, collated and stored. There are many complications around doing this, including, for example, the fact that certain forms of social media data can be removed, modified or erased by social media users and/or platform owners.

Data security

The process of information management is complicated by challenges associated with the secure preservation of different types of open source data. For open source materials to be actionable at any point in the future, they need to be safely and securely stored. This entails preserving data from both degradation and cyberattack, either of which would significantly undermine confidence in the validity of the original data. Moreover, data collection and storage needs to be conducted in such a way as to avoid any suspicion that the data have been tampered with at any stage. To this end, international organizations such as the OPCW have 'implemented steps to capture and protect results from open source searches directly related to the identification of perpetrators within the IIT's mandate', including through the development of a bespoke 'airgapped' file storage system accessible only through 'specific encrypted terminals'.[47]

Diversifying expertise

A further challenge to incorporating open source methods in treaty verification-related activities is ensuring both diversity of representation in the relevant processes, as well as localized, country-specific mechanisms that can contextualize open source data. Any system which relies primarily on Western expertise and focuses solely on Western adversaries is unlikely to foster widespread buy-in. Such acceptance is important if data are to be used at the international level and also resonates with the wider goal of maximizing diversity in the staffing of all international organizations. One first step

---

[47] OPCW. Note by the Technical Secretariat: *Second Report by the OPCW Investigation and Identification Team Pursuant to Paragraph 10 of Decision C-SS-4/DEC.3 "Addressing the threat from chemical weapons use" SARAQIB (Syrian Arab Republic) – 4 February 2018.* S/1943/2021. The Hague: OPCW. 2021. Annex 1, pp. 47–48. Available from: https://www.opcw.org/sites/default/files/documents/2021/04/s-1943-2021%28e%29.pdf [Accessed 4 August 2023].

to this process of diversification could involve treaty- or technology-specific international events with sponsorship for Global South participation.

While diversifying expertise in open source methods can help increase the quality of and support for the adoption of these technologies at the international level, it presents another set of challenges – More expert voices in open source methods in a highly contested information environment might also increase the scope for mis- and disinformation surrounding treaty verification activities, and might face problems relating to the differential access to and engagement with the internet in different parts of the world.

Reflections on WMD Treaty Verification in the Age of Google

The exciting prospects presented by open source research remind us that technological advances afford opportunities to international treaty regimes controlling and prohibiting WMD. However, they also present challenges to these regimes, and it is far from straightforward to assess when and how different regimes will be able to maximize the potential contributions of open source research.

Adopting innovations is a process, and often a slow one, particularly in international organizations dealing with the acutely sensitive issues of WMD treaty compliance (see footnote 11). At the international level, the integration of open source information and technologies into WMD verification regimes must take into consideration political as well as technological factors. In the current period of geostrategic tension and mistrust, these political considerations are significant.

However, they are not insurmountable. We should not give up on open source research as a means to support international WMD treaties. As some experiences have shown, it can be successfully integrated if the appropriate measures are put in place to validate the methods, authenticate and corroborate the data, and ensure data management and security. In the future, open source research could play an increasingly significant role as part of a 'new vision' for the verification of WMD treaties.

© 2024 World Scientific Publishing Company
https://doi.org/10.1142/9781800614079_0014

Chapter 4.4

Current OSINT Applications for Weapons Monitoring and Verification

Dan Liu and Zuzanna Gwadera

Abstract
This chapter considers open source research that can identify and track illicit weapons of mass destruction (WMD) proliferation and whether such efforts could be scaled up and harnessed to support the verification systems of international arms control, disarmament and non-proliferation treaties. It starts by examining two ways in which civil society is already engaged in researching patterns of illicit proliferation – specifically open source sanctions monitoring and trade data analysis. The chapter goes on to consider the desirability and possibility of incorporating non-governmental open source intelligence (OSINT) within WMD treaties and identifies precedents for such arrangements, as well as opportunities and constraints for them. It then presents two models for how OSINT might be included in additional treaty verification processes: The first considers arrangements for coordinating non-governmental OSINT, and the second explores building OSINT capability within international organizations. While there are undoubtedly complications to incorporating OSINT within international treaty verification, doing so could bring numerous benefits to international weapons regulations.

Introduction

Since civil society monitoring was conceived in the 1950s,[1] analysts have identified successive waves of new applications in open source

---

[1] Evan W. M. An International Public Opinion Poll On Disarmament and "Inspection by the People": A Study of Attitudes Toward Supranationalism, in Melman S. (ed). *Inspection for Disarmament*. New York: Columbia University Press. 1958, pp. 231–250.

This is an open access article published by World Scientific Publishing Europe Ltd. and distributed under the terms of the Creative Commons Attribution-NonCommercial 4.0 International (CC BY-NC 4.0) License.

intelligence (OSINT). In what Williams and Blum describe as the 'second generation'[2] in the early 2000s, the OSINT space dramatically expanded in scope and coverage. Despite this, it has fallen well short of the predictions of early theorists and practitioners.[3] As OSINT well and truly enters its conceptual 'third generation',[4] this chapter explores the current state of play of the technological landscape and OSINT ecosystem, focusing on non-proliferation and sanctions-monitoring applications. Building on this, we then explore the opportunities and challenges of scaling up and institutionalizing OSINT within the verification arrangements of international arms control, disarmament and non-proliferation treaties.

The chapter starts by detailing current applications for non-proliferation monitoring, focusing on red-flag monitoring and trade flow analysis that enable the scrutiny – and timely detection – of transfers and production of components that could be used to make weapons. In the second section, the chapter discusses previous experiences of using OSINT in treaty verification and the requirements for extending this approach. Finally, the chapter presents two possibilities for how OSINT could be scaled up to achieve broader coverage; The first is a decentralized system that would mobilize non-government actors and societal verification, while the second is a centralized framework that involves strengthening underempowered international institutions. In discussing these models, the chapter considers the difficulties of each, including by examining how funding constraints and the politicized nature of international institutions may erode perceptions of objectivity and trust, two core factors needed for open source treaty verification to operate effectively.

For the purposes of this chapter, verification is defined as the systems established by international weapons treaties to assess treaty compliance. Verification is thought to serve several functions, including deterring violations of, and building confidence in, a treaty. We adopt the definition of OSINT as 'intelligence produced from publicly available information that is collected, exploited, and disseminated in a timely manner to an appropriate

---

[2]Williams H. J. and Blum I. *Defining Second Generation Open Source Intelligence (OSINT) for the Defense Enterprise*. RAND Corporation. 2018.

[3]Remarks by J. Niles Riddel, Deputy Director Foreign Broadcast Information Service. First International Symposium National Security And National Competitiveness [speech transcript]. 2 December 1992. Available from: https://irp.fas.org/fbis/riddel.html [Accessed 31 July 2023].

[4]Williams H. J. and Blum I. 2018. *op. cit.*

audience for the purpose of addressing a specific intelligence requirement'.[5] While there are many different OSINT communities of practice, ranging from fully closed government capabilities to open civil society initiatives, this chapter focuses on OSINT conducted by non-governmental groups and its future adoption within international organizations.

Red Flags and Trade Network Analysis to Monitor Proliferation

Illicit proliferation does not generally involve the purchase of finished off-the-shelf weapons.[6,7] Instead, recent cases have comprised actors seeking component parts and technology needed for their own indigenous development of, e.g. weapons of mass destruction (WMD) and delivery systems. The international community often seeks to restrict access to constituent materials through sanctions lists, which are frequently seen as crucial tools for limiting proliferators' options and imposing economic costs on them. However, they can result in a 'cat and mouse' dynamic, in which the act of publishing lists of prohibited items and activities can prompt proliferators to adapt their methods in order to avoid attention and escape punitive actions. To evade sanctions and to circumvent trade control compliance, proliferators will change almost every aspect of their networks, including by using shell companies, intermediaries and agents across various countries' jurisdictions, and by organizing their activities over decades.[8]

Trade data can be useful in monitoring activities and materials related to proliferation. Analysis and screening of free and/or commercially available trade data has been an established part of non-proliferation and sanctions enforcement tradecraft since at least the early 1990s and provides visibility into the import and export of proliferation-sensitive, controlled and dual-use items, such as chemical precursors,[9] nuclear reactor components, critical

---

[5] National Defense Authorization Act for Fiscal Year 2006. 109–163. Sect. 931. 2006.
[6] Dall E., Keatinge T., and Berger A. *Countering Proliferation Finance: An Introductory Guide for Financial Institutions*. RUSI Guidance Paper. London: RUSI. 2017. p. 1.
[7] For information on work tracking corruption in the formal arms trade, see the chapter by Michie *et al.* in this volume (Chapter 5.3).
[8] Dall E., Keatinge T., and Berger A. 2017. *op. cit.*
[9] Chapter 4.2 in this volume (by Mathews) details open source research focused on the precursor chemical thiodigycol and how the Chemical Weapons Convention deal with this and other precursors.

Figure 1: The general red-flag methodology.

avionics or aramid fibres.[10] Across governmental and non-governmental monitoring of trade and sanctions, an overall process has organically emerged over the years. While each actor has their own unique mix of methods and tradecraft, almost all follow the fundamental workflow outlined in Fig. 1.

This chapter focuses on examples of the first two steps, since they ground and determine the overall process: (1) identifying red-flag indicators and (2) conducting investigations using network analysis.

Investigators across various disciplines, but especially in the financial and commercial space, use 'red-flag' approaches to guide and prioritize their investigatory work.[11] Fundamentally, red flags are diagnostic and observable signals that may indicate that an actor is deviating from standard or expected activity. Modern red-flag techniques are widely applied in the commercial sector to screen for signs of fraud and are akin to the decades-old 'indicators and warnings' techniques used by national intelligence and policing communities.[12]

As with all aspects of any monitoring system, the exact nature of red flags should be regularly updated, and the overall process must be dynamic enough to adapt at scale when proscribed behaviours change. Similarly, in keeping with wider indicator and warning systems, observation of red flags alone is insufficient to evidence a violation. False positives from imprecise

---

[10] German security agency efforts tracking Pakistani imports of nuclear critical material and equipment from customs information were key to unmasking the A.Q. Khan network. See Hibbs M. The Unmaking of a Nuclear Smuggler. *Bulletin of the Atomic Scientists*. 2006. 62 (6), pp. 35–41.

[11] Other chapters in this volume also consider the utility of 'red-flag' monitoring in open source research tracking weapons. See, for example, the chapters by H. Wilson *et al.* and Michie *et al.* (Chapters 4.1 and 5.3).

[12] Gentry J. A. and Gordon J. S. *Strategic Warning Intelligence History, Challenges, and Prospects*. Washington DC: Georgetown University Press. 2019.

indicator selection often occur and further investigation must proceed before researchers can confirm whether the red flags signify serious wrongdoing. Yet, red-flag signal detection, if set up correctly, can effectively trigger useful research and help investigators prioritize their work. Examples of red flags in open source trade analysis are as follows:

- a rise in the reported import of a chemical precursor into a country, which does not correlate with the needs of its civilian sector;[13]
- shipment of a controlled or dual-use good by a shipper or consignee with no history of shipping such an item;[14]
- incorporation of corporate entities that match or link sanctioned or designated entities.[15]

Detecting red-flag leads can trigger investigators to perform extra due diligence checks on the corporations and networks behind the suspect trade or commercial behaviour. Here, the acquisition of corporate registry information, business particulars and shareholder details can help build an understanding of the network of associations and ultimate beneficiaries involved in a trade, which is often necessary to confirm any sanctions breaches or violations of disarmament commitments. Investigators typically use network analysis for this, a tried and tested set of theories and practices that enable researchers to depict, understand and interrogate relationships between different actors and that is widely used in a variety of government, civilian and academic use cases.[16]

International relations theory has long recognized the potential of network analysis to provide precise descriptions of international networks, their actions and their effects.[17] In keeping with this, being able to detect and monitor the trade activity of proliferation procurement networks is critical to understanding and verifying the true state of a country's proliferation

---

[13] Conflict Armament Research. *Procurement Networks Behind Islamic State Improvised Weapon Programmes*. Ghent: Conflict Armament Research. 2020.

[14] Margolin J. and Bukharin I. *Trick of the Trade – South Asia's Illicit Nuclear Supply Chains*. Washington DC: C4ADS. 2020.

[15] Brewer J. *Study of Typologies of Financing of WMD Proliferation*. London: King's College London. 2017.

[16] Carrington P. J., Scott J., and Wasserman S. *Models and Methods in Social Network Analysis*. Cambridge: Cambridge University Press. 2005.

[17] Hafner-Burton E. M., Kahler M., and Montgomery A. H. Network Analysis for International Relations. *International Organization*. 2009. 63 (3), pp. 559–592.

status, regardless of its claims or ascension to any disarmament agreements. Effective operationalization of trade network monitoring systems, therefore, could be crucial to the success of any overall treaty verification.

Operationalizing Red-Flag Monitoring and Trade Network Analysis in Weapons Treaty Verification: Opportunities and Constraints

Various analytic communities use such techniques to examine wider compliance with sanctions or disarmament agreements (see footnote 17). For example, the Department of Safeguards of the International Atomic Energy Agency (IAEA) has been institutionalizing trade data analysis since at least the early 2000s;[18] various UN panels of experts on sanctions and arms embargo violations often incorporate trade data analysis as part of their portfolio of investigative sources and tools; and non-governmental research organizations also use these methods to support international non-proliferation and sanctions enforcement initiatives.[19]

Can such efforts be extended, and if so, what would be the best way to go about this? In particular, could the large and growing community of open source researchers contribute to weapons treaty verification arrangements?

An empowered and sustained civil society that can reliably and independently monitor red flags as well as publicly track trade of sensitive items and provide open source investigative capacity to uncover illicit networks, could make a meaningful contribution to building trust and transparency in international disarmament and arms control mechanisms. Currently, loose networks of people and organizations do this on an *ad-hoc* basis, often self-organizing through Twitter or other platforms.[20] Theoretically, these

---

[18] Chatelus R., Crete J. M., Schot P. M., Hushbeck E. C., and Heine P. *Safeguards Export-import Training: Adapting to Changes in the Department of Safeguards Over Six Years of Experience*. Vienna: International Atomic Energy Agency (IAEA). 2015. Contract No.: IAEA-CN–220.

[19] See for example, Brewer J. Proliferation Financing: The Potential Impact of the Nuclear Agreement with Iran on International Controls. *Strategic Trade Review*. 2016. 2 (2). Available from: http://www.str.ulg.ac.be/wp-content/uploads/2016/03/2.-Proliferation-Financing-The-Potential-Impact-of-the-Nuclear-Agreement-with-Iran-on-International-Controls.pdf [Accessed 14 May 2022].

[20] Several chapters in this volume provide examples of such emerging communities. See, for example, the chapters by Strick, Freeman & Koenig, and Ahmad (2.1, 2.5 and 3.1). Toler (Chapter 3.2) considers dangers of crowdsourced open source research and the possibilities of guarding against these.

arrangements could be formalized and harnessed by international treaties prohibiting weapons, thereby fulfilling societal verification functions in which public analytical communities would sit separately from international organizations and government verification efforts, yet would be an equally valued part of the information ecosystem, providing a means to support the overall work building confidence in treaty compliance.

There are precedents for such arrangements, in which non-governmental bodies are specifically mandated to augment an arms control regime, especially in the conventional small arms space. For example, UN Security Council Resolutions 2182 (2014), 2244 (2015), 2317 (2016) and 2385 (2017) mandate non-governmental organizational support for the Federal Government of Somalia (FGS) in the UN Security Council (UNSC)-mandated Joint Verification Team (JVT).[21] These teams conduct routine inspections and support local authorities' efforts to secure, track and manage weapons stockpiles.

However, there are significant technical and political constraints to non-governmental researchers getting involved in such initiatives.[22] The two largest technical limitations to scaling up current open source research are data availability and the means to process data, as discussed in the following section.

Data availability

Like any mass data analysis, a mandated open source verification effort focused on trade data and trade networks would need a constant, up-to-date stream of data that has as broad a coverage as possible. Although early open source theorists anticipated that open source information would be increasingly available (see footnote 2), since then the information environment has become ever more segregated, siloed and locked down. While there have often been good reasons for these developments, they have also impeded open source researchers' work accessing and understanding data.

---

[21] See also the chapter by Duke in this volume (Chapter 2.2) for details of non-governmental monitoring of small arms and light weapons in South Sudan and how this contributes to various national, regional and international non-proliferation and disarmament agreements.

[22] See also the chapter by Revill & Garzón Maceda in this volume (Chapter 4.4).

Type	Description	Example
Government Declared Data	Prepared and submitted by states to an international authority for non-proliferation purposes.	Compliance reports to UNSC resolutions. Responses to IAEA requests for information.
Government Recorded Data	Information collected by states for their own use, and which is not routinely submitted to international authorities for non-proliferation purposes.	Export licensing data. Customs data. Business registration information.
Business-Held Data	Information on a company's own products and customers, and commercially available market intelligence information.	Company sales reports.
Intelligence and Enforcement Derived Information	Information on specific procurement attempts, networks, or procurement requirements.	Suspicious activity reports from financial intelligence units.
Procurement Requirements Information	Information released by a programme for the purpose of seeking goods or services.	Public tendering information.

Figure 2: Categories of trade data (adapted from Stewart and Gillard).

According to Stewart and Gillard,[23] actionable trade data that lends itself to non-proliferation analysis can be thought of in terms of the categories shown in Fig. 2.

The ability of open source investigators to safely, ethically and legally access these different data types will depend on the data and regulatory environments in the place they are operating from and in the areas they are investigating. For example, a jurisdiction might have an open public tender gazette but keep their corporate registry information offline, making it impossible to access these records remotely. Others may have a highly searchable corporate directory online, but will include only limited information on their public tender processes. There are numerous legitimate secrets in commercial enterprises and national security bodies, and to protect these, many reports of suspicious activity that are sent by financial institutions to national financial intelligence units are not available to the public.

---

[23] Stewart I. and Gillard N. *Open Source and Trade Data for Non-proliferation: Challenges and Opportunities*. Vienna: International Atomic Energy Agency (IAEA). 2015. Contract No.: IAEA-CN–220.

Bill of lading information constitutes some of the most valuable market intelligence in the commercial sphere. It is frequently held by data vendors, who make it commercially available after procuring it from customs authorities, or shipping agencies. This type of data is often very expensive, increasing the financial burden of research, particularly research aiming to investigate transhipments or diversion of materials over time and in jurisdictions where data are not readily available. Additional constraints lie in the relatively incomplete nature of the coverage. Although bill of lading information is presented as encyclopaedic or exhaustive, it is often far from it. Many customs jurisdictions in Europe, Africa and the Middle East do not publish bills of lading.

Finally, the degree to which these data streams are made available in machine parsable formats greatly accelerates or limits the possibility of scaling up investigative workflows. Data availability and the permissiveness of the data environment also dictate whether investigators can set up a sophisticated surveillance and data collection architecture and passively wait for red flags to be raised or can proactively search to test databases for cases of red-flagged behaviours.

Processing, tooling and workflows

Data collection, fusion and analysis toolsets and platforms also have cost implications that can limit the size and growth of efforts to monitor trade. These can greatly facilitate and expand the capacity of individual analysts, but the standard analytical tools are currently very costly. Some collaborative platforms, resources and data-sharing arrangements have started to emerge among civil society open source researchers, providing invaluable spaces for the community to pool resources, work together and build a collective operating picture around common issues.[24] These are beginning to make a mark in lowering financial barriers and facilitating collaboration and analytical teaming, with some platforms having reached initial operating capability stage and already being used by the community to good effect. However, sharing commercially purchased information often has substantial data rights issues that cannot be overlooked.

---

[24] Several chapters in this volume give examples of the development of community tools and platforms. See, for example, the chapters by L. Wilson *et al.* and Bedenko & Bellish (Chapters 5.1 and 5.4).

Another major technical constraint is workflow. Currently, many analytical endeavours are limited by the rate an individual researcher can manually parse and filter data points. For example, entity- and network-focused investigations are heavily dependent on intense human analytical input, and without mass-machine-assisted analytical support to augment human analysis, this is unlikely to change. Such options are still in their early days and not widely adopted. Moreover, while they offer the promise that they will be able to help some aspects of research, they can bring with them other difficulties.

Red-flag monitoring, network analysis – and the large volumes of data processing both of these need – would seem to be ideally amenable to machine-assisted solutions, and indeed the commercial world is seeing some breakthroughs that can be adopted in this space. Yet, some parts of the workflow depicted in Fig. 1 do not lend themselves to automated analysis, especially the investigation and peer verification stages.[25] The complicated and dynamic ways in which proliferation networks hide and morph their corporate connections will make attempts to embed machine-assisted workflows *en-masse* technically challenging. For example, given that machine learning tools are trained to detect designated pathways, training datasets corresponding to those pre-defined instances have limited ability to detect novel proliferation strategies – and human interventions are needed for this. Further still, the consequences of potentially inaccurate attributions based on algorithmically derived evidence also complicates the adoption of such approaches legally and ethically.

Experiences of Using OSINT within Treaty Verification

As outlined in the previous section, the use of OSINT for verifying international weapons treaties is not new. In fact, it has previously been employed with varying degrees of formality. However, it is not widespread or uniformly accepted, for example, WMD-related arms control, non-proliferation and disarmament agreements have generally stopped

---

[25] See also the chapter by Withorne in this volume (Chapter 5.2) for a discussion on how to understand the relationship between machine learning and open source research.

short of incorporating non-governmental OSINT within their verification regimes. In 2001, Meier and Tenner[26] pointed out that OSINT-practising non-governmental organizations (NGOs) were hardly ever involved in WDM treaty compliance verification in any official capacity. Not much has changed since then; despite growing capabilities, open source reporting from civil society is generally only used semi-officially or completely informally. Most frequently, it happens when parties to international agreements or international verification organizations contract non-governmental groups to collect and analyze open source data relevant to particular missions. To date, perhaps the most prominent example of using OSINT as a treaty verification tool is the IAEA's employment of OSINT for safeguards monitoring mentioned above.

However, integrating non-governmental OSINT more firmly within treaty verification could provide all parties to an agreement with a broader and more robust picture of its implementation, thus enhancing the agreement's viability. For example, it could effectively function as an independent monitoring and evaluation component. While OSINT is not necessarily able to generate irrefutable proof of violations, it can provide valuable contextual information to help understand a country's activities and decision-making.[27] Woolf[28] highlights that, in general, a wider range of collected information will lead to more violations being detected, strengthening a verification regime's deterrent value. Furthermore, including non-governmental OSINT in treaty verification can serve as a confidence-building measure, allowing parties to get more clarity about each other's behaviour. Importantly, information obtained from open sources can be more easily discussed than that obtained clandestinely, and could thus provide more benign ground for dialogue about state party compliance. In time, all these factors could translate to strengthening global norms against prohibited behaviour.

---

[26] Meier O. and Tenner C. Non-governmental Monitoring of International Agreements, in Findlay T. (ed). *Verification Yearbook*. London: VERTIC. 2000. p. 217.
[27] Hobbs C. and Moran M. Armchair Safeguards: The Role of Open Source Intelligence in Nuclear Proliferation Analysis, in Hobbs C., Moran M., Salisbury D. (eds). *Open Source Intelligence in the 21st Century: New Approaches and Opportunities*. London: Palgrave Macmillan UK. 2014. pp. 65–80.
[28] Woolf A. F. *Monitoring and Verification in Arms Control*. Washington DC: U.S. Congressional Research Service. 2011. Report No.: R41201.

Embedding OSINT within treaty verification could also strengthen non-governmental OSINT practices, e.g. by providing practitioners with resources to collect and analyze greater quantities of more accurate data, and maintain better security. The latter is particularly important. Even though OSINT analysts only utilize publicly available sources, they often seek out and disclose information that could harm the groups or activities that they are observing, and risk being pursued by adversarial forces aiming to compromise investigations. Maintaining operation security is crucial for analysts, but insufficient resources may sometimes mean that organizations are unable to adequately protect their personnel. If managed well, institutionalizing OSINT as a treaty verification tool could help secure the funding necessary for both operation security (including training) and robust cyber-security infrastructure, and may provide an additional layer of legitimacy for the OSINT programme. The enhanced credibility that could result from official recognition in international weapons and disarmament agreements might also act as a deterrent to both state and non-state actors aiming to disturb or discredit work if, for example, there were in-built consequences to any attributable cyber-attacks.

Operationalizing OSINT as a Treaty Verification Tool

What would it take to include non-governmental OSINT within arms control, non-proliferation and disarmament treaty verification? It would first require mandating an OSINT-based component within a treaty's formal verification mechanism, thus providing a clear legal basis for when and how states parties and treaty organizations could invoke open source information collection and analysis. Developing a well-considered mandate is central to effectiveness, helping to ensure that analysts conduct relevant and robust research, as well as facilitating transparency and trust between parties.

One area where the international community has come close to doing this is the Additional Protocol (AP) that the IAEA adopted in 1997 to expand the safeguards verification it conducts within the 1968 Treaty on the Non-Proliferation of Nuclear Weapons (NPT), which is designed to ascertain that materials are not diverted from legitimate purposes towards illicit nuclear weapons programmes. Although the AP does not mention

OSINT specifically, its emphasis on comprehensive information acquisition and analysis paved the way for the Division of Safeguards Information Management (SIGM) acquiring OSINT capabilities.[29] It is important to note here that the IAEA safeguards are an enormous endeavour driven primarily by state parties' commitments to the NPT and closely defined by their safeguards agreements with the NPT. If future agreements, including those with fewer state parties and spanning even more politically sensitive areas, wanted to take this model a step further and enable non-governmental groups to contribute to such efforts, a clearly defined mandate would also be essential. The process of states parties negotiating and agreeing such a mandate would in the first place be required before non-governmental OSINT could contribute to verification, and once the agreement had been implemented, such a mandate could help prevent accusations of states parties abusing the system for their own benefit.

A second key factor to consider is finance. While generally the remote monitoring provided by online open source research can be cost-effective when compared to other treaty verification systems, it requires robust funding. In fact, inadequate resources are often cited as a major limitation for fully exploiting open source data.[30] A functioning OSINT programme needs highly skilled and well-trained personnel, physical space to work in, and access to relevant hardware, software and data. There are practical limitations to these, including the fact that they all come at a cost.

How an OSINT-based verification component within the context of a binding treaty would be organized is another question. Here we consider two feasible options.

Option 1: Decentralized model

Our decentralized model involves scaling up the current collaboration within non-governmental communities and empowering them to expand their capabilities and enhance their voices. This could involve one or more

---

[29] Ferguson M. and Norman C. *All-Source Information Acquisition and Analysis in the IAEA Department of Safeguards*. Vienna: International Atomic Energy Agency (IAEA). 2010. Contract No.: IAEA-CN-184.
[30] Salisbury D. Open Source Intelligence and Proliferation Procurement: Combating Illicit Trade, in Hobbs C., Moran M., Salisbury D. (eds). *Open Source Intelligence in the 21st Century: New Approaches and Opportunities*. London: Palgrave Macmillan UK. 2014. pp. 81–100.

NGOs working to support a treaty's verification mandate in close coordination with the treaty organization.

This option is more readily implementable than the second (detailed in the next section), as it taps into resources that, to an extent, already exist. Currently, there are several non-governmental open source research hubs focussed on international security.[31] These tend to congregate highly skilled data collectors and analysts, who excel at their mission and can be uniquely agile in responding to changing proliferation habits. But, as Persbo[32] notes, although NGOs tend to adapt easily and be cost-effective, their ability to be constructive monitoring and verification actors heavily depends on factors such as 'the size and composition of the organisation, staff training and experience, political support, and financial support'. These aspects could at least partially be addressed by mandating NGOs to conduct OSINT for verification of future weapons agreements and providing appropriate levels of consistent support for this work, which could yield a civil society-driven OSINT verification component that is well-equipped and capable of collecting and analyzing large amounts of information on the activities of all state parties in a neutral manner.

What further makes the decentralized approach perhaps more feasible is that the endeavour might be able to proceed without the enthusiastic political and financial support of state parties sceptical of the value of OSINT. While it would be naïve to expect these countries to readily offer funding and public endorsement, or easily consent to a mandated regime that facilitated this, they might agree to including non-governmental OSINT within a treaty's verification system as a condition for concluding a broader set of measures, either within the initial framing of a new treaty or the development of an existing one.

This option does involve several challenges. The first is logistical: The coordination of activities across several institutions is bound to be complicated. For example, among other things, contributing organizations are likely to need adequate communication channels and a shared

---

[31] See, for example, the chapters by Kristensen & Korda, Withorne, and Bedenko & Bellish in this volume (Chapters 2.3, 5.2, and 5.4).

[32] Persbo A. *The Role of Non-governmental Organizations in the Verification of International Agreements*. Geneva: UN Institute for Disarmament Research. October 2010. Report No.: 1020-7287 Contract No.: UNIDIR/2010/11.

information storage system. What presents a greater hurdle, however, is the presently unbalanced nature of OSINT cultures across different communities. The NGOs currently engaged in OSINT for arms control, disarmament and non-proliferation are primarily Western in their origin, location and approach, and accordingly, findings from these are unlikely to be politically acceptable to other parts of the world, including China and Russia.[33] Funding imperatives and realities may exacerbate this issue: NGOs are necessarily funding-driven, and it is likely that most funding for treaty verification OSINT will initially come from Western states.

Despite the relative Western-based homogeneity in the current landscape of non-governmental OSINT, a third hurdle is presented by the *differences* within this sector. Any individual NGO is unlikely to have large enough capabilities to single-handedly fulfil all aspects of an agreed mandate or be willing to be transformed into solely a treaty verification programme, and it is likely that the work would be carried out across several institutions. However, within the finite number of NGOs with relevant expertise, there are large variations. They differ in size and organization, and, as Nye points out, 'in accountability and sense of responsibility for the accuracy of their claims'.[34] They may also have different political leanings and views on issues related to a treaty verification mandate, and different institutional needs, including funding imperatives. While some redundancy may be desirable, for example, as a means for non-governmental OSINT to peer review each other's work, all these differences are likely to affect the choices NGOs make in data collection and reporting, and could complicate attempts to uncover the truth about treaty compliance/non-compliance.

There are, of course, ways to mitigate against all these challenges, including by developing a robust mandate clarifying processes and responsibilities in the first place, as described above. Another way to address the challenges

---

[33] An example of Russian scepticism about OSINT is the reaction to open source evidence of violations of the Intermediate-Range Nuclear Forces (INF) Treaty. While in this case *any* evidence would likely be rejected, Russian analysis specifically challenged OSINT, stating that while the method 'may seem convincing', it 'cannot serve as the basis for real-world political and military decisions'. See Kolbin A. How Open Source Intelligence Narrows Down the Opportunities for Dialogue on the INF Treaty. *Russia Confidential*. 2017. 242 (2), p. 2. Available from: http://web.archive.org/web/20220308231955/http://www.pircenter.org/media/content/files/13/14888922911.pdf [Accessed 25 August 2023].

[34] Nye J. The Rising Power of NGOs: Transnational Groups are Making their Voices Heard, and Governments and Corporations are Taking Notice. *Taipei Times*. 29 June 2004.

could be to coordinate training across organizations, to ensure maximum possible objectivity, transparency and coordination of groups and individuals, as well as to develop compatible working methods across contributing organizations.

Option 2: Building a bureaucracy

Beyond harnessing NGOs, another option – the 'centralized model' – could involve building on the IAEA's experience and forming an independent OSINT programme for treaty verification. This might originally be established for a specific agreement and then potentially grow and expand to form a multiple- or even pan-treaty OSINT verification organization. A programme like this could be attached to a relevant UN organ. For example, the OSINT capabilities for a future agreement limiting fissile material could be hosted within the technically oriented IAEA, or those for disarmament agreements could be organized under the United Nations Office for Disarmament Affairs (UNODA). Another option could be to have the United Nations Institute for Disarmament Research (UNIDIR) host the programme. As a well-established institute within the UN system that has long engaged in disarmament research, UNIDIR benefits from being seen as both legitimate and independent.[35] Funding for the open source effort could mirror that of the IAEA SIGM, which is financed partly from the IAEA's resources and partly from voluntary contributions from the Safeguards Member State Support Programmes.[36] As well as developing its own OSINT capability, a centralized arrangement could benefit from utilizing existing NGO expertise, including through talent procurement and access to relevant training.

While for either model for institutionalizing OSINT, hoping for immediate and tangible support could seem optimistic, the centralized model might meet with less opposition. Its biggest advantage is that, because it assumes hosting the OSINT verification component within the UN system rather than depending on Western NGOs, it could garner greater perceived legitimacy than the decentralized model, and so could potentially generate

---

[35] UNIDIR. *For a More Stable and Secure World* [online]. UNIDIR. Available from: https://www.unidir.org/about [Accessed 31 July 2023].

[36] Barletta M., Zarimpas N., and Zarucki R. Open Source Information Acquisition and Analysis in the International Atomic Energy Agency Department of Safeguards. *Nuclear Technology*. 2012. 179 (1), pp. 156–159.

more support and trust from sceptical states. As mentioned above, OSINT may serve as a tool for building transparency and mutual understanding. Attaching it to an international organization, even in a non-binding form, would help promote a norm for states to engage with open source information and use it to foster dialogue about treaty compliance. In time, it might also gain the trust of reluctant state parties.

A further benefit of operating from a single organization is that it may render a more cohesive team that is easier to manage on nearly all fronts, such as communication, information procurement and sharing, and coordination and dissemination of work. It could also make adopting appropriate cybersecurity measures more straightforward. In general, placing an OSINT verification programme within an international organization may help minimize cybersecurity risks, such as unintended data disclosure or cyber-attacks from malicious actors, as it could have greater oversight and control over systems for protecting against these.

The centralized model has its drawbacks, however. The first obvious one is that setting up a new OSINT programme could require a much larger upfront investment than funding several already existing organizations. Recruiting and training staff, setting up a working space and procuring the necessary software and hardware will involve significant costs. Given that the initial funding will likely largely come from voluntary contributions, it might be difficult to acquire sufficient finance.

Other obstacles stem from the nature of large bureaucracies. Even an exceptionally well-run bureaucracy is bound to be less agile and efficient than smaller and relatively less constrained organizations. This factor could have an adverse impact on the overall performance of OSINT activities, and especially on time-sensitive investigations. Operating in a highly politicized environment could exacerbate the issue. For example, Salisbury notes that the IAEA Outreach Programme must have a government's consent prior to collecting information from commercial entities within its territory (see footnote 30). In addition, bureaucracies are generally less likely to innovate in the long run, which may prove problematic for a field that is continuously expanding and modernizing. This may result partly from limited funding but also from broader systemic characteristics that do not favour rapid change and cutting-edge, risky solutions.[37]

---

[37] Based on an informal conversation with a colleague from King's College London.

Conclusion

The above discussion demonstrates that while OSINT could be leveraged as a treaty verification tool to a much greater extent than is happening now, there is no clear-cut way to achieve this. Whether one follows the speculative decentralized or centralized models presented here, or a mixture of the two, there are substantial obstacles. Overall, it is apparent that the biggest hurdles to institutionalizing and then operationalizing non-governmental OSINT as a treaty verification tool are political in nature. Since the status quo in the field is heavily Western-centric, a novel OSINT programme set up for treaty verification will likely fail to fully satisfy all state parties of a treaty, including by representing their competing views and approaches.

Nevertheless, as more states come to recognize the added value brought by OSINT to disarmament, non-proliferation and arms control efforts, they can work to make the idea more broadly accepted. To this end, one practical step could be to use OSINT in support of confidence-building measures (CBMs) included within international treaties. For example, the Biological Weapons Convention encourages member states to report on activities relevant to the treaty's content,[38] and OSINT could independently bolster this process. Another potential avenue for leveraging open sources for confidence-building is the Proliferation Security Initiative (PSI), a US-led global counterproliferation effort that has in the past served, for example, to plan future sanctions on North Korea.[39] Designed to 'involve in some capacity all states that have a stake in non-proliferation',[40] the PSI could serve as a platform for states to unilaterally share open source information that could help curb the spread of WMD and encourage others to do the same.

Without question, OSINT will never replace traditional verification measures. It certainly can, however, complement them, and could play

---

[38] Jeremias G. and Himmel M. Can everyone help verify the bioweapons convention? Perhaps, via open source monitoring. *Bulletin of the Atomic Scientists*. 2016. 72 (6), pp. 412–417.

[39] Niksch L. A. North Korea's Nuclear Weapons Program. Library of Congress Washington DC Congressional Research Service. 2005.

[40] Proliferation Security Initiative. *Proliferation Security Initiative: Statement of Interdiction Principles* [online]. Proliferation Security Initiative. 2018. Available from: https://www.psi-online.info/psi-info-en/botschaft/-/2077920 [Accessed 31 July 2023].

an interesting role spanning a verification tool and confidence- and trust-building mechanisms. Much of the foundation for a functioning societal verification component in disarmament, arms control and non-proliferation agreements already exists in the form of civil society actors working to apply OSINT techniques to understand weapons and proliferation. Fully tapping into this potential is a chance to create a more diverse and equitable OSINT, and more robust weapons treaty verification.

Part 5
Data, Methods and Platforms

© 2024 World Scientific Publishing Company
https://doi.org/10.1142/9781800614079_0015

Chapter 5.1

Identifying and Collecting Public Domain Data for Tracking Cybercrime and Online Extremism

Lydia Wilson, Viet Anh Vu, Ildikó Pete and Yi Ting Chua

Abstract

Collecting and making use of publicly available data is not always straightforward, particularly for interdisciplinary researchers who often lack skills to deal with technical issues that arise during the process. This chapter gives an overview of the challenges involved in identifying and collecting materials, and outlines a general technical framework for building effective and sustainable computer programmes to scrape, process and store online open source materials into structured datasets for research purposes. We also discuss the data licensing process, which is essential for experiment reproducibility, along with ethical considerations when working with the data to protect both researchers and the general population. We demonstrate, as a case study, how we collect and handle cybercrime and extremist resources at the Cambridge Cybercrime Centre – an interdisciplinary initiative combining diverse expertise at the University of Cambridge.

Introduction

Vast amounts of data are now publicly available online, free to download and store. This might suggest that we are working in a golden age of open source research,[1] but in fact there are numerous barriers to overcome –

---

[1] In line with most of the rest of this book, we use 'open source' in the social science sense of freely available data rather than the computer science concept of intellectual property and reusability.

This is an open access article published by World Scientific Publishing Europe Ltd. and distributed under the terms of the Creative Commons Attribution-NonCommercial 4.0 International (CC BY-NC 4.0) License.

technical, ethical and analytical – before using such data to carry out robust studies. This chapter shows the process from identification of material to interpretation of data, taking as a case study the process of creating databases of cybercrime and extremist content at the Cambridge Cybercrime Centre (CCC), within the University of Cambridge's Department of Computer Science and Technology.[2]

The CCC has been collecting data on cybercrime since 2015, from data traces of DDoS attacks[3,4] to scraping[5] conversations on underground forums discussing crimes, such as hacking and illicit marketplaces. These forums form the basis of CrimeBB, a large-scale dataset consisting of more than 99M posts and 11.6M threads made by over 4.6M users on 34 cybercrime forums in 5 different languages, English, Russian, German, Arabic and Spanish.[6] In 2019, the group expanded its collection to include extremist material, starting a new structured dataset, ExtremeBB, for this content.[7] Areas of focus have been extremist ideologies including white supremacy, manosphere such as incels (involuntary celibates) and lookism,[8] and online forums dedicated to trolling and doxxing.[9] Scraping has been expanded to collect data on far-right ideologies more broadly, and in 2021, jihadi material started to be added. As of April 2022, ExtremeBB contains nearly 48M posts in 3.5M threads from more than 390K active members on 12 extremist forums. These forums are scraped – and results are systematically processed and stored – on an ongoing basis, with the long-term aim of providing data to researchers looking at online extremism in the early-mid 21st century. As of the writing date (2022), access to ExtremeBB has been

---

[2]The Cambridge Cybercrime Centre [online]. Available from: https://www.cambridgecybercrime.uk/ [Accessed 12 July 2023].

[3]DDoS stands for Distributed Denial-of-Service, a type of attack on computer systems that makes them unavailable to intended users.

[4]Thomas D. R., Clayton R., and Beresford A. R. 1000 Days of UDP Amplification DDoS Attacks. *Proceedings of the IEEE Symposium on Electronic Crime Research (eCrime)*. 2017, pp. 79–84.

[5]The process of automatically collecting and extracting data from a website.

[6]Pastrana S., Thomas D. R., Hutchings A., and Clayton R. CrimeBB: Enabling Cybercrime Research on Underground Forums at Scale. *Proceedings of the World Wide Web Conference (WWW)*. 2018, pp. 1845–1854.

[7]Vu A. V., Wilson L., Chua Y. T., Shumailov I., and Anderson R. ExtremeBB: A Database for Large-Scale Research into Online Hate, Harassment, the Manosphere and Extremism. *The ACL Workshop on Online Abuse and Harms (WOAH)*. 2023.

[8]The term refers to techniques for enhancing men's physical attractiveness to women.

[9]The action of digging out and publishing information to expose identities, or finding personal, and previously private, information such as addresses to threaten individuals.

granted for 39 researchers in 12 groups from 10 universities and institutions around the world (excluding the team at Cambridge), while the figures are 170, 50 and 39 for CrimeBB, respectively.

There were various motivations for building these databases. First, many people do not have the skills to collect big datasets, putting such activities out of reach for many non-technical researchers. If people do have the necessary skills, it is still time-consuming for them to build datasets. Using large-data approaches without a pre-existing dataset would be impossible for a year-long MSc project, for example, but if data have already been collected, a researcher can bypass the collection step and focus on analysis. Further, such datasets are in general not widely available, making it difficult for others to check results, or for single teams to interrogate them via different techniques and analytical tools in order to compare research methods. Finally, complete longitudinal datasets are valuable for spotting how trends emerge and change over time, which is at odds with the current academic model of project-based funding. The databases developed by the CCC resist such short-term pressures, and will be useful to the wider academic community now and in the future.

This chapter shows the process of building the cybercrime and extremist databases, which are made freely available to researchers (subject to agreements to prevent misuse), and the further steps necessary to interpret the data. We start by considering the many ethical issues that need to be addressed for any work in this area. The chapter then broadly follows Jagadish et al.'s five steps in big data usage: 'acquisition, information extraction and cleaning, data integration, modelling and analysis, and interpretation and deployment',[10] describing our data identification, collection and storage methods, and discussing technical challenges and our processes for overcoming these. We then look at how the data are processed and made available to the research community, first by cleaning the data, and then providing the tools and expertise for a non-technical researcher to interrogate them. Finally, we look at interpreting the data, and demonstrate how interdisciplinary research works best for this work. Throughout the chapter, we show the complexities and possibilities of big data research. We encourage

---

[10] Jagadish H. V., Gehrke J., Labrinidis A., Papakonstantinou Y., Patel J. M., Ramakrishnan R., and Shahabi C. Big data and its technical challenges. *Communications of the ACM*. 2014, 57 (7), pp. 86–94.

interdisciplinary work to better understand the problem of online extremism and cybercrime in our societies.

Ethical Considerations

Discussions on ethical considerations and impacts from such data use are increasingly relevant.[11] Fundamentally, there is a balance to be struck between expectations of privacy on the side of users and the valuable information and understanding that can be gained from the research. There are no clear-cut guidelines to achieve this balance, as different contexts bring different considerations of potential harm and risk. Discussions on ethics can be broadly categorized into two groups for most research: (1) the general population and research subjects, and (2) the researchers themselves.

Ethical considerations: General population and research subjects

Although traditionally considered separately, the distinction between a general population and research subjects is increasingly blurred due to the nature of open source big data. For all research on people, informed consent is an unavoidable topic. In general, academic best practice stipulates that research subjects must voluntarily agree to participate, having been given details of the research, including its purpose, any potential risks associated with taking part and participants' rights.[12] However, under specific conditions, informed consent is not required. These conditions include (a) the use of secondary data where research subjects are in life-threatening situations where interventions by researchers are necessary before any possible consent; (b) circumstances in which research subjects cannot be identified; (c) cases where the research cannot be practically conducted with consent; and (d) times when the research poses no more than minimal risks to research subjects.[13]

---

[11] Other chapters in this volume consider ethical dilemmas within open source research and how practitioners approach these. See, for example, the chapters by Wilson, Samuel & Plesch, Duke, Freeman & Koenig, Ahmad, Michie *et al.*, and Bedenko & Bellish (Chapters 1, 2.2, 2.5, 3.1, 5.3 and 5.4).

[12] Bachman R. D., Schutt R. K., and Plass P. S. *Fundamentals of Research in Criminology and Criminal Justice: With Selected Readings*. Newbury Park CA: 2016.

[13] *ibid.*

With open source data, the issue of informed consent is further complicated by the public versus private nature of the data sources. Some argue that online platforms are publicly accessible and thus data collection without consent can be justified.[14] This view is reasonable for research that primarily involves observation only. However, researchers also need to take members' perceptions of the selected online community into account. For some communities, members may consider their publicly accessible postings to be private while other communities welcome the sharing of personal information.[15] Unless the research is conducted with care, research subjects may feel that their rights are being violated, which might prompt them to move towards more private or closed platforms, and thereby distort the composition and characteristics of the groups that they leave.

Leaked datasets, especially those containing classified data, also raise ethical dilemmas.[16] Some argue that it is ethical to use such datasets once they have been leaked. However, if leaked datasets provide access to otherwise personal data (e.g. mental health records), their use can harm individuals. For much publicly available data, additional measures are necessary to ensure the anonymity and confidentiality of individuals in the datasets, since secondary data analyses could compromise these aspects. A de-anonymization algorithm can reveal personal information, as Narayanan and Shmatikov demonstrated[17] a when they cross-referenced an anonymized Netflix Prize dataset with publicly available information, e.g. the Internet Movie Database (IMDB).

The first step to address these ethical considerations is to appoint a Review Board to ensure that human subjects are protected, and to help

---

[14] Holt T. J. Exploring Strategies for Qualitative Criminological and Criminal Justice Inquiry using On-Line Data. *Journal of Criminal Justice Education*. 2010, 21, p. 466.

[15] Garcia A. C., Standlee A. I., Bechkoff J., and Cui Y. Ethnographic Approaches to the Internet and Computer-Mediated Communication. *Journal of Contemporary Ethnography*. 2009, 38 (1), pp. 52–84.

[16] Thomas D. R., Pastrana S., Hutchings A., Clayton R., and Beresford A. R. Ethical Issues in Research Using Datasets of Illicit Origin. *Proceedings of the ACM Internet Measurement Conference (IMC)*. 2017, pp. 445–462.

[17] Narayanan A. and Shmatikov V. Robust De-anonymization of Large Sparse Datasets. *Proceedings of the IEEE Symposium on Security and Privacy (S&P)*. 2008, pp. 111–125.

devise systems that mitigate potential harms to subjects,[18] (and see footnotes 12 and 14), including, for example, refraining from naming particular websites to help ensure the anonymity of research subjects[19,20] (and see also footnotes 6 and 17). Minimizing and/or avoiding the use of long quotes can also lower the traceability of users and thus protect the participants' anonymity. Ultimately, when using open source data, researchers always need to consider ethical issues, especially with regard to potential harms, while weighing these against potential benefits.

Ethical considerations: Researchers

In addition to research subjects, researchers also need to consider, and protect, their own safety. Researchers examining violent extremism and cybercrime have a higher chance of witnessing, encountering and/or being asked to participate in illegal or criminal activities. For example, interviewees in a study by Holt and Copes[21] were asked about their intellectual property violations (e.g. illegal media downloads), which meant that the authors had knowledge of interviewees' illegal behaviour. In addition, the fieldworker for the study had to actively participate in the forums dedicated to intellectual property violations and demonstrate her knowledge in order to gain the trust of other forum members. In the example of extremism research, downloading terrorist content can be a crime, and it is essential that researchers engage with their research institutions to make sure that they have suitable protections.

Although there is wide variation in the severity and ramifications of crimes – e.g. drug offences and illegally downloaded material have different impacts and victim footprints – researchers exploring any illegal actions need to decide whether, when and how to report their findings to law enforcement authorities. Researchers may be tempted to report anything considered

---

[18] Franklin J., Perrig A., Paxson V., and Savage S. An Inquiry into the Nature and Causes of the Wealth of Internet Miscreants. *Proceedings of the ACM Conference on Computer and Communications Security (CCS)*. 2007, pp. 375–388.

[19] *ibid.*

[20] Holt T. J. and Copes H. Transferring Subcultural Knowledge On-line: Practices and Beliefs of Persistent Digital Pirates. *Deviant Behavior*. 2010, 31 (7), pp. 625–654.

[21] *ibid.*

a crime, but this might actually not be the right approach for several reasons. For example, in the case of terrorist content, intelligence agencies may be monitoring the same activities and might not want the extra burden of responding to researchers. For common crimes, local police may not have the capacity to pursue every report of minor infractions. Meanwhile, the relevant laws vary from country to country, and so researchers' decisions on whether to report will be affected by the jurisdiction they are based in. In many jurisdictions there is no legal obligation to report particular crimes, and so decisions must be made on a case-by-case basis.

One oft-posited rule is to report criminal behaviours when researchers have knowledge of a serious crime in which innocent third parties can be harmed, although this rule is rarely followed in reality.[22] For offline studies, researchers can tell research subjects to refrain from discussing illegal activity, and clarify reasons for this. But for open source intelligence where there is no direct interaction with research subjects, researchers need to establish guidelines and rules about when and what to report before data collection and analyses.

To protect themselves, researchers should also consider certain measures for the hardware and software used for research. These technologies could be compromised when visiting sites of online groups and communities that are infected with malicious software (see footnote 14). Such malware could also risk the anonymity of research subjects, if sensitive information is stored on affected devices. To minimize such occurrences, researchers should use different computers for storing and analyzing data.

In the context of our work compiling the CCC datasets, these ethical issues have been explicitly addressed. While discussing the CrimeBB dataset, Pastrana and colleagues (see footnote 6) delve into the ethical considerations of using web crawlers[23] to collect forum data, noting the challenges of breaking terms and conditions, bypassing CAPTCHA[24] and working to ensure that the research does not harm individuals. Before deploying

---

[22] Sandberg S. and Copes H. Speaking with Ethnographers: The Challenges of Researching Drug Dealers and Offenders. *Journal of Drug Issues*. 2013, 43 (2), pp. 176–197.

[23] A bot that systematically trawls the internet.

[24] CAPTCHA (Completely Automated Public Turing test to tell Computers and Humans Apart) is a challenge to determine whether the actor interacting with the content is a real human, for example, by requiring them to recognize distorted text. In the rest of the chapter, we will use the lowercase term 'Captcha' for ease of reading.

their web crawlers, the researchers submitted an ethics application, seeking permission for their work from the departmental Review Board. In the ethics application for the ExtremeBB dataset, harms to researchers were addressed by plans to holding regular meetings on these matters and to follow institutional guidelines. Information about institutional resources such as counseling services is also made available to researchers, to protect researchers by minimizing the effects of working closely with potential violent and extreme content.

Material Identification

The increased integration of technology into society has resulted in the creation of tremendous amounts of digital data. These range from user-generated content to personal identifiable information, in the form of websites, e-mails, blogs, forums, instant messaging, social media, and accounts on services such as Netflix[25–27] (and see also footnote 12). These data sources allow researchers to observe and examine behaviours and attitudes of online underground communities across platforms and over time[28] (and see also footnote 6). This section provides an overview of the methodological challenges this increase in data presents.

One major issue is identifying and selecting representative data from the ocean of available sources.[29] For example, researchers need to determine whether the conclusions derived from one platform are applicable to another platform dedicated to the same topic, or consider the generalizability of results derived from a subset of the whole platform population. The issue is further complicated by the reach of the internet, as there may be differences in digital rights and uses based on cultures, geographic locations, legal

---

[25] Burrows R. and Savage M. After the crisis? Big Data and the methodological challenges of empirical sociology. *Big Data & Society*. 2014, 1 (1). Available from: https://doi.org/10.1177/2053951714540280.

[26] Lazer D. and Radford J. Data ex Machina: Introduction to Big Data. *Annual Review of Sociology*. 2017, 43, pp. 19–39.

[27] Ozkan T. Criminology in the age of data explosion: New directions. *The Social Science Journal*. 2019, 56 (2), pp. 208–219.

[28] Bada M., Chua Y. T., Collier B., and Pete I. Exploring Masculinities and Perceptions of Gender in Online Cybercrime Subcultures. *Cybercrime in Context: The Human Factor in Victimization, Offending, and Policing*. 2021, pp. 237–257.

[29] Hughes J., Chua Y. T., and Hutchings A. Too Much Data? Opportunities and Challenges of Large Datasets and Cybercrime. *Researching Cybercrimes*. 2021, pp. 191–212.

provisions, and/or languages (see footnote 14). Another big challenge is the rapid migration of online communities, which could be a result of deplatforming or attempts to evade attention. A famous example is the deplatforming of Parler in January 2021 when it lost its hosting service, and was removed from Apple and Google.[30] This resulted in the migration of users from Parler to other well-known platforms that emphasized free speech, such as Gab.[31]

The CCC's recent effort in creating ExtremeBB illustrates the challenges presented by such migrations. We collect data on all aspects of extremism, irrespective of the direct research interests of the team, with the expectation that the resource will open up new avenues of research in the future. We began collecting data from extremist forums in 2019, starting with a range of sites with far-right ideologies, and in 2021 expanded this to include extremist Islamist data. The resulting database therefore comprises a wide range of research material, lumped together under the common rubric of 'extremism'. It is likely that researchers will use the data to assess one ideology at a time, although the database also allows for 'compare and contrast' analyses, which may yield some interesting results.

In collecting data from far-right online communities, the CCC drew on in-house expertise to compile a list of known sites, which is added to regularly. However, a different approach was needed to collect data on extreme Islamist communities, as these tend to be more fractured and shorter-lived because multiple actions are taken against them. Accordingly, the CCC found that experts who constantly monitor Islamist online communities were needed. These experts had different views about CCC's data collection and storage plans. Many welcomed the initiative, and began to collect and send on sources, beginning with Telegram and Discord channels that the CCC systems then scraped. Others, who were manually collecting material

---

[30] Fung B. Parler has now been booted by Amazon, Apple and Google. *CNN Business*. 11 January 2021. Available from: https://edition.cnn.com/2021/01/09/tech/parler-suspended-apple-app-store/index.html [Accessed 12 May 2022].

[31] Ray S. The Far-Right Is Flocking To These Alternate Social Media Apps — Not All Of Them Are Thrilled. *Forbes*. 14 January 2021. Available from: https://www.forbes.com/sites/siladityaray/2021/01/14/the-far-right-is-flocking-to-these-alternate-social-media-apps—not-all-of-them-are-thrilled/?sh=3c2cf25655a4 [Accessed 13 July 2023].

from official channels, preferred to stick to their own approach. Yet others were automatically collecting data but couldn't share for proprietary reasons.

With the help of some external experts, the ExtremeBB database is slowly building up, and a useful feedback loop has been created, whereby the team scraping the data can alert experts when channels are closed down. This type of collection requires continuous attention given the speed of emerging sub-groups of supporters on a variety of different platforms.

Data Collection

Open source, public domain data are in many cases readily available on the internet and require no special privilege to access (subject to local jurisdictions). Gathering these data at scale in the long term on a sustainable basis, however, can be tricky and time-consuming as most web administrators do not intentionally offer Application Programming Interfaces (APIs) that allow researchers to fetch data directly from their servers. Additionally, some data sources are only available through a special access mechanism; for example, using Tor[32] with an anonymous communication channel is a prerequisite to enter hidden websites.

However, such websites are basically still *public* and data can be collected from them in one way or another, albeit a manual collection process might take months or even years to complete. Although some data only need to be downloaded once (e.g. some documents or images), others are compiled continuously over time (e.g. chat and forum discussions) and thus require a long-term collection plan. Similarly, while a number of data sources are just a single file (e.g. a database) which can be downloaded by just one click, some are large, not well structured and non-trivial to gather (e.g. forum chats). In such cases, manual approaches would never be able to capture a useful sample of material.

Computer programmes can help to automate the processes of fetching, extracting, parsing and storing data, including, for example, web scrapers. Despite the existence of protection mechanisms on some websites, which

---

[32] Dingledine R., Mathewson N., and Syverson P. *Tor: The Second-Generation Onion Router*. Technical Report, Naval Research Lab Washington DC. 2004.

may significantly slow down and restrict the access of such automated bots, as long as the data are still public and can be seen by humans, they can also be seen by bots. This section outlines some of the technical challenges involved and suggests a general framework to build sustainable and efficient computer bots to automate data collection.

Challenges

To a technician, building a web scraper sounds simple and obvious: It involves using a web driver (most popularly Selenium and Puppeteer)[33] to access an identified webpage, then find and save relevant content. However, it may not be that straightforward in practice. The automated bot often mimics human behaviour by clicking and viewing the webpage, which, at scale, may generate a significant amount of requests towards the targeted server. The increased traffic may thus attract attention and be detected by administrators, who tend to protect their data from being crawled.

As a result, websites often adopt anti-crawling protection mechanisms, such as limiting the number of requests clients can send within a time period; using Captcha to prevent bots; blacklisting suspicious IP addresses, a range of IP addresses or the whole Autonomous System hosting these IPs; and more sophisticated techniques such as measuring timing between clicks and introducing non-visible malicious links to trap automated bots. Some websites also use DDoS protection mechanisms, limit sensitive content for registered users only, and require a paid (or reputed) account to access.[34] More sophisticated protections are offered by third-party providers (e.g. Cloudflare and DDoS Guard)[35] to block suspicious traffic, such as bot actions and DDoS attacks. These can detect and block web scrapers, for example, through infinite Captcha attempts.

While many defences can be bypassed with ease and do not impact scraping tools, some combined techniques may effectively slow down web crawlers.[36] It is thus challenging to make automated scrapers stealthy, in the sense that they can mimic human behaviour to avoid being detected, while

---

[33] Selenium [online]. Available from: https://www.selenium.dev/ [Accessed 13 July 2023]. Puppeteer [online]. Available from: https://pptr.dev/ [Accessed 13 July 2023].

[34] Benjamin V., Samtani S., and Chen H. Conducting large-scale analyses of underground hacker communities. *Cybercrime Through an Interdisciplinary Lens*. 2016, pp. 26, 56.

[35] Cloudflare [online]. Available from: https://www.cloudflare.com/en-gb/ [Accessed 13 July 2023]. DDoS Guard [online]. Available from: https://ddos-guard.net/en [Accessed 13 July 2023].

still being effective, sustainable and not causing negative consequences e.g. bandwidth congestion or a denial of services. Some sites often update their HTML structures (e.g. changing theme, adding new features or switching to new frameworks), thus the scrapers may need to be tailored regularly. Some data are short-lived, for example, chat channels and forum threads that only appear for a short period before being permanently deleted, and so real-time collection is sometimes necessary.

Technical solutions

Prior work has introduced some automated bot architectures for scraping online forums (see footnote 6). Here, we outline a more general framework to develop a web scraper on public domain sources, as depicted in Fig. 1.

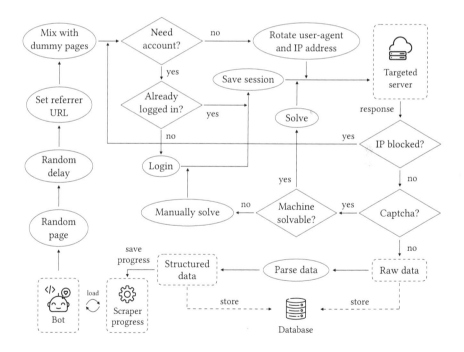

Figure 1: A general framework to build web scrapers for open source data collection.

---

[36] Turk K., Pastrana S., and Collier B. A tight scrape: methodological approaches to cybercrime research data collection in adversarial environments. *Proceedings of the IEEE European Symposium on Security and Privacy Workshops (EuroS&PW)*. 2020, pp. 428–437.

We do not describe technical details such as which programming languages and which programming libraries should be used, but instead overview some essential rules to bear in mind in order to make a scraper effective and appear natural. Note that the scrapers should be designed with ethical considerations in mind, as discussed above: The aim is not to flood targeted servers to gather the desired data as quickly as possible, but to automate tedious data collection.

First of all, it is necessary to make sure that the bot is set up with the correct web driver and communication tunnel. For instance, if the targeted website is only available on hidden webs (typically found with .onion domain), using a Tor browser with an anonymous communication channel (or setting up an onion routing)[37] is to be expected. Second, although timezone information is critical for longitudinal analyses, many websites do not clearly specify such information. Some display the date and time dynamically corresponding to the location of users, while others just show a fixed timezone. Thus, before starting the collection, manual effort is needed to figure out the actual timezone of the targeted websites.

When the bot starts, it chooses a page P of the targeted website to send requests to. Suppose that we need to visit a number of targeted pages, hitting them in a fixed order one by one (e.g. timestamp descending) is not a good idea as this would look like a robot's behaviour. Instead, P should be picked at random. After identifying P, the next important step is to add a random delay. The delay should never be a constant, as this could reveal repeated timing patterns that are easily detected. Then, a referrer URL should be set, which indicates the link that the bot has visited right before accessing P. This should look as genuine as possible; for example, by setting it to google.com, it will look like P has been discovered through a search and not by direct access. For different requests, the referrer URL should be also rotated periodically and appropriately; for example, setting it to the homepage or navigation URLs of the targeted website would be good choices. Next, it is important to mix P with a number of non-targeted pages, for example, by navigating to the site's homepage, clicking on some random adverts or unrelated URLs and then eventually visiting P. This will

---

[37] Reed M. G., Syverson P. F., and Goldschlag D. M. Anonymous connections and onion routing. *IEEE Journal on Selected Areas in Communications*. 1998, 16 (4), pp. 482–494.

potentially hide the actual intention of the bot and thus mitigate the chance of being detected.

The original IP address of scrapers can be mapped to a network and geographic location. Using a generic proxy service or setting up dedicated cloud-based servers to work as Virtual Private Networks (VPNs) will reduce the likelihood of the bot being linked to the researcher's institution. Similarly, when the targeted website does not require a registered account, it is beneficial to rotate the user-agent[38] and IP address frequently and randomly (sometimes, rotating the browser window's size is also recommended as this can be used to track users' behaviour). They should, however, be rotated together, as using the same user-agent from a particular IP for a long period makes the bot look more like a human. The rotation should not be done for every request but at an appropriate (and also, random) rate. If the targeted website requires logging in with a registered account, it is important to *not* rotate the IP as well as the user-agent for every request because it is unusual for one account to engage with many different IPs and user-agents. In this case, multiple accounts should be created to log into the site, so that each account can collect a subset of the targeted URLs, which should be divided randomly. For each account, the IP address and user-agent should remain constant throughout the collection process. IP addresses should be chosen from different geolocations, hosted by different Autonomous Systems (AS) and Internet Service Providers (ISP). After successfully logging in, the scraper should save the logged session by appropriate means (typically using cookies)[39] to make sure that the bot will not be asked to login again. Once this process has been done, the request to P is sent to the targeted server.

Servers' responses may vary. If an IP address is banned, another IP and user-agent should be chosen to resend the request and the blocked IP should not be used again (if the site asks users to log in, also rotate the account).

---

[38] User-agent is an intermediate software between servers and end-users helping them interact with websites. Not rotating the user-agent identification for a long period may lead to the bot being detected. A list of popular user-agents is available from a quick search, and it is better to use the common ones.

[39] Cookie, or HTTP, cookie, is a small piece of data stored in the client to identify the session of a user accessing a website, which tells the web server who is using the service so that the user does not need to log in repeatedly. It also helps web servers deliver personalized content better, as it knows who is accessing the websites.

Even when an IP address is allowed, the server may require Captcha solving to determine if the request has been made by robots. Captcha is perhaps the most challenging protection to bypass. While some Captchas are rather simple and can be cracked by modern machine learning algorithms (e.g. distorted text Captcha),[40] others are more challenging and typically hard for machines to bypass (e.g. reCaptcha, hCaptcha). Some Captcha solving services are available for a small fee;[41] however, one possible approach worth trying is using cookies (if the site allows) by (1) manually solving the Captcha, (2) saving the cookie session and then (3) attaching it back to subsequent requests. Some sites adopt a third-party DDoS defence layer (popularly Cloudflare and DDoS Guard), which requires additional effort to bypass. However, the same strategy as bypassing Captcha, plus incorporating a long enough delay (to wait for the DDoS check), may be effective to address this. Some third-party providers have started to offer sophisticated mechanisms to detect bot traffic, which aim at distinguishing 'good bots' (e.g. Google's bots for web indexing) and 'bad bots' (e.g. bots spying and stealing data for commercial uses). Fortunately, if research involves 'good bots', it is possible to get the bot's IP addresses whitelisted by contacting the third-party providers and explaining the research purposes.

After completing these steps, raw data are fetched from P. In any situation, a copy of the raw data (in HTML or other formats) should be stored locally. The scale of the data collection means that it is impossible to anticipate the fetched layout of P in advance, which makes data parsing (processing the raw data to store it in a format that is more readable and therefore suitable for analysis) cause unexpected errors. It is also necessary to parse the content offline later, if further information is required. In such cases, it will be critically useful to avoid sending a bunch of requests again, which takes time, causes unnecessary traffic towards the website and may increase the chance of the scraper being detected. After successful parsing, the structured data are stored in a database (or other system). Finally, the progress of

---

[40] Ye G., Tang Z., Fang D., Zhu Z., Feng Y., Xu P., Chen X., and Wang Z. Yet Another Text Captcha Solver: A Generative Adversarial Network Based Approach. *Proceedings of the ACM Conference on Computer and Communications Security (CCS)*. 2018, pp. 332–348.

[41] Motoyama M., Levchenko K., Kanich C., McCoy D., Voelker G. M., and Savage S. Re: Captchas-Understanding Captcha-Solving Services in an Economic Context. *Proceedings of the USENIX Security Symposium (USENIX Security)*. 2010, pp. 435–462.

the scraper should be recorded and persistently stored so that it can resume from the broken point if unexpected incidents happen, for example, the bot crashes, the internet drops out or there are other server errors. The scraper then repeats with a new page P' – normally, the next randomly selected page. It is always worth noting that each single page should be visited only once, and only what is exactly needed should be collected, to prevent flooding the targeted server with unnecessary traffic.

Once the scraper is running smoothly, setting a low rate limit (viz. a small number of requests per hour) is recommended to keep it indistinguishable from human users. This again helps ensure that the scraper will not be detected and the target site's administrators thus will not adopt additional protection layers or change their access policy which can impede or prevent data collection, such as making some of the site only available to 'premium' accounts. Boosting the processes by crawling in parallel may be feasible in some cases, but a completely different user profile and browser settings should be used for each bot. The choice of request rate heavily depends on how large the traffic of the targeted website is; thus, it is worth looking at the website traffic before increasing the rate limit or running bots in parallel. A rule of thumb is to build a scraper that keeps you under the radar, be patient and not greedy!

Data Usability

Data licensing and accessibility

A key component of research is reproducibility. When research is open, and based on open data, it can be interrogated by other scholars who can check conclusions, and thereby build confidence in findings and make the process more robust. Further, sharing collected data can be useful for multidisciplinary studies addressing different aspects of a problem. Moreover, making available the data collected through automated processes can mitigate obstacles faced by social scientists who often lack the technical backgrounds to build such tools themselves, enabling them to concentrate on analyzing the data in line with their own expertise.

The Cambridge Cybercrime Centre has robust ethical procedures to deal with scraped data that may contain sensitive personal information, and long experience in making such data available across multiple jurisdictions including the USA, the EU and China. Access is given to a data-sharing web platform from which authorized users can download the shared datasets. Along with the platform, we also provide detailed instructions on how to import and make use of the data to ensure that researchers from different backgrounds can get started with ease.

Before access is granted, users are required to complete legal paperwork to protect the data from misuse. The licensing regime was carefully developed in conjunction with legal academics, university lawyers and specialist external counsel. Once licensed, access to the most recent data snapshots will be automatically granted as they are published, without any further action by the licensee. The agreement includes requirements to inform the CCC about publications that draw on the data, and who is accessing them.

Data use by non-technical researchers

Open source data collection and sharing can ease the collective burden of identifying and gathering datasets, and save months or even years of researcher time.[42] Online cybercrime and extremist forums in particular lend themselves to collaborative, interdisciplinary research. However, translating the high-level research questions and the desired goals of research projects into actionable steps is a non-trivial task, given the complexity and size of the datasets alongside the technical requirements needed to work with them. The characteristics of the forum data render manual analysis infeasible, and often necessitate the application of data science methods and tools.[43–46]

---

[42] See also the chapter by Withorne in this volume (Chapter 5.2).
[43] Pastrana S., Hutchings A., Caines A., and Buttery P. Characterizing Eve: Analysing Cybercrime Actors in a Large Underground Forum. *Proceedings of Research in Attacks, Intrusions, and Defenses – 21st International Symposium (RAID)*. 2018, vol. 11050, pp. 207–227.
[44] Motoyama M., McCoy D., Levchenko K., Savage S., and Voelker G. M. An analysis of underground forums. *Proceedings of the ACM Internet Measurement Conference (IMC)*. 2011, pp. 71–80.
[45] Caines A., Pastrana S., Hutchings A., and Buttery P. J. Automatically Identifying the Function and Intent of Posts in Underground Forums. *Crime Science*. 2018, 7 (1), pp. 1–14.
[46] Portnoff R. S., Afroz S., Durrett G., Kummerfeld J. K., T. Berg-Kirkpatrick, McCoy D., Levchenko K., and Paxson V. Tools for Automated Analysis of Cybercriminal Markets. *Proceedings of the World Wide Web Conference (WWW)*. 2017, pp. 657–666.

The most immediate aspect that might pose an impediment to analyzing such data is size, exacerbated for researchers from non-technical backgrounds. We surveyed existing users of CCC's datasets to understand this aspect; they reported technical challenges with data exploration and download prior to analysis.[47] Thus, research aimed at automating the overall process or individual steps of data analysis, for example to identify posts on cybercrime forums related to transactions, is a highly valuable contribution for both technical and non-technical scholars.[48]

Stemming from these insights and the desire to develop tools for interdisciplinary analysis of underground forums, the Cybercrime-NLP (CC-NLP)[49] project was created. One of the aims of CC-NLP is to develop a web application, PostCog, that provides a user interface allowing licensees to explore CrimeBB and ExtremeBB with ease and without the need to develop substantial new technical skills.[50] To support longitudinal data analysis and understand underground forums at scale while taking into account the unique characteristics of the language used and interactions taking place on these forums, CC-NLP aims to create tools to allow automatic analysis of posts in the datasets. These tools, which will be integrated with PostCog, will provide answers to questions around generalizability, and will contribute to social scientists being able to discover useful and interesting themes within the data. Finally, the project involves engaging with research communities in various disciplines to understand and address their data analysis needs.

Data preparation

A necessary step for using open source datasets, like those offered by CCC, is data preparation, regardless of methodology to be used to analyze it (e.g. quantitative versus qualitative). In order to apply quantitative techniques such as natural language processing and machine learning, the datasets require further preparation. For example, in the study of masculinity and

---

[47] Pete I. and Chua Y. T. An Assessment of the Usability of Cybercrime Datasets. *Proceedings of the USENIX Workshop on Cyber Security Experimentation and Test, (CSET).* 2019.
[48] Motoyama M., McCoy D., Levchenko K., Savage S., and Voelker G. 2011. *op. cit.*
[49] The project title refers to the application of Natural Language Processing techniques.
[50] Pete I., Hughes J., Caines A., Vu A. V., Gupta H., Hutchings A., Anderson R., and Buttery P. PostCog: A tool for interdisciplinary research into underground forums at scale. *Proceedings of the IEEE European Symposium on Security and Privacy Workshops (EuroS&PW).* 2022.

hacker forums by Bada and colleagues (see footnote 28), several preparatory steps were performed on posts extracted from an underground hacking forum, before analyzing the dataset with a natural language processing programme. These steps included (a) removing unique content such as quotations, website links, programming codes, images or references, (b) removing 'normal' content such as stop words (a, the, of, in, etc.), numbers and punctuation, (c) removing capitalization of words, (d) text lemmatization, and (e) converting text into tokens (smaller chunks than the whole posts extracted from the dataset).

For qualitative methodologies and techniques, it is also necessary to adjust the data in order to efficiently and feasibly perform data analysis. An obstacle for qualitative methodologies is often the time required to perform in-depth analysis on large volumes of data. One possible solution is to incorporate sampling techniques. For example, while performing a modified grounded theory approach to identify key gender-related concepts in the underground hacker forum, Bada and colleagues (see footnote 28) included new samples of posts at each stage of coding to ensure that the categories identified at these points are consistently found throughout the data.

Data interpretation

Researchers can also encounter challenges when interpreting the output of analyses. Given the ongoing debate in the social sciences between quantitative and qualitative approaches,[51] there needs to be a shift in discussions towards how these methodologies are complementary and not mutually exclusive, especially with the emergence of online and open source data as well as improved technical knowledge and tools.

Here, we give examples of how such a mixed methods approach has been applied to research using underground forum data. In the paper mentioned above, Bada and colleagues (see footnote 28) applied both data science and qualitative approaches to examine the construct of masculinity and

---

[51] Buckler K. The Quantitative/Qualitative Divide Revisited: A Study of Published Research, Doctoral Program Curricula, and Journal Editor Perceptions. *Journal of Criminal Justice Education*. 2008, 19 (3), pp. 383–403.

its relationship to the hacker subculture. Through the use of natural language processing techniques, the authors performed an exploratory analysis of the entire sample, which consisted of more than 490,000 posts. The outputs were then compared with the qualitative results derived from a modified grounded theory approach. When comparing findings from both approaches, the authors discovered overlaps in perceptions of gender, as well as how gender is discussed in a specific context, such as social engineering.

Quantitative methods can also be accelerated by qualitative theories to provide insights into the way online communities (often considered as groups of users) are established and develop over time. This method has been used in our recent work on the evolution of a cybercrime marketplace, in particular how it responded to the COVID-19 pandemic.[52] The findings suggested a stimulus of trading activities in this marketplace at that time, explained by the fact that people spent more time online during lockdowns due to missing school or being jobless, and faced the boredom of being confined to their room.

Conclusion

This chapter has presented an automatic data collection framework for cybercrime and extremist resources, and ways to maximize their use. With appropriate care, the vast amounts of data that are freely available online can be used by researchers in a multitude of disciplines to answer many questions about online crime and extremism. Collaboration is key, and not just because of the number of skills required for the separate stages of data identification, collection, sharing and interpretation, but also because without sharing datasets it is impossible to replicate research, a cornerstone of scientific activity. Open source research is at its heart a shared endeavour, and datasets from the Cambridge Cybercrime Centre contribute to this, providing resources that can be used both for original research and also to verify the findings of others. It is an ongoing process, requiring constant attention

---

[52] Vu A. V., Hughes J., Pete I., Collier B., Chua Y. T., Shumailov I., and Hutchings A. Turning Up the Dial: The Evolution of a Cybercrime Market Through Set-up, Stable, and COVID-19 Eras. *Proceedings of the ACM Internet Measurement Conference (IMC)*. 2020, pp. 551–566.

to keep the sources and tools updated – one of enormous value to a wide research community.

Acknowledgement

We are grateful to Richard Clayton and our colleagues at the Cambridge Cybercrime Centre for their useful feedback and valuable comments on an early draft of this chapter. Icons used in the figures are designed and provided for free by Freepik, Darius Dan, Vitaly Gorbachev and Pixel Perfect.

Chapter 5.2

Assessing the Relationship between Machine Learning and Open Source Research in International Security

Jamie Withorne

Abstract

The growth of information technologies, digital data and the internet has led to a vast increase in open source data. The scale of expansion is such that it can be difficult, or even impossible, for open source researchers to access and process all relevant data manually. Accordingly, many are looking to automated tools to help with these tasks. One such tool is machine learning – the use of algorithms that 'learn' how to categorize and classify data. This approach has huge potential, but it is also not necessarily straightforward to deploy effectively. This chapter explains core components of machine learning, and how it can be usefully integrated within open source research.

Introduction

International security researchers, practitioners and commentators are paying increasing attention to open source research[1] as a possible source of information about global and local security risks. There is also growing awareness of and excitement about the possibilities afforded by machine

---

[1] This chapter takes open source research to mean research using tools and information that are publicly available either for free or commercially, as detailed later.

This is an open access article published by World Scientific Publishing Europe Ltd. and distributed under the terms of the Creative Commons Attribution-NonCommercial 4.0 International (CC BY-NC 4.0) License.

learning as a new and powerful tool for automating data processing tasks. At the nexus of these two activities is a sense of optimism that machine learning can begin to solve some of the challenges associated with conducting open source research, in particular, those associated with the large and ever-increasing quantities of digital data available through the internet.

Despite this enthusiasm, there is not always sufficient understanding of the technical requirements underpinning open source research and machine learning, which can lead to misunderstandings about what each can do. While both are undoubtedly useful and can complement one another, neither is a panacea for solving all problems associated with big data. Failure to recognize this can impede efforts to effectively harness the potential of each.

This chapter demystifies the use of machine learning in open source research, by providing robust accounts of both and by demonstrating how they can work together. It starts by defining open source research and machine learning, recognizing the subtleties of the different terms, and identifying some of the ethical issues embedded within them. It then considers how machine learning can help open source researchers to process more data more efficiently, by providing a research framework that demonstrates how to effectively integrate machine learning into existing open source research processes. Finally, the chapter considers other work at the intersection of open source research, machine learning and international security, and future possibilities and inherent limitations.

Definitions

Both open source research and machine learning are types of data-driven exploration, aimed at uncovering useful insights into material realities. Specifically, they can both be classified as types of data analysis, meaning that they are primarily concerned with the process of transforming data into useful information that can inform actions. This distinction between data and information is typically understood in this way: Information is 'organized or structured data, which has been processed in such a way that the data now has relevance for a specific purpose or context and is therefore meaningful'.[2] Notably, both data and the information that can be derived from them incorporate assumptions and biases; they can be interpreted and understood differently by different individuals.

Open source research generally implies a type of research that is conducted using open source data or information, i.e. data or information that are legally collectible and publicly available. Accordingly, any research that relies on publicly available datasets, like those provided by the United States Census Bureau for example, is classified as open source research.[3] While terms such as open source analysis, open source research and open source investigation are often used interchangeably, each has different connotations. For example, the term open source intelligence (OSINT) is often associated with national intelligence collection and processing.[4] For this reason, this chapter uses the broader term open source research.

Machine learning algorithms are computer programs that can automatically improve their ability to perform a specified data analysis task. They 'learn' in the sense that they incrementally improve the degree to which they can correctly perform a task on a set of 'training data'. This 'training' adapts the algorithm's parameters until it is able to perform its task effectively, before being assessed on a second set of 'test' data that were not available to it during training. Once trained and tested in this way, the algorithm can be deployed to perform its task on new data that need to be processed. However, the algorithm's continued success will always depend on the extent to which the new problems that it is asked to address resemble the data on which the system was initially trained and tested.

Machine learning has been defined as 'the process by which a computer system, trained on a given set of examples, develops the ability to perform

---

[2] Rowley J. and Hartley R. *Organizing Knowledge: An Introduction to Managing Access to Information*. Farnham: Ashgate Publishing Ltd. 2006, pp. 5–6, cited in: A. J. Nash, The Differences Between Data, Information, and Intelligence, *United States Cybersecurity Magazine*. Spring 2017. Available from: https://www.uscybersecurity.net/csmag/the-differences-between-data-information-and-intelligence/ [Accessed 12 July 2023].

[3] United States Census Bureau [online]. Available from: https://data.census.gov/cedsci/ [Accessed 12 July 2023].

[4] See the chapter by Vogel in this volume (Chapter 3.4) for a discussion on the development of OSINT in the US intelligence community.

a task flexibly and autonomously'.[5] Recently, the phrase machine learning has been used loosely in such a way as to imply it is mystical. For example, Google has historically branded their machine learning products with phrases like 'the life-changing magic of making with machine learning'.[6] However, to be clear; machine learning is not magic. Rather, at its core, it is a data-driven process rooted in advanced data analytics and statistics.

Processes

Both open source research and machine learning involve methodologies – general strategies applicable to multiple types of data and use cases – as well as individual tools or techniques. They are also *iterative*, meaning that a researcher and/or algorithm will undertake individual component steps multiple times during a single analysis, and *repeatable*, meaning that additional researchers and/or algorithms should be able to follow the same analysis process to arrive at the same or similar findings.

Throughout these steps, it is important that researchers identify any bias that exists in their data, information and methods. In a similar vein, it is crucial that they recognize any assumptions, or conclusions drawn without sound corroborating information, that are made throughout the work. It is vital that assumptions are considered to both ensure robust answers and so that researchers can verifiably and transparently demonstrate how they arrive at their findings.

The open source research process

Open source research is a thoughtful and deliberate analytical process that requires identifying a research question, exploring and collecting data, and data management, analysis and evaluation.

The first step is to clearly identify what needs to be achieved or accomplished by outlining a research question and assessing if this question can

---

[5] Stephens M. A machine-learning revolution, *Physics World*. 4 March 2019. Available from: https://physicsworld.com/a/a-machine-learning-revolution/ [Accessed 12 July 2023].

[6] Markowitz D. The life-changing magic of making with ML. *Google Cloud*. 17 February 2021. Available from: https://cloud.google.com/blog/topics/developers-practitioners/life-changing-magic-making-ml [Accessed 12 July 2023].

be usefully addressed using open source data or information. Specifying a research question can contribute to the overall success of the research. Establishing the reason why data are being collected and analysed not only helps organize the rest of the research but also establishes an awareness of intent that can be a useful ethical consideration.[7] If, for instance, a research question involves investigating an individual, it is important to be mindful of their privacy rights and set a limit on the type of data that are collected and analysed. Sometimes, an individual's private data can be legally accessed through open source research. In these cases, researchers should have a clear strategy on what they plan to do with sensitive data so as not to exploit or compromise it.[8]

Researchers from the James Martin Center for Nonproliferation Studies (CNS) have conducted extensive open source research on nuclear nonproliferation issues. In a report published in 2016, they focused on the research question 'are 2014 allegations that Iran built a secret underground centrifuge facility true?'[9] The research then aimed to explore whether open source research could assist in confirming or refuting allegations of illicit centrifuge facilities in Iran – technologies that could be used to enrich uranium for nuclear weapons. Noting that there were similar accusations about potential covert centrifuge facilities surrounding North Korea's nuclear programme in 1998, the report explains that the 2014 Iran situation was deemed more amenable to investigation, because advances in information technology meant that there were more relevant data available for this research question than for the 1998 North Korea case.

After establishing the research question, it is important to explore and identify freely available and proprietary sources of data and information that are relevant to it. For many research questions, there exist a vast amount of potentially useful open source data, only some of which are free to use.

---

[7] Bazzell M. *Open Source Intelligence Techniques: Resources for Analyzing Online Information*, 7th edn. Washington, DC: Michael Bazzell. 2019, p. 560.

[8] Other chapters in this volume consider ethical issues encountered in open source research and different approaches to these. See, for example, chapters by Wilson, Samuel & Plesch, Duke, Freeman & Koenig, Ahmad, Toler, L. Wilson *et al.*, and Bedenko & Bellish (Chapters 1, 2.2, 2.5, 3.1, 3.2, 5.1 and 5.4).

[9] Lewis J. Applying New Tools to Nonproliferation: Nuclear Detective Story [resource collection]. *Nuclear Threat Initiative*. 20 September 2021. Available from: https://www.nti.org/analysis/resource-collections/applying-new-tools-to-nonproliferation-a-nuclear-detective-story/ [Accessed 12 July 2023].

That is, some are owned by an individual or entity, and arrangements need to be made with the owner before the data can be used – which usually involves paying for the data. While much open source research can be done using free information, researchers may find it useful to explore and assess the availability of specialized or proprietary data that have been curated in a way that aligns with the project's identified needs. Because owners of proprietary data may have already conducted a large amount of preliminary data processing, using such data can help streamline the overall research process (although it should be noted that doing so could mean that the collection and curation procedures may be more opaque than situations in which researchers complete these steps themselves). At this stage, it is also crucial to 'knoll' the data collection and analysis tools and methods that can be used to address the research question. Knolling is the process of organizing resources so that they are easily accessible. Preparing tools and methodologies at the outset of research will lead to more effective data collection and processing (see footnote 7).

The CNS Iran case study demonstrates the intricacies of data collection in open source work. Since the investigation focused on exploring allegations about the location and nature of alleged proliferation in Iran, it was useful to start by looking at satellite images of places of concern. The report notes that the research started with satellite imagery provided in a news brief, which in turn led the researchers to purchase similar or related imagery from a data provider – while satellite imagery is sometimes freely available through services like Google Earth, high-quality images are often proprietary. The report goes on to describe that the satellite imagery led to more questions than answers because it displayed inconsistent visual identifiers. To deal with this confusion, the reporters knolled additional resources to begin to address their underlying research question more efficiently. Knolling here included collecting tools and data that could be useful to the research question, including techniques for corporate analysis, 3D modelling of suspect sites and social media analysis.

The next step in the open source research process is analysis. In this step, data are examined to identify potential answers to the original research question. Analysis of the data can yield information by revealing patterns, networks or connections between data. Analysis can also reveal data points that have been duplicated and missing pieces of data.

In the Iran case study, after collecting satellite imagery and creating a 3D model of the buildings at the facility in question, the researchers also found information on the technical construction requirements for centrifuge facilities. The researchers then conducted their analysis, comparing the alleged site to other facilities worldwide to determine potential visual indicators that could reveal the presence of uranium enrichment facilities in satellite imagery. By doing this, the researchers were able to assess whether satellite images of the site did or did not show the ventilation or electricity installations necessary for a centrifuge facility. This led to the conclusion that there was *no* centrifuge facility at the alleged site.

The final stage in the open source research process is to evaluate the findings. This can involve multiple techniques, including conducting peer reviews to authenticate the conclusions drawn and ensure they are reliable. As noted, ethical considerations should be woven throughout the research process, including at this stage. Publishing or publicly presenting results could inadvertently or deliberately reveal sensitive or harmful information about actors associated with an investigation, such as personal information that is potentially incorrect or misleading. For example, in the Iran case study, a legitimate business was situated at the site of the alleged centrifuge facility. Had the investigation drawn a different conclusion (i.e. that there *was* a centrifuge facility located there), the business could have received severe reputational damage. Instead of rushing to conclusions, the CNS research team meticulously examined all their collected data and further evaluated their findings with an individual who had physically visited the site.

A machine learning process

Beyond establishing a broad technical understanding of machine learning, it is also important to grasp how and when it can be applied. The most crucial prerequisites for applying machine learning are computational power and a sufficient amount of relevant data. While much open source research meets these requirements, it is not always amenable to machine learning, and machine learning cannot solve all the challenges associated with open source research.

There is a tendency to think of different machine learning processes and applications as autonomous and abstract. However, humans are integral throughout. Ultimately, a person decides what data should be used to 'train' the machine learning model, defines the model's training categories and tells the model what sort of tasks to undertake. People are also required to choose or create the data to feed into a machine learning model, to assess the significance and validity of the results, and to interpret and apply the findings of the model.[10] Considering this, the process of applying machine learning very closely mirrors the open source research process, albeit it is often carried out using more advanced analytical techniques and technologies. From this perspective, the machine learning process can be summarized as collecting data, formatting data, building a model, training the model, assessing the model's findings, and applying the results.

The Intersection of Open Source Research, Machine Learning and International Security

There is significant potential overlap between open source research and machine learning. Specifically, based on the above definitions and discussion, it is possible to identify a hybrid framework for incorporating machine learning into open source research centred on data collection, data management and data analysis.

To begin this hybrid process, a crucial first step is to determine if machine learning should be used within an open source research project, and if so, how and when it should be employed. It is important to ask, 'how exactly might machine learning be applied to make the open source research process more effective and efficient?', and consider the following aspects:

- Data type, quality and quantity – is there a large enough set of relevant data for machine learning to be analytically useful? Research that relies on geospatial data is likely to have access to large datasets as there is a substantial amount of good-quality satellite imagery, and it could

---

[10] Schuman L. AI and National Security: Examining First Principles – A Conversation. *The Sunday Show*. Tech Policy Press. Available from: https://techpolicy.press/ai-and-national-security-examining-first-principles-a-conversation-with-lucy-suchman/ [Accessed 12 July 2023].

be viable and beneficial to use machine learning to process this. Conversely, for research that has access to fewer and less clean data, machine learning is less useful. For example, it is unlikely that machine learning would be useful for analysis of the ranges of North Korea's missile tests as there are a limited number of cases to assess. It is also important to think about whether the data are labelled or organized in a way that a machine learning model can recognize. Moreover, it is useful to consider if there is a foundational 'ground truth' that can be used to train the model, i.e. unambiguous data that are recognized as objectively correct.

- Technical expertise and efficiency – does the open source research team have technical experience of working with machine learning so that they can use it to streamline, rather than bottleneck, their work? If the process of understanding machine learning requires more resources (time, money, etc.) than traditional approaches, or than the research team has, it may not be beneficial to employ machine learning.
- Identification of precedents – has a similar research question and open source process been conducted using machine learning, and were the results analytically useful? If previous research has been done, could the same trained model be deployed to new research questions? Would employing a similar method and/or model to a new, albeit related, research question be a useful contribution?
- Will machine learning help uncover information that is important in answering the research question? Much machine learning can achieve results that would be impossible using manual approaches alone, or address components of a study faster and cheaper than manual approaches, but this may not be true across all cases.

If, after weighing these considerations, a researcher chooses to employ machine learning, they should clearly establish their intent for doing so, helping to ensure that the machine learning will remain useful to the overall research goal. Researchers should also clearly identify where they wish to apply machine learning. Machine learning is most likely to be of use within an open source research project's data collection, management and analysis stages. Each of these steps will be dealt with in turn.

Data collection

Data collection is arguably the most important step during open source research as it ultimately determines success. Open source research based on irrelevant, poor-quality or incorrect data will arrive at findings that are also irrelevant, poor quality or largely incorrect. It is possible for some open source research projects to use machine learning to improve their data collection, thereby improving the overall research; machine learning could be used to collect large amounts of relevant data very quickly. For example, after the type of data necessary to answer the research question has been identified, and if a suitable training dataset exists, researchers could train a machine learning model to automatically distinguish between relevant and irrelevant data discovered online by a web crawler, or web scraping tool. This could assist in automating the data collection and quickly building large datasets. It is also possible that a machine learning model could be trained to automatically label each piece of data in a collected dataset, e.g. adding the label 'potential missile silo' or 'no missile silo' to each gathered satellite image. Note, however, the concern that if the machine learning model deployed to expedite the data collection has not been accurately or fully trained, it could introduce and potentially perpetuate bias with respect to the types of data being identified, collected or labelled.

Data management

Data management – sometimes also called data processing, structuring or cleaning – is the step in both machine learning and open source research where the researcher must make sure their dataset is clear and consistent so that it can be analysed in a coherent fashion. After data have been collected, they must be formatted homogeneously so that information can be extracted from them more effectively. This can be a tedious task for people, and machine learning can be applied to streamline the work.

For example, analysts from the Center for Advanced Defense Studies and the Nuclear Threat Initiative used machine learning models to automate data management for a case study on illicit financing and nuclear trade.[11]

---

[11] Arteburn J., Dumbacher E., and Stoutland P. Signals in the Noise: Preventing Nuclear Proliferation with Machine Learning & Publicly Available Information. *Nuclear Threat Initiative*. 2021.

They created a series of predictive machine learning techniques to screen collected publicly available trade data for shipments of concern, as well as to automatically adjust for variance in the data so that the format of the data was automatically standardized. In doing so, the analysts were able to detect more high-risk transactions than would have been detected by humans alone and were also able to do so more rapidly.

Integrating machine learning within open source data management is also relevant to the wider field of security. Researchers at Forensic Architecture used machine learning to sift through thousands of social media videos of Russian activity in Ukraine during the 2014 Ukraine conflict.[12] In this case, the researchers built a machine learning model that looked through the collected videos frame by frame and was trained to recognize images of military vehicles, specifically tanks. By doing so, the researchers drastically reduced the number of videos individual analysts had to view to identify the origin of the military assets.

Data analysis

After a dataset has been effectively managed so that it is coherent and consistent, then the actual analysis of these data can be undertaken to garner information needed to answer the defined research question. Analysing the data includes identifying any patterns within the set, and/or pieces of connected data, that can help shape answers or highlight any gaps that need additional research. While open source analysis is often done by a human to ensure that conclusions are relevant and accurate, machine learning can also be useful here. That is to say, machine learning can be applied to the dataset as an initial form of analysis, to identify patterns and make predictions. The researchers deploying the model can then interpret the model's results and further apply them to their investigation of the posed research question.

While machine learning is data analytics in and of itself, in this proposed integrated framework, applying machine learning can be classified as using machine learning to conduct a discrete proportion of the analysis, where the

---

Available from: https://media.nti.org/documents/Signals_in_the_Noise_-_Preventing_Nuclear_Proliferation_with_Machine_Learning__PAI.pdf [Accessed 12 July 2023].

[12] The Battle of Ilovaisk: Mapping Russian Military Presence in Eastern Ukraine. *Forensic Architecture*. August–September 2014. Available from: https://ilovaisk.forensic-architecture.org/ [Accessed 12 July 2023].

findings are then further considered, interpreted and applied by the open source researcher. For example, researchers at Stanford University were able to successfully apply a machine learning image recognition model to detect activity at a key nuclear facility in North Korea. The researchers conducted extensive traditional geological and satellite imagery analysis to monitor activity at North Korea's main uranium mine.[13] To further ensure that their analysis was as robust as possible and that it was conducted in a timely manner, the researchers also employed a machine learning image recognition land-use model. Here, the algorithm detected and labelled key natural features in the satellite imagery, classifying the visual indicators of mine expansion and operation as 'other'.[14] Notably, while the algorithm recognized changes in the landscape, it was not able to identify whether the changes were specific to mine expansion and activity without interpretation from trained geologists. In this case, the machine learning model conducted the initial analysis and identified a changing pattern in the data, which was then further developed and applied by individual researchers.

While machine learning can be a useful analytical aid in open source research, there are limitations. A machine learning model will only be as good as the data and parameters it is trained on; it could miss important patterns if they are not present in the original training data or if the model's parameters prevent it from identifying them. Moreover, machine learning can only extrapolate from the training data that are directly input into it; it can only produce findings relevant to wider, as yet unseen data to the extent that the new data contain the same features and patterns as the training data to which they have been exposed. Consequently, the quality of its input will impact the quality of its findings. Considering this, open source research should not rely on machine learning to generate definitive results – comprehensive analysis will likely require further contextualization as well as subject matter expertise. Further, all machine learning analysis should be evaluated against other research to check that its results are not unexpected,

---

[13] Park S., McNulty T., Puccioni A., and Ewing R. C. Assessing Uranium Ore Processing Activities Using Satellite Imagery at Pyongsan in the Democratic People's Republic of Korea. *Science and Global Security*. 14 October 2021. https://doi.org/10.1080/08929882.2021.1988258.
[14] Tucker P. North Korean Uranium Mining Picked Up From 2017 to 2020. *Defense One*. 4 November 2021. Available from: https://www.defenseone.com/technology/2021/11/north-korean-uranium-mining-picked-2017-2020/186620/ [Accessed 12 July 2023].

and if they are, it should be determined why this is and whether it means that the initial model needs to be changed.

Wider Understanding of Machine Learning and Open Source Research

There is a growing body of literature examining open source research and machine learning in international security. For example, researchers at the Universidade Nove de Julho in São Paulo have conducted a literature review examining publications discussing both open source issues and artificial intelligence (AI).[15] They found that the number of publications detailing both open source research and AI has grown consistently since around 2015, with groups in the United States and the United Kingdom publishing the most. Of these, 41% focused on cybersecurity applications whereas only 15% focused directly on military issues or traditional conceptions of security. The remaining identified publications focused on various topics including social media, language and translation, and business and industry.

Most of the existing literature on open source research and machine learning concentrates on the potential implications of these emerging disciplines and explores what the future intersection of these fields might look like, rather than examining *how* the two might work in combination. For example, organizations like the Congressional Research Service[16] and the Center for New American Security (CNAS)[17] have released reports detailing current global AI capabilities and their potential impact on national and international security. They mainly provide a literature and capability

---

[15] Evangelista J. R. G., Sassi R. J., Romero H., and Napolitano D. Systematic Literature Review to Investigate the Application of Open Source Intelligence (OSINT) with Artificial Intelligence. *Journal of Applied Security Research*. 7 May 2020. Available from: https://doi.org/10.1080/19361610.2020.1761737.

[16] Sayler K. Artificial Intelligence and National Security. Congressional Research Service. 10 November 2020. Available from: https://fas.org/sgp/crs/natsec/R45178.pdf [Accessed 12 July 2023].

[17] Horowitz M. C., Allen G. C., Saraville E., Cho A., Frederick K., and Scharre P. Artificial Intelligence and International Security. Center for New American Security. July 2018. Available from: https://csdsafrica.org/wp-content/uploads/2020/06/CNAS_AI-and-International-Security.pdf [Accessed 12 July 2023].

overview rather than discussing particular technological advances and best practices for how to use these technologies.

Similarly, working groups have been established by organizations including CNAS[18] and Stanford University,[19] with the intent of fostering discussion around AI's potential impact on security. Very few of these incorporate discussions of machine learning and open source research working together. One notable exception is an interim US National Academies of Sciences report on nuclear proliferation and arms control monitoring, detection and verification, which recommends that both open source assets and advanced data analytics (such as machine learning) are more routinely employed for non-proliferation security purposes. However, in keeping with the wider trend, this report does not detail how best to apply or integrate these two interrelated disciplines, a gap that this chapter aims to begin to fill.

There have been discussions on how to integrate machine learning into the narrower field of open source intelligence (OSINT) – open source information used by national intelligence agencies. For example, one author notes that within OSINT, machine learning has been used to sift through news sites and monitor trends, conduct sentiment analysis for campaigns and fact-check fake news.[20] Moreover, analysts at Recorded Future have provided an outline for how to incorporate AI into the intelligence cycle.[21] Similar to the framework presented in this chapter, this outline suggests that machine learning has the most potential to be useful in the intelligence collection, management and analysis stages of OSINT. The report also suggests that machine learning will eventually become central to the intelligence cycle in combination with existing techniques, which raises questions about whether

---

[18] See, for example, Artificial Intelligence and Global Security. Center for New American Security. Available from: https://www.cnas.org/artificial-intelligence-and-global-security [Accessed 7 July 2023].

[19] AI and International Security. Stanford University Human-Centered Artificial Intelligence. 26 February 2020. Available from: https://hai.stanford.edu/events/ai-and-international-security [Accessed 12 July 2023].

[20] Sutherland M. The Augmentative Effect of AI in the Open Source Intelligence Cycle. *Security Distillery*. 17 July 2017. Available from: https://thesecuritydistillery.org/all-articles/the-augmentative-effect-of-ai-in-the-open-source-intelligence-cycle [Accessed 12 July 2023].

[21] The Recorded Future Team. How Artificial Intelligences is Shaping the Future of Open Source Intelligence. *Recorded Future*. 9 January 2019. Available from: https://www.recordedfuture.com/open-source-intelligence-future/ [Accessed 7 July 2023].

machine learning in broader security-based open source research might follow a similar trajectory.

When existing publications discuss the technical aspects of machine learning in open source research, they tend to classify its contributions in three main categories: data review, data collection and automation. For example, researchers conducting reviews of scientific literature have presented an 'open-source machine learning framework for efficient and transparent systematic reviews'.[22] Their work focuses on using machine learning models to accelerate the screening of titles and abstracts of scientific literature. This has security implications, as such a model could greatly enhance strategic knowledge by helping to comprehensively conceptualize proliferation security concerns. Similarly, researchers at Sustainalytics have developed a machine learning model tool to monitor and collect news media sources, which could also be used to monitor relevant security-related news and global affairs.[23] Lastly, research has been conducted to create machine learning models for automating data gathering and conducting open source research techniques like geolocation.[24]

Future Research and Conclusions

As technology continues to advance, it is likely that machine learning and open source research will continue to grow and develop new ways to support one another as analytical disciplines, with novel applications and in an increasing numbers of domains. However, as the fields progress, it is important to consider the limitations of what machine learning can achieve in open source research.

This chapter presents a framework for how best to integrate machine learning into open source research. The framework is not intended to be a

---

[22] van de Schoot R. *et al.* An open source machine learning framework for efficient and transparent systematic reviews. *Nature Machine Intelligence.* 1 February 2021, pp. 125–133. Available from: https://www.nature.com/articles/ s42256-020-00287-7 [Accessed 12 July 2023].

[23] Brutain A. and Dumitrescu S. Machine Learning Powered Open Source Intelligence. *Sustainalytics.* June 2019. Available from: https://ndrconf-archive.codecamp.ro/wp-content/uploads/2019/06/Sustainalytics-Presentation-Final73627.pdf [Accessed 12 July 2023].

[24] Ponder-Sutton A. M. The Automating of Open Source Intelligence. In Layton R. and Watters P. A. (eds). *Automating Open Source Intelligence: Algorithms for OSINT.* 2016. Available from: https://doi.org/10.1016/B978-0-12-802916-9.00001-4.

blueprint for replacing human-centred research. Rather, it is one component of multiple analytic options. Analysis generally works best when it accommodates multifaceted approaches; the framework shows how machine learning can facilitate other parts of research, by saving time and effort at various stages of open source data collection, management and analysis. The framework does not guarantee sound results; conclusions drawn could still be subject to bias and should be thoroughly evaluated to ensure they are not misleading, incomplete or incorrect.

Future research could be done to identify how the presented framework could be developed to include mechanisms to authenticate the accuracy of open source data and information, and to consider how machine learning might be applied to help achieve this. This is particularly important given that the world has increasingly been operating in a contested information environment, heavily populated with mis- and disinformation. As a result, it has become more difficult to both authenticate and ensure the accuracy of open source data.

Research could also address the lack of technical know-how and availability of suitable datasets within the field of international security. Future work could helpfully shape and build security-relevant, multimedia, labelled, open source datasets and provide security analysts with technical training on both open source research and machine learning.[25] After a more rigorous international security data landscape has been fashioned, it would also be useful to explore how researchers can effectively collaborate to apply machine learning in their security analysis.

Machine learning and open source research are exciting and emerging practices. However, they are not magic or panaceas, and should be considered with nuance through a technically oriented lens. Ultimately, as technology develops, it is likely that open source research and machine learning will continue to advance, expanding their potential for novel applications. While this expansion of applications can create opportunities for security analysis, it is important to first understand what they are, and are not, capable of.

---

[25] See also the chapter by L. Wilson *et al.* in this volume (Chapter 5.1) for details of a project aimed at facilitating the use of datasets by people that do not have a technical background.

Chapter 5.3

Shadow World Investigations: Tracking Corruption in the Arms Trade

Rhona Michie, Paul Holden, Andrew Feinstein and Alexandra Smidman

Abstract

Shrouded in national security-imposed secrecy and uniquely underregulated, the shadow world of the global arms trade is a hotbed of corruption and other illicit practices. Unfortunately, these same features make it incredibly difficult for investigators – whether they be journalists, law enforcement professionals or non-governmental researchers – to gather the necessary information to uncover these practices and hold perpetrators to account. This chapter presents Shadow World Investigations and its work uncovering corruption in the arms trade. It describes open source resources useful in researching potential corruption, illustrates their use through real-world examples, and explores how and when closed sources can contribute to open source research.

Background and Introduction

The global arms trade spans numerous entities, including the groups that develop and make weapons, the supply chains that provide requisite components, the brokers that facilitate deals and the organizations or individuals that buy the arms. These multi-site, high-value contracts usually include a complex mixture of public and private involvement, and their details are often classified. This combination of circumstances can provide the perfect environment for corruption – that is, the abuse of transactions for the private gain of individuals, shielded from outside scrutiny or legal accountability.

This is an open access article published by World Scientific Publishing Europe Ltd. and distributed under the terms of the Creative Commons Attribution-NonCommercial 4.0 International (CC BY-NC 4.0) License.

Because of these complexities, investigators must use creative means to identify and track corruption. Shadow World Investigations was established in 2019 for this purpose. Its founders Andrew Feinstein and Paul Holden were first drawn into monitoring corruption through open source investigations because of their research into a South African arms deal in 1999, and they have worked together investigating corruption since 2008.[1] Feinstein and Holden had at first assumed that, as a young democracy governed by anti-apartheid activists, South Africa and its officials were particularly naïve and susceptible to corruption. However, as they looked further into the companies and individuals involved in the 1999 arms deal, they realized that not only was this happening all over the world but that it was in fact the *modus operandi* of the arms trade. It is estimated that 40% of all corruption in global trade takes place in the arms trade.[2]

What happened in South Africa was the direct result of a global trade run by a tiny elite of politicians, corporate executives, military and intelligence leaders, intermediaries and enablers, all of whom operate with virtual impunity. Shadow World Investigations has shown that this pattern exists across the globe and that on numerous occasions corruption beneficiaries actively seek to destroy democratic processes and sometimes even create or exacerbate conflict in order to make excess profits. Feinstein and Holden now work together at Shadow World Investigations to research and bring transparency to global corruption and the arms trade, and train other people in how to conduct similar work.

This chapter shows how Shadow World Investigations leverages open source materials and tools to track down corruption, particularly but not exclusively in the global arms trade. It first outlines how researchers can build a detailed picture of the 'formal' arms trade, then overviews how

---

[1] Feinstein was a South African Member of Parliament and the senior African National Congress member on a financial oversight committee when, in 2000, the Auditor General alerted the committee to a 1999 arms deal in which South Africa spent roughly $10 billion on equipment that it didn't need and in which it is estimated over $300 million in bribes were paid. Holden has a background as a research historian. They both worked to uncover the details about exactly what had happened and who was involved in the 1999 South Africa deal and its consequences, as detailed in Feinstein's first book, *After the Party: A Personal and Political Journey Inside the ANC*. New York: Verso. 2010, and two books by Holden, *The Arms Deal in Your Pocket*. Johannesburg & Cape Town: Jonathan Ball Publishers. 2008 and *Devil in the Detail* (written with Hennie Van Vuuren, published by Jonathan Ball Publishers. 2011).
[2] Roeber J. Hard-wired for corruption: The Arms Trade and Corruption. *Prospect Magazine*. 2005, 113.

they can recognize the signs of corruption using open source information, before detailing tools to scrutinize these 'red-flag' warnings.[3] While the chapter focuses on our open source research – defined as research that uses publicly available methods and information – it also includes some pointers for working with closed sources, as the most effective investigations usually involve a combination of different approaches.

Section I: Understanding The Formal Arms Trade

Many national and international rules and laws regulate the global arms trade; these have different enforcement mechanisms and differing degrees of compliance. Shadow World Investigations monitors the 'formal arms trade' (i.e. trade that, in theory at least, conforms with these regulations), as opposed to the 'informal arms trade' or arms trafficking (i.e. trade that happens outside established regulatory frameworks). Although the formal arms trade perpetrates a multitude of illicit practices, the fact that it involves 'legitimate' trades means that elements of it are represented in publicly available datasets, as well as in the decision-making records that are generated in accordance with regulations. These can be used to track the formal arms trade, and determine patterns and behaviours within it. This is the first step in uncovering corruption; once researchers become accustomed to the way the formal trade operates, they are better able to identify anomalous weapons transfers and recognize the 'red-flag' signals of illicit or corrupt transactions (as discussed in Section II).

Here, we list resources featuring information about the formal arms trade in three sections: The first comprises electronic databases about the international arms trade; the second includes databases containing exclusively USA data; and the third lists resources that can help researchers identify particular weapons. While all the resources we include are invaluable, the chapter's lists are presented in order of how often we consult them, with the most frequently used resources appearing at the top of each list.

---

[3]Several other chapters in this volume describe open source research focussed on identifying 'red flags' that could indicate wrongdoing. See, for example, the chapters by Liu & Gwadera, and H. Wilson *et al.* (Chapters 4.4 and 4.1).

International data

- The Stockholm International Peace Research Institute (SIPRI) compiles databases on arms transfers, military expenditure and arms embargoes.[4] It also tracks military assistance between states. It is perhaps the resource we refer to most in our work tracking the formal arms trade. SIPRI's website allows users to generate bespoke trade registers that describe, in considerable detail, major weapons transfers between states. SIPRI's database does not contain data on small arms; it only tracks military matériel the size of vehicles and drones at the smallest end to submarines, air carriers and jet fighters at the other.
- The United Nation's Commodity Trade Statistics (UN Comtrade) database is a collection of self-reported data from 170 countries.[5] It can be filtered by importers and exporters, as well as by commodity type. Small arms transfers are accorded their own UN Comtrade code, and these codes can be used to search and filter the Comtrade database.
- The Peace Research Institute Oslo (PRIO)[6] hosts the legacy site for the Norwegian Initiative on Small Arms Transfers, which built a database of the international authorized small arms trade until October 2017. The database is no longer updated, but researchers can still search its library for historical data.
- The UN Register of Conventional Arms (UNROCA) collates data submitted by states about their imports and exports of major arms.[7] It started collecting this data in 1991; the database can be filtered by country.
- National Arms Control Reports filed in parliaments. Several countries produce annual reports on arms imports and exports for their legislators. Many of these are publicly available; if not, they can sometimes be obtained through Freedom of Information requests (see below for more

---

[4] Stockholm International Peace Research Institute. *SIPRI Arms Transfers Database* [online]. Available from: https://www.sipri.org/databases/armstransfers [Accessed 28 May 2023].

[5] *UN Comtrade Database* [online]. Available from: https://comtradeplus.un.org/ [Accessed 28 May 2023].

[6] PRIO. *NISAT Database on Small Arms Trade* [online]. Available from: https://www.prio.org/data/2 [Accessed 28 May 2023].

[7] United Nations. *UN Register of Conventional Arms* [online]. Available from: https://www.un.org/disarmament/convarms/register/ [Accessed 28 May 2023].

information on these). SIPRI's website lists countries that produce reports and links to their reports.[8]
- UN Security Council Reports on internal country situations, produced by independent experts,[9] provide useful leads and information on arms and arms dealers.
- The South Eastern and Eastern Europe Clearinghouse for the Control of Small Arms and Light Weapons (SEESAC) produces reports on arms exports in its region,[10] and maintains a database of all registered arms brokers compiled from information supplied by countries in its area.[11]

USA-specific data

These US resources document prospective arms sales rather than completed ones; some sales may never materialize, and those that do can take years to transpire. Because of this, any research using these resources should be supplemented with information from alternative databases such as those listed above, to confirm whether deals actually went ahead.

- The Defence Security Cooperation Agency (DSCA) maintains a database of all 'Major Arms Sales' by year.[12] Researchers can click on each headline to review the official transmittal letter to Congress about a particular sale, which then reveals the value, recipient country, major weapons systems and occasionally also the companies involved. The database allows searches by country, which may help locate and identify sales.
- The Program Acquisition Cost by Weapon System is a document published by the US Department of Defense that lists the Pentagon's major procurements.[13] Many of these are exported because the Pentagon often acts as a broker: negotiating arms deals with foreign entities, collecting

---

[8] Stockholm International Peace Research Institute. *National Reports on Arms W] Exports* [online]. Available from: https://www.sipri.org/databases/national-reports [Accessed 28 May 2023].
[9] *Security Council Report* [online]. Available from: https://www.securitycouncilreport.org/ [Accessed 28 May 2023].
[10] SEESAC [online]. Available from: https://www.seesac.org/ [Accessed 28 May 2023].
[11] SEESAC. *Brokering Database* [online]. Available from: https://www.seesac.org/Brokering-Database/Brokering-Database-1/ [Accessed 28 May 2023].
[12] Defense Security Cooperation Agency. *Major Arms Sales* [online]. Available from: https://www.dsca.mil/press-media/major-arms-sales [Accessed 28 May 2023].
[13] Under Secretary of Defense (Comptroller). *DoD Budget Request* [online]. Available from: https://comptroller.defense.gov/Budget-Materials/ [Accessed 28 May 2023].

the money from buyers and passing this on to suppliers. The value of this document is that it describes the principal and secondary contractors involved in producing each weapons system.
- The US Department of Defense issues lists of contracts[14] daily, and allows searches on individual terms, such as company names or keywords.

Useful sources for identifying arms

When tracking armaments worldwide it can be useful to recognize different weapons systems, identify types of arms used and establish where they originate. The following tools can help with these tasks.

- The Omega Research Foundation is a UK-based research organization which identifies arms and ammunition, torture and surveillance equipment.[15] It has visual guides to weapons on its website and can be contacted for additional information.
- Bellingcat is an investigative non-profit whose website includes useful how-to guides on verifying information about weapons, and which provides access to a community with experience in arms identification.[16]
- The Small Arms Survey Report on Documenting Small Arms is a useful introduction to the basics of identifying small arms.[17]
- RiotID publishes guides to identify non-lethal weapons, in particular tear gas and impact munitions.[18,19]

Section II: How Corruption Happens and What to Look for in Procurement Processes

We track arms sales through routinely monitoring the sources listed in Section I, as the baseline of our investigations. After that, identifying

---

[14] US Department of Defense. *Contracts* [online]. Available from: https://www.defense.gov/News/Contracts/ [Accessed 28 May 2023].

[15] Omega Research Foundation. *What We Do* [online]. Available from: https://omegaresearchfoundation.org/ [Accessed 28 May 2023].

[16] Bellingcat. *Latest Investigations* [online]. Available from: https://www.bellingcat.com/ [Accessed 28 May 2023].

[17] Small Arms Survey [online]. Available from: https://www.smallarmssurvey.org/ [Accessed 28 May 2023].

[18] Incidentally, RiotID is publishing a downloadable board game where players work to expose excessive use of force by police against protesters around the world.

[19] Riot ID [online]. Available from: https://riotid.com/ [Accessed 28 May 2023].

corruption involves scrutinizing these sales for 'red-flag' indicators. Most such signals will be found during procurement, including within bidding processes and contract negotiations. Further information comes from tracing the flow of funds once a contract begins. This section lays out some of the major red flags that we look for.

Intermediaries

Most corrupt procurement involves consultants, agents or brokered agreements; the Organisation for Economic Co-operation and Development (OECD) estimates that three quarters of corruption cases involve the use of agents or intermediaries.[20] In this context, possible leads are provided by newly formed companies, or companies that are registered in tax havens, as intermediaries can register such companies to broker deals, and then possibly engage in corrupt activity while avoiding scrutiny. Similarly, 'consultancy' arrangements can also indicate corruption; often supposed maintenance services or subcontracts mask a range of bad practices. Meanwhile, following funding flows can enable researchers to find evidence of payments significantly exceeding what would normally be considered reasonable for intermediary or consultancy services. In corrupt deals, an intermediary may have a close connection to influential people in the importing and exporting countries involved.

The 2010 case of AgustaWestland's VVIP helicopter deal in India[21] clearly demonstrates how the restructuring of bid specifications and the use of intermediaries can signal corruption. AgustaWestland (now Leonardo Helicopters) is a subsidiary of Finmeccanica (now Leonardo), a company historically embroiled in corruption scandals across multiple jurisdictions. In 2010, the Indian government needed to acquire new helicopters for their VVIP squadron, which is tasked with carrying the President around the country. Their existing helicopters could not fly high enough to pass over the Himalayas and access the north of the country, and so the original contract specified a minimum flying height of 6000 metres.

---

[20] OECD. *OECD Foreign Bribery Report: An Analysis of the Crime of Bribery of Foreign Public Officials*. OECD Publishing. 2014. Available from: https://doi.org/10.1787/9789264226616-en.
[21] Corruption Watch. *The Anglo-Italian Job: Leonardo, AgustaWestland and Corruption Around the World*. June 2018.

AgustaWestland used three agents in this deal, two of whom had relationships with senior figures in the Indian Air Force. All three were paid tens of millions of dollars for their role. On 8 February 2010, AgustaWestland signed a deal with the Indian government to provide 12 AW101 helicopters – a helicopter only certified to fly to 4500 metres and thus still unable to pass over the Himalayas. An incentivized contact of AgustaWestland in the Indian Air Force had intervened to change the technical specifications for the procurement. Our investigations initially focussed on uncovering these details and thus showed that the procurement process had resulted in an acquisition that was not fit for its intended purpose. Section III shows how Shadow World Investigations further tracked the details of the individuals and companies involved.

Offsets

Offsets are contractual obligations for supplier companies to invest in purchasing countries' defence or civilian sectors to 'offset' the cost of a contract. These arrangements are heavily criticized for distorting trade, as they leverage alluring promises of investment to convince countries to buy weapons they don't need or that do not suit their strategic demands. The World Trade Organization bans the use of offsets as a selection criterion for contract evaluation in every sector except defence, which illustrates the favour granted to this area.[22]

Over and above this trade-distorting effect, offsets are a major avenue for corruption, in two main ways. Firstly, officials and/or politicians may be promised that they will be given offset-related contracts, giving them a financial incentive to ensure that a deal is done. Secondly, offset arrangements provide the means to hide illicit financial flows into a country throughout the life of a deal. Offsets require that defence companies move money and assets into the country buying weapons. This process can be abused to disguise bribery payments as legitimate offset transactions. Furthermore, given that offsets create the expectation of money flows from a defence company into a country, such financial transfers do not attract the same scrutiny that they otherwise would.

---

[22]Brauer J. and Dunne J. P. (eds.). *Arms Trade and Economic Development: Theory, Policy and Cases in Arms Trade Offsets*. London & New York: Routledge. 2004.

Offsets were a key element of the above-mentioned AgustaWestland's VVIP helicopter scandal in India. The company created a series of sham offset contracts in order to launder money for the payment of bribes. The money laundering systems were complex; essentially, funds were registered as relating to offset agreements for engineering services connected to the helicopters, but in fact were used to pay Indian Air Force officials. In this way, AgustaWestland was able to send money to various Indian officials through intermediaries, in the process securing the officials' support and distorting procurement decision-making.

Bidding and post-employment

In many corrupt arms deals, malfeasance is apparent from the bidding process. Common corruption indicators include single-bid tenders (where only one company is pre-selected to submit a bid for a contract); rewriting and restructuring bid specifications; direct interventions by political players including cabinet ministers; and the threat, or actual filing of, legal complaints and reviews.

Yet another signal for corruption is the 'revolving door' of people between government and industry positions, i.e. the promise of employment to officials once they leave government, and offering industry representatives access to power, or influential roles, in exchange for arranging payments to regulators, legislators and/or political parties. Online search tools (such as the ones discussed below) can be used to help identify individuals who have gone through the revolving door between the public and private sector.

Monitoring procurement

Researchers can track procurement processes via open sources, as certain information about procurements and tenders is uploaded to publicly available databases in many jurisdictions. Along with some of the US resources listed above, key tools include the following.

- EU – Tenders Electronic Daily (TED).[23] EU countries are bound by regulation to publish advertisements and awards for public contracts. These

---

[23] TED – Tenders Electronic Daily [online]. Available from: https://ted.europa.eu/ [Accessed 28 May 2023].

can be searched via the EU's official tender database. EU countries must supply information about who won a contract, what was paid, what the deliverables were and the criteria on which it was awarded. Researchers can also search by company and see all their contracts.

- Opentender is a transparency project that allows search and analysis of tender data from 33 jurisdictions (27 EU member states, the EU institutions, Georgia, Iceland, Norway, Switzerland and the UK).[24] It is part of the EU Horizon 2020 funded Digital Whistleblower project DigiWhist, which analyses public procurement in the EU.

Section III: Digging Deeper; Discovering Corruption Using Open Source Investigations

As well as monitoring the arms trade and spotting red flags that might indicate corruption, further research is needed to determine whether corruption has taken place, follow the trail of corrupt deals and gather appropriate evidence. This often requires investigating specific deals and cases, and establishing what relationships might exist between the entities and individuals involved. We do this in a variety of ways, including through using company research, court records, advanced searches and tools to visualize and manage large amounts of information.

Corporate registries

Deep corporate research can be paramount in establishing details about the ownership of a company, as well as finding networks and relationships between companies and their directors. Shadow World Investigations relies on a range of public databases to do this, including the following.

- OpenCorporates is a global database of openly available corporate information across many jurisdictions, derived from company registers worldwide that have been scraped for as much information as possible.[25] As well as allowing researchers to find relevant information, OpenCorporates

---

[24] Opentender. *Making Public Tenders More Transparent* [online]. Available from: https://opentender.eu/start [Accessed 28 May 2023].

[25] OpenCorporates. *The Largest Open Database of Companies in the World* [online]. Available from: https://opencorporates.com/ [Accessed 29 May 2023].

searches are useful because results are provided in the form of a link to the original company registry, which can be used to acquire detailed company documentation, and can enable follow-on trails (e.g. some registries allow researchers to download or purchase company documents such as Annual Returns).
- The Open Ownership Register includes company data and disclosures from millions of companies across over 200 jurisdictions, and allows for searches by company or individual.[26]
- The International Consortium of Investigative Journalists' Offshore Leaks Database includes a range of leaked documents such as the Panama Papers and the Paradise Papers.[27] It can be used to track the relationships between individuals and companies, by searching for them, and then exploring connections.
- The UK's Companies House provides information about all UK companies.[28] Researchers can search by company or individual names, allowing them to find all the companies an individual is associated with.
- Government-published gazettes contain information about changes to company directors and other corporate information. Many governments publish these online.
- Dan O'Huiginn's Panama archive lets investigators search by company director name (which is not possible on the official site of the Panama corporate records).[29] From this, they can identify companies of concern, and then search for these on the official Panama papers site to find complete company register entries, as well as associated scanned documents.

An example of a case in which company research uncovered important details is when a huge cache of emails was leaked from various businesses owned by the Guptas, a family of businesspeople, in 2017 (#GuptaLeaks).

---

[26] Open Ownership. *Register (Beta)* [online]. Available from: https://register.openownership.org/ [Accessed 29 May 2023].

[27] International Consortium of Investigative Journalists. *Offshore Leaks Database* [online]. Available from: https://offshoreleaks.icij.org/ [Accessed 29 May 2023].

[28] GOV.UK. *Companies House* [online]. Available from: https://www.gov.uk/government/organisations/companies-house [Accessed 29 May 2023].

[29] *Search Panama Company Records* [online]. Available from: http://panama.ohuiginn.net/ [Accessed 29 May 2023].

Following this, our investigation into state capture[30] in South Africa intensified. We discovered records of payments to a company based in India called the Worlds Window group, each referenced with seemingly meaningless keywords such as 'exim', 'agro' and 'impex'. A company search on OpenCorporates, filtered by jurisdiction, found 16 companies in India called Worlds Window – and it became clear that each reference on the payments referred to the name of a subsidiary company of the Worlds Window group. From there, OpenCorporates showed us the addresses, registration dates and a list of directors associated with the different companies. Most importantly, it also provided a link to the original source – in this case, the corporate registry held by the Indian Ministry of Corporate Affairs. This gave more detailed information including company filings, annual reports[31] and even the names of senior management.

Court records

Court records are also often crucial in determining a matrix of facts about a company's structure, beneficial owners and connections. It can be useful to look at any court records involving particular companies, not just corruption cases.

Most countries provide some means of searching for documents from court cases, even if they don't provide access to full texts. These can be found by consulting relevant domestic departments of justice or by using a site such as WorldLII (see below). Court websites are frequently fairly opaque, and often no translation is provided, so this kind of investigation can take time and effort. Nevertheless, there is much to be gained by dogged pursuit.

The following list provides a snapshot of what is available.

- PACER/RECAP.[32] PACER is a useful source of transcripts, founding affidavits and evidence from the United States of America. Each PACER

---

[30] State capture refers to the corruption of all levels of a state to the point where procurement and policy decisions are influenced to benefit the corrupters, facilitated by the systematic destruction/dilution of state oversight mechanisms that threaten this process.

[31] When looking at a company's annual financial reports, it is vital to read the notes: This is where accountants will attempt to explain away anything untoward.

[32] PACER Public Access to Court Electronic Records. *What Can We Help You Accomplish* [online]. Available from: https://pacer.uscourts.gov/ [Accessed 29 May 2023].

search and document download costs a fraction of a dollar; however, many are also available through the RECAP project, a public sourcing project in which participating individuals upload PACER document downloads, thereby creating an entirely free database that is searchable just like PACER. If researchers require a document that is not yet available here, RECAP will direct them to where to buy it from PACER.

Shadow World Investigations used PACER in its research into a South African mobile phone provider called MTN Group, which had won a contract to become the second mobile supplier to the Iranian government. The loser of that contract, Turkcell, brought a case under the US Alien Tort Statute,[33] claiming that the contract had been awarded because of large-scale bribery. In order to build its case, Turkcell had paid a private investigator and gathered significant first-hand evidence of the alleged corruption, including information suggesting that MTN's senior officials had convinced the South African government to help smuggle weapons into Iran to ensure MTN won the contract. All these findings were posted as part of the court case. We were able to download from PACER a 70-page summary of the alleged corruption, and the entire dossier of supporting evidence. NB: It is often worth researching the losing companies of any contract – they will be angry and may reveal an important trail!

- World Legal Information Institute (WorldLII) links to court registries around the world and gathers judgements in one place.[34] It runs on a regional basis: Participating courts send their judgements to Legal Information Institutes around the world, who collate them either on regional sites (for example, SAFLII runs for Sub-Saharan Africa and is indexed on WorldLII) or directly onto WorldLII itself. Most regional sites also provide information about how their legal systems work, as well as links to individual courts. It can be daunting to figure out different court systems; to help with this, WORLDLII also lists NGOs familiar with various structures who can help with navigation.

---

[33] If both companies have facilities in the US, the loser of a contract can pursue a damages claim if they believe they have been cheated out of business.

[34] WorldLII. World Legal Information Institute [online]. Available from: http://www.worldlii.org/ [Accessed 29 May 2023].

The research into the AgustaWestland/India helicopter scandal described above illustrates how useful these court records can be. At the time of our investigation, we knew there had been one arrest: A certain Gautam Khaitan had been arrested for money laundering. Searching on WorldLII gave us links to the official records of the court which heard the case. We then searched these records to find the arrest warrant, which in turn provided hitherto unknown details, including names of key individuals and companies involved. Those names then informed further investigations using the various techniques detailed in this chapter.

During the AgustaWestland investigation, we also learnt that there was an Interpol red notice warrant issued for a key agent in the deal, and from reading news coverage in India we discovered that a court was dealing specifically with India's Central Bureau of Investigation cases. Although the court website had limited functionality, with no keyword search feature, we realized that the court was uploading PDF files of their judgements daily, and by trawling through these we found the relevant one. One 100-page document proved indispensable, setting out details from the corruption scandal that we hadn't previously been able to track down.

- Legal journals, e.g. LexisNexis.[35] These are not free to use (although they are open in the sense of being publicly available) and can be very expensive; however, some libraries have subscriptions, and it is worth checking what is available.

Historical deep dives and document aggregators

- The Wayback Machine is an archive of imprints of websites from certain dates, that lets researchers find old versions of particular URLs that have been saved.[36] It can also be used to save internet web pages, which is vital if investigators need to reference something online at a later date, especially if there is a danger of it being deleted or altered (documents can be removed even from trustworthy websites like company registries).

---

[35] LexisNexis. *Browse Featured Products* [online]. Available from: https://www.lexisnexis.co.uk/solutions/legal-magazines-and-journals.html [Accessed 19 May 2023].

[36] Internet Archive. *Wayback Machine* [online]. Available from: https://archive.org/web/ [Accessed 29 May 2023].

- DocumentCloud: A public aggregate data store where journalists share the source of their information on the public web.[37]

We have found the Wayback Machine to be invaluable, as, whenever a corruption scandal arises, often the companies involved immediately remove compromising information from their website, and then lie about the changes believing that they won't be caught out. Certain court systems even allow the Wayback Machine as evidence in court applications, as, unlike screenshots, it is considered forensically solid.

The Wayback Machine is also useful in correcting false statements, as illustrated by independent scrutiny of Dominic Cummings. In May 2020, Dominic Cummings, then Chief Adviser to the UK Prime Minister, claimed that he had warned of the 'possible threat of coronaviruses and the urgent need for planning' in 2019, before the start of the pandemic.[38] A BBC journalist searched the Wayback Machine and discovered that the reference to coronaviruses in the piece had in fact been added on 14 April 2020.

Advanced searches

Shadow World Investigations uses advanced search features as well as simple keyword searches.

- Google 'dorks': Google's search function can be refined to focus searches on specific websites, or to add or remove specific words from searches, amongst other things. The modifiers are colloquially called 'dorks'; Google provides a guide to such advanced search features.[39]
- Penetration Testing tools (Pentest):[40] Pentest provides the ability to do two free searches of a particular website using a range of Google dorks. It is a quick and easy way to perform multiple dork searches simultaneously.

---

[37] DocumentCloud. *Turn Documents into Data* [online]. Available from: https://www.documentcloud.org/home [Accessed 29 May 2023].

[38] Cummings D. Press Conference. Watch again: Dominic Cummings Makes Rare Statement as Calls for his Resignation Grow | Coronavirus. *The Telegraph* (YouTube). 2020. Available from: https://www.youtube.com/watch?v=-mSyZGy8LX8&t=2123s(35:09) [Accessed 29 May 2023]. Islam F. Coronavirus: Why Did Dominic Cummings Say He Predicted It? *BBC*. 26 May 2020. Available from: https://www.bbc.co.uk/news/business-52808059 [Accessed 29 May 2023].

[39] Together Learning. *Powersearching: What is Google Powersearching?* [online]. Available from: https://sites.google.com/view/togetherlearning/learn/digitalliteracy/powersearching [Accessed 29 May 2023].

[40] Pentest Tools. *The Essential Penetration Testing Tools, All in One Place* [online]. Available from: https://pentest-tools.com/ [Accessed 29 May 2023].

- DuckDuckGo:[41] We use DuckDuckGo in conjunction with Google, as it complements Google in several dimensions. Google offers the 'right to be forgotten' – people can take themselves off search results so that websites with their name on don't show up when they are Googled. While DuckDuckGo also offers the right to be forgotten, it is a lesser-known search engine and is therefore often overlooked by those wishing to be removed.
- Online sector-specific forums: These can also be extremely useful, providing a gateway to proactive discussions and in-depth analysis of a company's assets, investors, management, connections and performance.

Visualizing relationships and managing data

Open source research can yield huge amounts of information and it is crucial to keep on top of the data collected, although this can be challenging. Shadow World Investigations uses specialist relationship-mapping software. This lets us track and visualize the connections we discover, and can help us notice links that we would otherwise miss. Useful packages include the following.

- yEd Graph Editor (works on PC, MAC and Linux).[42] This is a relatively simple (and free) way to build visualizations of process flows and uses a powerful analysis and import function through MS Excel. It has different styles of representation for different types of relationships, and allows users to see visualizations forming as they trace various elements.
- dtSearch Desktop can handle up to a terabyte of documents and sources in a single index, which can be searched in seconds.[43] It is capable of opening obscure attachment formats, including those related to accounting tools like Imprest or Tally.

---

[41] DuckDuckGo. *Tired of Being Tracked Online? We Can Help* [online]. Available from: https://duckduckgo.com/ [Accessed 29 May 2023].

[42] *yWorks. yEd – Graph Editor: High-quality Diagrams Made Easy* [online]. Available from: https://www.yworks.com/products/yed [Accessed 29 May 2023].

[43] dtSearch [online]. Available from: https://www.dtsearch.com/ [Accessed 29 May 2023].

Section IV: A Note on Closed Source Investigations

Open source information is central to our work. However, we also use closed source investigative methods and believe that open and closed source research work best alongside each other.[44] Corruption tracking tends to require numerous human sources of information, such as people who are prepared to share their knowledge of deals they know or suspect to be dubious. It is important when using information from human sources that it is corroborated and not trusted blindly. We do this by checking it against either at least one other independent trustworthy source, or with documentary evidence, or both.

It is paramount to protect human sources, as they are likely to be taking risks in providing information.[45] Shadow World Investigations has developed a rigorous protocol for this, which starts with offering and, if requested, maintaining anonymity. It also requires open, honest and trust-building dialogue; we are careful that we never mislead our sources about our intentions, and we have found that being upfront about the nature of our research doesn't deter sources from working with us. Similarly, we ask contacts to be clear about what they do and don't want to be in the public domain, and in cases where there are safety concerns, we give people the option to review written material that quotes them before publishing. Further, where possible, we signpost them to legal and other resources (for example, whistle-blower support organizations who provide such assistance).

Many of these human sources are identified as part of the processes described above. Other than this, Shadow World Investigations maintains a capacity to find and connect with closed sources in several ways, including the following.

---

[44] Other chapters in this volume similarly emphasize the utility of hybrid approaches that use both open and closed sources. See, for example, the chapters by Strick and Triebert (Chapters 2.1 and 2.4). H. Wilson *et al.* (Chapter 4.1) discuss the sometimes porous boundaries between open and closed sources.

[45] See also the chapter by Duke in this volume (Chapter 2.2) for a discussion of the risks faced by local weapons monitors in South Sudan.

- Informal media networks. A network of investigative journalists is essential to our work, enabling us to share information and analysis with others who are tracking the minutiae of the arms trade and cases involving potential or actual corruption.
- Losers and participants in underhand procurement processes can report on classified details of both formal and informal procedures. As noted above, court documents can be particularly valuable for finding such people, as these will often reveal ex-employees and competitors who came off worse in a deal. Disgruntled intermediaries are also worth looking for.
- Members of the legal fraternity, especially prosecutors, are sometimes willing to disclose useful information, particularly when they have been involved in cases where political interference has stymied their efforts. We identify such individuals through court dossiers as described above.
- Diplomats and former diplomats who may have been involved in facilitating transactions are sometimes willing to share their experiences with us.
- Parliamentarians who contribute to oversight bodies can be a useful source of information, not least as they have access to parliamentary libraries, including reports and records of parliamentary committees and sittings. Information on who these people are, and how to identify them, is usually publicly available online.
- Freedom of Information (FOI) requests. Many countries have legislation enabling non-governmental entities to ask for information about the public sector; such FOI requests can be a means of transforming closed or obscure information into open sources. Shadow World Investigations has used such legislation to access information that would otherwise be hidden from the public. The process of making an FOI application can be complicated, and we tend to partner with non-governmental organizations that specialize in doing this.
- Industry specialists, company employees and whistle-blowers. Two of the most valuable tools for finding and contacting such people are LinkedIn and the Wayback Machine (which, as detailed above, provides past versions of companies' websites which often display key figures on their management teams).

- National intelligence sources. While these can be useful, Shadow World Investigations treats any information from intelligence communities with a great deal of caution, as such organizations often have multiple agendas.

Conclusion

Convictions in corruption cases are rare, and in arms trade corruption cases they are rarer still. Nevertheless, it is valuable to ensure that verified information about corruption is available in the public domain. From there, it can inform possible prosecutions and/or campaigns aimed at holding to account corrupt politicians, officials and companies, as well as improve regulatory and/or enforcement environments and impact policy agendas.

This is what inspires our work. In addition to publicizing often unknown information, we work with prosecutors and political figures globally, as well as legal and civil society organizations, to litigate strategically in an effort to ensure that companies, governments and/or individuals are charged in relation to the vast criminal malfeasance that we see, especially in the arms trade. It is worth bearing in mind that when it comes to court cases, success – in the form of greater media attention, a focus on malfeasant organizations and/or individuals – is possible even without legal victory.[46]

---

[46] Shadow World Investigations offers training in open source investigative methods (detailing some of the methods introduced in this chapter) and online security (demonstrating tools to protect investigators online). For more information, see our website.

Chapter 5.4

Democratization of OSINT: The Vision, Purpose, Tools and Development of the Datayo Platform

Veronika Bedenko and Jonathan Bellish

Abstract

The availability of open source data and the tools for its analysis (referred to as OSINT) have proliferated over the last decade with the growth of big data, modern computer science and social media. However, high-quality OSINT continues to depend on high-value skills related to linguistics, intelligence community tradecraft and technical programming skills. As well as these underlying skills, OSINT can also benefit from 'democratization', that is, mobilizing communities to process large amounts of open source data and/or work across disciplinary boundaries. This chapter explores ways in which this can be achieved, using the work of Datayo as a case study. Datayo is a platform dedicated to providing an OSINT workspace accessible to professionals and hobbyists alike. This chapter highlights the genesis of and motivations behind Datayo. It then provides an in-depth overview of how Datayo has been utilized by the Open Nuclear Network for OSINT-informed nuclear risk reduction. Finally, this chapter addresses ethical challenges facing the democratization of OSINT.

Introduction

The use of open source data as the basis for analysis (OSINT) is not a new concept and has long predated the internet age.[1] It is widely cited

---

[1] For examples of open source research before the widespread use of digital tools and data, see the chapters in this volume by H. Wilson *et al.* and Mathews (Chapters 4.1 and 4.2).

This is an open access article published by World Scientific Publishing Europe Ltd. and distributed under the terms of the Creative Commons Attribution-NonCommercial 4.0 International (CC BY-NC 4.0) License.

that OSINT as an official institutional practice began as a defence-oriented enterprise in 1941 when the United States decided to establish the Foreign Broadcast Monitoring Service (FBMS) with the purpose of monitoring and analyzing propaganda programmes of the Axis powers.[2,3] From those early days of open source data analysis, which primarily focused on monitoring and translating foreign media sources, the situation has changed dramatically. With the rapid development of technology, the creation of the internet, the introduction of social media and the proliferation of media outlets and mechanisms for transmitting information (and disinformation), the challenge facing analysts has shifted from how to collect data to how to process it. It is becoming critical for OSINT analysts to be equipped with high-value skills related to linguistics, tradecraft and technical programming to be able to turn such data into meaningful analytical insights.

Tools that have previously been available only to government intelligence agencies are now becoming widely accessible to the public, either for free or for a price (such as the newspaper content behind paywalls). This opens the OSINT field to a broader audience, from the private business sector and non-governmental organizations (NGOs) to individual researchers and hobbyists. However, the challenge still persists: How to derive intelligence from the never-ending, constantly shifting stream of massive amounts of data from an ever-increasing range of sources? The authors contend that one possible solution is further democratization of OSINT through collaboration.[4]

Democratizing Open Source Intelligence Through Collaboration

Context and motivation behind collaborative OSINT

Most of the important questions in connection with information analysis are what early information theorist Warren Weaver described as *problems*

---

[2]Williams H. and Blum I. *Defining Second Generation Open Source Intelligence (OSINT) for the Defense Enterprise.* RAND Corporation. 2018.

[3]For more information about the development of OSINT within the US Intelligence Community, see the chapter by Vogel in this volume (Chapter 3.4).

[4]Several other chapters consider collaborations within open source research. See for example the chapters by Freeman & Koenig, Ahmad, Carboni & Raleigh, H. Wilson *et al.* and L. Wilson *et al.* (Chapters 2.5, 3.1, 3.3, 4.1 and 5.1). Toler (Chapter 3.2) warns of the dangers of irresponsible crowd-sourced research.

of organized complexity.[5] These are problems that cannot be solved using science or statistical methods alone, and require 'mixed teams' with diverse expertise and skill sets working in a collaborative, iterative and somewhat open-ended fashion towards understanding and resolving problems.[6]

Within some government intelligence agencies, these mixed teams can be assembled within single institutions with thousands or tens of thousands of employees and billions of dollars in annual budget. However, OSINT insights that are developed from start to finish by a single institution suffer from a 'black box' problem, whereby the rationale for their findings is frequently not shared or shareable outside of the institution.

Many non-governmental OSINT practitioners have also adopted an institutionally driven approach, resulting in sporadic and siloed efforts in which particular groups focus on isolated parts of a case rather than taking a more holistic perspective. When government insights and external OSINT insights differ, they can appear to third parties as duelling assertions. In high-trust societies, the official position will almost always prevail, and in low-trust societies, such duelling assertions merely deepen the existing political conflict between 'pro-government' and 'anti-government' factions.

In the absence of government-level resources, many non-governmental OSINT practitioners have found that they must adopt a collaborative, networked approach if they wish to build the kinds of mixed teams needed to develop valid insights able to withstand public scrutiny. Such 'collaborative OSINT platforms' exist in the realm of humanitarian action,[7] human rights[8] and environmental conservation.[9] However, while there are examples in the peace and security sphere of open dataset aggregation and analysis platforms,[10] it has proved harder to develop joint systems which combine data,

---

[5]Weaver W. Science and complexity. *American Scientist.* 1948, 36, pp. 536–544.
[6]*ibid.*
[7]For example, HDX. *The Humanitarian Data Exchange* [online]. Available from: https://data.humdata.org/ [Accessed 20 July 2023].
[8]For example, Amnesty International. *Amnesty Decoders* [online]. Available from: https://decoders.amnesty.org/ [Accessed 20 July 2023].
[9]For example, *Allen Coral Atlas* [online]. Available from: https://allencoralatlas.org/ [Accessed 20 July 2023].
[10]For example, The GDELT Project. *Watching Our World Unfold* [online]. Available from: https://www.gdeltproject.org/ [Accessed 20 July 2023]. Intelligence Fusion. *Tailored threat intelligence data and bespoke software solutions for global security teams* [online]. Available from: https://www.intelligencefusion.co.uk/ [Accessed 20 July 2023].

machine learning and collaborative human analysis. This is an important niche that should be filled if OSINT insights are to be produced at the speed, and on the scale, of the peace- and security-related problems they could address. It is this niche that the One Earth Future (OEF) foundation was hoping to fill in 2017 when it began to explore what would ultimately become Open Nuclear Network (ONN) and its Datayo platform.

Collaborative OSINT in the nuclear field

The United States tested its first nuclear device in 1945 in Alamogordo, New Mexico, followed shortly by the first Soviet Union test (1949) and subsequently those of the rest of the five permanent members of the UN Security Council (the UK 1952, France 1960 and China 1967). The development of nuclear weapons went hand in hand with calls for international controls against such powerful and dangerous weapons, which led to the creation of the 1968 Treaty on the Non-proliferation of Nuclear Weapons (NPT). Various verification mechanisms have been established to help ensure that states parties abide by their NPT obligations, and to build confidence in treaty compliance.

However, determining if a state has ever engaged in proliferation activities in the past or has such intentions in the present or, potentially, in the future is not a trivial task because of the very secretive nature of nuclear-weapons-related activities and the dual-use nature of associated technologies and materials.[11] OSINT has become one of the tools governments and relevant international organizations, such as the International Atomic Energy Agency (IAEA), use to monitor nuclear-weapons-related developments. As OSINT tools have become more widely available, individual researchers and NGOs have joined the monitoring efforts.[12]

At present, a number of NGOs and think-tanks conduct open source research to investigate nuclear weapons and proliferation issues, including (but not limited to) the James Martin Center for Nonproliferation Studies

---

[11] Hobbs C. and Moron M. Armchair safeguards: The Role of Open Source Intelligence in Nuclear Proliferation Analysis. In: Hobbs C., Moran M., and Salisbury D. (eds.). *Open Source Intelligence in the 21st Century: New Approaches and Opportunities*. London: Palgrave Macmillan. 2014.

[12] For further information about open source research focussed on monitoring nuclear weapons, see also the chapters by Kristensen & Korda and Withorne in this volume (Chapters 2.3 and 5.2). Chapters 4.3 and 4.4 (by Revill & Garzón Maceda and Liu & Gwadera) consider whether and how open source research could be harnessed by international treaties that ban weapons of mass destruction.

(CNS), Center for Strategic and International Studies (CSIS), 38 North, the Institute for Science and International Security (ISIS) and the Federation of American Scientists (FAS),[13] to name a few. Some of their findings, especially those involving analyses of satellite imagery, attract a lot of public and sometimes also government attention.[14]

Members of the nuclear-weapons-related OSINT community tend to collaborate with each other in their research and there are two notable reasons for that. First of all, the community of nuclear non-proliferation experts is relatively small and tightly knit. Second, accurate analysis of nuclear-weapons-related developments in various countries based on the open source data requires a very broad set of expertise (e.g. technical, cultural and linguistic). Thus, it is only natural that research collaboration in the nuclear-weapons-related OSINT field is self-organizing and relatively widespread. Such collaboration can obviously happen 'behind the scenes' through private channels, but often one can see such interactions in public domains. Researchers discuss their findings on Twitter, Facebook and other social media, create semi-public channels on Slack, write their own blogs and interact with their readers in comments sections, and crowdsource feedback or seek additional expertise through other public means.

With that in mind, OEF decided to go beyond monitoring and analysis for research purposes, and established ONN. Open Nuclear Network is an experimental initiative tasked with the ambitious goal of reducing nuclear risks primarily by deriving actionable insights with the help of open source data analysis through Datayo – its in-house platform for collaborative OSINT.

Collaborative OSINT Using Datayo

Datayo – Idea and development

The seed of the idea for Datayo came when a recently retired senior government official made an offhand and somewhat flippant remark about how

---

[13] See the chapter by Kristensen & Korda in this volume (Chapter 2.3).
[14] Gayeon Ha, Gyunyoung Heo, Jooho Whang. A Preliminary Study for Knowledge-Based Management for Nuclear Activities using Open-Source Satellite Imagery. *Transactions of the Korean Nuclear Society*. Goyang, Korea. 24–25 October 2019. Available from: https://www.kns.org/files/pre_paper/42/19A-170-%ED%95%98%EA%B0%80%EC%97%B0.pdf [Accessed 20 July 2023].

we should just 'put a bunch of webcams up in North Dakota to see for ourselves if the silo doors are open'. From this remark came a core insight; over the past two decades, the quality of remote sensors had improved dramatically and their costs had fallen precipitously. This created an opportunity for NGOs to gain access to data previously available only to governments. These data did not rely on classified sources and methods and thus could be shared between adversarial governments and across government departmental boundaries, and delivered by impartial outsiders to a given conflict situation. After almost a year of validation by dozens of experts, practitioners and former practitioners, OEF was convinced that a project to leverage this capacity was viable and worthy of investment.

The next key breakthrough came via the N Square innovation network, a collaboration between the Carnegie Corporation of New York, the MacArthur Foundation, the William and Flora Hewlett Foundation, the Ploughshares Fund and the Skoll Global Threats Fund, whose mission is to cultivate partnerships among nuclear experts and cross-sector partners. The OEF design team was involved in N Square's inaugural cohort, which was convened in Stinson Beach, California, for a week-long design session. It was there that the idea for Datayo was born, in partnership with design strategists, OSINT experts, corporate risk consultants, and professional communicators and storytellers. Over the course of the next year, the team developed the idea through further iterations, and by the fall of 2018, the team was ready to present an initial model at the Rhode Island School of Design. The mock-up included shared datasets, collaborative workspaces where users could asynchronously comment on developments and a 'Mechanical Turk' platform where users could help train algorithms.

At that point, armed with $100,000 in seed investment from the Carnegie Corporation of New York and the Skoll Global Threats Fund, and a $1.5 million commitment from the OEF Board, One Earth Future launched ONN, the team that would develop and implement the Datayo project.

Open Nuclear Network's nuclear risk reduction concept

Building further on the general idea of setting up an open source collaborative platform for security-related research, OEF established ONN. Its goal was to be an open and non-partisan nuclear risk reduction programme, utilizing empirically grounded analysis and domain expertise to monitor potential catalysts of conflict involving nuclear-weapons-possessing states. ONN's main goal is to reduce the risk that nuclear weapons are used in response to error, uncertainty or misdirection. In order to achieve this goal, ONN devised a formula for nuclear risk reduction which consists of two elements.

The first element, as already mentioned, is open source data analysis. Decision-makers in states engaged in conflicts, or non-military confrontations, that could lead to the use of nuclear weapons, need access to high-quality, shareable information that enables them to make the best decisions in the face of such high-stake situations. ONN analysts produce operational insights using unclassified sources, leveraging publicly available data and technology.

The second and equally important aspect of ONN's concept is the engagement of decision-makers through a set of trusted intermediaries within its bespoke 'Engagement Network'. The members of the Network are predominantly former senior civilian or military government officials, prominent academics, and other experienced and well-regarded practitioners from the field. With the help of the Engagement Network, ONN transmits its analyses to top government officials.

One of the most significant factors contributing to the risk that nuclear weapons could be used – either deliberately or by accident – is asymmetric access to information, whereby adversaries have differential access to shared, timely and reliable information. While intelligence services exist precisely to minimize informational shortfalls, they do so for their respective governments; they have to protect their sources and methods, and they cannot freely share their information. In a stand-off relationship, adversaries may be incentivized to not be fully transparent about intentions and capabilities or to present them ambiguously. Such uncertainties and misunderstandings are critical risk factors for conflict escalation. With the increasing public availability of data from unclassified open sources, and rapidly advancing analytical capabilities, civil society can and should provide alternative sources for trustworthy information and analysis. For example, NGOs could provide independent assessments of the capabilities of the parties to a conflict, and this could contribute to alleviating the core challenge of asymmetric access to information.

To address information asymmetries in a transparent and verifiable manner, open source capabilities are especially useful as the process through which a specific assessment has been made can be reviewed and confirmed. Commercially available satellite imagery allows NGOs to continuously monitor activities around the globe and to track changes. Movements of troops, military vehicles and large equipment, and the renovation and upgrading of relevant sites are all now observable via rapidly developing and commercially available remote sensing capabilities.

To bring all the necessary data streams to perform such open source analysis in the most transparent, verifiable and reproducible manner, ONN is developing its in-house open source data platform for collaborative OSINT – Datayo.

Datayo as a platform for risk reduction OSINT

Datayo creates a platform for ONN analysts to streamline their daily work routine. It provides a space where different types of data can be overlaid and new analytical insights derived. To test its risk reduction concept, ONN is currently concentrating on applying it to the Korean Peninsula situation. To be more specific, ONN has identified a number of possible pathways for conflict escalation involving the Korean Peninsula[15] and, for each of these, it has specified a number of indicators that need to be monitored in order to spot escalation.[16] Monitoring such indicators provides data that allow the analysts to see, understand and contextualize any significant changes that could lead to crises – particularly focused on changes that move events along the escalation pathways.

As an example, one of the identified escalation pathways is the occurrence of natural disasters and accidents which could, in turn, lead to a humanitarian crisis in the country and, in an extreme scenario, to the Democratic People's Republic of Korea (DPRK) regime collapse. To stay ahead of the game and detect the earliest signs of the development of such a scenario,

---

[15] See *ONN's Nuclear Risk Reduction Approach for the Korean Peninsula*. ONN. 6 November 2020. Available from: https://opennuclear.org/publication/onns-nuclear-risk-reduction-approach-korean-peninsula [Accessed 20 July 2023].
[16] *ibid.*

the following monitoring activities were envisioned:

> ONN would monitor any natural disasters and incidents that could affect the agricultural sector and thus lead to food shortages. Among the most common are such natural disasters as floods, droughts, typhoons and wildfires. Due to geographic proximity and similar climate zones, weather forecasting assessments and relevant measurements conducted by ROK [Republic of Korea] forecasting agencies would be applicable to the DPRK and are actually also produced for the DPRK [Democratic People's Republic of Korea] specifically (e.g. from the Korea Meteorological Administration). In addition to monitoring official forecasting and statistical data, ONN would also process and analyse satellite imagery of affected areas in order to comparatively assess the scale of the incident. Among other indicators for monitoring, ONN will be tracking customs data (to assess the amounts of imported goods to make up for food shortages), numbers of defectors/refugees fleeing the DPRK (this could serve as an indicator of the severity of a crisis), market prices for food products (primarily rice) and official government requests for humanitarian assistance.[17]

All the data streams necessary to perform the described monitoring activities are accessible to the Datayo analytical team. Further, Datayo can crowdsource interpretation of the data in instances where monitoring requirements go beyond the expertise of the core Datayo team. This is just one possible example of how a platform such as Datayo could be instrumentalized for very specific analytical purposes.

At the current stage, Datayo is still a tool in the making and it is being constantly upgraded and readjusted to better suit the analytical needs of the ONN team. Once the platform proves its usefulness for conducting open source data analysis to ONN and the selected group of vetted users who currently have access to the platform, ONN will consider opening it up to a broader audience, creating a collaborative all-in-one platform for other researchers in the field. Right now, the team is working on identifying the different data streams within the OSINT domain that could be useful in spotting critical changes along the escalation pathways, and finding existing and potential analytical tools (e.g. big data analysis, crowdsourcing, counterintuitive data mixing and visual analysis) that could be acquired or created for processing and visualizing data.

---

[17] *ONN's Nuclear Risk Reduction Approach for the Korean Peninsula*, ONN. 6 November 2020. Available from: https://opennuclear.org/publication/onns-nuclear-risk-reduction-approach-korean-peninsula [Accessed 20 July 2023].

Datayo tools

Datayo combines different types of data layers and workspaces where users can perform analyses. On the main workspace (see Fig. 1), mapping data are combined with optical satellite imagery from various providers (e.g. Planet and Maxar) and other types of Geographic Information System (GIS) data that can be visually displayed (e.g. ship and flight tracking data, notices to airmen and radio frequencies detection data). Users can also perform basic measuring activities and initiate a discussion with other users regarding a data point of interest, either by tagging particular users or opening the discussion up to anyone who is interested.

The main workspace also supports the function of creating a custom list of locations of interest which could automatically redirect a user to the requested place (without needing to enter geographical coordinates). For each of those locations, it is then possible to create a gallery of imagery to track changes at a specific location and easily access previously reviewed imagery which a user can also annotate.

Other workspaces contain archives of relevant text and visual (photo and video) data which can also be annotated by users. More importantly, the data can be processed in Datayo's *analytics workspace* to draw insights from large volumes of data.

For example, performing text analysis would allow a user to extract information, relationships, patterns and meaning from large amounts of textual data. This analytical method helps to automatically identify differences and commonalities across many texts, which would be too labour intensive for a researcher to process manually (see example in Fig. 2). It also helps find, for example, particular phrases, names of individuals, places and specific policies. A very practical use case for this method would be, for example, using libraries of common names to identify people mentioned in texts and checking them against sanctions lists. Furthermore, through analyzing text data, Datayo users are also able to create network maps which can help reveal relationships between different actors (see Fig. 3).

The Datayo platform is constantly developing, and it is the users who will define what data are the most relevant to the platform, as well as what datasets and tools could be added to enhance analysis. As technology develops and new types of data become available, Datayo's tools and datasets will change in parallel.

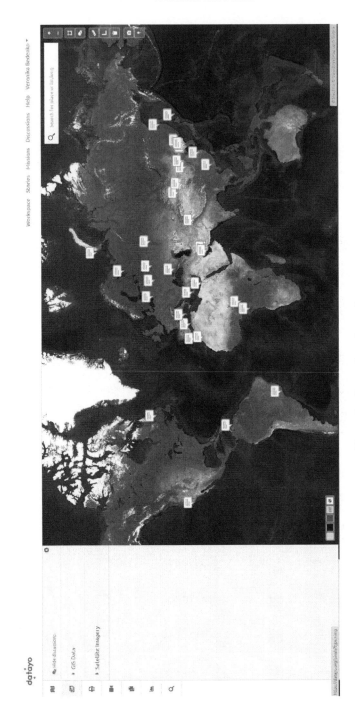

Figure 1: Datayo's main workspace.

Democratization of OSINT: the Datayo Platform

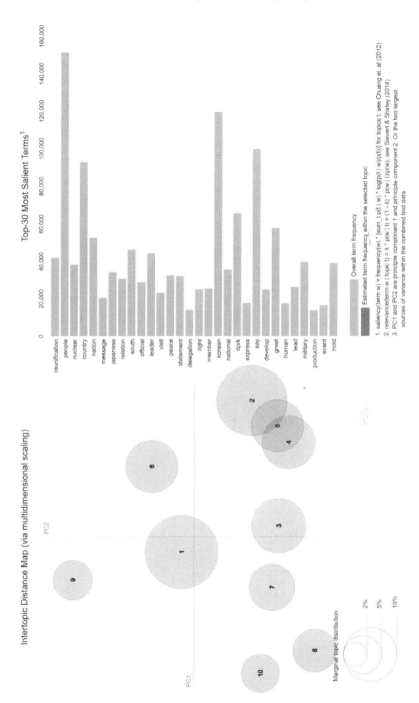

Figure 2: Example of text analysis result from Datayo's analytics workspace.

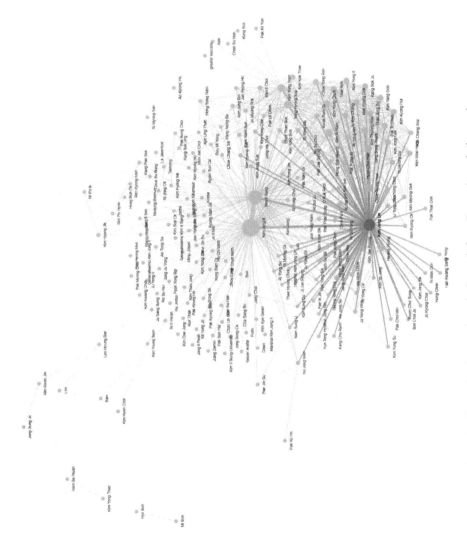

Figure 3: Example of network analysis result from Datayo's analytics workspace.

Ethical Considerations for Collaborative OSINT

Researchers working in the field of OSINT have access to resources that previously have been exclusive to governments. This is particularly apparent in collaborative OSINT efforts, where independent individual researchers make up a working team with diverse expertise, mimicking the setup of government intelligence agencies. We are already living in a reality where open source analysts can craft intelligence products, break news, add evidence to reporting, offer insights and provide accurate information to the public on issues critical to peace and security. However, with the power to influence public discourse comes responsibility.

There are no universally accepted norms of ethical principles for open source research, although, as evidenced by feedback from open source practitioners, there is a clear need for them.[18] In July 2019, ONN joined the Stanley Center for Peace and Security in a joint project aimed at exploring the landscape of ethics in the field of open source information analysis, especially as it pertains to research related to nuclear weapons. The main takeaway from the project was that there was a clear need for such norms to provide 'moral guidance to practitioners, enhancing public trust in their work, and deterring unethical behavior'.[19]

Open Nuclear Network is committed to serving the public good. In this context, the principles of transparency, accuracy and independence are paramount to its mission. Following the joint Stanley Center–ONN initiative, ONN has drafted its own code of ethics, offering a model approach and key principles for ethical open source analysis.[20,21]

It is ONN's belief that ensuring the accuracy and fairness of its work is of primary importance. Factual information must at all times be distinguished from commentary, criticism and advocacy. All ONN staff are obliged to abide by the laws and regulations of the jurisdiction in which they are

---

[18] *The Gray Spectrum: Ethical Decision Making with Geospatial and Open Source Analysis*. Stanley Center and Open Nuclear Network. July 2019. Available from: https://stanleycenter.org/wp-content/uploads/2020/01/RRNW-TheGraySpectrum120-web.pdf [Accessed 20 July 2023].
[19] *ibid.*
[20] ONN's Code of Ethics. Available from: https://oneearthfuture.org/code-ethics-0 [Accessed 20 July 2023].
[21] Several other chapters in this volume detail ethical issues within open source research and different approaches to these. See for example the chapters by Wilson, Samuel & Plesch, Duke, Freeman & Koenig, Ahmad, and L. Wilson *et al.* (Chapters 1, 2.2, 2.5, 3.1 and 5.1).

located, as well as the laws of Austria and the United States (where ONN is situated) and, to the extent relevant, the extraterritorial laws that may apply to them by virtue of their citizenship(s).

Some of the core principles of ONN's code of ethics include the following:

- Always use primary sources and original data when possible;
- Never plagiarize other people's work;
- Assess source material to avoid undue bias;
- Respect the privacy of all the individuals/entities involved;
- Never jeopardize the safety/security of others;
- Treat all data sources critically;
- Never spread misinformation and disinformation;
- Never publish information that escalates conflict;
- Always distinguish between fact and opinion;
- Prioritize accuracy over speed;
- Always acknowledge mistakes and correct them in a timely fashion.

The notion of ethical principles for OSINT research still remains a grey area, allowing relevant entities to set their own boundaries and redlines of what is considered appropriate. We would like to encourage further discussion on this topic and raise awareness of its importance among current practitioners and the next generation of professionals in the field.

Conclusion

The field of OSINT has changed dramatically over the past 20 years, providing analysts with capabilities that were previously exclusive to governments. Analysis performed by NGOs, think-tanks, researchers in academia, and even individual researchers and hobbyists alike, can now meet the level of national intelligence.[22] Furthermore, open source intelligence produced by independent entities offers the comparative advantage of being shareable.

---

[22] Zegart A. Spies Like Us: The Promise and Peril of Crowdsourced Intelligence. *Foreign Affairs*. July/August 2021. Available from: https://www.foreignaffairs.com/reviews/review-essay/2021-06-22/spies-us [Accessed 20 July 2023].

Open Nuclear Network intends to leverage the power of open source analysis by further democratizing the field through its Datayo platform. Crowdsourcing analytical expertise from different domains should empower Datayo users to produce more insightful, unbiased and error-free analytical products, which in turn would inform meaningful substantive conversations among allies and adversaries on the most sensitive topics.

However, it is critical that the analysis produced from open source data is in line with the best ethical principles. This area still remains in an uncodified grey spectrum that is worth closer attention, and further collaboration among members of the OSINT community is required to develop universally accepted norms around ethical principles of open source research.